JAMES I. ROBERTSON, JR.

GENERAL A. P. HILL

James I. Robertson, Jr., Alumni Distinguished Professor of History at Virginia Tech, is the recipient of the Bruce Catton Award and the Freeman-Nevins Award, as well as other honors for teaching and research in Civil War history. A native of Danville, Virginia, Robertson teaches the largest Civil War history class in the world and is the author/editor of many books and more than one hundred fifty articles on the Civil War period. Among his publications are *The Stonewall Brigade, Civil War Sites in Virginia,* and *Tenting Tonight: The Soldier's Story.*

GENERAL A. P. HILL

GENERAL A. P. HILL
THE STORY OF A
CONFEDERATE WARRIOR

James I. Robertson, Jr.

VINTAGE CIVIL WAR LIBRARY
VINTAGE BOOKS
A DIVISION OF RANDOM HOUSE, INC.
NEW YORK

First Vintage Civil War Library Edition, July 1992

Library of Congress Cataloging-in-Publication Data
Robertson, James I.
General A.P. Hill: the story of a Confederate warrior / James
I. Robertson, Jr. — 1st Vintage Civil War library ed.
p.   cm. — (Vintage Civil War library)
Originally published: New York : Random House, 1987.
Includes bibliographical references and index.
ISBN 0-679-73888-6
1. Hill, A. P. (A. Powell) 2. Generals—United States—Biography.
3. Confederate States of America. Army—Biography. 4. United
States—History—Civil War, 1861–1865—Campaigns. I. Title.
II. Series.
E467.1.H56R63   1992
973.7'42—dc20
91-58060 [B]   CIP

Book design by Jo Anne Metsch

Manufactured in the United States of America
10 9 8 7 6 5 4 3 2 1

To Libba, Beth, Jim, and Howard—
for being all the things you are

Acknowledgments

A. P. Hill was a pivotal figure in every major Civil War battle in the eastern theater from 1862 to 1865. Nevertheless, he has been such an obscure figure for the past 125 years that the best photograph of him has never been published until now. One reason for this neglect is that until a collection of Hill's writings was discovered in the preparation of this book, historians believed that none of the general's papers had survived. In addition, comparatively few veterans of the Light Division or the Third Corps published wartime letters, diaries, or reminiscences, and so little research material seemed to exist. In reality, however, dozens of unpublished letters and memoirs by men who fought under Hill have for years lain unused in various archives and libraries. Hill's newly discovered writings, and these heretofore unpublished observations by the men who marched, fought, and suffered with "Little Powell," form the base of this book.

With the help of such previously unused sources, Hill's own story can be told for the first time. Therefore, the overriding object of this study has been to portray people and events as Hill himself saw them. Thus does "Stonewall" Jackson, for example, appear here in a more negative light than usual.

Shortly after beginning research on Hill, I learned that Mrs. Alice B. Daniel of Somerset, Va., a descendant of the Hill family, had some material on the Confederate leader. This material turned out to be a literary gold mine, consisting of some of Hill's Mexican War and Civil War letters, a prewar diary, and detailed family correspondence a Richmond newspaperman had assembled for an aborted biography in the 1930s. Mrs. Daniel placed all of the papers at my disposal. Her kindness, assistance, and hospitality will always be remembered. The Hill Papers have since been deposited at the Virginia Historical Society.

Much additional information, as well as copies of portraits of Hill's wife and a daughter, came from another descendant, Henrietta Towler Millns of Raleigh, N.C. Her help and enthusiasm throughout this study were extraordinary.

Dr. Richard E. Bullock of Virginia Tech headed the "medical team" that painstakingly studied the established facts of Hill's malady and developed an explanation for the lifelong deterioration of his health. Assisting in the diagnosis were Drs. Richard J. Desjardins of Virginia Tech, Richard J. Duma of the Division of Infectious Diseases at the Medical College of Virginia, and David P. Minichan, Jr., of Jefferson Surgical Clinic in Roanoke. Their skill in solving a century-old puzzle cannot be overpraised.

Robert K. Krick, chief historian at the Fredericksburg-Spotsylvania National Military Park, provided many leads from his vast research holdings on the Army of Northern Virginia. Portions of eight chapters of this book profited greatly from his scrutiny. Chris Calkins of the Petersburg National Battlefield went out of his way to help by lending much material on Hill's 1864–1865 activities, by taking me on a step-by-step tour of Hill's ride to death, and by reviewing the Petersburg portion of the narrative for accuracy. There were others who cheerfully read blocks of this study and offered beneficial suggestions: John E. Damerel of Richmond; Dennis E. Frye of Harpers Ferry National Historic Park; Willard S. Gilley of Williamsburg; John Hennessy, formerly of the National Park Service; William F. Mallory of Richmond; Harry W. Pfanz, whose knowledge of Gettysburg is awesome; and Edmund Raus of the Manassas National Battlefield Park. Anyone who denigrates "local historians" has never had the privilege of knowing any of the above authorities.

Library staffs are the arteries of any scholarly undertaking. That was certainly the case with this work. To the ever-helpful personnel at Duke University, the Library of Congress, the Museum of the Confederacy, the National Archives, the New York Public Library, the North Carolina State Archives, the University of South Carolina, the U.S. Military Academy, the Virginia Historical Society, the Virginia State Archives, and the College of William and Mary, I owe and extend sincere thanks. I especially want to single out the Southern Historical Collection at the University of North Carolina. It was the most fruitful depository for manuscript material on and by Hill's men, and I am deeply grateful for permission to quote extensively from its collections.

Genuine feelings of indebtedness also go to these friends, who helped in a variety of ways: Calvin M. Applegate, James D. Birchfield, Kent Masterson Brown, Mary C. Fray, Roland Galvin, Russell P. Green, William W. Hassler, Vicki K. Heilig, Howard W. Kympton, Jr., Thomas R. McAnge, Burton Milward, Michael P. Musick, Sandra V. Parker, David F. Riggs, Ben Ritter, Mrs. Reid S. Towler, James H. Tubbesing, and Waverly Winfree.

The maps in this book are the work of Gary L. Hall of Raleigh, N.C. Cartography and the Civil War are his hobbies. Hall is gifted in both areas and, as I found, generous with his time and talent.

Historian Allan Nevins once said of Richard B. Harwell, "He is the most honest scholar in the country." Rick has been a veritable godfather to me throughout my career. My indebtedness to him is exceeded only by my respect for him. He gave encouragement to this project from the start; he then gave his editorial expertise to several of the chapters. He remains that rarest of individuals: a true friend.

Robert D. Loomis, Vice-President and Executive Editor of Random House, Inc., fully substantiated the old adage that a good editor makes an average author look respectable. From the beginning to the end of this study, it was a pleasure working with him. My thanks also to Virginia Avery, my copy editor at Random House.

To Beth Brown, my unofficial copy editor and one who eagerly analyzed every line of every page, I blend appreciation with all the love a father could have for his daughter.

My wife, Libba, has been my most constant companion throughout this undertaking. Whether examining manuscript material on research trips, feeding my garbled copy into the orderly world of a word processor, reading finished chapters with all the benevolence of the Spanish Inquisition, or maintaining silence through months of neglect, she deserves front-rank recognition for sacrifices above and beyond the call of duty. I hope she knows how grateful I am.

James L Robertson, Jr.

Virginia Polytechnic Institute
and State University

Contents

Maps

GENERAL A. P. HILL

Stormy Road to Manhood

Artillery flashes broke the darkness and outlined trees along the horizon. The deep bark of cannon, hours earlier only a rumble, accelerated into a roar. Even the spring air seemed heavy and stale. Another killing time was about to begin.

Sleep would not come to Lt. Gen. A. P. Hill that first night in April 1865. Fear was hardly the reason. Fellow officers knew Hill as "always ready and impatient to fight," a "brilliant corps commander and devoted patriot." For the past three years, Hill had been the hard-hitting embodiment of the Confederacy's military might. He had been singled out as "one of the bravest officers of an army noted above all things for undaunted courage and intrepid valor." Yet for both Hill and the Southern army, the days of brilliant successes were in the past.[1]

Now, in the Civil War's fourth spring, Hill lay in bed and stared through the blackness at the ceiling of the cottage he had called home for the past eight months. His wife, Dolly, heavy with child, moved uncomfortably beside him. Their two infant daughters were sleeping in an adjacent room. Hill thought of all he should be doing. His sector of the lines in front of Petersburg was the key to Robert E. Lee's defenses. U. S. Grant's Union army was about to launch a major attack—no doubt about it—and Southerners behind their breastworks were probably too few and too exhausted to beat back the blue flood this time.

Hill shifted painfully in bed. He ought to make another inspection of his lines, but that would only confirm his apprehensions. Besides, he did not think he could stand the exertion. The stabbing pain in his sides and the dull ache in his back were getting worse again. He felt feverish from the pressure deep inside his body. Perhaps he should go back to the latrine. Yet he knew that would be a waste of time and effort. The siege of illness the last two months still lingered. Just breathing now sapped his energy.

So he lay there that Saturday night and let memories shove pain aside. Soon the waves of Federal cannon fire began to sound like the thunderstorms Hill had watched with awe as a child back in Culpeper.

The Hill family was representative of the landed gentry of north-central Virginia. Two centuries prior to the Civil War, the Hills had planted their roots in the rolling piedmont country of the Old Dominion. The taproot of the family stretched back to twelfth-century England and may have touched royalty. Some evidence suggests that the Hulls (as the family name was first spelled) were descended from Hamlet Plantagenet, a son of King Henry II. Succeeding generations maintained respectability but without excess wealth. The colonization of Virginia seemed to offer unlimited opportunity, and in 1630—barely twenty years after the first settlement at Jamestown—Henry Hill of Shropshire and his brother William migrated to America. They settled in what became Middlesex County, where the Rappahannock River empties into Chesapeake Bay. Both brothers raised tobacco and children in large quantities.

As the family expanded in the ever-expanding country, it was inevitable that some members would seek new horizons. In 1740 Russell Hill, a great-grandson of William, moved inland to the land between the mountains and the flat country. He became an original settler of Culpeper County, Va., created in 1748 after being officially surveyed by George Washington. Russell Hill carved out an estate in the area known as the Wilderness, dubbed it Stranger's Rest, and followed in the family footsteps by becoming both prosperous and prolific.

A neighbor and associate of this Hill was an extraordinary Capt. Ambrose Powell: Indian fighter, Kentucky explorer, justice of the peace, sheriff, legislator, and close friend of President James Madison.[2] Russell's son Henry (1743–1815) married Anne Powell, daughter of the prominent Virginian. Henry Hill served in the

Revolutionary War under Col. "Light Horse Harry" Lee and then built Millwood, an estate of several thousand acres in nearby Madison County, Va. Henry Hill has been described as "a very large man," a description that certainly fits the wealth and influence he ultimately possessed.[3]

Five children came from the marriage of Henry Hill and Anne Powell. One son, Ambrose Powell Hill (1785–1858), served in both houses of the Virginia legislature in addition to being elected captain of the Culpeper Minute Men militia. Another son, Thomas Hill, born October 3, 1789, also crossed back into Culpeper County to make his fortune. His November 1811 marriage to Fannie Russell Baptist was a merger of two proud lines. She was a native of Mecklenburg County and was descended from the Earl of Gainsboro in Charles II's reign. Fannie Hill was a nineteen-year-old bride when she arrived at Thomas Hill's new estate, Greenland, ten miles west of the town of Culpeper Court House.

Husband and wife soon developed contrasting life styles. Thomas Hill became a highly esteemed merchant, farmer, and politician. An acquaintance recalled that he "was a splendid looking man, tall, taciturn, noted for his courage, famed for his hospitality and beloved for his character." People called him Major out of respect. Fannie Hill, on the other hand, was a small, frail, bespectacled introvert who had difficulty controlling her emotions. She tended to keep to herself, preferring to sit by the window, knitting or gazing out across the fields. Most of her married life she spent battling "ills real or imaginary," a family member stated, and she was "much petted by her husband and children."[4]

The union of Thomas and Fannie Hill produced seven children: four sons followed by three daughters. At eight in the morning on November 9, 1825, the last son was born. He was appropriately named Ambrose Powell Hill, Jr. Powell (as he was called throughout his life) enjoyed a pleasant childhood. Being the youngest son and closer to his mother than the others, Powell Hill was more tolerant of her hypochondria. The lad enjoyed the outdoors with his father. Hunting and fishing were favorite pastimes. Moreover, "the Major" took Hill from the cradle, figuratively speaking, and put him on a horse, and the boy learned to ride as quickly as he learned to walk. As a result, Powell Hill became what a Richmond artillerist years afterward would term "a perfect picture in the saddle and the most graceful rider I ever saw."[5]

In the mid-1830s, Major Hill moved his family into the town of Culpeper Court House to be nearer his expanding mercantile business. The Hills settled into a large, three-story brick residence at the corner of Main and Davis streets. Before the age of ten, Hill was enrolled in a one-room school operated by the Reverend Andrew Broadus. Hill was a receptive student—"self reliant, forceful and bright," boyhood chum (and later Confederate general) James L. Kemper said of him.[6]

While keeping his mother company, the lad grew fond of reading. Books on the life and campaigns of Napoléon Bonaparte fascinated him, and he often organized neighborhood boys into miniature armies and played war. At the age of twelve, Hill was sent to Black Hills Seminary. There he joined other well-to-do boys, such as the future Baptist leader John A. Broadus. Black Hills was a private boarding academy three miles northwest of Culpeper Court House. Its major attraction was a schoolmaster who seemed straight out of an English novel. Albert Gallatin Simms was small in stature and wide of girth, a devout Baptist who quoted Latin mottoes on all occasions, and a chewer of tobacco who had deadly aim within ten feet of a cuspidor. Every boy, on arriving in class for the day's lessons, had to be prepared to read a chapter from the Bible. Simms frowned on levity and wielded the rod regularly, but most of his students remembered him as a rotund and bespectacled gentleman with "a wonderful faculty of imparting knowledge." Hill readily absorbed much of that knowledge; a classmate said that Hill's "devotion to his studies" exceeded that of "all his fellow students."[7]

Religion was another matter. The Hills had maintained their allegiance to the Church of England after they came to America, and the family gravitated after the Revolution to the Episcopal Church. In 1840, however, a "new light" Baptist revival movement swept through north-central Virginia. A descendant of the fiery evangelist James Ireland became remarkably effective in the area as a "Crusade for Christ." He converted Fannie Hill, who signed the pledges and plunged eagerly into the austerity of her new faith. Suddenly dancing, boisterous conduct, card-playing, and all forms of theatrics were banned in the Main Street home (although Major Hill adamantly refused to give up his occasional mint julep).[8]

Teenaged Powell Hill revolted against such curtailment of pleasure in his family. He felt unjustly confined to a cloistered life, and his youthful resentment caused him to become irreligious.

In the years that followed, he attended church service more from duty than from devotion. Furthermore, he always looked with disapproval on anyone who—like "Stonewall" Jackson, for instance—practiced religion with excessive intensity.

As fifteen-year-old Powell Hill spurned religion, he moved rather naturally toward the military. Southerners then were traditionally more martial-minded than other Americans. In the antebellum years at least one military academy could be found in every Southern state. Undoubtedly, too, the impressionable Hill listened with rapture to family stories of the exploits of such soldiers as Henry Hill and Ambrose Powell. His father encouraged him; his mother protested loudly that Hill was too young and loving to foresake home for a military life. Yet Hill, both determined and persuasive, soon won her grudging assent. With that, the wheels were put in motion to secure Hill an appointment to the nation's leading military school: the United States Military Academy at West Point, N.Y.

On September 13, 1841, in a petition to Secretary of War John C. Spencer, thirty-one citizens of Culpeper County expressed "pleasure in testifying to the intelligence, energy of character . . . and moral worth" of Powell Hill. The next month the county's most powerful political figure, John S. Barbour, informed Spencer that Hill's acceptance at West Point "will give to the public service an acquaintance both of hope & value." Uncle Ambrose Powell Hill lauded him as "a youth of promise." A family friend in Richmond wrote his congressman: "Possessing a sense of propriety and moral firmness that always must protect him from wrong doing, he has at the same time an amiability of heart and amenity of manners that endear him to all his acquaintances."[9]

Such endorsements bore fruit. On April 26, 1842, Hill wrote the secretary of war: "I have the honor to acknowledge the receipt of your communication of the 19th of April informing me that the President has conferred upon me a conditional appointment of Cadet in the service of the United States, and to inform you of my acceptance of the same."[10]

In late June, Hill prepared to leave Culpeper for West Point. The one attribute of a future officer that he possessed was confidence. A half year shy of his seventeenth birthday, he was tall and noticeably thin, with hazel eyes, a high forehead, and chestnut hair swept to one side. His father's going-away present was a Bible in which was inscribed: "Ambrose Powell Hill: Peruse this every day." The keepsake from his mother was unique. It was a small ham bone, which was to be a good-luck charm. Hill carried it with him all his life. Schoolmaster Simms bade him farewell by shaking his hand solemnly and intoning: "My boy, remember: Dulce et decorum est pro patria mori!" Hill often repeated the translation: "It is pleasant and fitting to die for one's country."[11]

At first glance, West Point was an awesome and foreboding place. The boat trip up the Hudson River was scenic but long; finally, at a sharp bend in the river, a small pier jutted into the stream. From the landing, the ground rose precipitously 160 feet skyward. Atop that ridge, situated on a forty-acre plain surrounded by wooded mountains, stood the cluster of buildings which was the Academy. West Point had been America's largest fort in the Revolutionary War. George Washington considered it the most important position in the colonies. Following national independence, the need for a professional training ground for army officers became acute. In 1802 (after strenuous objections from pacifistic Thomas Jefferson), the United States Military Academy opened for classes.

Chaos and mismanagement marked its first decade and a half. That changed abruptly in 1817, when Sylvanus Thayer became superintendent. Thayer upgraded standards, curriculum, and faculty to such a degree that by the 1830s the Academy had developed into a model military college as well as the foremost engineering school in America. Its star professor in 1842 was Dennis Hart Mahan. His Engineering and Science of War course was the seedbed of strategy and tactics for scores of cadets who later became Civil War generals. Thus, when Powell Hill arrived at West Point on July 1, 1842, the Academy was enjoying its greatest prestige and, with some 225 cadets, its largest enrollment.

Hill found himself in a class of eighty-five plebes. He quickly made friends with fellow Virginians Birkett D. Fry and Dabney H. Maury. Only a day or two after their arrival, the three teenagers were in conversation at the doorway of South Barracks when another new cadet entered the building. Tall, clad in homespun, with huge muddy boots, and staring at the ground, the plebe appeared awkward and ill at ease. "That fellow," Maury jokingly said, "looks as if he has come to stay."

On learning that the stranger was likewise a Virginian, named Thomas J. Jackson, Maury walked over and introduced himself. Yet, he later stated, "Jackson received me so coldly that I regretted my

friendly overtures and rejoined my companions, rebuffed and dis-
comfited."[12]

Hill and Jackson were never friends at West Point. Hill was of a
higher social status in Virginia than Jackson—and both knew it.
While Jackson had to study long and hard to survive West Point,
education came easier to Hill. Jackson scorned levity; Hill sought a
good time. Jackson practiced religion with a fervor Hill detested. In
a little book of axioms that Jackson kept (and practiced) was the
statement "It is not desirable to have a large number of friends."

Hill made friends easily at West Point. Numbered among his
close acquaintances were future Civil War generals Darius N. Couch,
John G. Foster, David R. Jones, Dabney Maury, Samuel B. Maxey,
I. Newton Palmer, George E. Pickett, Jesse L. Reno, George Stone-
man, Samuel D. Sturgis, Truman Seymour, Cadmus M. Wilcox—and
his roommate in number 36, Pennsylvanian George B. McClellan,
who was fifteen. Of a "gentle nature and high culture," McClellan
"went at once to the head of the class and remained there until the
end, enjoying the while the affection and respect of all." He and
Hill quickly became "on terms of great intimacy." McClellan's ease
with studies unquestionably helped Hill over the rough academic
road of that first year at the Academy.[13]

The full West Point curriculum then included mathematics, engineering, natural philosophy, astronomy, drawing, French, chemistry,
mineralogy, geology, military tactics, English and rhetoric, geography, history, and ethics (including law). Mathematics was far and
away the most important subject because it was the steppingstone
for advanced work in several other fields. Hence, it counted the
most when academic grades were tabulated. Examinations in January
and June were traumatic for the majority of cadets because six
months of work were summed up in those grades. At the end of the
first grading period, in January 1843, McClellan was at the top of
the class, Jackson at the bottom. Hill stood midway academically.
In cadet conduct he got off to a bumpy start.

An army officer of that day observed: "From the moment of entering the Academy, discipline is with [the cadet] always. It rises with
him in the morning at reveille, it attends him through the day, and
he lies down at night under its ever-present care. He learns that
'duty' is the one great law of life, and this law is embodied in every
lesson of every day."

Discipline was indeed strict. The cell-like rooms, spartan in furnishings, with mattresses on the floor, were expected to be impeccably neat at all times. So was the cadet uniform, which consisted of gray coat trimmed in black, bedecked with a profusion of brass buttons, and topped by a high leather collar and stiff leather hat. Daily marks were given for deficiencies at recitations; demerits followed any violation of regulations. Most of the offenses were trivial—an unbuttoned coat, giggling on the parade ground, not being cleanly shaved, and so forth—but the demerits added up ominously. A cadet who amassed one hundred demerits in six months was subject to dismissal from the Academy.[14]

Hill picked up the usual demerit here and there in his first term, but two major infractions—ten demerits for "not walking post properly" and eleven demerits for being "absent from reveille roll call"—sent him plummeting to the rank of fifty-fourth in behavior He then applied himself diligently for the next six months, made the honor roll for good conduct, and ended his first year at the Academy ranked thirty-ninth in his class.[15]

The one surviving letter of Hill's from that first year at West Point is startling, for it contains a sad mixture of forced humor, a sense of abandonment, love, and homesickness. For nine months he had heard nothing from his family and seen no one. He was extremely anxious for news from home, he said, "though if you never wrote me, that should not deter me from expressing my tender love and filial respect for such kind parents." Yet he was hurt because he had not received a single communiqué from the family. "I expected, at least, to be remembered with a feeling of some sort for one short year, but alas! for the frailty of human hopes."

Seeking parental attention, Hill momentarily became lighthearted: "Spring has just begun to put forth its budding beauties. Old heavy headed winter has taken his departure at last, though he has prolonged his visit to a greater length than was agreeable. The cheerful singing of the birds, the cloudless days and cool bracing air causes the blood to leap through the veins with exhilarating warmth."

Like most cadets, Hill had a low opinion of the post physician. "Our surgeon hardly ever has his services put in requisition, except when some poor fellow has studied himself in a headache and then the invariable remedy is a bread pill. Thank God! that so far I have kept clear of his skirt."

The letter closed with a soulful plea from a homesick lad of sixteen. "Do you intend visiting the Point this spring? Let me beg of you to muster up courage enough to undertake a two days journey. You cannot tell how happy I would be to see you. Do come! Tell Pa I shall consider this letter for him also, as he has not answered. Your affectionate son, A. P. Hill."[16]

The 1843–1844 year at West Point was, for Hill, a marked improvement. He devoted increased time to his studies while paying more attention to cadet regimens. By year's end, he had risen to twenty-third in his class of sixty-six cadets. He was pleased at his progress. Added to this, one of the great joys on reaching the status of a second-classman was a two-month summer furlough. Henry Heth spoke for his fellow cadets when he wrote: "I think those two months were among the most enjoyable of my life. The Duke of Wellington . . . could not have felt more exalted . . . than the West Point cadet, dressed in his furlough coat, with brass buttons, when strutting along the streets, or on entering the parlor of some young miss."[17]

That summer of 1844 was a generally pleasant time for Hill. The "lithe figure and manly bearing" of the cadet evoked the envy of many of Culpeper's youth; he listened quietly at home to lectures from his all-wise father and complaints from an always unwell mother, renewed old acquaintances, and enjoyed the leisure of summer.[18] He started back to West Point in an eager if not exhilarated mood. Then occurred the tragedy of his life.

Hill contracted venereal disease.

The place was probably New York City, through which Hill had to pass on returning to the Academy. Superintendent Henry Brewerton had repeatedly warned the cadets of the evils of the city. The "harems of pleasure in Church and Mercer streets" were notorious. Yet it is natural that the eighteen-year-old Hill, full of youthful exuberance, would have been attracted to the excitement of New York before returning to the sobriety of West Point.[19]

On September 9, 1844, Hill was officially admitted to the Academy Hospital "with Gonorrhea contracted on furlough." By the mid-1840s, the disease was easily identifiable. Three days to two weeks after contact, the male experienced "the urge to urinate frequently, with burning pain and with much thick pus in the urine." Treatment consisted of regular doses of copaiba, which one authority described as a "thick, yellowish-brown, spicy-smelling liquid—with an ungodly taste—used for everything under the sun, most especially gonorrhea." This medication (and all others until the advent, in the 1940s, of penicillin) was useless.[20]

Although gonorrhea in some people runs its course and leaves no lasting effects, Hill was not among the fortunate. In the weeks following hospitalization, he began having other, more serious complications: severe pelvic pain, fever, and difficulty in urination. The urethral strictures produced by the gonococcus had led to painful prostatitis. On November 19, Hill hobbled home on a convalescent furlough, which was repeatedly extended as months passed and he failed to improve in health. In March 1845, his family physician in Culpeper requested another extension by attesting: "I have carefully examined this cadet, and find that the disease of the prostate glands &c. under which he labored prior to his leaving the Military Academy still continues, and that in consequence thereof I conceive him to be incapable of military and academic duties."[21]

A few days later, however, Hill formally requested of the Academy commandant that his sixteen-dollar monthly stipend as a cadet be forwarded to him without further delay. Hill might have been physically—embarrassingly—ailing, but insistence on his rights under the law was evident even at this early age.[22]

The attacks of prostatitis would increase in frequency through the years, cause periods of excruciating pain and incapacitation, and ultimately lead to another, potentially fatal, illness. Hill's condition improved by the late spring of 1845, and he prepared to return to West Point. He was disappointed when, on June 23, a six-man faculty board at the Academy reviewed Hill's record and concluded that the long absence from classes had left him deficient, especially in philosophy and chemistry. The committee directed that Hill repeat his third year.[23]

The decision was difficult for Hill to accept. It meant saying goodbye to beloved classmates, who would now graduate a year ahead of him. It also meant having to make new friends among a younger class while trying to catch up in his studies. Hill did both, admirably. Many in the class of 1847 he already knew, so he had merely to strengthen the bonds of friendship. Virginian Henry Heth, Hoosier Ambrose E. Burnside, Georgian Julian McAllister, and Hill became an inseparable foursome in their last two years at West Point. Moreover, Hill's spirits were such in the summer of his return that he carried on by letter a tongue-in-cheek romance with a young lady. Hill described himself in part by writing:

"Dear Georgia, Now do not draw up and put on a dignified reserve at the 'Dear,' for you know you have given yourself to me for better, for worser, richer for poorer and I say the Lord save you from the bargain you've made; but the banns have been published and with the blessing of 'Uncle Sam' we'll be married some time before the millenium. Now I am going to give you some little insight into my 'cranium' so that your leap into matrimony may not be made entirely in the dark.

"First of all, I am a terribly jealous fellow, and now that you are summoned by so many handsome young beaux, the green eyed devil allows me no peace at all. . . . I am also remarkably fond of a good dinner, so buy one of Mrs. Randolph's cookery books and set yourself to studying. Also take a few lessons from Jim Clay in making sherry coblers, as I should like one always immediately before dinner. Also buy a drum and be taught the art of making music on a sheepskin, for I can never *retire* or rise without the sound of the drum. And a good many alsos which it is not necessary for you to know yet awhile."[24]

On September 4, 1845, Hill was caught using tobacco in his room and was confined to quarters as a result. A week later, on the other hand, Hill and Charles Griffin received promotions to sergeant. Hill's conduct the remainder of the year was nearly flawless: twice he made the honor roll. At the end of the third year, Hill ranked eighteenth in his class. He stood twenty-first in engineering, sixteenth in ethics, twentieth in artillery, sixteenth in infantry tactics, and twenty-first in geology. Yet any personal pleasure was lost in the excitement that swept through the corps of cadets that spring. United States forces invaded Mexico. The class of 1846 was ecstatic. "War at last sure enough!" Hill's former roommate, George McClellan, exclaimed. "Aint it glorious! 15,000 regulars and 50,000 volunteers!"[25] Hill watched with envy as his first Academy friends went south to seek military fame.

In the senior year, Hill and Julian McAllister were roommates. "They had a room over the commandant's office," Heth remembered, "and it was never inspected."[26] Heth and Burnside likewise roomed together. These four cadets, through practical jokes and boisterous conduct, became the social leaders—and hence the "party managers" —of their class. Their antics more than compensated for the lack of organized athletics at the Academy.

The two Virginians—Hill and Heth—spent much of the summer

of 1846 courting two young (and apparently forward) ladies staying at the West Point hotel. Both cadets became lax in conduct their senior year. Heth, for example, received reprimands for everything from "vulgar and offensive language" to "making improper use of the coal pile." Hill was not far behind. He averaged over ten demerits a month, knowing that misconduct marks in the final year were not taken seriously by Academy officials.[27]

Hill was eager to get to Mexico and do his share in the war. "I expect soon to enter upon the arena of strife," he wrote to his parents in March. Then to his mother he penned more personal lines. "It would make you laugh to see how eager the embryo heroes in grey coats are to flash their maiden swords, and calculating the chances of the old officers being knocked in the head, and their promotion. For my part I have a lucky bone from an old Virginia ham, and with that with me, shall feel as safe as by your side."[28]

June 19 was graduation day for the class of 1847. McAllister ranked fourth in the final standings, Hill was fifteenth, Burnside stood eighteenth, and Heth had the dubious honor of bringing up the rear. Twenty-one-year-old Powell Hill was the epitome of what an army colonel described as the new West Point graduate: "a very young officer with a full supply of self-esteem, a four-story leather trunk filled with good clothes, and an empty pocket." The $64.50 that Hill was to receive monthly was not going to fill that pocket rapidly.[29]

The Academy graduate went home to await orders. They came on August 11. He was one of thirteen in his class assigned to the artillery branch of the U.S. Army. Among the other twelve brevet second lieutenants were future Union generals James B. Fry, John Gibbon, Romelyn B. Ayres, and Charles Griffin. Two weeks later, Hill was promoted to second lieutenant in the 1st Regiment, U.S. Artillery, and ordered to report for duty in Mexico. He was to replace 1st Lt. Thomas J. Jackson, West Point class of 1846.[30]

The trip southward was exciting: by train from Richmond to Wilmington, N.C., from there by ship to Charleston, thence overland through Savannah, Macon, and Columbus on to New Orleans. Hill enjoyed five days of sightseeing at the Mississippi River port before boarding a troop ship for the final leg of the journey to Vera Cruz, Mexico. There he received assignment to Capt. Francis Taylor's horse artillery company, which was to be part of Gen. Joseph Lane's brigade. Late in September, however, Hill temporarily took charge of two hundred cavalrymen and a train of thirty wagons for the trip inland through Cerro Gordo to Lane's camp in the highlands of Jalapa.

As the only member of his West Point class to be seeing action in Mexico, and filled with exuberance over the prospects of battle, Hill adopted a flamboyant uniform. He wore a flaming red flannel shirt and coarse blue soldier's trousers stuffed into red-topped boots, to which were attached an immense pair of Mexican spurs. On his head, at a jaunty angle, rested a huge sombrero. His weapons, hardly less conspicuous, were a long artillery saber, a pair of horse pistols in enormous leather holsters, plus a pair of revolvers and a butcher knife, all stuck in a wide black belt. By his own admission, Hill resembled something between a strutting bandito and a mobile arsenal.[31]

The war, unfortunately for Hill's dreams, was in its final stages. The Mexican capital had fallen days earlier; Mexican politicians with any remaining influence were looking for some way to secure peace. Meanwhile, even though no longer president, General Santa Anna was defiantly leading bits and pieces of his army into battle. He besieged the American garrison at Puebla and forced Lane to move his command to the relief of that post.

Lane's long column was winding slowly through the arid mountain country when, on October 9, he received word that most of Santa Anna's force was at Huamantla, twelve miles to the north of Lane's line of march. Hill was then acting adjutant of Maj. Samuel P. Heintzelman's battalion. To his chagrin, he was among those left behind to guard the wagon trains after Lane dispatched a mounted contingent to Huamantla. The Americans engaged in a running fight through the town and occupied the place for a few hours. Suddenly, the Mexicans counterattacked in force, inflicting twenty-four casualties and driving the Americans back on their main column.

In retaliation for the killing of fourteen of his men, Lane turned his men loose on Huamantla. Hill was appalled at what followed. "The soldiers rendered furious by the resistance rushed through the town, breaking open the stores, houses and shops, loading themselves with the most costly articles, rendering themselves brutish by the drinking of aguardiente. The women screaming and running about the streets, imploring protection, was a sight to melt a heart of stone." The young lieutenant's conception of an army of gentlemen-soldiers was shattered. "Twas then I saw and felt how perfectly unmanageable were volunteers and how much harm they did," he stated.

Some two hundred soldiers were too drunk to get back to camp. The next morning, when the march resumed, straggling was rampant. Hill tersely noted: "My arm was perfectly sore from beating the men into obedience [with] both fist and sword."

The advance continued toward Puebla. A portion of the besieging Mexican army fell back eighteen miles to Atlixco. Part of Lane's force reached there late in the afternoon of October 12 and began a close-range artillery barrage. Hill was in the action and he observed: "The smell of gunpowder has some peculiar property which acts with powerful effect on the nerves of those Mexicans. They soon 'vamoosed.' " As green-clad soldiers raced out one end of town, municipal authorities scampered out the other end to surrender Atlixco. In the meantime, and despite a collective hangover, Lane's other regiments reached Puebla and broke the long siege.

Mopping-up operations followed; and in the process of "disinfesting" the area of guerrillas and bandits (as Gen. Winfield Scott put it), Hill wrote down a number of revealing observations. He was leading his men from Atlixco to Puebla when "a band of Guerrillas had the impudence to rob a number of pack mules, driven by their own countrymen within full view of our train. A small party of dragoons dashed out upon them and succeeded in killing thirteen. One of the teamsters, an insolent scoundrel, drew his revolver on a wagon master, and shot him through the arm, killing a soldier who was standing behind him. He was arrested, of course, and made a rare show for the good people of Puebla by dangling at a rope's end, and dancing the Cachuca on nothing."

Mexican women Hill found to be almost as pretty as American girls. "They have more beautiful feet, small almost to deformity, and the sweetest eyes in the world, but they have not the pure rosy complexion of ours, the lily vieing with the carnation for the rivalry, and lips on which 'kisses pout to leave.' " In contrast, Hill considered Puebla's male element "the most expert robbers and assassins in Mexico, and though the city contains upwards of seventy churches, the wonder of sanctity does not seem much to pervade them." Everywhere one turned, Hill noted, there were beggars. "I believe they compose half the population of Mexico, and it has got to be a common saying that now we've whipped the people, we have got to support them." He then closed a long descriptive letter with the revelation: "The night spent here will ever be memorable in my history, from the terrible attack made on me by an army of fleas and the great danger of my utter annihilation."[32]

Disease killed six times more American troops in Mexico than did Santa Anna's armies.[33] Operating in hot country, with practically no hospital equipment, the raw troops suffered epidemiclike waves of diarrhea, dysentery, typhoid fever, and yellow fever. Hill came close to being one of the 12,800 fatalities. He managed to avoid infection from the 3,000 sick soldiers he encountered scattered all around Vera Cruz, Jalapa, and Puebla, but contaminated water soon took its toll on him. Sometime in November, shortly after reaching his new quarters at Mexico City, he fell dangerously ill with typhoid fever.

For six weeks he battled the disease—its high fever, vomiting, severe headaches, and total prostration. Because of the severity and length of the seizure, and particularly the resultant high fluid loss, the typhoid attack could only have aggravated the prostatitis with which Hill was already afflicted. Yet he survived the bout with typhoid fever and looked back on it rather philosophically. "Twas a matter of toss up" whether or not he would "shuffle off this mortal coil," he told his father. He also reassured his sister: "I am well now, and as every body must have an acclimating spell, I am glad mine is over."

The twenty-two-year-old lieutenant returned to duty with his regiment and occasionally tasted the limited social life of the Mexican capital. "The ladies of Mexico *are* beautiful, oh, how beautiful," he declared. "However, very few of them ever read Wayland's 'Moral Science.' " He teased his father at one point by asking: "How would you relish a Mexican daughter-in-law? . . . Tis Sunday again, and the bells (belles) called me to my devotion."

Not all of the attractions were to Hill's liking, however. "I went to see a bull fight last evening," he wrote, "and came away thoroughly disgusted with this great national amusement of the Mexicans. Tis a cruel, most cruel sport, and how the ladies can so defame those feelings given them by Nature, as to look on with the utmost delight, cry 'bravo' and clap their pretty little hands, is mystery to me." Hill concluded his account of the spectacle by asserting: "I have seen human blood flow in streams, but this turned me sick at heart."

The war with Mexico officially ended February 2, 1848; on the last day of that month, Hill brought his parents up to date on his activities and opinions. For a time he had been billeted in luxury in Santa Anna's private chapel at the national palace. However, "twas not permitted to remain in this little sancture long, for as soon as the promotions came, I was gazetted to another company." As for his daily routine: "I generally rise at six, take a cup of chocolate, go out to the battery, drill until ten, breakfast at eleven, drill again at the manual of the piece from two till four, see that the horses are all groomed, so that you cannot soil a white glove by nibbling them, then dine at five, and smoke cigars till bed time."

Hill then offered judgments on some of his superior officers, and he did it with a bluntness that became characteristic of him. "Gen. [William J.] Worth is a weak headed, vain glorious, but brave man, perfectly reckless of the lives of his soldiers and his own, as witness the battle of Molino. Gen. [Gideon J.] Pillow is as soft as his name and will no doubt be dismissed from the Army for barefaced lying. Gen. [William O.] Butler is now in command, a general of mushroom growth, over whom I, young as I am, can claim some three years military experience. . . . I am now attached to Maj. Gen. [Robert] Patterson's division and like the old gentleman much better than any other mustang. He is affable and polite to his young officers, throwing into his manner very little of that hauteur which his men are so apt to think necessary to sustain high rank."

The last letter from Mexico closed with the observation "I have not had an opportunity to try [Mr. Simms's] maxim—'Dulce et decorum est pro patria mori'—and hope the trial may be long spared me."[34]

2

Love Affairs
and War Clouds

Hill spent most of the year 1848–1849 on garrison duty at Fort McHenry, Md. This installation was the principal defense for Baltimore harbor and had already been immortalized in Francis Scott Key's poem "The Star-Spangled Banner." Hill's duties there were light and pleasant. This one-year assignment led to his first serious romance.

Of all of the children of Thomas and Fannie Hill, no two were closer than Powell and his sister Lucy Russell. Perhaps there was a natural attraction between the last son and the last daughter; or their personalities may have been the most compatible. In any event, and despite some eight years' difference in their ages, Hill and "Lute" adored each other. Thus, with Hill at Fort McHenry and Lucy enrolled at Patapsco Female Academy in nearby Ellicott City, brother and sister saw much of each other—and in the process Hill met Lucy's classmate Emma Wilson.

It was a match between a maturing army officer from Virginia and a teenaged debutante from Baltimore; and with Lucy eagerly playing matchmaker, attraction moved swiftly toward first love for them both. The couple did not become engaged, as family legend has it, for the courtship ended more abruptly than it began. The Wilson family had no objections to a dashing officer escorting their daughter, but they did not regard the Hills as of equal social status. When a love affair became evident, the parents intervened and convinced Emma to direct her affections to someone else. The extent of Hill's disappointment is not known; two years later he could rationalize: "Love which will not keep, you know, is not worth having."[1]

Hill left Baltimore in the autumn of 1849 for an assignment in Florida. Again he was going into the tail end of a conflict. In 1835 Seminole Indians and runaway slaves had retreated into the Florida Everglades and defied American control. Seven years of guerrilla fighting raged in the swamps; over 1,500 soldier casualties made it the costliest Indian struggle in the nation's history. Despite the capture of the halfbreed chief Osceola (who was treacherously seized under a flag of truce), ambushes and search-and-destroy missions continued sporadically into the early 1850s. The American army was still trying to immobilize the Seminole threat when Hill arrived in the Everglades. He soon became regimental quartermaster for the 1st U.S. Artillery. Yet not even staff appointment and a later promotion could compensate for the almost six years of misery, boredom, and poor health that Hill experienced in Florida.

His duty station was Fort Clinch, situated on the Withlacoochee River northeast of Tampa Bay and headquarters for one of the seven military districts in the state. The artillerists were employed mostly in constructing roads and bridges from the fort to various outposts and garrisons. Hill's principal activity was to prepare monthly statistics on persons hired and materials expended in the quartermaster chores. The routine was so dull that for seven months Hill kept a small diary. Its entries contain few references to military matters. Rather, Hill voiced complaints about the alien environment into which he had been thrust.

For example, on October 16, 1848, he noted: "My God, will these mosquitoes never satiate their vampirean appetite for blood? Buggy, Buggy, Buggy. There is no peace for the wicked, saith the good book. Mosquitoes were especially sent on earth as a torment to the wicked. Wonder if Noah had any in the ark with him!" Nine days later, he wrote: "Went to a cracker's house, a grass widow, and inquired if she had any thing at all in the eatable line to sell. Answered as short as pie crust, 'No,' and slammed the door in my face. Thought I must have looked like the devil, that anything in the shape of a man could frighten a woman."

The heavens opened the following day. "Jehu! how the rain patters against this canvass tenement of mine! A soldier's life is always gay—What an infernal lie. Tis sometimes most confoundedly not, and rain always throws a *damper* upon my spirits." October 28 was Sunday, but "no sounds of church bells cheerily calling the pastoral flock to imbibe pure thoughts from inspired tongues." Later that day, Hill and a fellow officer went on a sightseeing tour. They proceeded a mile to a "cracker's" house. "Went in & made ourselves at home. Nearly split my throat bawling at the old woman who was deaf & shamed my eyes looking love to the daughter, who was confoundedly pretty. Wish to Heaven that old woman had been blind instead of deaf."

Hill became poetic over the dense foliage of western Florida: "Earth is so kind here. You have only to tickle her with a hoe and she laughs with a harvest." He found the families sometimes of equal productivity. Accompanying a census-taker one day, Hill was shocked when they came to one cabin alive with the "squalling of children." He added: "My God! The eruption of the Huns into Italy would but feebly portray the living stream which gushed forth from the door to greet our arrival."

With very few diversions available, Hill's consumption of alcohol increased noticeably. In mid-November 1849, on the return leg of a long patrol through rain and swamps, he candidly described the effects of his drinking. "The brandy bottle, a quart out, was full when I started," he declared, "but being so cold, wet, and thoroughly chilled, I drank all of it and came into camp and they tell me just rolled right off my horse." Hill barely remembered Christmas Day that year. After partaking freely of eggnog at the fort, he and a fellow officer decided to grace another party with their presence. "Wilson & myself mounted our horses [on a] clear moonlight night and rode nine miles to a dance.—And such a dance! Much excitement and whiskey the foundation of it all." Three weeks later, Hill went on a strenuous march through the swamps. That was bad enough, but the theft of his bottle along the trail was infuriating. "Some scoundrel stole my whiskey from my wagon while I was in advance. May it choke him, confound him!"[2]

By May 1850, Hill was both angry and pessimistic over the present and the future. He poured out his frustrations in a letter to his father. "We have already been in Florida eight months, wintering in tents, and the season for an active campaign allowed to pass in inactivity. The time which should have been devoted to forcing the Indians out, has been consumed in trying to talk them out, and the Indians as a matter of course have out-talked us, lying being the chief ingredient in their diplomacy. . . . For six months I have been in the woods, no society, clothes all worn, salt provisions, occasionally a deer, and at present no prospect of a termination. . . . I am heartily tired of it. With a grasping spirit, we are continually acquiring more territory, and our army is actually smaller than before the Mexican War. . . . In case we get Cuba, God help us! I shall go home and maul rails."[3]

To make matters worse, sickness then struck the young lieutenant. Although it has long been commonly assumed that Hill fell victim to yellow fever, which ravaged the American army in Florida, it is more likely that stress, overindulgence, and the debilitating effects of the climate combined to provoke a severe attack of prostatitis.[4] For several months Hill was unable to perform any duties because of weakness and the pain that shot up through his body when he attempted to mount or ride a horse.

While trying to regain his health, Hill wrote an outraged letter to one of his brothers, Baptist, concerning slavery and threats of Southern secession. In August 1850, Hill learned that a Culpeper mob had lynched a young black accused of murdering a white man. Hill was livid at what residents of his hometown had done. "Shame, shame upon you all, good citizens," he asserted. "Virginia must crawl unless you vindicate good order or discipline and hang every son of a bitch connected with the outrage." (Hill's wife stated after the war that he "never owned any slaves and never approved of the institution of slavery, but [he] thought the Government should not take the slaves from their masters without paying something for them.")

In that same 1850 letter, Hill commented on the widespread talk of national disunion. His reaction was as much personal as patriotic. "If the Union is dissolved I shall make tracks for home, and offer my service to the Governor, and intimate my modest desire for a brigade at least. I've been a sub long enough, and wish now to seek the bubble reputation at the cannon's mouth."[5]

Either Hill's poor health or a rotation of duty assignment led late in 1850 to his transfer to the remote outpost at Key West. Life there was as lonely as the routine was drab. For a year he did little more than hunt, fish, and submit monthly reports to the U.S. Quartermaster Department. An occasional bout of prostatitis limited his activities. On September 4, 1851, Hill was promoted to first lieutenant.[6] That did little to assuage either his pugnacity or his restlessness. Only a week later, he pursued two deserters and finally cornered them as they hid in the hold of a ship. Sailors sympathetic to the fugitives looked on menacingly as Hill ordered the two on deck. One emerged very slowly and snarled, "It is not worth while to be in such a hurry about it."

"I thought it very necessary to be in a hurry," Hill wrote, "so I raised my sabre and struck him so hard as to fell him, and drawing my pistol told the other fellow to lift his companion up and take him on deck. He did so in quite considerable of a hurry, I can tell you."[7]

Such interludes relieved monotony, but Hill's major concern continued to be his health. To a friend the following month he declared: "I do not wish to remain here another summer. I have thus far weathered it safely *though it has been nip and tuck*, but I do not like to tempt fate too much. She might give me the slip next time and leave me to be carried out feet foremost."[8]

By November, however, Hill became so bored that he requested a transfer. The War Department responded by sending him to frontier duty at Camp Ricketts, in the extreme southern tip of Texas.[9]

Hill was initially unimpressed by the country along the Rio Grande, and his opinion did not improve during the year he spent there on patrol duty. Only a few months after his arrival, displaying his more cultivated background, Hill vented his contempt of the Texas settlers. "One who has not been here, and daily mixed with the people living on this frontier can have no conception of the state of society, the quintessence of ruffianism and scoundrelism that has been squeezed out from the states and sprinkled along the Rio Grande. Human life is but held as a feather in the list of possessions. . . . I was in Brownsville but some ten days and four men were shot down in the streets. Two gentlemen, they call them down here, whacked out their six shooters not ten steps from our camp the other day, and blazed away at each other until one got a bullet in the bread basket which has forever stopped all desire on his part to fill it. And this is the country to annex which both blood and treasure has been poured out freely as the rains from Heaven. . . . My regret is that [these residents] do not destroy each other fast enough and finally shoot out the entire race. The world would be no loser, and certainly Heaven no gainer."[10]

Following a bitterly cold winter in which at times Hill slept underneath seven blankets, he welcomed spring and a resumption of patrols. He demonstrated in a number of ways that he was a good soldier when given the opportunity. One afternoon his detachment was lounging on the bank of the Rio Grande. Gen. William S. Harney's boat arrived at the landing. Hill went aboard and saluted the general.

Harney asked, "How long will it take you to pack everything and be on board with the company?"

"One hour by the watch, sir," Hill replied.

"Very well, sir," said Harney, "I'll give you three hours."

Hill wrote with pride that his fully packed company was aboard the ship sixty-five minutes later.[11]

News from home became disturbing. Fannie Hill was not well, and her psychosomatic maladies were becoming more disruptive. Hill tried to reassure her through his father. "Tell my dear mother to cheer up. The world has many days of happiness in store for her yet." In July 1852, Hill wrote a light but affectionate letter directly to his invalid parent. "And how is my dear, good old mother? How progressed the demon of the imagination in magnifying her ailments? They all write me from home that your health is good. Now say, is it so? Or are they mistaken as usual, and only fooling me?" Hill then momentarily displayed his childhood love for her: "Will you long as affectionately to throw your arms around me, once more, as I have longed, oh so *much*, to be again an inmate of the old yellow room?" He closed with touching words: "Good bye. God bless you. Your afft. Son, Powell."

Despite years of duty far afield, Hill's ties to his hometown remained strong. He was in charge of a battery which was to fire a Fourth of July salute to the thirty-one states. Hill confided that he ordered an extra volley: *"One for old Culpeper! and home!"*[12]

Hill returned to duty in Florida later that year. He was first at Fort Barrancas in Pensacola harbor, and on at least one occasion he temporarily commanded the garrison there. Yet the old discontent with Florida remained. He expressed the hope to Lute that he would soon be ordered northward. "Heaven grant that it may be so, as it only needs a 'Swamp' order to make it so. This is dull and the sand is deep, but the Everglades are duller, and the water deeper." By then he had wearied of the idea that America could conquer the Seminoles in an all-out offensive. " 'Twould be unwise in Uncle Sam to engage in such an expensive war as 'twould prove to be, and only to drive out a few poor, lazy harmless devils from the country that no white man could, or would live in."[13]

Fannie Hill died in 1853. Hill's memories of her thereafter became more dear; so did the little ham bone she had given him as a good-luck charm, which was always in his pocket. The emptiness and the sorrow would have been more acute had not Hill's duties increased significantly. Later in 1853 he and his unit—Battery D, 1st U.S. Artillery—shifted over to Fort Capron, at the mouth of the Indian River in the northern part of the Florida peninsula. Hill was second-in-command of the small garrison. That winter an armed truce went into effect between the army and the Seminoles. Construction began immediately on a new line of outposts from Fort Jupiter on the Atlantic coast westward across the peninsula so as to confine the Indians more securely within the Everglades region.

Throughout 1854, backbreaking work continued in the swamps and heat. It was normal army duty at a frontier post, but it was not Hill's idea of a soldier's life. He later complained that, "God's curse being upon" him, he spent month after month "building bridges, cutting roads, grubbing roots and fighting mosquitoes." Yellow fever and typhoid fever quickly struck in epidemic proportions. The mortality rate among the soldiers was such, one officer stated, that "there were hardly enough strong men remaining to bury the dead." Hill mercifully escaped the first onslaughts of the two diseases. In fact, his major concern in the first weeks of 1855 was to gain promotion. "I have been serving so long as a subaltern that now I am ambitious of the title Captain," he informed Lucy.[14]

Then Hill collapsed from yellow fever, prostatitis, or both. His affliction was so severe that he was ordered home to recuperate. Lt. John M. Schofield, who was recovering from typhoid at the Fort Capron base hospital, later recalled that when Hill arrived there en route to Virginia, he fell desperately ill with yellow fever. Schofield stated: "I had to send a barge to Jupiter for some medicine. . . . Mr. Jones, the sutler, and some of the men helped me to nurse him night and day for a long time. At length he recovered so far as to continue his journey."

By the time Hill was sufficiently well to travel, Schofield had received transfer orders. The two officers departed for home together. However, on the St. John's River steamer, Schofield had a recurrence of typhoid fever. "Hill cared for me tenderly, and kept me at Savannah awhile, and then some days at Charleston." Hill insisted that his new army friend accompany him home to Culpeper. There Schofield remained until he was well. Hill's father lent his help by insisting that a brandy mint julep start each day for the patient. "Under its benign influence," Schofield wrote, "my recovery was very rapid."[15]

Hill was the "gay lieutenant, social and sportive," during his long recuperation at home. A neighbor observed that "he still wore the charm which captivated the child, and that even the stern duties of mature manhood did not destroy the wonderful gentleness of his fine gray eye." How many romantic adventures he had at this time is unknown, but one of them was a widow "who showed him motherly love." Hill's physical disability, however, became the overriding issue. The length of his incapacitation suggests that following recovery from yellow fever the old prostate disease reappeared. His health "becoming very much impaired," Hill found it impossible to return to field duty. He therefore requested transfer from the 1st U.S. Artillery to a desk job. "By the kindness of Secretary [of War Jefferson] Davis," he was detailed for special duty in the United States Coast Survey offices at Washington, D.C.[16]

On November 23, 1855, he began his new assignment. The Coast Survey was part of the U.S. Navy, but Hill, an Army man, was a logical choice because of the engineering experience he had gained in Florida. The five years he spent in the Coast Survey office brought various duties and consistent praise. Hill was part of a team that carried out the triangulation of the Hudson River around the Albany area. He also was a leader in improvements made in map printing. Very quickly, an early biographer stated, Hill "acquired a reputation for dispatch of business and urbanity of manner, so very rare, that Congress remarked upon it." A friend added that "Lieutenant Hill was faithful and attentive to his duties, and a great favorite with all his brother officers, as well as in the refined circle of society in which he moved."[17]

In that "refined circle of society" occurred a number of flirtations and brief romances. One was between Hill and a Miss Carrie. It ended more abruptly than the young lady desired. Hill gingerly backed away with what he considered a farewell letter. "No doubt, Miss Carrie, you imagine that the old adage out of sight, out of mind, is the one rule governing me with those I am proud to number among my friends. If indeed your imagination has taken this, I must call it wild flight. You wrong me, for even I, together with the many warm friends you secured to yourself during your stay here—have often thought of you—mentioned you—and that too in terms which would most certainly please one who loved to be well thought of." Hill wrote in a rambling style for three more pages and then closed by sending "kindest remembrances to Miss Redfield, and believe me your true friend."[18]

Then came the celebrated love affair with Ellen Marcy. Everything about Ellen Mary Marcy was attractive. She was the daughter of Maj. Randolph B. Marcy, an 1829 West Point graduate and professional soldier famed for explorations of the West, including the Red River country. Ellen was twenty-one, blond, blue-eyed, and sprightly. In the winter of 1855–1856, while Major Marcy was on assignment in Texas, Ellen and her mother lived at Willard's Hotel in Washington. The two ladies were regulars at capital social functions, with Ellen luring one suitor after another. But there was a hitch.

His name was George B. McClellan. This West Point classmate of Hill's had accompanied Marcy on the Red River survey, and both Major and Mrs. Marcy had been extremely impressed with the young officer. Both parents, in short, wanted him as a son-in-law. McClellan had dutifully and rather feebly conducted a courtship of Ellen; then he went to the Crimea as a military observer for the War Department. It was at that time, when Ellen and the headstrong Mrs. Marcy were unattended, that Lieutenant Hill appeared on the scene.

At first he was but another escort for Miss Nelly. However, the couple soon fell in love, Hill proposed, and Ellen accepted. Hill had already presented Ellen with an engagement ring before the Marcys were aware of how serious the affair was. Then both parents reacted with anything but joy. From Laredo, Tex., Major Marcy wrote his daughter: "Did my affection for you merit such a breach of confidence? . . . I forgive you, but I should expect that you at once abandon all communications with Mr. Hill. If you do not comply with my wish in this respect, I cannot tell you what my feelings towards you would become. I fear that my ardent affection would turn to hate. Do nothing, therefore my dear child, without choosing between me and him."[19]

Marcy employed every persuasion. He urged his daughter to wait at least six months before committing herself to wedlock. The major painted harsh pictures of life on the frontier as an army wife. He pointed out Hill's Southern upbringing amid a detested slave environment. Moreover, Hill's means were limited. "I received a letter from Mr. Hill in which he says he is worth $10,000. This is something but not much," Marcy sneered. In contrast, McClellan was a captain; "his talents and well known high character with the warm friendship which exists between us would have caused me to discard all other considerations and given you to him."[20]

By then, McClellan had returned to America. Learning of the situation, he went to Hill for clarification and then politely retired from the contest.

Now Mrs. Marcy took action—and with a vengeance. Somehow, through a check of service records or via army gossip, she learned of Hill's contracting venereal disease while at West Point. Mrs. Marcy thereupon leaked the scandal, if not to the public, then at least to the family. Typically, Hill was outraged at what he regarded as a personal affront. Moreover, he believed that he was completely cured of all effects of gonorrhea. He expressed his hurt—and confessed his helplessness—in a four-page letter to Major Marcy:

"My Dear Sir: I have been most deeply injured but the peculiar nature and unknown source of the calumny prevents my seeking that redress which would be most pleasing and most satisfactory. You know that last Spring I asked that you would consent to my marriage with your daughter, to which you postponed giving a decided reply. This was made by me in all honor and good faith, and I supposed then and now that your opposition touched not my personal character. Mrs. Marcy has evidenced a decided hostility to my suit, which though it pained me much, yet was conceded to her as her right, and I was silent as long as I conceived the grounds of her opposition to be such neither you nor I should blush to hear. I now find that I have been in grievous error.

"I have heard from truthful lips and with delicacy, that Mrs. Marcy's objections . . . are that from certain early imprudences (youthful indiscretions I suppose), my health and constitution had become so impaired, so weakened, that no mother could yield her daughter to me, unless to certain unhappiness. This is the substance. The ornaments may be imagined. Nor do I do Mrs. Marcy the justice to believe that this has been told her, and that she without weighing the matter calmly has believed it, for I have ever thought her a woman of good feeling though somewhat warped against me. . . . The charge is simply indicative, yet fatally blighting.

"True or untrue the mere rumor is sufficient to make a man bow his head in shame. Hence I cannot meet and refute it, as in any other case, and as my inclination would lead me to do in this, for this would give it the publicity I desire to avoid. At present, I hope it has reached but few, and these I wish to scotch it, if not kill it. I can trace no farther back than your wife, and to you as the proper person I address myself. If this charge were true, and knowing it to be so, I had asked your daughter's hand, my honor indeed [would] be but a name, and my simple denial would be unnecessary. . . .

"I ask it of you as one gentleman from another, as one officer who has been wronged, from a brother officer, that your wife correct this false impression with whomever she may have had any agency in hearing it. I think too that in justice both to herself and myself she should make known the name of her informant to be used by me as I see fit."[21]

Marcy weakly assured Hill that his wife's alleged statements were a "base fabrication." At this point, McClellan found himself drawn into a war of words between the Marcys and Hill. Mrs. Marcy apparently concluded that McClellan was the one who told Hill of her publicizing the gonorrhea incident. McClellan promptly wrote Mrs. Marcy: "As a matter of course I transmitted to Hill *none* of the remarks you made; I thought that you would regret what you had written before the letter reached me—that reflection would convince you that you had been unjust to him, & that you had said unpleasant & bitter things to me in reference to one of my oldest & dearest friends.

"Under no circumstances would I repeat such things. If a gentleman had made use of such expressions to me about Hill, I should have insulted him, & made the quarrel my own. . . . I wish you to understand distinctly that after the first conversation I had with Hill —commenced by myself—no other words have passed between us on the subject."[22]

By then too much damage had been done. On July 31, 1856, Ellen informed her father that the affair with Hill had ended. She returned the engagement ring to Hill, who gave it to his sister Lucy. Engraved on the ring were the words "Je t'aime."[23]

The year 1857 for Hill began with sadness but ended happily.

His father died on January 6. That loss, coupled with the death a year later of his eponymous uncle, severed a number of cherished ties and left Hill feeling lonelier than ever. Yet there were rewarding times. In April he was a groomsman at the Richmond wedding of his West Point friend Henry Heth. This event first introduced Hill to a Richmond society he came to know well in the years ahead. Hill and fellow officer Earl Van Dorn then made a brief inspection tour of Texas. His work in the Coast Survey elicited commendation from Superintendent Alexander D. Bache: "Lieutenant A. P. Hill continues to occupy this position (viz, general assistant), and the interest as well as ability, displayed by him in performing the requirements of the office cannot fail to meet your warmest commendation."[24]

It was also in 1857 that Hill found the lady with whom he would share the remainder of his life. One evening Hill attended a Washington party given by a friend, Dr. Wood. There he met Kitty Grosh Morgan McClung. Born July 25, 1834, to one of Kentucky's most prominent families, Kitty Morgan grew up with her brothers and sisters in an imposing home, Hopemont, at the corner of Mill and Second streets in Lexington. Kitty's Negro mammy had nicknamed her Dolly because she resembled a large china doll. Although in Kentucky she was always called by her proper name, to Hill she was never anything but Dolly.

Family members described her as a "sparkling and vivacious" woman with "blue eyes & chestnut hair, a lovely talking voice," and one who "sang like a nightingale."[25] Dolly was also opinionated and outgoing. On June 14, 1855, while Hill was ardently pursuing Ellen Marcy, Kitty had married Calvin McClung, a cousin who had become a fairly prosperous merchant in St. Louis. McClung had a sense of humor and delighted in pointing out how marriage had calmed down his Kentucky belle. In a letter to her family, he wrote: "Tell Aunt Betty that Kitty has not spoken a harsh word of any person since she left Lexington. Quite a reformation!" A couple of months later, he noted the hearty appetite his bride was displaying. Then McClung feigned disappointment because he recently had a chance to take a trip "and would have gone but for the idea of leaving Kitty all alone. So much for being married."[26]

McClung died suddenly. A year later, the captivating widow of twenty-three journeyed to Washington to visit friends. There she met the thirty-two-year-old lieutenant in the Coast Survey. Hill was smitten almost immediately. To Lute he confided: "You know that I am so constituted, that to be in love with someone is as necessary to me as my dinner, and there is now a little siren who has thrown her net around me, and I know not how soon I may cry 'Percavvi!' and yield up my right to flirt with whom I please. She is a sensible little beauty, and if the spasm will stay in me long enough, and she will say 'yes,' why I don't believe I could do better. Alas, though, I much fear that the good things of this world are unequally distributed in her case. Her beauty and sense are her only dowry!"[27]

As Hill meticulously courted Dolly McClung in 1858, he also campaigned hard to fill the vacancy of "Captain in the Subsistence Department." In October he laid his case before Secretary of War John B. Floyd: "I base some claim to the position sought upon the following facts, which are of record—a service of nearly twelve years as a Lieutenant, seven of which have been in the unhealthy climate of Florida, and performing duty in the Commissary Dept. . . . During the Mexican War I was the only officer of my class [at West Point] who arrived in Mexico in time to participate in any of the engagements . . . and whilst every Officer of the Army in the War, I believe without a single exception, and many who were not in the war at all, received brevets or rewards for their services, I received none. That this did not occur from any misconduct or failure to perform service on my part I am sure the evidence of others will bear me out."

Twenty-two members of the Virginia Senate endorsed Hill's application. So did a Washington resident, James Chilton, who told Secretary Floyd: "I have known Lieut. Hill almost from infancy and I have never known a more gentlemanly young man, or one of better habits and principles." Florida senator Stephen R. Mallory added his voice to the chorus. "From long personal knowledge of you as an officer and a man," he wrote Hill, "I must frankly say that I know of no officer of any grade more competent than yourself to the faithful discharge of its duties."[28]

His position as an army officer working in a navy-associated office was probably the major factor that blocked Hill from getting the promotion. Hill's frustrations would doubtless have been keener had not the romance with Dolly McClung moved toward marriage. Late in the spring of 1859, Hill lightheartedly poured out his feelings for Dolly to George McClellan, still a close friend. "I'm afraid there is no mistake about it this time, old fellow, and please God, and Kentucky blue-grass, my bachelor life is about to end, and I shall swell the number of blessed martyrs who have yielded up freedom to crinoline and blue eyes. I have gone in direct opposition to the advice of the Elder Welles and mean to put my trust in a 'widder,' with the firm belief that there must have been some moral obliquity obscuring the vision of the parental Welles, or else he never saw such a widow as mine. She is young, 24 years 7 mos., gentle and amiable, yet holy, and sufficiently good looking for me—and what's more—I know that you will like her, and when you come to know her, say that I have done well.

"I believe that her income is close to mine—and if this be so I am glad for her sake, and if not I shall not be disappointed. I expect to be married in Lexington, Ken., on the 18th July, and if you could ride down from Chicago, you know that there is no [one] whose presence would delight me more."

Hill then switched the subject to the now-gone love affair with Ellen Marcy. "I have heard a report lately which has annoyed me a good deal, that the Marcys had given their consent for my marrying Miss Nelly, and that I had declined. Now you would of course know that this was untrue, but others might believe it. If you should ever hear it, please flatly contradict it for me. The last communication I ever had with Miss Nelly, about two years ago, she positively and without leaving a ray of hope rejected me—and that's the truth. This much is certainly due her."

The letter closed with "best love" to "Old Burn" (West Point classmate Ambrose Burnside) and Hill declaring to McClellan: "Believe me as ever, your friend."[29]

Powell Hill and Kitty Morgan McClung were married July 18, 1859, at the Morgan home in Lexington. Dolly was stunningly beautiful in a flowing gown; Hill, now sporting a large mustache, was a fitting bridegroom in full-dress blue uniform with gold braid and large epaulets. No one in the Hill family could attend the ceremony, so John Hunt Morgan (another future Civil War notable) served as best man for his new brother-in-law. The Reverend J. H. Morrison of Christ Episcopal Church in Lexington officiated. Dolly's strong allegiance to this denomination now brought Hill full circle back to the Episcopal church, although his interest in religion remained lukewarm.[30]

Following a brief visit to Culpeper, the newlyweds settled into a life together in Washington. It was an exceedingly happy marriage from first to last. Army pay was poor, promotion was exasperatingly slow, and living conditions on a lieutenant's salary were anything but luxurious. However, Dolly's income eased the financial pressures, and the social whirl of the capital was exciting, especially for a couple who made friends so easily because they loved each other so obviously. Their union "was an ideal one," a daughter later observed, "as Father was a man of unusually fine traits, gentle & courteous, a wonderful sense of humor, and a charming man."[31]

Dolly complemented her husband so naturally that the two became inseparable. Not even war could keep them apart. Whenever possible, she would accompany Hill in the field from one theater to another. She acquired a well-known habit of staying too long and too close to the front lines because of her insistence on being with her husband.

The first rumbles of that approaching war burst into an explosion only three months after the marriage. Militant abolitionist John Brown's raid on the federal installation at Harper's Ferry, Va., failed pitifully, but reaction from an aroused South was instantaneous. In Hill's home county of Culpeper, a resident asserted, "patrols were increased, mass-meetings were held, military companies were raised and equipped and everything was done to put the State in readiness for war." Hill watched these developments with the apprehensions shared by a majority of Americans north and south.[32]

On May 22, 1860, in the midst of national uncertainties, McClellan and Ellen Marcy were married in New York City. Hill was a groomsman at the wedding. His best wishes for the couple were sincere and strong, for he himself had at last acquired a wife he adored.[33] Later that year, Dolly gave birth to a daughter, who was christened Henrietta (in honor of Dolly's older sister). She was the first of four children—all girls. Netty, as Hill lovingly called her, was born with fragile health and had a tragically short life.

The election of Abraham Lincoln as president of the United States sparked the secession of South Carolina and brought the national situation to a crisis. Six other Deep South states quickly followed South Carolina's lead. Hill viewed outright war as imminent. On January 2, 1861, in the midst of an extended furlough, he wrote his sister, still "isolated" in a Baltimore school. "I have been sick for two weeks, and today for the first time begin [to] feel like myself again. I got your letter with the sweet little present for Netty. . . . Poor little thing, she is suffering with a terrible cold and threatened with croop. Dolly is scared, of course, and can think of nothing else. . . .

"Tell Carter to prepare to pack up his traps unless he desires to live in the Northern confederacy, for surely the end is approaching."[34]

Fellow officers at the Coast Survey sought to reassure Hill that if he remained at his job, he would not be ordered to bear arms against his native region. However, the issue with Hill went much further. He had always loved his native state. Back in 1847 he had asserted: "There is one regiment on which I would stake my life, and that is the one from dear old Virginia. I would fight for its honor and reputation as soon as for my own." Convinced that Virginia must inevitably go the way of her Southern sisters, he resolved to leave the Army near the end of March, but as the fractured nation seemed to hasten toward hostilities, Hill saw no need to delay. On February 26, he submitted his resignation. He had examined his alternatives. Defense of slavery and secession held no attraction. However, family ties, Virginia traditions, disenchantment with the federal government, and allegiance to the land of his forefathers were all deeply instilled in Powell Hill. There was no real choice to make: he must cast his lot, for good or ill, with the Old Dominion and the new Confederate States of America.

The General
Emerges

Hill took Dolly and little Netty home to Culpeper. They stayed with his older brother Baptist at his home a block off Main Street. Culpeper had the aura of "a quiet, tidy-looking city, filled with the luxuries and comforts of life, and abounding in the highest souled generosity." Yet appearances were deceiving. Anxiety was high there and throughout Virginia. Like other families, the Hills waited and watched as war slowly swept into view. A Richmond editor commented on the situation of men like Hill: "The large number of officers who have resigned in both Army and Navy is one of the most striking evidences of the hopeless dissolution of the Government we have yet seen. These two branches of service have always been composed of the *elite* of American society." The editor added that the dream of restoring the Union "is the wildest of all spectres that ever rove at midnight through a lunatic asylum."[1]

In early April another Virginian observed: "We scarcely hear anything talked of but war. Even clergymen whose mission it is to preach 'peace on earth and good will to men' are infected by the belligerent spirit now prevailing, and they divide their time between the Sermon on the Mount and conversations upon the subject of fighting." At a mass meeting in Orange Court House, a few miles down the road from Culpeper, a huge crowd thundered approval of a resolution that stated in part: "Virginians, to arms! War is begun! . . . Fly to arms, and by bold and prompt action let us drive from the high places . . . these destroyers of our peace and enemies of our institutions."[2]

As heavy rain fell on April 14, word came that Fort Sumter had fallen to Confederate forces. The news "caused the most intense excitement" in Culpeper. Years of sectional debate and threats were over. So were years of peace. Hill, who admitted to being "thoroughly Southern upon the question of the War," tendered his services to Gov. John Letcher as Virginia severed its ties with the Union.[3] The thirty-five-year-old Hill journeyed to Richmond with the hope that his experience would qualify him for a general's stars, but to his great disappointment he was told that a generalcy was out of the question.

A reporter passing through Culpeper in the last week of April wrote: "The military spirit of Culpeper is fairly aroused, and almost every train bears away some of her gallant sons to join their companies in arms at Harper's Ferry. . . . The ladies, God bless them, are busy night and day making up clothes for the absent ones, and for those who are preparing to leave." Hill was among those departing. He had been ordered to join units rendezvousing at Harper's Ferry, where the Shenandoah and Potomac rivers merge, a site that was the key to the Valley of Virginia. Hill reached there early in May, not knowing exactly what he was to do. He must have had the same impression as another young officer: "Harper's Ferry is a beautiful and romantic place. Its appearance is quite lively and animated; nothing but *soldiers soldiers* every place."[4]

On May 9 Hill received appointment as colonel of infantry in the Confederate army, and he was assigned command of the 13th Infantry Regiment. The former artillery officer and coastal survey assistant moved at once "to organize, equip, drill, and discipline his regiment," wrote the young chaplain of the unit, "until it was soon pronounced the finest in the service"—which was not saying much under the circumstances.[5] One of Virginia's most famous veterans, Gen. Joseph E. Johnston, later admitted that the "army" at this point "was simply a vast mob of rather ill-armed young gentlemen from the country. . . . The Companies, unarmed, untrained, and hardly even organized, . . . were in theory drilled and disciplined and made into soldiers by a little handful of available West-Pointers and lads from the Military Institute at Lexington." Adding to the confusion was the fact that "measles, mumps, and other diseases, to which new troops are subject" became so prevalent "that the average effective strength of the regiments of the army did not exceed five hundred men."[6]

The 13th Virginia was not "localized," as were most 1,000-man regiments in the Civil War. Six of the ten companies were from the

Culpeper-Orange vicinity. Two other companies were organized in remote Hampshire County. One came from nearby Winchester. The tenth was an "orphan" company from Maryland. A member of the regiment wrote that these were days "of 'holiday' soldiering, where we were all quartered in houses, where we drilled in dress uniforms and white gloves, where every private soldier had his trunk, and each company had enough baggage for a small wagon train."[7]

Hill met the challenge of commanding 700 raw recruits by personal example, repetitive duties, and hard work. Battle drill and dress parade occurred several times daily. The colonel showed early that he treated officers and soldiers alike. On May 25, Hill issued a stern warning: "The Colonel having requested that officers must attend the drill at 1/2 past 9, and some of them having failed to be present, he now orders that every officer of his Regiment not otherwise on duty appear at this drill at 1/2 past 9. Any officer failing to appear, and without a good cause, will be arrested and reported to Head Quarters. And the same order will hold good as to the evening parade."[8]

Only long marches broke the camp regimen, but they hardly offered relief. The 13th Virginia was far afield one afternoon when a hailstorm began pelting the column. Hill would not stop the march. "Many thought the end of the world was at hand," Hill's adjutant commented; and when darkness at last brought a halt, every man "was cold and wet to the skin, and covered with mud from head to foot." The regiment trudged back to its camp the following day, "as footsore and broken down a lot of men as is often seen."[9]

Chaplain J. William Jones, fresh out of seminary, eagerly asked permission to hold religious services. Hill refused. "A good fighter now is more desirable than a good preacher." Jones bemoaned the fact that between daily drill and nightly picket duty, he had no opportunity "of wedging in a sermon."[10]

The colonel's hard-driving routine slowly molded the ten companies into a single command with a "forward spirit" and "veteran-like appearance." Discipline remained firm, but there were occasional light moments. One cold, rainy night Hill decided to ride out and personally inspect his picket line. He dismounted near a post and walked silently up to the sentry, whose musket was propped against a tree and who was thrashing his arms about in an effort to get warm. Hill almost walked into the guard before he was seen. The man jumped in surprise, then chuckled: "Damn it, sir, what do you mean by running against a sentinel? Couldn't you see him? But, my friend, I forgive you, for nobody but a damned fool would have thought a sentinel necessary on such a night as this!"[11]

Hill enjoyed a laugh at this retort, and he had no qualms about his men taking an occasional drink, as he did; but he drew the line sternly when the whiskey was bad or was drunk in distracting quantity. One of his first interregimental directives made that point clear. "Sir—you will move your company into a Hotel known as Shorters. My Regiment is being poisoned by the liquor that is being sold to the men and it must be broken up. You will take as much room as may be necessary for your company, even if it should include the whole house. If the liquor is not removed by the Proprietor immediately, you will take the Regimental wagon and move [the whiskey] to Hd. Qrs. for the final disposition of the Colonel commanding."[12]

The Virginian became an easily recognizable figure among the thousands of troops encamped at Harper's Ferry. Neatly polished black boots came almost to the hips. Disdaining full uniform, Hill preferred calico or checkered shirts, which Dolly sewed for him. Nor did he have any use for the kepi, the cap popular in that day. Instead, Hill chose a black felt hat, which became a trademark. His accoutrements were narrow saber attached to a belt on one side, revolver on the other side, plus oversized buckskin gloves, which he was inclined to wear year-round. Quite often a pipe protruded from his mouth. Hill now was letting his hair grow longer, and he was following custom by developing a large beard. His horse in the early stages of the Civil War was a black stallion named Prince.[13]

In command of Confederate forces at the northern end of the Shenandoah Valley was fifty-four-year-old Joseph E. Johnston. A small, lean, gray-headed professional soldier from Virginia, Johnston had a trim mustache and goatee, in keeping with a dignity that he wore like a protective shield. Johnston was reserved, but Hill had known him for many years and liked him. Another officer in camp whom Hill remembered from prewar days was Thomas J. Jackson. His aloofness bordered on eccentricity, and no indications exist that the two very different colonels had much to do with each other that spring.

Hill's first nine months as a Confederate officer required unusual patience and determination. Disappointments began in June, when he missed the action of the Romney expedition.

While the forces of Johnston and Federal general Robert Patterson (the same Patterson whom Hill had praised in the Mexican War) warily eyed one another at a distance, Col. Lewis Wallace and his 11th Indiana occupied the railhead at Cumberland, Md. From there the Federals made a descent on Romney, only forty-three miles from Johnston's headquarters at Winchester. Wallace seized Romney after a spirited fight. Hill, with the 13th Virginia and the 10th Virginia, had just fallen back from Harper's Ferry to Winchester when Johnston ordered him, leading those two regiments, along with Col. John C. Vaughn's 3rd Tennessee, to "move toward Romney without delay, and take the best measures in his power to retard the progress of the Federal troops."[14]

Hill advanced rapidly in anticipation of his first battle. However, by the time he had completed the tedious march over the mountains to Romney, Wallace had fallen back eighteen miles to New Creek. The Union stab had been blunted, but Hill was not satisfied. He dispatched two companies from the 13th Virginia and two from the 3rd Tennessee—all under Vaughn—toward New Creek. Vaughn was to attack any small force he encountered there and burn the strategic Baltimore & Ohio Railroad bridge over the Potomac River.

"I am happy to assure you," Hill stated to Johnston in his first official report, that the instructions "were carried out to the letter." Vaughn marched his companies all night and on June 13 found 300 Federals posted on the north side of the river. A Richmond correspondent dramatically described the early-morning assault. "Our brave fellows, in the face of the enemy, forded the stream, waist deep, drove them off in the utmost confusion, capturing two pieces of loaded artillery and a stand of colors, destroyed the railroad bridge at that point and returned to Romney, making the march of thirty-six miles and gaining a brilliant victory within twenty hours."[15]

Federal losses were three killed and several wounded. Two Confederates were casualties in the affair, reported a newspaper. A Tennessean caught a spent bullet in the arm, picked it out with his knife, and continued in pursuit of the Federals. A member of the 13th Virginia fared worse. He "was seriously injured by dropping some fire from a pipe which he was smoking amongst some cartridges. He will recover."[16]

Meanwhile, back in Romney, a young commissary officer announced to Hill that no beef was available for that day's ration.

"Very well," replied Hill. "You can report back to your company. We have no earthly use for a commissary who, in a [rich] country like this, cannot furnish regular rations for the men."

Hill then called for his horse and left camp. Some time later he returned, "driving a herd of fine beeves" in front of him. Loud cheers went up from the soldiers: "Colonel Hill is the Commissary for us!"[17]

The colonel then triumphantly marched his men—many of them hobbling barefooted because of blisters—back to the base camp at Winchester. He had commanded three regiments, carried out orders explicitly, and shown calm skill in the pursuit of Wallace. Additionally, Hill in a short space of time had produced a regiment hailed as among the best in Johnston's army. All of these factors pointed to quick promotion to brigadier general. However, most of the accolades for the successful foray into northwestern Virginia went to Vaughn; word then came out of Richmond that the Old Dominion already had a disproportionate number of brigadiers in service and would get no more for the time being. Hill's close friend John Barbour of Culpeper visited him in Winchester and gave reassurances that he was exerting all of his political influence in Richmond to get Hill promoted. "You will never succeed," a dejected Hill replied. "President Davis does not like me. If he has his way, I will remain in command of my gallant little regiment until the war closes."[18]

His disappointment became more acute when Johnston a few days later reorganized his forces after new units and new officers arrived. The Winchester army was divided into four brigades. Jackson, Barnard Bee, and Francis S. Bartow led three of them. Hill's 13th Virginia, along with the 10th Virginia, 1st Maryland, 3rd Tennessee, and Grove's Battery, constituted the Fourth Brigade, under a Marylander, Arnold Elzey.

Sultry weather descended upon the army as it stayed at Winchester. Alarms of reported Federal advances were regular occurrences, a correspondent reported. "Our troops were frequently drawn up in order of battle, and always 'fell in' as the bridegroom hastens to the wedding." At least one member of Hill's regiment disagreed sharply. "We confronted Patterson for days," he wrote, "marching from point to point . . . until we were all disgusted and began to feel the Yankees would not fight."

This same soldier acquired a toothache and asked to go to a Winchester dentist. "No, Sergeant," Hill responded. "Wait until tomorrow. You may have it filled with lead before night."[19]

By early July, with each day seeming hotter than the last, Hill's regiment was encamped in woods four miles from Winchester. It was a preferred site, a visitor noted. "The location is cool, pleasant and agreeable, and just far enough from town to keep the soldiers orderly. . . . The men are all well and in good spirits, and seem to enjoy a soldier's life exceedingly, and make no complaint, except they want a little 'fire-water,' which they cannot get, as none is allowed to be brought into camp."[20]

Whether because Hill was unrealistic or because he was insistent that his men be properly outfitted, he submitted a requisition on July 11 for 700 uniform coats, 700 pairs of trousers, 700 caps, 1,400 pairs of socks, 1,400 pairs of drawers, 700 pairs of shoes, and 1,400 flannel shirts. The request was apparently approved, but no evidence remains to show that the items were delivered.[21]

Soon after one in the morning on Thursday, July 18, 1861, the troops were awakened and told to dismantle their camps and pack quickly. The men were unaware that Johnston had received a directive from Richmond to join Gen. P. G. T. Beauregard's army at Manassas with all haste. The Union's largest force had left Washington and was on its way to where the Manassas Gap Railroad joined with the Orange and Alexandria line. Battle was a certainty.

Leaving some 1,700 sick and wounded soldiers at Winchester, and with Col. J. E. B. Stuart's cavalry screening the move from Patterson, Johnston led his brigades eastward toward Manassas. The route was through the Blue Ridge Mountains at Ashby's Gap, then across the Shenandoah River to Piedmont, a station on the Manassas Gap Railroad only thirty-five miles from the vital junction with the Orange and Alexandria. Shortly after the 13th Virginia left Winchester at the tail end of Johnston's column, Hill halted the regiment and informed his men that they were rushing to Beauregard's aid. "This gave the men new life," one of them later asserted, "and we marched with light hearts to Piedmont. . . ."[22]

That was not exactly the way it happened. The march was hot, dusty, and accordionlike. So many delays occurred the first day that Johnston despaired of reaching Beauregard in time. It took Hill's men almost ten hours to march thirteen miles because every time any portion of the force stopped, Hill's regiment at the rear had to do so as well. The jerky movement continued into the night.[23] A soldier in the Maryland regiment wrote home: "In that forced march . . . we knew no distinction between night and day, but marched during both without rest almost, and almost entirely without food." At dawn on the nineteenth, Elzey's brigade reached the Shenandoah River. The men paused awhile before fording the stream in water up their chests. Rain soon began falling. Sometime in the wet darkness of July 19–20, Hill and his soldiers arrived at Piedmont.[24]

"Everything was bustle and confusion" at the station as eager troops waited to board the one train running shuttlelike between Piedmont and Manassas. Disappointment then blunted enthusiasm: Elzey's brigade was ordered to remain at Piedmont as depot guard until all other troops had departed. For twenty-four hours the men stood or sat impatiently by the track. Hill's regiment and the sister units finally boarded the now-deteriorating train and began an agonizingly slow ride. It was Sunday, July 21; and as the train neared Manassas, the sound of battle grew louder. The great contest had begun.[25]

At twelve-thirty, the cars ground to a halt at Manassas Junction. The battle arena was six miles away. Troops rapidly detrained, threw knapsacks into a pile, and, under a broiling sun, started across the country at double-quick. Excitement was high, anticipation keen. This was to be the moment of glory! Then, for Hill and his regiment, came a demoralizing shock. The 13th Virginia, the smallest of Elzey's regiments with only 550 men present, was ordered to leave the brigade and proceed to the right so as to guard Manassas and the lower fords of Bull Run from possible Federal flank attack.

The Virginians "were all disgusted," one of them later commented. "The war [was] to close and we to have no part in it!" Hill was furious. His chance to take a leading role in the war would be gone if the Yankees gave up after one battle, as was expected. So the troops waited and listened and fumed as the afternoon wore along and shouts of Confederate victory eventually filled the air. Another disappointment now marked Hill's military career. He must have wondered if he was under some sort of curse.[26]

Rain poured on Monday the twenty-second as Hill's regiment continued to perform guard duty. Johnston and Beauregard then moved the troops forward to take advantage of the Federal rout. Soldiers in the ranks saw a different reason behind the march. "We were literally starved out of Manassas," one of them recalled, "and were forced to advance to Fairfax Court House in order to get supplies which the Union army had left in abundance." Johnston admitted that the forward movement was imperative. "Until the 10th of August, we never had rations for more than two days, and sometimes none; nor half enough ammunition for a battle."[27]

Hill's men arrived at Fairfax on July 24 and remained encamped there into the autumn. The colonel quickly requisitioned fifty tents for his companies as they settled into dull routine. For Hill, however, early August was a time of unblemished happiness. Back in May, Dolly had gone to live with an uncle in Nashville. Now Hill received word that on August 1, Dolly had given birth to a second daughter. She was named Frances Russell, had her father's chestnut hair, and later "sang like a bird" despite a slight lisp. Hill would call her Russie.[28]

The weather fluctuated in August. When cold rain was not falling, the temperature soared to one hundred degrees or higher. The general tone in camp became "miserable and gloomy." Transportation breakdowns and commissary incompetence combined to produce regular shortages. The troops on one occasion went three days without rations, "except what little they could buy or beg of the citizens of the thinly settled country." Typhoid fever, measles, mumps, diarrhea, dysentery, and jaundice began to scourge the encampments. A South Carolina soldier observed: "The green corn, it was said, did the army more damage than the enemy did in battle. Wagons and ambulances went out daily loaded with the sick." Fairfax was soon more hospital than town.[29]

The regiment spent one week marching along the perimeters of the Confederate position. Rain made the outing a nightmare. Hill often dismounted on the march and allowed a more weary soldier to ride awhile and regain his strength. One night the troops made camp during a downpour. Later in the evening, Hill rode up to the sergeant of the guard, who was obviously tired. The man never forgot that Hill "directed me to lie down and sleep and he would call me every two hours or when wanted." Such acts, the sergeant asserted, gave the men in the 13th Virginia an "exalted opinion" of their colonel.[30]

Skirmishes picked up in frequency along the northern Virginia line as North and South geared fully for war. On August 25, with Hill incapacitated by illness, part of his regiment plus some of Stuart's cavalry advanced under fire and seized Mason's Hill. From the top of this strategic eminence Washington could be seen. Several men in the regiment were wounded in subsequent picket encounters. A quick strike at Bailey's Cross Roads on September 3 by portions of Hill's regiment netted eight Federals without a shot being fired. Not even a drenching rain on the return march could dampen exhilaration. "Our regiment is now in fine condition," one of Hill's men wrote a newspaper, "and under the leadership of that accomplished soldier and gentleman, Col. A. P. Hill, who has won the enthusiastic admiration of every man under him, you will hear from us whenever we may meet our hireling foe."[31]

This was one of the first notices of Hill by the press. The oversight was due in the main to the fact that Hill's regiment was in a mixed brigade. Camped nearby was Gen. James Longstreet's all-Virginia brigade, which had also won laurels at Manassas. Its activities in camp and on picket dominated the columns of Richmond newspapers that autumn.

On September 2, Hill wrote a long letter to Lute. He hoped soon to rent a home in Richmond for Dolly and the children, he said. Then, changing the subject, he asked his sister (as well as the rest of the family) to quit teasing Dolly about his first love affair. "I should bargain for one thing, that you all did not plague Dolly about Emma Wilson, for she is very sensitive and easily affected by such things. I want to send to Nashville for her now, before the weather gets too cold, and would do so immediately if I could only get some place to board her. . . . She is uncomfortably situated, her uncle's home in Nashville being crowded by people flying from Kentucky.

"We are still lying on our arms here, in a perfect state of sluggishness so far as the cause is concerned. To be sure, we are having little brushes occasionally in which my Regiment has had its full share, and we are just as far from a settlement of our difficulties as we were before the battle of Manassas.

"Gen. [E. Kirby] Smith has assumed the command of our Division of the Army, and I hope that his young and vigorous counsels may at least force us to be killed on the field rather than be dying of these pestilential fevers."[32]

Sickness then forced Hill temporarily to turn over command of the 13th Virginia to Maj. James B. Terrill—and this indisposition cost Hill another chance at military recognition. On September 11, a Federal force of 1,800 infantry and cavalry, along with a heavy battery, tried to establish an outpost at the village of Lewinsville.

"Jeb" Stuart learned of the move and responded by advancing with 305 men of the 13th Virginia, a section of artillery, and two companies of cavalry. Stuart caught the Federals unprepared and sent the 13th Virginia charging into their exposed right flank. Fighting lasted ninety minutes before the Union soldiers "took to their heels in disorganized flight." Eighteen of their number were casualties. The Confederates suffered no losses. While Stuart received most of the credit for the affair, Major Terrill came in for praise that would have gone to Hill had he not been struggling in Fairfax to regain his strength.[33]

Hill was back in command a week later. He longed now to see his wife and his daughters, one newborn, the other always sickly. However, Dolly and the girls were then at her parents' home in Kentucky, separated from him by Union forces. When they would be able to get to Virginia was uncertain. On September 19, Hill led his regiment in a grand review for Johnston and other officers. The army commander told Hill afterward that he had never seen regular army troops drill so well. At five that afternoon, Dolly Hill was present in spirit at a special flag presentation. A member of the regiment stated: "The flag is a beautiful silk banner, the handiwork of the accomplished lady of our Colonel, and will be prized and defended as the gift of a fair daughter of unhappy Kentucky, bidding us a hearty 'God speed' in fighting the battles of the South." The flag was made of material from Dolly's wedding dress. It waved proudly over the 13th Virginia until captured in battle. Dolly thereupon sewed another standard for the regiment.[34]

It soon became obvious that the Union army—now commanded by Hill's former close friend George B. McClellan—was not going to make another invasion of Virginia that year. A Richmond editor announced sarcastically: "McClellan consistently thinks no more of attacking the Confederate Army . . . than of attacking the man in the moon." Nevertheless, 41,000 Confederates could not remain, strung out as they were, in advanced positions. This was especially true of the area north of Fairfax Court House. "This country," a soldier wrote home that autumn, "is in a sorry condition, the fences all burnt up, the houses deserted, the crops annihilated, and everything showing the footprints of war."[35]

The 13th Virginia, with the rest of Elzey's brigade, fell back to within two miles of Manassas. Scores of tents and lean-tos popped into view at a site the men dubbed Camp Hill. In the months ahead, the troops did little but perform camp guard, endure week-long stints on the picket line four miles away, and participate in grand reviews for generals and visiting dignitaries. At one such review, a reporter wrote, two of the regiments "gave a specimen of the Yankees running at the battle of Bull Run. It was truly a laughable scene, and created shouts of applause."[36]

Sometime in November, Hill smuggled his family through the lines from Kentucky to Culpeper and dashed there himself for a quick visit with his wife. He had to rush back to the Manassas line for two reasons. First, the brigade commander, General Elzey, was absent much of the time, and whenever he was gone, Hill acted as temporary brigade commander. The experience was good for him. As for the men, one of the chaplains stated that Hill "so mingled rigid discipline and kind consideration for the command as to win the respect, admiration and love of the whole brigade, as he had always had of his own regiment." A member of the 1st Maryland was apparently referring to Hill when he wrote of a Virginia colonel who unexpectedly "came in and sat down with us [privates], and talked to us in as friendly a way as if we had been his equals in rank."[37]

Secondly, and naturally, under the circumstances, Hill again became a leading candidate for promotion to general's rank. His division commander, Kirby Smith, made a strong effort to have Hill assigned to a vacant brigadier's slot. That appointment, however, went to a non-Virginian. Hill's preoccupation with his own advancement irritated several members of the 13th Virginia. Some soldiers reacted adversely to the idea of Hill's leaving the regiment; others took umbrage at being "neglected." One private went so far as to assert that during this time Hill "was regarded by many of his Regiment as very *ambitious for promotion*. . . . I don't think he ever afterwards paid a visit to his old Regiment. . . . I have always remained impressed with the idea that his greatest motive power was promotion and military distinction."[38] Such an opinion was shared by few men who knew Hill. His ambitions were as real as those of other commanders, but they were not dominating.

On December 18, Elzey's brigade received long-awaited orders to go into winter quarters. Hill's regiment encamped in a pine thicket, which steadily disappeared as log cabins came into existence and the need for firewood increased with cold weather. A Virginia soldier in the brigade spoke for most of his compatriots when he ended the year by writing home: "We lead the *dullest imaginable* life here. Shut out from the world, hid away in a pine thicket, we have nothing to think of but the loved ones at home."[39]

A week later, Hill expressed violent anti-Northern feelings in a letter to a friend. "What changes, my God what changes since last we met. Even though we looked forward to this rupture, yet how little idea we had of the reality of things as they now are, and how many of our old friends, upon whom we would have staked our last dime, have shown the cloven foot, and are now most bitter in this war of subjugation. Yet, notheless, by the blessing of God, and hearts that will never grow faint, we will whip the damned hounds yet— and then God grant that a gulf as deep and as wide as Hell may interpose between us." Hill noted that the men were "in fine condition, and better still are confident of success, and mean to fight for it."

Dolly, he added, "is now in Culpeper, and though within 20 miles of me, I have seen her but once since April. She has another *little girl*, so will have a good supply of sweethearts for you."

Hill closed by stating that "we all are persecuted, and for what? Nothing but to get politicians out of a damn bad scrape they have talked themselves into."[40]

The weather was miserable that first winter of the war. Rain, snow, sleet, fog, and mud preoccupied those men not struck down by sickness. Roads became impassable; carcasses of horses reportedly sank out of sight in the mire. "Oh! the mud! the mud!" a soldier who later served under Hill wrote in his diary. "I have heard some of the soldiers wish that Manassas Junction was sunk to a very warm place which I shall not mention."[41]

Long-deferred promotion came to Powell Hill in that dreary period.

Reorganization in command structure that winter had become necessary through a combination of illness and transfers. Early in February, Johnston placed the "well qualified" Hill first in a list of colonels he recommended to the War Department for elevation to brigadier. Promotion came that month.[42] Leaving the 13th Virginia was no easy thing. Almost singlehandedly, Hill had converted those hundreds of inexperienced volunteers into a unit so professional that even the highly critical Gen. Jubal Early later stated, "They can do more hard fighting and be in better plight afterwards than any troops I ever saw."[43]

Williamsburg
and a New Hero

Late in February 1862, Hill bade farewell to his regimental officers
and men. Then the new general proceeded to army headquarters.
There he found Johnston wrestling with the necessity of having to
withdraw his forces from northern Virginia. McClellan's massive
Army of the Potomac now numbered in excess of 150,000 men.
Johnston had barely a third of that number. So, early in March,
Johnston ordered his brigades to consolidate on the line of the Rapidan and Rappahannock rivers. With all of those preparations and
movements to be accomplished, it was not until March 24 that Brigadier General Hill got his new command: Longstreet's former brigade,
consisting of the 1st, 7th, 11th, and 17th Virginia regiments, along
with the Loudoun Battery of artillery.

Several days earlier, knowing those orders were on the way, Hill
had spurred his horse Prince southward and joined the brigade at
its camps around Orange Court House. A general's wreath now
surrounded the three stars on his lapel. Yet the steel glint in his eye,
the black felt hat and calico shirt, the sword buckled to his side—all
were the same. The troops soon learned that this new general possessed a strong character, despite his thin physique. On March 26,
Hill issued his first directive as a general. It was short and to the
point. "The undersigned assumes the command of the First Brigade.
All orders and regulations heretofore existing will continue in force
unless otherwise specifically ordered."[1] This low-key approach to
command was one reason why Hill at the time was so unknown

behind the lines. A Richmond newspaper even announced the promotion of "A. P. Hall of North Carolina."[2]

The general spent much of his time becoming acquainted with the officers and men in his brigade. He even spent an evening at a cotillion in Orange Court House, where he demonstrated surprising agility on the dance floor. This brief interlude ended on April 2 with the receipt of marching orders. McClellan was on the move, albeit reluctantly. President Lincoln, like most Northerners, had tired of waiting. The president ordered McClellan to advance into Virginia, strike for Richmond, and bring an end to the potentially terrible war. McClellan vacillated as long as he could; then he suggested a roundabout move whereby his huge army would proceed by boat down the Potomac River and Chesapeake Bay to the tip of the Virginia peninsula formed by the York and James rivers. From there, presumably, McClellan would sweep unimpeded up the peninsula some seventy miles and seize the Confederate and Virginia capital, thereby knocking the Old Dominion out of the war and probably ending the sectional struggle. If McClellan honestly expected to pull off such grandiose tactics while Johnston innocently or helplessly remained in northern Virginia, that expectation was one of the most mistaken assumptions of the entire Civil War.

Johnston knew when the Union army made its first moves, and he was kept fully informed by spies of McClellan's offensive thereafter. To check this invasion meant transferring the Confederate army east of Richmond and as far down the peninsula as possible. A rapid repositioning by both armies began. For the Confederates, the situation was perilous. "The loss of Virginia is a thought which should not be admitted into the head of any person of authority in the Confederate States," one editor asserted. "If the Confederacy loses Virginia it loses the backbone and right arm of the war." There was irony in this confrontation between Johnston and McClellan. Before the war, they had been such intimate friends that in their regular correspondence Johnston usually began his letters "Beloved Mac."[3]

Hill's brigade began its march on April 3 and made as good time as rain and mud allowed. The men covered nine miles the first day, passed Verdiersville, and bivouacked alongside the road the next day. When the weary and mud-caked column reached Louisa Court House on the sixth, Hill at his own expense treated every man in his command to a drink of whiskey. A two-day rainstorm began the following afternoon. Suffering in the ranks became acute. A chaplain's letter asked rhetorically: "How would you enjoy sleeping if it had to be effected out in the woods, in a driving rain, with a soggy, spongy soil for a bed, and no covering for a blanket? I have waked up at midnight under such circumstances and found half the regiment standing silently and gloomily around the camp-fires, while now and then the barking, hectic cough of some afflicted soldier preached a sermon on death."[4]

On the sixteenth, Hill's regiments arrived at Richmond and embarked on boats down the James to King's Landing, near the beautiful colonial town of Williamsburg. From there the men slogged through ankle-deep mud to the Confederate entrenchments in front of Yorktown. Gen. John B. Magruder and some 12,000 troops had been uneasily confronting McClellan's ever-increasing army as Union regiments disembarked daily at the Yorktown piers. Magruder's troops were frantically strengthening their works as Johnston with equal haste was rushing every company, battalion, and regiment he could find to the defense of the peninsula.

Commanding the division to which Hill's brigade belonged was a man soon to become one of Hill's principal nemeses for the duration of the war—and long after Hill's death. Maj. Gen. James Longstreet, a powerful man more than six feet tall, with cold blue-gray eyes and an irritating air of self-assurance, had been a reasonably good-natured officer in the war's first months. However, in January 1862 his family fell victim to a scarlet fever epidemic in Richmond. Three of his four children perished within days and were buried by friends as Longstreet hovered over his critically ill wife. This tragedy so sobered the general that he became uncommunicative and reserved. Between such a person and the normally genial, outgoing Hill, friction was inevitable.[5]

Initially, all went well between the two headstrong officers. On April 20, Longstreet ordered Hill and his 2,512-man brigade to take charge of repairing and completing the thin line of earthworks that formed the division's sector at Wynne's Mill. Hill had permission to commandeer all other troops he needed. Water was to be drained from the trenches; slats were to be placed on the trench floor for better footing. "The boards of any old house in the neighborhood will answer for this object," Longstreet stated matter-of-factly.[6]

For two weeks Confederates slaved at their task with only limited results. One of Hill's privates commented: "The service on the Peninsula was arduous and disagreeable; in the muddy trenches, or back in the woods, lying on the rain-soaked ground, or marching along the cut-up and muddy roads, was trying indeed, and caused no little sickness among the troops." Despite the danger of picket fire, some of the men preferred "a prone position out in the open to the pits half filled with water by the almost incessant rain. The trenches themselves filled with water and could not be drained." Hill was always present to give instructions and personal assistance. Occasionally Johnston would ride along the lines and acknowledge cheers. A private in the 11th Virginia observed: "He always reminded me of a gamecock trimmed and gaffed ready for the main."[7]

Johnston realized by the first days of May that his line, although being strengthened daily, could not withstand an artillery bombardment of the magnitude McClellan was planning to launch from land batteries and gunboats. The Confederates would have to fall back slowly and jab at McClellan whenever possible while waiting for additional reinforcements. Therefore, under cover of darkness on Friday, May 2—after McClellan's men had been digging emplacements for a month—Johnston began withdrawing his forces from the Yorktown line. Stuart's cavalry galloped back and forth to serve as a rearguard antenna. Hill's men left their trenches at Wynne's Mill, moved westward two miles, and bivouacked until four the next afternoon. The brigade resumed its march and halted after darkness at Lebanon Church to await the passage of the last units. At two in the morning Hill ordered his men to fall in behind the army. A member of the 7th Virginia recalled: "We were soon on the road, in the mud, floundering and pushing toward Williamsburg, about twelve miles distant, reaching there early next morning after an all night march. The command halted in front of the grounds of the Eastern Hospital for the Insane."[8]

By late Sunday afternoon, most of the 56,000 Confederates under Johnston had passed through the second-line earthworks east of Williamsburg. The silence of the plodding march under heavy skies suddenly ended. Sharp musketry announced that pursuing Federals had made contact with Stuart's horsemen. Johnston detached two of his brigades and sent them back to the Williamsburg trenches to blunt the Federal advance. Meanwhile, Hill's brigade marched out of the deserted and already decaying town. The troops bivouacked in a muddy expanse a mile or so to the west. At two in the morning rain began pelting the regiments.

May 5 was a nasty Monday in which a cold downpour limited

visibility and thoroughly drenched everything. It was also the day that Hill got his first taste of battle in the Civil War.

A mile east of Williamsburg, running north to south, was the main defense line for the town. Its anchor was an extended entrenchment called Fort Magruder, which covered the high road from Yorktown. Thirteen square earthworks strengthened the line on either side of Fort Magruder. Protecting the approach to the main fort were a moat, a line of abatis, rifle pits, felled timber, and another row of rifle pits only a few yards from a wide forest.

Hill's men were up at dawn that day. They were weary from the previous days' marches; yet like Hill, one of them stated, the troops "were in the very best of spirits and anxious to 'fight and have done with it.' "[9] At seven-thirty the Federal division of Gen. Joseph Hooker poured out of the woods toward the Confederate positions. Federals drove Gen. Richard H. Anderson's thin outer line back into Fort Magruder. Other bluecoats clambered over four of the redoubts to the left of the fort. The whole Southern line was in jeopardy. With more Union regiments fanning out into the open, Longstreet (commanding the rear guard of the Confederate army) sought to reconsolidate the Southern defenses. Gunfire now rolled in waves across the country. Only a limited number of cannon could be brought into play by either army. A Federal officer noted that most of the artillery "were buried up to the axles [and] were with difficulty drawn out of one deep rut, only to fall immediately into another."[10]

The men in Hill's brigade could hear the tumult of battle three miles away. They grew first apprehensive and then restless as the minutes passed and they did nothing. Finally, at eight-thirty, a courier dashed up in the rain to Hill. Longstreet needed his brigade at the front with all dispatch. The Virginians were to form in the rear of the Confederate line, Hill recalled, "that I might support either the right or left of our line as the occasions demanded."

That day Hill was wearing a dark blue blouse, pinched at the waist by his sword belt. He had attached a sprig of pine to his hat, either for good luck or for identification. Thus clad, Hill doubletimed his men back into Williamsburg, where they dropped all baggage before continuing out of town toward the sound of combat. Hill later reported: "I moved the brigade across the fields under a heavy fire of artillery, which was borne with all the steadiness of veterans and formed it in line of battle in rear of the redoubts and in supporting distance of General Wilcox."[11]

The brigade was in an open hollow perpendicular to the York-town road and to the right of Gen. Cadmus Wilcox's brigade. Gen. Roger A. Pryor's regiments were to Hill's right. It was ten in the morning. For the next hour Hill's soldiers strengthened the muddy works as best they could while Federal long-range guns and superior artillery battered their position. The Confederates tried to fight back, but inferior and malfunctioning guns were no equal for the Union firepower. Longstreet saw that to continue the contest would be suicidal. Besides, his wagon trains could not clear Williamsburg before nightfall. His best alternative was to attack. Orders to that effect went out to brigade commanders Hill, Anderson, Wilcox, and George E. Pickett.

This was the moment for which Hill had waited. At last he was to demonstrate leadership ability under fire, to lead his men to victory in battle. Hill quickly directed the 7th, 11th, and 17th Virginia to advance into action. Men cheered at the order, "and with fixed bayonets, steady pulse and rapid steps," wrote one of them, "the defenders of Virginia's sacred soil moved through mud, along a ravine, and up a hill."[12]

By now the Federals of Hooker's division had taken strong cover behind trees and thickets. They unleashed close-range volleys of musketry into Hill's ranks. The Confederates could see little because of the smoke and rain, but they continued forward unflinchingly. At that moment, some troops appeared through the mist a hundred yards obliquely to the left. Col. James Kemper, one of Hill's boyhood chums and commander of the 7th Virginia, tried to make positive identification but could not. Hill, now dismounted (as he so often was in battle), walked up rapidly. Kemper pointed to the troops. Hill gazed through his field glasses, then said: "Yes, they are Yankees. Give it to them!"

Kemper repeated the order, and "a deafening roar" of musket fire came from the Virginians. The Confederate advance picked up speed, with their general leading the way. "As [Hill] went forward, waving his pistol over his head, looking back over his shoulder and calling on the men to follow," a soldier stated, "he made a splendid picture of the heroic and gallant soldier that he was."[13]

The 17th Virginia, Hill noted with pleasure, moved forward "with

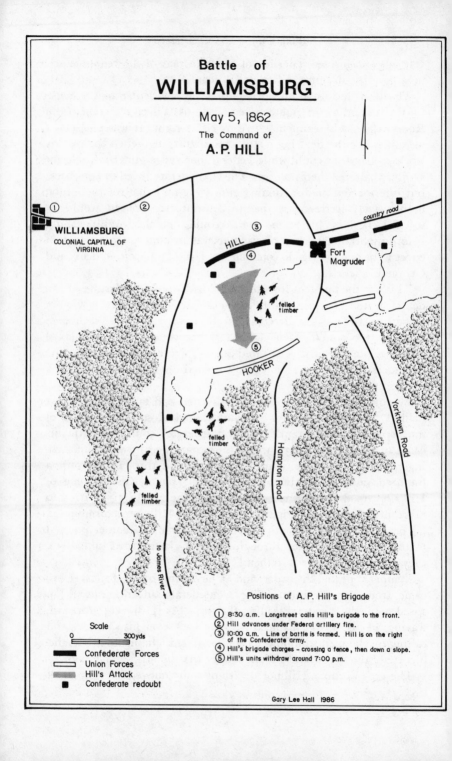

Battle of
WILLIAMSBURG

May 5, 1862

The Command of

A.P. HILL

country road

① WILLIAMSBURG
COLONIAL CAPITAL OF
VIRGINIA

②

③

HILL

④

Fort
Magruder

felled
timber

⑤

HOOKER

felled
timber

felled
timber

Hampton Road

Yorktown Road

to James River

Positions of A.P. Hill's Brigade

① 8:30 a.m. Longstreet calls Hill's brigade to the front.
② Hill advances under Federal artillery fire.
③ 10:00 a.m. Line of battle is formed. Hill is on the right of the Confederate army.
④ Hill's brigade charges – crossing a fence, then down a slope.
⑤ Hill's units withdraw around 7:00 p.m.

Scale
0   300 yds

Confederate Forces
Union Forces
Hill's Attack
Confederate redoubt

Gary Lee Hall 1986

great steadiness and gallantry" and took almost a right-angle position on Kemper's left. The 1st Virginia, meanwhile, had swerved farther to the left. It became intermixed with Wilcox's men and had more than its share of another fight. Col. Samuel Garland's 11th Virginia hurriedly moved up on Kemper's right to extend the line even more. Now Hill's brigade, three regiments wide, swept across the rain-laden field. One soldier described the charge: "The whole line rushed forward over a fence and down a slight slope in the ground, about fifty yards, and was met by a close and deadly fire from the enemy, whom we could not see, but the sharp, quick 'sip, sip' of the minie balls . . . told plainly that they were in very close quarters. . . . Now the men were falling on every hand. The firing was kept up here for some little time, the men sitting or kneeling on the ground, loading and shooting into the bushes in front whence the balls were coming." Then, according to Hill, "The enemy was forced back step by step—my own men eagerly pressing them—until the enemy reached an extensive field of felled timber, which afforded them excellent cover." This defense, plus Federal reinforcements, compelled the Southerners to stop and improvise a line of their own. They easily repulsed a quick Federal counterattack.[14]

For the next two hours, war in all its fury swirled around the two sides, separated by only forty-five yards. Rain still fell; blood flowed into water puddles. In one battery, gunners sank to their knees trying to man the pieces. At least twenty-three bullets riddled the flag of the 7th Virginia, yet, Colonel Kemper later asserted, his men "killed and captured of the enemy more men than the regiment numbered when marched into action."[15] Hill was present throughout those two hours of fighting. A story long persisted that he "saved by his own hand an unknown private who was struggling in personal combat." Hill certainly was inspiring that day. "In the midst of the renewed uproar," a private recalled, "General Hill came down the line. He stood bolt upright between the contending fires, looked around awhile, then went off to the left, returned, looked once more intently into the timber as if to say this nest must be cleaned out." In those moments, Hill was "erect, magnificent, the god of war himself, amid the smoke and the thunder."[16]

In midafternoon Hill got reports "that our ammunition was being exhausted," whereupon "the enemy was again charged with the bayonet by the whole brigade and utterly routed." Among the captures was a Federal cannon with the engraving "To Hell or

Richmond." However, Hill's assault was not "utterly" successful. It actually produced some confusion in Hill's line; and by five in the evening, with ammunition critically low, Hill felt it expedient to pull his regiments back. The Federals had been beaten to a standstill. Nothing else could be done in the gathering twilight. The brigade's organization, Longstreet wrote with admiration, "was perfect throughout the battle, and it was marched off the field in as good order as it entered it." Some of the Virginians replenished cartridges and muskets from Federal dead, who, Hill boasted, "were plentifully and opportunely strewn around."[17]

Night closed as Hill, felt hat sagging and blouse waterlogged, led his men to the rear. Over on the far left, the forces of Confederate general D. Harvey Hill and Federal general Winfield S. Hancock had hammered at each other for hours until both were too exhausted to achieve victory. A surgeon observed that the whole battlefield "was filled with wounded, whose groans and cries made the night hideous."

Hooker's division, against which Hill and other brigades on the right fought for seven hours, suffered total losses of 334 killed, 906 wounded, and 330 missing. Hill's casualties were 67 dead, 245 injured, and 14 missing—the highest Confederate brigade loss in the battle. Yet the immensely proud brigadier reported the capture of 160 Federals, 7 battle flags, and (with the help of the 9th Alabama) 8 pieces of artillery. His regiments, Hill added, "fought with a heroism that, if persisted in, must ever drive back the foe from our soil."[18] Equally important, Hill had fully demonstrated his prowess in battle. He had accepted responsibility, seized the initiative, fought gallantly, and exceeded what was asked of him. With the possible exception of Richard Anderson, he had been the most conspicuous Confederate in this first engagement of the Peninsular Campaign. Both armies would know him henceforth. Richmond newspapers would not misspell his name again.

May 6 dawned sunny and bright, as if Mother Nature was trying to compensate for the trauma of the previous day. Hill's men resumed their westward march before daybreak. The mud was bottomless. The column had to halt several times and form battle lines to check the Federals until the long procession of wagons and artillery could struggle to safety. By nightfall the brigade had covered only seven miles. Leaving Burnt Ordinary at four the next morning, Hill again had to halt in line of battle for much of the day. The men then marched all night and on May 8 reached the Chickahominy River. Soldiers eagerly grabbed the first rations they had had in two days. A short march on the ninth brought Hill's troops to Bottom's Bridge. "A fearful rain set in during the night," wrote a soldier in the 1st Virginia, "and we were almost swimming in water the next morning."[19]

For six days the men encamped while they overcame hunger and weariness. Yet the Virginians under Hill were still capable of humor. One afternoon an aged minister, long white hair and beard blowing in the breeze, walked into camp. A member of the 7th Virginia hollered out good-naturedly, "Boys! Here is Father Abraham!"

"Young man, you are mistaken," the preacher replied in a calm tone. "I am Saul, the son of Kish, searching for his father's asses, and I have found them!"[20]

On May 10, Hill submitted his first official report of participation in a battle. Hill's exaggeration in his enthusiasm can be understood and forgiven. He referred to Williamsburg as "one of the most obstinately contested battles ever fought"; he praised anyone deserving of any praise; he even expressed a high opinion of the use of the bayonet in battle. "The superior nerve and enthusiasm of our men," Hill asserted, "will ever drive [the enemy] back when the bayonet is resorted to."[21]

The brigade shifted on May 15 to a new camp on Clark's farm, near Darbytown. It was an advantageous move, all agreed. The site was "on higher and dryer ground, with better water." But there was little time now for relaxation.[22] McClellan's massive army was steadily approaching Richmond via every road and opening on the peninsula. Federals in large numbers were also driving southward through the Shenandoah Valley. Still other Union forces were in position outside Washington and ready to strike from the north. The object of that mighty Union effort was the city that was capital of both Virginia and the Southern Confederacy. Richmond newspapers were begging for all men to rally in defense of the South's most vital metropolis. "There is no time to be lost. The enemy are at our gates. Who will take the lead and act, act, act? . . . A city destroyed may be rebuilt and flourish again. Liberty once lost is irrecoverable."[23]

Most of Hill's men labored day and night to strengthen defenses;

some were detailed to recruit troops as expeditiously as possible. The weather, if not rainy, was hot, humid, and buggy, and sickness was an inevitable result.

Amid that anxiety and confusion, Hill received an unexpected present: another promotion.

Brigades from all over the Confederacy were rushing to the defense of Richmond. So quickly did one after another report to Johnston for duty that the army's chain of command grew shaky. For example, both the Georgia brigade of Joseph R. Anderson and the North Carolina brigade of Lawrence O'B. Branch were then stationed along Richmond's outskirts, but neither had yet been given official positions in the Army of Northern Virginia. Johnston therefore requested that President Davis appoint additional major generals to handle the divisions into which brigades in the army were organized.

Davis concurred that several new division commanders were needed. The president perhaps remembered Hill's efficiency when Davis was secretary of war in the 1850s; he was quite aware that Hill had distinguished himself at Williamsburg. The president acted promptly. Rain was falling on Monday afternoon, May 26, when Hill learned that he had been promoted to the rank of major general.[24]

Hill had entered Confederate service hoping for quick appointment to high command. It had not developed. For nine months he had gloomily marked time as a colonel, watching chances for glory go to subalterns. Then, in rapid fashion, came brigade command and his first taste of battle. Now the man who wanted to be a general in charge of large numbers of troops—the officer who had led a brigade in but one engagement—found himself at the head of a division. He had jumped from regimental colonel to division major general in precisely ninety days.

Beginning in late May, Hill would be leading twenty times the number of men he had commanded near the end of February. Not only was he the youngest major general in the Confederate army; he was also assuming broad and unfamiliar responsibilities as the Confederacy faced its worst military crisis to date.

The Light Division's
First Attack

Hill assumed division command as if he had been born for it. He established his headquarters at "Mrs. Jones' home" near Stony Run, then sent a cryptic message to Branch: "I assume the command of this division. I send you General Johnston's order." The following day, without a murmur of complaint from Hill, his division doubled in size with the additions of Charles W. Field's Virginia and Maxcy Gregg's South Carolina brigades. Both units were returning to Richmond from guard duty at Guiney's Station, south of Fredericksburg. Within a week, W. Dorsey Pender's small North Carolina brigade joined the division; on June 12, James J. Archer's regiments also became part of Hill's command. The new major general must have enjoyed being at the head of the largest division in the Confederate armies, but he had much work to do.[1]

None of the brigades had ever acted with each other in combat. Once again Hill had to become acquainted with new units and new officers. Some of the brigadiers he had never met, and none of them did he know well. McClellan's slowly advancing army became of secondary concern to Hill as he sought to become acquainted rapidly with his brigades and their generals.

Joseph R. Anderson led the 14th, 35th, 45th, and 49th Georgia regiments. Anderson was thirty-nine, a West Point graduate, and prewar superintendent of Richmond's indispensable Tredegar Iron Works. He was untested in the field and would serve but a short time. His brigade was lacking in battle experience.

59

Lawrence Branch was not a professional soldier. A Princeton-educated attorney and former congressman, he was a few years older than Hill. Branch would prove to be a hard-hitting brigadier as well as a good follower. Hill came to admire him greatly. Branch's brigade—the 7th, 18th, 28th, 33rd, and 37th North Carolina—would achieve a record for valor equaled by few units North or South.

Like Hill, Charles Field had his ancestral roots in Culpeper County, although he was born in Kentucky. He was graduated from West Point two years behind Hill and was teaching cavalry at the Academy when war came. Charlie, as everyone called him, was stocky, congenial, and full of humor. Field was probably the best of the three professional soldiers then commanding brigades in Hill's division, although his performance seemed always to be solid rather than brilliant. His Virginia brigade included the 40th, 47th, and 55th regiments, plus the 2nd Battalion.

The most striking of the six brigades were the Carolinians of Maxcy Gregg. These troops in the 1st, 1st Rifles, 12th, 13th, and 14th South Carolina were men of privileged backgrounds—physicians, attorneys, and landed gentry full of dash and spirit. The 1st South Carolina had encamped at Richmond in the early days of the war, and at its departure for the front, the regiment thanked the ladies of Richmond with a public notice that concluded: "We go cheerfully to meet the foe; rest assured that our vile enemy shall never desecrate your homes until they have first trodden over the bodies of our regiment."[2]

The brigade commander was just as colorful. Maxcy Gregg had supported slavery and secession. He was a lawyer from Columbia, an authority on astronomy, and an officer motivated by sheer patriotism. Gregg was jocular, thickset, and blue-eyed, with graying hair that made him look older than his mid-forties. He appeared quiet and slovenly until battle began; then an all-but-total transformation took place. Gregg became one of only two brigadiers who had free access to Hill.[3]

Dorsey Pender was the other. He was then twenty-eight, erect, with a thin frame, an olive complexion, a pointed beard, and a kindly expression that belied his strict sense of discipline. However, men who did their duty found Pender good-natured. Devoted to his wife and infant daughter, he daily poured out his heart in letters home. He and Hill liked each other because both were ambitious, intense, and at their best in combat (where Pender customarily could be seen astride a horse, enjoying a cigar as he watched his units in battle). Those regiments—the 16th, 22nd, 34th, and 38th North Carolina—would reflect their general's devoutness as well as his gallantry.[4]

Archer's brigade was a strange mixture. The 1st, 7th, and 14th Tennessee anchored the unit, to which the 5th Alabama Battalion and the 19th Georgia were also attached. This heterogeneity characterized the brigade commander as well. James J. Archer was a Marylander who graduated from Princeton, served awhile in the regular army, became a successful attorney, returned to the army, and then in 1861 took command of the 5th Texas. A slightly built man with thin face and elongated beard, the humorless Archer was another dependable but unexciting brigadier. He and Hill had little in common and were never close.

The man selected to command the nine artillery batteries in Hill's division was awesome-looking Maj. Reuben Lindsay Walker. Eight years older than Hill and descended from another prominent Virginia family, Lindsay Walker stood six feet four inches tall. He had long hair, a sweeping mustache, and an imperial beard. Piercing black eyes stared from a face with a habitually grave expression. No other artillerist in Confederate service had more organizational skill than Walker. He participated in sixty-three engagements without suffering injury. After the war, whenever someone asked Walker if he had been wounded, he would draw himself up and reply: "No sir, and it was not my fault!"[5]

Those who saw the most of Hill in the Civil War were the members of his staff. The group of advisers and aides began to take permanent shape with Hill's rise to divisional command. His brother Baptist was major and commissary; a nephew, Francis T. Hill, served as aide-de-camp; brother-in-law Richard C. Morgan and James W. Ratchford were assistant adjutants general; R. J. Wingate held the important post of inspector general; and James G. Field was division quartermaster.

Also on the staff were three persons especially close to Hill. Murray Forbes Taylor was a VMI cadet who was helping to drill one of Hill's new companies at Harper's Ferry when he caught the colonel's eye. Taylor joined Hill's regimental staff and remained with him thereafter, as did George W. Tucker, a Maryland cavalryman whom Hill appointed chief of couriers. Tucker was fearless and indefatigable; he also served his general with open admiration.[6] A volunteer aide to Hill in the latter stages of the Peninsular Campaign was John M. Daniel, editor of the *Richmond Examiner*. The contrast in appearance between Hill and Daniel was almost ludicrous. Hill was slight, and wore a calico shirt or short jacket along with a shapeless plain black hat. Daniel, tall with long black locks, was given to uniforms that brought back visions of English cavaliers in the days of Elizabeth I. While Hill was openly friendly, Daniel was composed of equal parts of cynicism and egotism. "He hated the world at large," it was said, "but loved his few friends with an ardor which shrank at nothing." That last statement would have a painful relevance to Hill in the days ahead.[7]

Few generals in the Civil War were as solicitous of, or as affectionate toward, their men as Hill. In his relations with his brigade and regimental commanders, however, he maintained a polite distance. Hill never referred to any of them by first name. Embracing a comrade or slapping someone on the back was alien to his nature. Although he did not demand any formality, his presence and aura evoked it, so that—with the exception of Gregg and Pender—his officers were strictly formal with him. This aloofness no doubt brought periods of loneliness, but Hill regarded it as a necessary concomitant of discipline.

On May 27, his first full day in command of a division, Hill confronted a military setback. Branch had been ordered to guard the Virginia Central Railroad north of the capital. He had barely posted his men at Peake's Crossing on the rail line when Federals came out of the rain and attacked. Branch blunted the assault, then launched a disjointed counterattack. "Our Regiment was ordered to charge the Yankee Battery after marching to the double quick at charge bayonets for about 300 yards," a member of the 18th North Carolina recalled. The men were too exhausted to deliver a concerted and energetic attack. As a result, that one regiment took 200 casualties.[8] The 37th North Carolina had almost as many losses, including three brothers killed. A Confederate in that unit complained to his wife: "We was Defeated through General Branchs bad management. He was told by a Citizen that the enemys force was small & he believed it but No person else did. he did not even use the [whole] force that was at his command."[9]

Hill labored far into the night to shore up that segment of his line. At one in the morning, with his troops in strong position to continue the battle the next day, Hill wearily lay down to rest. The

Federals fell back under cover of darkness and put an end to the affair.[10]

The following day, Hill received orders to shift his division south of the swollen Chickahominy River to the vicinity of Meadow Bridges and Mechanicsville. His troops, and the division of Gen. Gustavus W. Smith, were to assault McClellan's right (northern) flank before Gen. Irvin McDowell's anticipated arrival with Union reinforcements. When McDowell retired instead to Fredericksburg, Joe Johnston decided to assail the other flank of the Federal army. Thus, Hill and his division missed the May 31–June 1 battle of Seven Pines, in which the troops of Longstreet and Smith fought desperately through swamps and mud, all to no avail. Late in the second day's action, Johnston fell seriously wounded. The army momentarily was leaderless.

June 1 was also the day that Hill first used a nickname for his new command. At the top of a brief communiqué he sent to Branch were the words "Headquarters, Light Division."[11] The exact origin and intent of the title are unknown. Possibly Hill wanted his men to have a reputation for alacrity and agility; or the name may have been nothing more than an antonym for the largest division in the Confederate armies. A soldier in Field's brigade eventually came to his own conclusion: "The name was applicable, for we often marched without coats, blankets, knapsacks, or any other burdens except our arms and haversacks, which were never heavy and sometimes empty." Nevertheless, Col. William McComb of the 14th Tennessee later said, "we became very proud of the 'Light Division,' " in large part because "Gen. A. P. Hill was an ideal soldier."[12]

Hill met the new army commander the next day. Morale inside the ranks of the Army of Northern Virginia (as it had been called since April) had dipped with the announcement that Gen. Robert E. Lee had been named to succeed Johnston. Up to that point in the war, Lee had been little more than a "paper shuffler" in Richmond; although he had spent his adult years in the military, his combat capabilities were still an unknown quantity. To entrust the South's most important army to an unproved field officer seemed preposterous. Yet when Lee summoned his generals to a get-acquainted session at his headquarters the day after he assumed command, he instantly stilled much of the unrest.

Then fifty-five, Lee was a strikingly handsome man just under six feet tall. His black hair was beginning to gray, and he was in the process of growing a beard, which gave his appearance a slight but rugged scraggliness at the moment. His dignity, self-assurance, and easy grace won instant respect. A chaplain who came to know him well observed: "It was impossible to be in this officer's presence, and to note his air of self-poised strength and repose, without feeling that he was a person of great elevation of character and of broad and commanding intellect."[13] Moreover, audacity—the willingness to attack when the opportunity permitted—was evident in Lee's conversation at this first meeting. Hill rode back to his lines both impressed and optimistic.

For most of the next three weeks, Hill concentrated on his brigades and batteries. His first task was to consolidate his huge division. Orders and directives poured forth in a never-ending stream. Staff officers were kept galloping from one brigade to another. Hill himself daily visited the camps, his slender frame sitting a horse naturally, his deep-set eyes taking in everything, whether he was riding in silence or dismounted and talking to an officer. In spite of high rank, Hill still wore a plain uniform—which, noted a staff officer, "often led to amusing blunders."[14]

Hill would not tolerate either lax discipline or usurpation of authority. Barely a week after assuming division command, he issued a directive that all indiscriminate musket-firing in camp was henceforth strictly prohibited. "This applies to those on picket also," he stated. "The sentinel can always load his gun quickly when he's watchfully notified of danger approaching."[15]

His anger flared quickly when a surgeon took it upon himself to grant furloughs to two of Hill's regimental officers. Hill heard about it and had his adjutant general dispatch the following note to brigade commander Archer: "I am directed by the Maj. Genl. cmdg. to call your attention to the two enclosed papers given by Surgeon Wright & to say that such ignorance upon the part of Surgeon Wright is unpardonable or, if not ignorance, then such assumption of authority should be severely dealt with. He directs that you inquire into it & also order Lt. Col. [John K.] Howard and Capt. [William H.] Williamson immediately back to camp."[16]

The Light Division's position was a sweeping arc north and northeast of Richmond. Hill's left rested on the Richmond, Fredericksburg & Potomac Railroad. The line then curved gently for some twelve miles before anchoring on the New Bridge Road. Most of the division was on high ground just south of the Chickahominy, which a

Richmond newspaperman classified as "a stream rather above the dignity of a creek and not fully up to that of a river."[17]

At first the soldiers muttered over Lee's order to construct earthworks. They were enthusiastic recruits; they had not joined the army to dig ditches. Hill and common sense soon convinced them that safety was preferable to idleness, but the learning process was agonizing. Mosquitoes, the swampy terrain, impure water, exposure, poor rations—all began to take their toll. Forty percent of Gregg's brigade fell ill; typhoid fever prostrated half the gunners in the Pee Dee Artillery. Capt. Robert G. Haile of the 55th Virginia fussed in his diary about the "horrid and unnatural state of affairs that this war has produced"; but he quickly added: "I am still willing to suffer any and every hardship rather than submit to the abolitionists who are now invading our soil. . . . Our battle cry should and will be victory or death."[18] Haile would be killed in action less than two weeks later.

Discipline and hard work inside the Light Division brought praise. One of Lee's inspectors visited the encampments and then wrote: "Hill's defences are as well advanced as those of any part of the line. His troops are in fine condition. . . . Hill is every inch a soldier, and is destined to make his mark."[19]

A brief and barbed exchange of correspondence between Hill and Federal general McClellan also occurred at this time. Writing to his wife on June 8, McClellan told of the Confederates' requesting a truce to retrieve the bodies of some officers killed in action. "Well, whom do you think the letter came from?" McClellan quipped. "From no one else than A. P. Hill, major-general commanding the Light Division." McClellan the next day stated with satisfaction: "I had another letter from our friend A. P. H. (A. P. Hill). . . . In my reply sent this morning I ignore Hill entirely and address mine to the 'Commanding General,' etc."

Hill also sent a letter to McClellan concerning a one-on-one exchange of prisoners. McClellan promptly replied—to Lee. A week later, the Union commander did assure Hill that the exchange would take place at once. "This has not been done," Hill grumbled to Lee a few days later.[20]

Industry and anxiety characterized both armies as they confronted each other in the first few weeks of June. On Sunday morning, June 22, as the surgeon of the 40th Virginia was writing his fiancée that "a second Waterloo is at hand," Hill received a sealed dispatch from Lee.[21] The division commanders were to meet at Lee's head-quarters the following afternoon. The waiting—the atmosphere of expectancy in the Confederate camps—was ending.

Lee's headquarters was the widow Dabb's home on Nine Mile Road, just inside the eastern Confederate defenses of the capital. The first of the division commanders, Maj. Gen. D. Harvey Hill, arrived just before noon that Monday. North Carolinian Harvey Hill was slight, stoop-shouldered, and dyspeptic. He was caustic and usually critical. Harvey Hill was still in the front yard when he spied another officer, "dusty, travel-worn, and apparently very tired." When the man looked up and nodded silently, Harvey Hill recognized his brother-in-law, Gen. "Stonewall" Jackson. This was a shock. Jackson had just completed a spectacular campaign in the Shenandoah Valley that had evoked superlatives from both North and South. Supposedly 150 miles away, he had galloped all the way to Richmond—that day he had ridden 52 miles in fourteen hours. A man who made little conversation, Jackson was quieter and more undemonstrative than usual as a result of fatigue.[22]

Powell Hill and heavy-set, opinionated James Longstreet soon arrived together. They too were surprised to see Jackson. The conservative Longstreet must have looked on the risk-taking Jackson with skepticism; for Powell Hill, it was a reunion with a man who had been his antithesis since West Point. Now their differing personalities were even more pronounced: the colorless, uncommunicative Jackson, seemingly impervious to criticism, and the colorful, outgoing Hill, engaging but acutely sensitive.

Lee greeted each man warmly before closing the door to his upstairs quarters. This was the first time in the war that the five generals had been together. The men surrounding Lee were all bearded; their uniforms were blanketed with dust. Longstreet was the oldest at forty-three; Harvey Hill was forty; Jackson, thirty-eight; and Powell Hill was the youngest at thirty-seven.

The meeting began at three in the afternoon. Four hours later, as the sun set, the battle plan was completed. What Lee had in mind was a two-pronged sweeping movement of 56,000 troops converging on the Federal right flank. That portion on McClellan's army numbered 35,000 men on a strongly fortified five-mile front. Their primary responsibility was to guard eleven bridges spanning the Chickahominy.

Lee's forces were going to execute a large-scale rotating turn to the southeast, with elements assailing en echelon (in steplike formation) from the left. Powell Hill would send Branch's brigade seven miles northward to a forward position at Half Sink, an unguarded crossing of the Chickahominy. Jackson, meanwhile, would shift his Valley army across Virginia to a point southeast of Ashland. He would make contact with Branch so as to establish a link with Powell Hill's division. Branch and Jackson would then advance southeastward on parallel roads. When their approach became known to Powell Hill, he would force the crossing of the Meadow Bridges and strike eastward for Mechanicsville.

That would clear Mechanicsville Bridge for Harvey Hill and Longstreet to join in the assault. Harvey Hill's division would pass behind Powell Hill's men and provide support for Jackson; Longstreet would fall in behind Powell Hill. The whole force would then move swiftly down the north side of the Chickahominy to New Bridge, where the flanking columns would link with the divisions of Gens. Benjamin Huger and John B. Magruder. That would reunite Lee's Confederates, after which a large part of McClellan's army could be attacked from different directions and, it was hoped, could be crushed.

Lee's objectives were to shatter the Federal corps on McClellan's right, destroy the York River Railroad supplying the Union army, cut McClellan off from his base, and thus force him to fight at a disadvantage if battle did erupt. But the Southern war plan had snags. Coordination among Jackson, Branch, and Powell Hill was crucial to the whole trap Lee hoped to spring. Since Longstreet and the two Hills were already in the area, the date of the attack was left to Jackson, who had to move his men from the Shenandoah Valley. June 25, he said with no elaboration. Longstreet snorted that such a schedule was too tight. When Lee agreed, Jackson relented. His men would be on line by the morning of the twenty-sixth.

Still, not everyone was comfortable. Timing was vital in the campaign, and Jackson's assault was deemed the key to turning McClellan's right. Lee apparently wanted maneuver rather than combat to accomplish the first stage. Evidence suggests that Lee anticipated no major action near Mechanicsville, particularly since Hill was not to advance until Jackson had swept around the Union line.[23]

Hill agreed to the plan and said little else. He was the new division commander and the junior officer in the room. He was content to listen; but once his division moved into the important pivotal spot, he would demonstrate audacity, not merely dependability, in handling a division under fire. Now if that eccentric Jackson would just carry out his part of the strategy . . .

On the twenty-fourth Hill placed his men on battle alert: "Brigade commanders will direct their commissaries tomorrow (Wednesday) to draw two days' rations (Hard Bread) to be issued cooked and put in Haversacks. Each Brigade will select one Battery for service. . . . No wagons will be taken along except one for each Regt. and battery for ammunition, and the wagons mentioned for forage. Knapsacks will be left behind in camp with the sick, Artillery as well as Infantry, the men taking but one blanket. . . . All men on extra or daily duty in and around the camp who can be possibly spared must take their place in ranks. Brigade commanders are urged to see that their men are in good fighting condition. These orders are precautionary and, as far as they can be, confidential."[24]

Rain showers drenched the Chickahominy camps throughout Wednesday morning as men prepared for action. Federal artillery barked sporadically all day, leading to some apprehension that McClellan might be aware of Lee's gamble. At 5:30 P.M., orders came down the line. Six brigades and nine batteries—14,000 troops —in the Light Division left their encampments and began marching for the first time as a unit. One of the South Carolina soldiers recalled that "the gleaming bayonets, and waving flags, the rumbling of the artillery, and the steady tramp of the men, were both exhilarating and imposing."[25] Men Hill had never seen until five weeks ago were now confidently following him toward battle. He himself was spearheading a major offensive for the first time. His whole life had been pointing to this moment.

Thursday, June 26, broke clear and mild. The air was still and promised to get hot. At sunrise, a Pennsylvania soldier later commented, "nature seemed loath to rouse from her dreamy slumber." That morning the editor of the *Daily Dispatch* in Richmond wrote, "It is generally expected that operations of great moment will take place to-day."[26]

Hill had his division massed in the woods along the Meadow Bridge Road. At daybreak his brigade commanders passed the word: "If this battle is lost, Richmond must fall!"[27] The major general that morning sat easily in the saddle and stared northward. He was wearing a red calico shirt, which the men in time called his battle shirt. The black felt hat was slouched forward over his face and, of course, the sword dangled at his side.

From the beginning, Hill had assumed that the great turning movement would commence shortly after dawn. Certainly, he reasoned, the assault would be under way by eight in the morning. Yet that hour arrived and all remained quiet. Hill began to have apprehensions about Branch. The North Carolinian was dedicated but inexperienced. Shortly after eight, Hill sent him a gentle reminder: "Wait for Jackson's notification before you move unless I send other orders."[28]

Two more hours passed; still no word from Jackson. Around ten, Jackson informed Branch that he was crossing the Virginia Central Railroad six miles fom Ashland. According to Lee's original schedule, Jackson was running six hours late. Worse, Branch never relayed the message to Hill. The Tarheel brigade suddenly encountered Union infantry, and Branch's attention was occupied with the brisk and confusing fight that ensued—and all of this was too far away to be heard along the Chickahominy. In fact, at noon McClellan wired authorities in Washington: "All things very quiet. . . . I would prefer more noise."[29]

Inside the Light Division, the stillness grew heavy and then oppressive. The sun rose higher as the hours dragged. It got hotter, so that by early afternoon the waiting soldiers were sweating from heat as well as from nervousness. One o'clock came and went; two o'clock passed without activity. Hill was now edgy and growing agitated. He believed—as did several other officers—that the whole plan was about to fall apart. Where was Jackson? Why had he not heard from Branch? Time was running out as Lee's army sat poised on a limb. *Where was Jackson?*

Now it was three in the afternoon. Hill's nerves were wound tight. His patience was exhausted. Lee was two miles away. It would be too time-consuming to try to confer with him. McClellan would fall back, or would himself attack, if the Confederates waited any longer. Hill felt compelled now to cross the Chickahominy and initiate the turning movement. To delay longer would be to "hazard the failure of the whole plan."[30] Surely, by the time he made contact, Jackson would be there.

Hill turned to Charles Field and gave the command. The burly Kentuckian took the lead with his brigade. Archer and Anderson got their men on the road close behind. Field's Virginians "rushed across the bridge at double-quick, and with exultant shouts drove the enemy's pickets from their posts." In their nervousness, they also unloosed a volley of musketry into an abandoned camp. Tent poles, canvas, pots and pans went flying in every direction.[31]

The Federals fell back from the river to Mechanicsville, a crossroads cluster of houses which sat in the open surrounded by tilled ground. The brigades of Gregg and Pender swung off to the right to provide flank protection for Hill's main thrust, which was now moving across a mile and a half of open ground toward Mechanicsville. Federal batteries on the other side of the village began firing. The regiments in Field's brigade "were momentarily thinned by the most destructive cannonading I have yet known," the brigadier stated in his official report. "Our only safety from this fire lay in pushing forward as rapidly as possible and getting so close to the enemy's infantry as to draw the fire upon his own troops should it be continued."[32]

Hill now dispatched Capt. William J. Pegram's battery to support Field. Pegram unlimbered his six guns and began replying to the Federal pieces. Within minutes, shells from some thirty Union cannon were raining upon Pegram's position. Four of his six guns were disabled, half the battery's horses were slain, and fifty of ninety artillerists were killed or wounded in seemingly as many seconds.

Pegram's valor does not compensate for Hill's dereliction in this case. Just prior to Lee's counteroffensive, the artillery had been reorganized so that batteries would be attached to divisions rather than brigades, thereby providing greater concentration of artillery fire when needed. Hill, however, had followed earlier custom by sending a single battery to a brigade. He did this throughout the battle, with costly results.[33]

The sight of the Federals abandoning Mechanicsville led Longstreet and Harvey Hill to put their troops in motion. They naturally assumed that Powell Hill and Jackson had made contact and were executing the turning movement. Lee accompanied the men of Harvey Hill and Longstreet as they crossed the Chickahominy and proceeded up the Mechanicsville Turnpike. Hill's troops were securing Mechanicsville when Lee arrived. The commander rode down the main street, which was cluttered with abandoned equipment, and learned for the first time that Hill had attacked without Jackson.

Lee found himself—as the old cliché goes—"holding a tiger by the tail." Two-thirds of the Confederate army was now north of Chickahominy; battle had already been joined, and Richmond was virtually unguarded. There was nothing to do but go ahead with the assault. The offensive must be continued, even without Jackson, and despite the fact that Lee had hoped to avoid a major confrontation with entrenched Federals.[34]

By then, Union forces were consolidating a mile east of Mechanicsville. This previously prepared main defense line was as awesome a position as any in the Civil War. Beaver Dam Creek flowed sluggishly southward and formed a marshy valley where the Cold Harbor Road crossed it. This millrace of Dr. Ellerson's grist mill created a natural barrier to any troops advancing on an east-west line. North of Ellerson's Mill, Beaver Dam Creek was waist-deep and bordered on both sides by swamps. To get across it from the west meant to traverse open land, stumble through soggy bottomland, and then scale the bluff on the opposite side. There Gen. FitzJohn Porter had carefully deployed his corps. Any troops moving toward him, Porter observed, "presented their flanks, as well as their front, to the fire of both infantry and artillery, posted behind intrenchments." With 30,000 infantry and eighty pieces of artillery banked up in tiers along the crest of the bluff, Porter's line was simply unassailable in front.[35] Hill, of course, did not know that.

Branch's brigade rejoined Hill at Mechanicsville near six that evening. Jackson's whereabouts were still a mystery, but Porter's whereabouts were not. The sun was starting its descent, and if momentum was to be maintained, Hill had to push hard and fast. President Davis and an entourage had arrived on the field and were with Lee. As all watched, Hill moved three of his brigades eastward toward full battle. His soldiers, wrote one, "made the hills and valleys and woods ring with their Confederate yells as they eagerly pressed forward with anticipation of coming victory."[36]

Hill's strategy was to strike hard at the Federal right flank, where Jackson was momentarily expected to appear. Anderson's brigade moved obliquely in that direction, with David G. McIntosh's battery accompanying the infantry so as to keep the Federals occupied. (Predictably, the success of this Pee Dee Artillery was limited. Typhoid fever had debilitated the unit, and "the cannoneers actually tottered

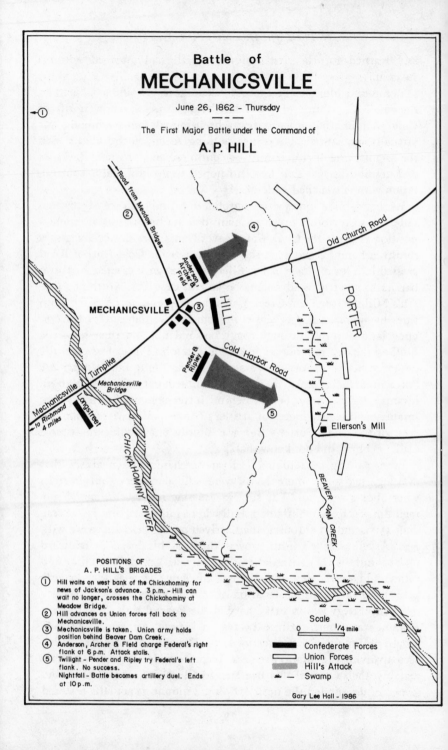

Battle of
MECHANICSVILLE

June 26, 1862 - Thursday

The First Major Battle under the Command of

A. P. HILL

Road from Meadow Bridges

Old Church Road

PORTER

Anderson, Archer & Field

MECHANICSVILLE

HILL

Pender & Ripley

Cold Harbor Road

Mechanicsville Turnpike

Mechanicsville Bridge

Longstreet

to Richmond 4 miles

Ellerson's Mill

CHICKAHOMINY RIVER

BEAVER DAM CREEK

POSITIONS OF
A. P. HILL'S BRIGADES

(1) Hill waits on west bank of the Chickahominy for news of Jackson's advance. 3 p.m. - Hill can wait no longer, crosses the Chickahominy at Meadow Bridge.

(2) Hill advances as Union forces fall back to Mechanicsville.

(3) Mechanicsville is taken. Union army holds position behind Beaver Dam Creek.

(4) Anderson, Archer & Field charge Federal's right flank at 6 p.m. Attack stalls.

(5) Twilight - Pender and Ripley try Federal's left flank. No success.
Nightfall - Battle becomes artillery duel. Ends at 10 p.m.

Scale

0   1/4 mile

Confederate Forces

Union Forces

Hill's Attack

Swamp

Gary Lee Hall - 1986

in serving their guns.") Archer's brigade marched down Old Church Road and swung off to the left to support Anderson. Field posted his soldiers on Archer's right. Gregg, Pender, and Branch were held in reserve.[37]

One Union soldier was struck with awe as "from the woods, out of the swamps, down the roads, along the entire front, with shriek and yell, flashing fire, thunder, and curling smoke," the Confederates surged forward. However, as Hill's three brigades approached Beaver Dam Creek, Union batteries unleashed a converging fire that ripped great holes in the once-orderly columns. Federal infantry then sent sheets of musketry into the Southern ranks. The charging lines hesitated, reeled back, and sought shelter in swamps and thickets. Then they came on again and got within a hundred yards of the Federal works, only to recoil from the same unweatherable fire. "We fought under many disadvantages," color-bearer Martin Ledbetter of the 5th Alabama Battalion commented. "It was with great difficulty that we made our way through [the] entanglement of tree tops, saplings, vines, and every other conceivable obstruction, under a heavy fire."[38]

Within a half hour, dead and wounded were strewn all over the ground to the west of Beaver Dam Creek. Hill, not utilizing the concentrated firepower of his nine batteries, continued sending massed infantry against fortified infantry and superior artillery. "The battle now raged along my whole line," he stated; and he was in the middle of it, hatless, begrimed, oblivious to danger as he urged men forward by personal example. The 35th Georgia of Anderson's brigade actually punched across the creek and established a beachhead of sorts. No reinforcements could come to its support. Hill soon began to see the futility of attempting to smash the Federal right and center. "Their position along Beaver Dam Creek," he conceded, "was too strong to be carried by a direct attack without heavy loss, and expecting every minute to hear Jackson's guns on my left and in rear of the enemy, I forbore to order the storming of their lines."[39]

Twilight came. Longstreet and Harvey Hill were now on the field with their divisions, but smoke, noise, death, and uncertainty rendered any strong cooperation all but impossible. To Hill at this point came Capt. Thomas W. Sydnor. A cavalryman intimately familiar with the topography of that region, Sydnor would pen a widely distributed letter about his role in the battle some thirty-five years after the war. Sydnor had warned Lee that quicksand abounded along the creek bottom north of Cold Harbor Road. He now informed Hill (he later stated) that because portions of Anderson's and Archer's brigades were near that dangerous area, Lee wished Hill not to advance but to maintain his position.[40]

If this verbal directive was in fact issued, Hill must have concluded that it applied only to the Confederate left, who were near where the quicksand was. The other end of the line, near Ellerson's Mill, still offered a final opportunity at sundown. Hill ordered Pender's brigade, just coming on the field, to assail the Federal line on that flank. In support, Hill sent Roswell Ripley's brigade from D. H. Hill's division. The Union center and right were demonstrably strong, Hill reasoned; the left must be the weak point, and there was time to overrun it before night fell.

What followed was the bloodiest setback of the day. Pender made somewhat of a mess out of his part of the attack. His brigade came under heavy artillery fire as it turned south off the Cold Harbor Road and it fell apart. The 16th North Carolina sidled to the left; the 34th North Carolina veered to the west and got itself overlapped by Federals. This left the 38th North Carolina to make the attack. An officer in that regiment wrote: "The heat was intense and the double-quick march exhausting, but the charge was kept up over the open field until the regiment reached the summit of the last elevation. . . . The Yankee batteries were upon the summit of the opposite hill with their supporting infantry in their intrenchments, and the old field pines in front cut down and piled across the stumps which were about three feet high, forming an almost impassable barrier." Yet the North Carolinians charged.

Shells came screaming through the air; volley after volley of musketry slammed into Pender's ranks. Men fell and the hillside rapidly became blanketed with bodies. "To take the works was impossible," that same officer concluded.[41] The 38th North Carolina fell back, leaving 152 of 420 men on the field. As for Ripley's part in the assault, he got only one of his regiments pointed toward the Union position. The men mistakenly charged down a hill straight into Federal artillery. At a range of seventy yards, grapeshot "mowed down whole files of our men." That unit (44th Georgia) took 335 casualties out of 514 men engaged.[42]

Nightfall ended the infantry activity, but cannon duels angrily persisted until ten o'clock. Barns, houses, and haystacks were all ablaze, giving a brief but eerie glow to the battlefield. When the guns finally grew silent, a soldier in the 16th North Carolina noted, "our surroundings were a solitary desert of horror. . . . Nothing could be heard in the black darkness of that night save the ghastly moans of the wounded and dying."[43]

Hill, fatigued and sweaty, left the front and rode through the wreckage of battle back to Mechanicsville. There Lee met with his division commanders to assess the day's actions and to plan for tomorrow. Jackson's nonappearance was still the critical issue. Lee would note in his official report of the campaign: "In consequence of unavoidable delays, the whole of Genl. Jackson's command did not arrive at Ashland in time to enable him to reach the point designated on the 25th. His march on the 26th was consequently longer than had been anticipated."[44] Put another way, Jackson had established an unrealistic timetable for his march, and his failure to keep Lee posted on his whereabouts put him in an even more unfavorable light.

Lee made no mention that evening of Hill's having launched an attack without permission or support, nor was the commander critical in his written report. Lee would demonstrate many times that he appreciated a general who fought and, if he erred, did so on the side of aggressiveness rather than vacillation.

It is difficult to imagine what was going through Hill's mind when he lay down after eighteen hours in the field. He did not write his official report of Mechanicsville until eight months later. By then, at least, he had satisfied himself of the propriety of his decision. He stated that the battle ended with "my brigades resting along the creek, the object of this attack, viz, clearing the way for Longstreet, having been fully accomplished." On the other hand, Hill's exasperation (if not anger) with Jackson was unmistakably clear. He closed his report with the blunt observation: "It was never contemplated that my division alone should have sustained the shock of this battle, but such was the case."[45]

Especially in war, the verdict of contemporaries and of history rests almost entirely on success or defeat. This axiom was illustrated many times in the Civil War. Two weeks before Mechanicsville, Confederate general "Jeb" Stuart had reconnoitered the northern flank of the Union army, then impulsively returned to Richmond by leading his cavalrymen on a circuitous trip behind the Army of the Potomac. The South praised Stuart not because of the daring involved in the "Ride around McClellan" but because the feat was successful. No one raised any question of impetuosity on Stuart's part. Hill sent his brigades across the Chickahominy with equal fervor. The results were not so positive. Criticism, questions about his competence, and the like promptly gushed forth. Had Hill won the battle, particularly against such heavy odds, he would have been hailed for valor and audacity. Rarely does middle ground exist when analyzing a battle. It did not after Mechanicsville.

Hill was adjudged "impetuous" and "exceedingly imprudent" in starting a battle "contrary to orders." He "threw caution and Lee's plans to the winds," and the results "could have been disastrous for the whole army." The blood shed along Beaver Dam Creek "was wasted in vain" and had "a most dispiriting effect" upon the Confederate army. The battle was a "slaughter," the battlefield a "butcher pen." One author even offered the preposterous theory that Hill attacked because he had "a score to settle" with McClellan over losing Ellen Marcy![46]

If Hill followed the human tendency to shift responsibility, he had cause. Branch had proved to be a missing link in the chain of command. When Branch made contact with Jackson's forces at three in the afternoon, he sent no communiqué to Hill. A little later, when the Carolinian received word that Hill was advancing on Mechanicsville, he failed to inform Jackson.[47]

And what of Jackson? To put all the blame on Hill for a premature attack is to overlook Jackson's tardy arrival as well as his failure to do anything when he did arrive. Jackson's 15,000 men were strung out for five miles along two parallel roads. They were a mighty hammer raised to strike McClellan's exposed flank. Yet, the strong-minded Longstreet asserted, "Jackson came up, marched by the fight without giving attention, and went into camp at Hundley's Corner, half a mile in the rear of the enemy's position of contention." The rationales advanced by Jackson's aides—that the general "was moving in the dark" and that his mere presence in the area could force the Federals to abandon their works—are transparent. "Had Jackson been in position that day," a respected staff officer stated, "the enemy would have melted before us. He had promised to be there on the morning of the 26th."[48]

Hill's lunge over the Meadow Bridges was precipitate, but it was not insubordinate. He waited some eight hours for a battle plan to unfold. As the hours passed, Lee showed no inclination to alter the highly fragile strategy. Hill then crossed the Chickahominy to execute his orders—to drive the Federals from Mechanicsville so as to clear the river passages for Harvey Hill and Longstreet. Such an advance would put Hill in position to cooperate with Jackson when (not if) the latter appeared. If Hill had not moved out, Jackson might have been left all alone for Porter to assail.

At Mechanicsville the real problem was that once Hill's men seized the village, it was difficult not to press after the Federals as they fell back to Beaver Dam Creek; however, the steadfastness of the Union troops brought unexpected failure.

The *Official Records* do not give Hill's casualties at Mechanicsville. The figure quoted most often is 2,000 and comes from Federal general Porter, who put his own losses at but 361 men.[49] In reality, only two regiments in the Pender-Ripley attack took severe losses. Hill's total casualties appear to have been about 1,400 men, or 10 percent of his command. That figure is high but hardly constitutes a "slaughter" in a "butcher pen."

In one circle Hill was acclaimed the hero of the hour. A Richmond editor wrote on June 27: "In the battle of yesterday, he displayed, in the highest degree, all the talents of a commander, with the exception of proper caution of his own life, which he exposed from the first shot to the last, with the recklessness of a trooper."[50]

Forging a Reputation on the Peninsula

Weariness after a battle is bone-deep and long-lived. The men in the Light Division spent the night of June 26 on the battlefield where they had stopped fighting. Any sleep was short and sporadic. Before dawn on Friday the twenty-seventh, Federal artillery unleashed a "terrific" bombardment of two hours' duration. "We could do nothing but stand and take it," one of Hill's men recalled.[1] The cannonade died away shortly after sunrise. Lee became convinced that Porter was aware of the Lee-Jackson vise and had abandoned Beaver Dam Creek earthworks. He ordered Hill to advance his division in that direction. Hill moved promptly at eight in the morning—the same hour when Jackson's men were leisurely breaking camp a few miles to the north.

Gregg's South Carolinians were the only brigade in the Light Division unused the previous day, so Hill put them in the lead. The courtly Gregg, hard of hearing but dedicated to the core, set a brisk pace. His men marched through the area where Pender and Ripley had charged the day before. Heavy fighting had occurred near a bridge, and there dead Confederates were found standing knee-deep in mud. The Carolinians quickened their pace. Hill noted with pleasure how Gregg's men "handsomely dashed" across Beaver Dam Creek and "cleared the pits of the few men left as a blind."[2]

Hill now edged all of his brigades forward. Men bleary-eyed from lack of sleep advanced slowly along the dusty road, which snaked toward Gaines's Mill on Powhite Creek. That stream was the next logical defensive point for the Federals. Gregg's regiments passed through abandoned camps where food and other needed supplies lay for the taking. The soldiers continued forward without stopping. "Our ardor," one of them boasted, "prevented us from pillaging as freely as we learned subsequently to do."[3]

By ten o'clock the South Carolinians had advanced a mile and a half and were in sight of an intersection marked by Walnut Grove Church. Suddenly they caught artillery fire on their left. Two men fell wounded. Gregg was preparing to send part of his brigade in battle array in that direction when he learned that the fire was from another Confederate column. Jackson had finally arrived on the scene. Gregg was neither relieved nor impressed. He sent an officer to alert Jackson to the situation so as—Gregg stated with some disgust—"to avoid the risk of further mischief."[4]

Hill galloped up to Walnut Grove Church at the road junction. Moments later, Jackson and his staff came down the other road and dismounted. One of Jackson's aides wrote that the two generals exchanged "pleasant greetings." That is quite doubtful. The Light Division had taken a painful beating twenty-four hours earlier largely—Hill believed—because of Jackson's nonappearance; and now Jackson was late again. Moreover, the Valley warrior, whom a newspaperman characterized as "sullen, unsocial . . . unimpressive, silent, emphatic," was not given to pleasantries in battle or behind the lines.[5] The two generals in all likelihood saluted that morning and said no more than necessary.

Fortunately, another contingent of horsemen arrived at the church. Robert E. Lee dismounted quickly and greeted the two major generals in friendly fashion. While Lee and Jackson wore uniform coats, a courier observed that none of the officers were dressed in a manner to denote their status as generals. The "spare and short" Hill was the most unpretentious of the three. The officers chatted awhile before the Light Division began filing by. Jackson's chief of staff thought that those men looked remarkably fit after the fighting they had undergone the previous day. A moment later, Hill touched his hat to Lee and Jackson, remounted Prince, and joined his lead regiment.[6]

Jackson's tardiness forced Lee to alter his battle plan for the day. With D. H. Hill's men, Jackson now had fourteen brigades—more than Powell Hill and Longstreet combined. Lee thought Porter's divisions would make a stand at Powhite Creek. He therefore wanted

Jackson to march swiftly to Cold Harbor, three and a half miles to the east. That would put Jackson in the rear of Porter's position—that is, where Lee assumed it to be at this time. He could then assail it as Hill and Longstreet drove the Federals southward across the peninsula. Hill was to follow Porter's line of retreat and maintain contact with the rear guard. Longstreet to the west would parallel Hill's route, with Jackson swinging out to the east in an arc.

At noon, after a march of seven miles under a blazing sun, Hill's skirmishers reported Federals in some strength east of Gaines's Mill and behind Powhite Creek. Hill displayed "his usual impetuous ardor," an officer wrote, and quickly fanned out Gregg's brigade in line of battle. Snowden Andrews's battery shelled the woods along the creek. Then, Hill wrote, Gregg "immediately filed his brigade across [Powhite Creek], forming lines successively as each regiment crossed." Gregg tightened his ranks and sent them yelling across open country in what Hill termed "the handsomest charge in line I have seen during the war."[7]

The thin line of Federals Gregg saw falling back from Powhite Creek caused the inexperienced brigadier to underestimate Porter's strength and intentions. Hence, the South Carolinians went charging at full speed under a sun that was getting hotter. The brigade began to lose cohesion as panting soldiers fought to keep up. Federals disappeared into a line of woods at the foot of a ravine. Without pause, the Confederates, yelping like dogs, bounded down the slope and stumbled right into a barrage from hidden guns on the crest overlooking Boatswain's Creek. The whole hilltop came alive with Federal fire. Gregg managed to get his exhausted men all huddled at the base of the ravine; and as they caught their breath, Gregg enthusiastically sent a courier to tell Hill he "had brought the enemy to bay" and to ask permission to attack this Federal line.

Hill said no. The "reckless impetuosity" so often attributed to Hill was not evident at Boatswain's Creek that noon. Naturally, Hill wanted to press the issue, but there was no wild excitement about him now. Power lay in weight of numbers. He wanted the entire Light Division to show its might. So he instructed Gregg to hold his position; then he dispatched Branch's brigade to form on Gregg's right, with Anderson, Pender, Field, and Archer taking positions in turn on the right. Artillery batteries were rushed into place to take aim on the Union line. Quickly the six brigades were poised. But what Hill did not know was that he was massing against

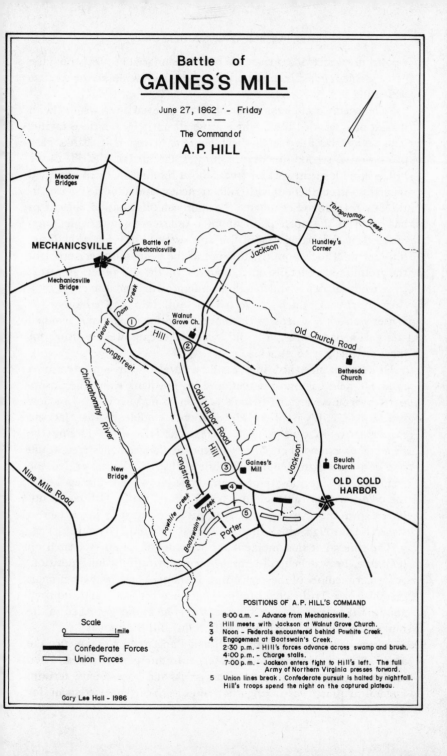

Battle of
GAINES'S MILL

June 27, 1862 - Friday
– – –

The Command of
A. P. HILL

Meadow
Bridges

Totopotomay Creek

MECHANICSVILLE

Battle of
Mechanicsville

Jackson

Hundley's
Corner

Mechanicsville
Bridge

Dam Creek

Beaver

Walnut
Grove Ch.

Hill

①

②

Old Church Road

Longstreet

Bethesda
Church

Chickahominy River

Cold Harbor Road

Hill

Jackson

Nine Mile Road

New
Bridge

Longstreet

Gaines's
Mill

③

Beulah
Church

**OLD COLD
HARBOR**

④

⑤

Powhite Creek

Boatswain's Creek

Porter

POSITIONS OF A.P. HILL'S COMMAND

1 8:00 a.m. – Advance from Mechanicsville.
2 Hill meets with Jackson at Walnut Grove Church.
3 Noon – Federals encountered behind Powhite Creek.
4 Engagement at Boatswain's Creek.
   2:30 p.m. – Hill's forces advance across swamp and brush.
   4:00 p.m. – Charge stalls.
   7:00 p.m. – Jackson enters fight to Hill's left. The full
           Army of Northern Virginia presses forward.
5 Union lines break. Confederate pursuit is halted by nightfall.
   Hill's troops spend the night on the captured plateau.

Scale
0 _____ 1 mile

▬▬ Confederate Forces
▭▭ Union Forces

Gary Lee Hall - 1986

a position even stronger than the one he had faced at Mechanicsville —the Boatswain's Creek area did not even show on the maps Lee was using.[8]

"The enemy occupied a range of hills," an eyewitness wrote, "with his left on a wooded bluff, which arose abruptly from a deep ravine. The ravine was filled with sharpshooters, to whom its banks gave protection. A second line of infantry was stationed on the side of the hill, behind a breastwork of trees, above the first. A third occupied the crest, strengthened with rifle trenches, and crowned with artillery." An aide to Lee noted: "To approach this position, the troops had to cross the open plain about a quarter-of-a-mile wide, commanded by this triple line of fire and swept by the heavy batteries south of the Chickahominy. In front of the Federal center and right the ground was generally open, bounded on the side of our approach by a wood of dense and tangled undergrowth, and traversed by a sluggish stream which converted the soil into a deep morass."[9] Porter's entire V Corps, with another division as backup, manned crescent-shaped works. All told, 35,000 Federals were waiting for the Confederates to attack.

Hill's front stretched in the sultry haze for three-quarters of a mile. He held back no reserves, and his left flank would be unsupported for however long it took Jackson to make contact. Lee now rode up to Hill's position. He expressed confidence that Jackson would arrive in time to add strength to Hill while forcing the Federals to extend their lines to meet his threat. Longstreet would also be attacking the Union left while Hill struck the center. No one seems to have been aware of the natural impediments: steep banks, the creek, swampy ground, and felled trees. Finally, Hill could not have known that Porter was massing his forces squarely in the face of the sector through which the Light Division would advance.

The general at that moment was a model of calmness. Seated on his horse, he watched columns of men moving into final position. A former member of the 13th Virginia shouted hello as his regiment marched past. Hill called him over, grasped his hand, and inquired about "the boys of the old Thirteenth." The soldier returned to the ranks shouting: "Little Powell will do his full duty today!"[10]

At one o'clock Lee ordered Hill and Longstreet to commence the attack. Longstreet almost immediately encountered difficulties. When his troops were not struggling across creeks and over swampy terrain, Federal artillery was raking the columns. Yet the excitement for battle that Hill had displayed the day before was not there now. He would wait for Longstreet, even though he knew full well that Porter's bluecoats were buttressing their lines with every passing minute. Hill waited . . . and waited . . . and the minutes became a half hour . . . then an hour . . . and still no activity on his right. Finally, Hill concluded that he could wait no longer. If the Federal position was not assailed quickly, it would become too strong to break. Around two-thirty Hill signaled for his batteries to open fire; as layers of smoke mingled with oppressive heat, Hill sent his brigades forward. Longstreet would write petulantly that Hill "deployed his men and opened the attack without consulting me." The truth of the matter is that—as at Mechanicsville—time was a factor working against the Confederates, and only Hill seems to have been aware of it. He had no intention of adding to the problem.[11]

First Gregg, then Branch attacked, followed by Anderson and Archer. Across the way, Porter watched Hill's well-formed lines advance from under cover of woods. "Dashing across the intervening plains, floundering in the swamps, and struggling against the tangled brushwood," the Union commander observed, "brigade after brigade seemed almost to melt away before the concentrated fire of our artillery and infantry; yet others pressed on, followed by supports as dashing and as brave as their predecessors." Hill realized the worst. "The incessant roar of musketry and deep thunder of the artillery told me that the whole force of the enemy was in my front."[12]

He was not exaggerating. Longstreet gave no support. Further, "as Jackson's movements were unaccountably slow," Lee's chief of staff commented, the Federals were able to concentrate solely on Hill's brigades.[13] For the second day in a row, Hill's division was fighting in a death trap at the bottom of a watery ravine.

Intense fighting ran the length of Hill's line. So did gallantry and sacrifice. On the left, Gregg's men got into a killing match. The colonel of the 1st South Carolina Rifles reported: "My men, although now under three cross-fires, and falling thick and fast from one end of the line to the other, never once faltered." The Palmetto brigade then charged and actually pierced the Federal line, "some of the men having it hand-to-hand, clubbing their rifles, then dispatching four or five with the bayonet." Yet they were driven back by superior numbers. Gregg rallied his troops, and a close-range struggle ensued. "There was no cheering," one soldier noted. "Every man was fighting with his mouth closed and standing his ground with all the courage he could command—and never anywhere do I recall a heavier fire than on the left of our line, General A. P. Hill, that magnificent fighter . . . showing himself the man he always was." Two of the South Carolina regiments lost more than a third of their complement in barely an hour's fighting to gain a foothold on the hill.[14]

Gen. Henry W. Slocum's division now reinforced Porter's front. Massed Federals were blasting the gray ranks with precision. Hill's men, dashing across open ground and into marshlands, struck repeatedly at the Federal position. Nowhere could they gain a permanent breakthrough. Yet they continued to attack with what a Union writer called "a disregard of death never surpassed."

Branch all but lost control of his brigade as the North Carolinians floundered among the bushes and over the swampy ground. Some men wandered to the rear; others took whatever cover was available. There was also bravery. Two color-bearers in the 7th North Carolina fell one after another. Col. Reuben Campbell dashed forward, seized the flag, carried it to within "a stone's throw" of the Federal lines, and was killed. A lieutenant picked up the standard, only to be slain. By nightfall, the treasured banner had thirty-two bullet holes in it.[15]

Hill rushed in Pender's brigade to help his fellow Carolinians. Pender's men pounded the Union lines until his regiments were in fragments from the futile efforts. Anderson's troops, in the center, made three different assaults and achieved nothing but casualties. On the right, Archer's men charged in spurts: dashing thirty yards, lying down, dashing another thirty yards, until they were within a stone's throw of the Union works. Then Archer, in shirtsleeves, waved a sword over his head and yelled: "Forward, everybody! We are going through!" But Federal artillery and infantry zeroed in on the Confederates and, wrote a Billy Yank, "mowed them down like grass." The several cannon that Hill had placed in position were no match for Porter's fifty guns, but they performed heroically. One of the Pee Dee Artillery pieces fired 239 rounds and became so heated that the barrel bent at the trunnions and the cannon had to be abandoned.[16]

It was four in the afternoon. Battle had raged for two hours. "Men never fought better, or died more bravely," a Confederate later claimed. Hill's left flank, having reached desperately all day for Jackson's helping hand, was being enveloped by swarms of Federals under dour, hard-hitting George Sykes, a former West Point classmate of Hill's. Now came an order from Hill: stop the attacks; lie down where you are. "These brave men had done all that any soldiers could do," Hill reported. "From having been the attacking I now became the attacked, but stubbornly, gallantly, was the ground held."[17] However, the Light Division was slowly being destroyed for lack of support.

An hour passed, fraught with exhaustion and uncertainty. The roar of gunfire was continuous. Then, shortly after five, word came down the line: Jackson was filing into position on Hill's left. His troops had spent much of the day countermarching to reach the field. ("The Chickahominy is not much like the royal Valley of Virginia," one of Jackson's men admitted, "and we always felt lost in it.")[18]

Jackson would testify thereafter that he was in no hurry on June 27 because he expected Hill and Longstreet to drive the Federals into his arms. Hill must have shaken his head in disbelief and anger at the statement. As far as he was concerned, Jackson was at least thirty-four hours late committing to battle. Most astounding of all is that Jackson apparently never comprehended what transpired until his chief engineer explained the battle to him step by step—eight months later.[19]

Lee now arranged his united forces carefully. Darkness was rapidly approaching when Lee gave the signal at seven o'clock. For the first time, the full Army of Northern Virginia swept forward in attack. Hill's battered ranks could do little more than follow the strong, fresh front line. Yet there was fire still in the major general. Hill was riding with Lee in the rear of the line when he spied a frightened captain hiding behind a tree. One of Lee's aides described what happened next. "Genl. Hill leaped from his horse in fierce anger, denounced the coward, took his sword from him and attempted to break it over his knee. The sword was of as bad metal as the man who wore it and bent instead of breaking. Genl. Hill hurled it as far as he could, remounted his horse and rode on into the charge."[20]

The Federal divisions, which had waged one of the most steadfast defenses of the war, now broke under the pressure of Lee's full army. Porter's men fled southward toward the safety of the Chickahominy. The pursuit, Hill stated, was "only stopped by night-fall and the exhaustion of our troops."[21] McClellan had lost 7,000 men and 22 guns in the battle; his entire line had been turned; his supply and communication links with the York and Pamunkey rivers were in danger; the York River Railroad was about to be severed. The mammoth Army of the Potomac was in retreat toward the James River, and Lee was trying to get his victorious Confederates close enough to deliver a killing blow.

Hill won high praise, both from Lee and from the usually gruff Longstreet. The latter, who provided scant help at Gaines's Mill, later proclaimed: "The Confederate commanders, except A. P. Hill, claimed credit for the first breach in General Porter's lines. . . . The troops of the gallant A. P. Hill, that did as much and effective fighting as any, received little of the credit properly due them. It was their long and steady fight that thinned the Federal ranks and caused them to so foul their guns that they were out of order when the final struggle came."[22]

In sustaining Lee's attack almost singlehandedly on June 27, Hill suffered 2,688 men killed and wounded.[23] This figure was about two times his losses at Mechanicsville and represented 20 percent of the Light Division. Perhaps this was a small price for protecting Lee's army that Friday and bringing the South its first victory in the critical Peninsular Campaign. He could not be accused of rashness or impetuosity at Gaines's Mill. His hard-hitting tactics and relentless pursuit of victory had gained Lee's eye as well as the praise of the South. Hill was now receiving the attention and fame he had sought throughout his adult years.

Hill spent the night in the Federal works on the Watts House plateau. Unseasonable heat continued the next day as the men in the Light Division rested, attended to the wounded, buried the dead, and confiscated supplies. Capt. William Morris of the 37th North Carolina wrote that the Yankees "burned Every thing they could but they left any amount of Camp Equippage & . . . we could pick up anything you would want, Napsacks, Haversacks, guns & all kinds of clothing scattered for miles wide in the direction they went." The battlefield itself was sickening. A lieutenant in another of Hill's Tarheel regiments noted: "Hundreds of horses were lying around, some not dead, some with legs shot off, trying to get up, moaning and crying like children begging for help."[24]

At sundown on June 28, a violent rainstorm swept across the peninsula. Rumbles of thunder muffled angry exchanges of gunfire to the south as Lee and McClellan prepared for the next round. Hill's troops were standing helplessly in rain-drenched woods when Hill joined the other generals at Lee's headquarters. The army commander had quickly formulated new strategy to intercept McClellan before the Union army could get to the James and the cover of gunboats.

Lee knew that McClellan would slow down and be most vulnerable when he attempted to move his men across White Oak Swamp. That was the moment for Confederates to strike, from three directions: Jackson would impede the retreat by assailing the Federal rear; Magruder and Huger would move eastward and slam into McClellan's exposed flank; Longstreet, commanding his own and Hill's division, would make a forced march southeastward down the Darbytown Road to its intersection with the Long Bridge Road, then northeastward until he made contact with the lead elements of the Union army. To buy time for this major shift of two divisions, Lee directed Magruder, Huger, and Jackson to apply pressure as the Federals funneled over Grapevine Bridge at White Oak Swamp.

Sunday, June 29, was a day of sheer frustration. Hill and his men, behind Longstreet, filed to the south side of the Chickahominy and tramped over the steaming countryside for hours. Dust and heat caused scores of men to stagger from the road. On the columns plodded until nine that night, when Hill's brigades wearily bivouacked amid a thunderstorm on Atlee's farm. Longstreet and Hill were on schedule, despite the blistering pace and the cumbersome wagon trains struggling behind them. The same could not be said for the other wings of the Southern army. Jackson that day seemed in a daze and barely made a weak stab at the Federals; around Savage Station, Magruder was too inept and Huger too slow to give McClellan more than minimum concern. That left the Union army intact and in force as it continued toward the James River—and the two Confederate divisions in its front.

Hill's troops resumed their march early on a cloudless, hot Monday. Lee soon joined the Longstreet-Hill column as it wound through timber to the Long Bridge Road. The Confederate line turned left and increased its step toward the Quaker Road junction, which was known variously as Glendale and Riddell's Shop. White Oak Swamp lay two miles farther north. Longstreet's soldiers halted a half mile from the road intersection. Hill had stopped his men three-fourths of a mile behind Longstreet's and was tightening the ranks when one of Lee's staff officers arrived. Longstreet was not up yet, he said; Hill was to take command of all troops. Hill summoned

Gen. Richard H. Anderson, Longstreet's senior brigadier, and the two men rode forward to inspect the terrain that might become a battlefield.

The Long Bridge Road curled between low ridges as it climbed gently to high ground, on which was the largest estate in the area, Frayser's Farm. Woods with thick underbrush, broken often by small clearings, stretched off on either side of the road. Hill rode back to make troop dispositions. It was near noon. A quick probe by gray-clad skirmishers brought word that Federals were "in force and position, ready for battle." Hill placed Longstreet's own division in front, as the commander would have wanted. The Light Division moved up in close support. Longstreet now arrived on the field and resumed command. He called up Branch's brigade to protect his right and confidently instructed Hill "to hold the rest of his troops in readiness to give pursuit when the enemy has been dislodged."[25]

About two-thirty the sound of a cannon from the White Oak Swamp sector to the north convinced Lee, Hill, and Longstreet that Jackson's troops were attacking. President Davis, once again on a battlefield, now joined Lee in a clearing beside Long Bridge Road. Suddenly Federal cannon fire began blasting holes in the area perilously close to where the two leaders were, seated on horseback. Up dashed Hill. Displaying little courtesy, he exclaimed, "This is no place for either of you, and, as commander of this part of the field, I order you both to the rear!"

"We will obey your orders," Davis chuckled. The president and Lee rode back a short distance, halted, and continued to watch developments. Artillery fire grew more intense. In a moment, Hill galloped up again, and this time his anger was obvious. "Did I not tell you to go away from here?" he shouted. "And did you not promise to obey my orders? Why, one shell from that battery over yonder may presently deprive the Confederacy of its President and the Army of Northern Virginia of its commander!" This time Davis and Lee gave more heed to the young general and retired from the field.[26]

Artillery fire continued; but as the minutes passed, no sound of battle was heard from Magruder, Huger, or Jackson. The afternoon of inactivity wore on: three, three-thirty, four, four-thirty. It was Mechanicsville all over again—opportunity was slipping away because of tardiness and or lack of cooperation. This time Lee himself decided to attack with what he had. It seemed the only alternative to permitting McClellan to march, unhindered and undisturbed, past the Confederate front. Longstreet and Hill between them had fewer than 20,000 men; at least twice that many Federals were nearby in battle formation. Directly in front, straddling the road, were the 6,000 Pennsylvania Reserves of Gen. George McCall. This division had defeated Hill at Mechanicsville and borne the major share of the fighting at Gaines's Mill. Three other divisions completed the Union battle line on Frayser's Farm.

At five o'clock, with no more than a third of Lee's army at hand, Longstreet opened the attack. Lee and Hill joined the burly Longstreet in a small field to watch what they hoped would be the closing of a trap. Confederates buckled the enemy line and seized several guns. Federals rallied and counterattacked. Backward and forward the two lines swayed. Soon Union soldiers began surging toward both of Longstreet's flanks. The front line, because of its position, could neither advance nor retreat without great cost. Longstreet could wait no longer "in the hope that Jackson and Huger would come up on our left, enabling us to dislodge the Federals, after which Hill's troops could be put in fresh to give pursuit." A call went out to Hill, "ever watchful and on the alert," one of Longstreet's officers said in relief.[27]

The sun was beginning to set when the Light Division leaped into the contest. Field advanced straight up the road, Pender right behind him. Gregg fanned out to Field's left to buttress the already fighting Branch, while Archer moved to cover Pender's flank. Hill held Anderson's brigade in reserve. The men plunged ahead screaming the rebel yell as enthusiastically as they had done at Mechanicsville. And everywhere, one participant reported, Hill was "among the men, leading and cheering them on in his quiet and determined manner. He saw the overwhelming numbers with which they had to contend, but calmly planning his designs, he was fiery in the execution of them, giving counsel, as if in private life, but mounting his horse and dashing to the front whenever his battalions began to swerve before the masses of the enemy."[28]

Field's Virginians dashed ahead so eagerly that Pender's North Carolinians lost contact. Pender kept his troops advancing steadily but cautiously. Without warning, a regiment appeared seventy-five yards away, double-quicking from right to left. Yankees! Pender ordered his men to open fire, and he expressed satisfaction when a volley of musketry "scattered them in every direction." Meanwhile,

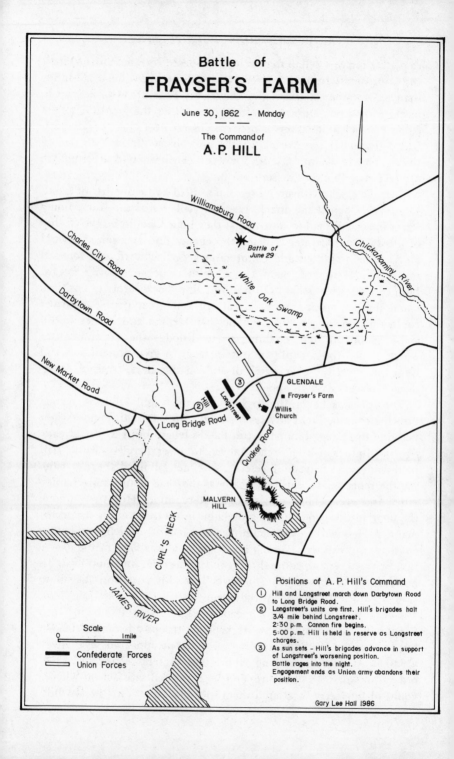

Battle of
FRAYSER'S FARM

June 30, 1862 – Monday

The Command of
A.P. HILL

Williamsburg Road

Charles City Road

Darbytown Road

New Market Road

Battle of June 29

White Oak Swamp

Chickahominy River

① ② Hill ③ Longstreet

Long Bridge Road

GLENDALE
■ Frayser's Farm
Willis Church

Quaker Road

MALVERN HILL

CURL'S NECK

JAMES RIVER

Scale
0 _____ 1 mile

■ Confederate Forces
▭ Union Forces

Positions of A. P. Hill's Command

① Hill and Longstreet march down Darbytown Road to Long Bridge Road.

② Longstreet's units are first. Hill's brigades halt 3/4 mile behind Longstreet.
2:30 p.m. Cannon fire begins.
5:00 p.m. Hill is held in reserve as Longstreet charges.

③ As sun sets – Hill's brigades advance in support of Longstreet's worsening position.
Battle rages into the night.
Engagement ends as Union army abandons their position.

Gary Lee Hall 1986

Field's regiments were alone and now close to the enemy lines. Still they charged forward with bayonets into the Union ranks. One of the Pennsylvanians stated: "A terrific contest ensued. Bayonets thrust and parried; muskets were clubbed; pistols, daggers, and bowie knives were freely used as the hostile currents surged in the turmoil of death, around and among the guns and caissons."[29]

One "murderous and destructive fire" knocked down seventy-five men of the 40th Virginia simultaneously. In the 60th Virginia were brothers Eli W. and Robert A. Christian. Four Federals attacked Robert and bayoneted him several times. The dying soldier, however, killed three of his assailants, and his brother took care of the fourth Yankee. The 47th Virginia of the same brigade captured several cannon and turned the guns so as to help Gregg's hard-pressed lines on the left. When Pender's men soon fought their way to Field's side, the troops "commenced cheering vociferously."[30]

Just at twilight in that smoke-filled inferno a lone Federal horseman rode accidentally into the ranks of the 47th Virginia and was promptly seized. He was Gen. George McCall, whose division in the Federal center had fought so bravely and inflicted heavy losses on the Southerners. The Virginians angrily leveled their muskets at the general. McCall turned to Robert Mayo and begged: "For God's sake, Colonel, don't let your men do me any harm!"

Mayo retorted angrily that his soldiers were not barbarians, and with that McCall was hustled off to a Richmond prison.[31]

Battle still raged in the gathering darkness. A Massachusetts chaplain was shocked. "The roll of repeated volleys, the rapid reports of the batteries, the crash of solid shot through the trees, and the clatter of canister and spherical case striking against trunks and branches, mingled with the yells of the combatants and the cries of the wounded, in one deafening and terrific uproar, appalling alike to ear and heart." Muskets became so overheated that men set ramrods against trees in order to force charges into the barrels. Oliver Wendell Holmes, Jr., of the 20th Massachusetts asserted that fully two-thirds of the muskets in his company became fouled through heat and dirt.[32]

Hill had followed closely every step of the conflict. At one point, he had repaired his line "by personal appeals so ardent that tears started to his eyes."[33] He also showed emotions of a different kind that afternoon. Part of Branch's brigade began breaking under the weight of numbers. An irate Hill galloped forward, seized the flag of the 7th North Carolina, and shouted at the men moving to the rear, "Damn you, if you will not follow me, I'll die alone!"

As staff officers sprang to protect the general, the foot soldiers paused. One of them pointed at their commander, still standing in his stirrups. "Lead on, Hill! Head the North Carolina boys!" Branch's line regrouped speedily.[34]

Increased gunfire from the Federal positions gave the impression that reinforcements were at hand. Hill now summoned his final reserve, Anderson's Georgians. He warned the brigadier to advance carefully and to refrain from firing as long as possible so as not to unloose volleys into sister units. Moreover, Hill told the poised soldiers, cheer as loudly as you can so as to deceive the enemy into thinking that heavy fresh regiments are at hand. Anderson's troops carried out instructions to the letter. The Georgians charged up the road, reserved their fire until they were but seventy paces from the Union works, and then yelled like a tribe of Indians. "In less than five minutes," Hill wrote proudly, "all firing ceased and the enemy retired."[35]

There were the usual nighttime horrors after the battle ended. "The shrieks and groans and cries for help which came up from that valley of death were appalling," one soldier commented. This time Hill's men were too tired to care. Most of them simply dropped to the ground where they stood; and without food or covering, too weary to think, they sought to rest. Captain Morris of the 37th North Carolina later told his wife: "Strange as it may seem to you I Never slept sounder in my life. We was so worn out that as soon as we stopped fighting we Could hardly keep awake."[36]

Frayser's Farm was a struggle that might have ended differently. "Could the other commanders have cooperated in the action," Lee observed with disappointment, "the result would have proved most disastrous to the enemy." Lee made reference in his official report to "Huger not coming up, and Jackson having been unable to force the passage at White Oak Swamp" as the principal causes of the empty victory.[37] The army commander was hardly alone in the judgment that Hill and Longstreet had maintained a furious but unequal contest. Gen. Harvey Hill sneered: "There were five divisions within sound of the firing, and within supporting distance, but not one of them moved." He was right. Some 50,000 Confederates were nearby, most of them within three miles of Frayser's Farm, and they merely listened. Down in the ranks of the 18th North Carolina, one of Hill's privates angrily wrote in his diary that the Federals managed to escape the trap. "*All* due to the negligence, drunkenness & stupidity of some few cowardly Braggarts."[38]

The Confederates lost 3,300 men in the battle. All they got for their efforts, one authority wrote, "was a causeway of dead bodies, some hard-won Federal ordnance and a bit of shell-torn woods."[39] Actually, Hill and Longstreet inflicted more losses than they took, and captured eighteen cannon and a Federal general. But the real objective—trapping McClellan's army in a vise—was not accomplished.

Hill nevertheless emerged from the fight with hero status. His battle conduct had been exemplary. He and Longstreet had demonstrated unusually good coordination in a two-division attack across broken country. A Mississippi soldier proclaimed Hill "a general of genius" because "had it not been for the scientific handling of his men few would have slept uninjured on the torn and bloody field on Monday night." The soldier then added prophetically that Frayser's Farm "will prove the never-fading honour of Hill, if the impetuous spirit of that gallant soldier does not meet with an untimely fate."[40] Longstreet was understandably guarded in the praise he gave. With the exception of Branch's men, he reported, "the other brigades of [Hill's] division were prompt, and advanced to the attack with an alacrity worthy of their gallant leader. . . . Maj. Gen. A. P. Hill deserves much credit for the condition of his new troops and the promptness and energy displayed in throwing his forces forward at the proper time and to the proper points."[41]

Just before dawn on July 1, Magruder's unmarked regiments relieved Hill and Longstreet. Lee shortly thereafter joined Longstreet, Jackson, and the two Hills at Willis Church. The division commanders said little to one another until Lee announced his determination to attack one final time at Malvern Hill. Harvey Hill protested, to no avail. Powell Hill and Longstreet were allowed to give their battered divisions much-needed and certainly deserved rest. Throughout the stunning Confederate defeat that followed, the Light Division was in reserve, dodging "nail kegs" (as the big shells from Union gunboats in the James River were called).[42]

The battle of Malvern Hill brought the Peninsular Campaign to an end. McClellan's grandiose plan had come to naught; Richmond still stood defiant. The Light Division spent a week on guard in the woods around Malvern Hill. When it was clear that McClellan would not resume the offensive, Hill's troops marched to the Laurel Church area south of Richmond and encamped. "Here," a member of Gregg's brigade observed, "the results of exposure to sun and rain, of hard fare and tiresome marching, and, perhaps, in no inferior degree, of excitement and anxiety, speedily manifested themselves. Diseases of various kinds broke out among the troops. . . . The camp-hospital and the quarters were filled with sick men."[43] During this period of inactivity, the recent campaign was appraised.

No one wanted to admit it, but the Confederates had stumbled to a military success. Strong organization and coordination were glaringly absent throughout Lee's first campaign. Often the commander was unaware of the overall situation. Each of the battles did not begin until late afternoon. Fighting time, and the quest for victory, were brief. Once combat erupted, the division commander on the field was in charge, rather than Lee. Yet these things all appeared petty compared with the final results. Lee had not only stopped the seemingly unstoppable Federal army; he had sent it reeling in confusion to the muddy bank of the James. The overall leadership qualities exhibited by Lee stamped him as a premier general and as permanent commander of the Army of Northern Virginia.

High also on the list of those receiving accolades was Powell Hill. In the commanding general's official report, Lee lightly passed over Hill's decision to do battle at Mechanicsville and lauded his assaults at Gaines's Mill. Lee used an adjective that future writers often applied to Hill. Hill, he stated, advanced into battle "with the impetuous courage for which that officer and his troops are distinguished."[44]

Impetuous Hill was, at Mechanicsville, and less so at Gaines's Mill and Frayser's Farm. He had marched promptly, executed movements effectively, rushed once into an attack without proper caution, and always fought hard. On the peninsula he showed that hesitation was not in his makeup. He was a fighter who would slam into whatever loomed in his path. Because Hill had been heedless, a bit headstrong, or "impetuous," he had in the end provided the punch that sent McClellan's right wing staggering behind the Chickahominy. Not to attack at Mechanicsville could have been disastrous for Lee's army, Richmond, and the Southern Confederacy. Some of the early writers went to excess in characterizing Hill at that time as "a household name" and his division as a unit "made of steel, rather than flesh and blood."[45] In truth, Hill needed seasoning; his temperament required more control. However, he clearly emerged from the Peninsular Campaign with the reputation of being one of the best combat officers Lee had.

The price of gaining such renown had been high. Although Hill put total casualties in the Light Division for this Seven Days campaign at slightly more than 4,000 men killed and wounded, his actual losses were about 5,500 troops. Moreover, Hill led by personal example; he expected his brigade and regimental commanders to do likewise. Consequently, in this shakedown campaign, losses among officers were heavy. Six colonels and three majors were killed; two brigadiers (Anderson and Pender), eleven colonels, and six lieutenant colonels were wounded.[46]

The men in the ranks had now acquired both experience and pride. Allen Redwood of Field's brigade boasted that "the soldiers were quick to learn the ways of war; the same men, who under the cannonade of the 26th of June . . . had almost suffered a panic, four days later stormed those death-dealing lines with the steadiness and determination of veterans. Before the battle, they had scarcely known and even cared less to what division of the army they belonged; *now* if you asked one of them he would answer, with a perceptible pride in his mien and voice, that he was one of Hill's 'Light Bobs.' "[47]

Dolly, Netty, and little Russie joined Hill in Richmond. Everything should have been pleasant. Yet crises produce frayed nerves, and in those early July days, Confederates began fighting the Seven Days battle all over again. Generals Harvey Hill and Robert Toombs argued almost to the point of fighting a duel. Georgia's Henry Benning complained so long and loudly over the new conscription act as to court arrest. Lee became the target of occasional sniping in newspapers. The worst and most damaging incident, however, involved Hill and Longstreet. It shattered a friendship and impaired the harmony of the high command thereafter.

The seed of the dispute was John M. Daniel, the "half genius, half misanthrope" editor of the *Richmond Examiner.* Daniel had attached himself to Hill's staff late in May, and his affection for the general was unbounded. Following a slight wound at Gaines's Mill, Daniel settled down as a wounded hero in Richmond and, through the pages of his paper, began to inflate Hill's acomplishments. It was Hill alone who achieved "the investment of Mechanicsville," and his division "stood successfully, opposed to at least four times their number."

Daniel's account of Frayser's Farm appeared a couple of days later, and the editor pulled out all the stops. Among his more glaring statements: "The battle was fought under the immediate and sole command of General A. P. Hill, in charge of both divisions. . . . the heroic command of General Hill pressed on with unquailing vigor and a resistless courage, driving the enemy before them. This was accomplished without artillery, there being but one battery in General Hill's command on the spot, and that belonged to General Longstreet's division, and could not be got into position. . . . Catching the spirit of their commander [Hill], the brave but jaded men moved up to the front, replying to the enemy's cheers with shouts and yells. . . . One fact is very certain, and that is that the battle of Monday night was fought exclusively by General A. P. Hill and forces under his command."[48]

Longstreet was a proud and jealous officer—"habitual critic of everyone but himself," his biographers concede. His resentment flared instantly when he read the *Examiner* article; his participation as well as his leadership had been ignored. Longstreet wrote a short but scathing rebuttal, which he asked his handsome young chief of staff, Moxley Sorrel, to sign and mail. Sorrel, equally livid, did so, and the letter appeared in the rival Richmond *Whig*. It stated in part: "No one in the army has any objections to Major Gen'l. A. P. Hill being supplied with all the notoriety that the 'Examiner' can furnish, provided no great injustice is done to others. . . . The 'eight thousand' claimed to have been lost by General A. P. Hill's Division alone, will cover the loss of the entire army during the week's campaign. . . . Exaggerated statements of casualties like these made by the 'Examiner' are calculated to be of great injury to the army, both at home and abroad."[49]

Now Hill became angry. He had had nothing to do with the manufacture of Daniel's stories, and his fierce pride in the achievements of the Light Division probably led him not to deny any aspects of the stories. Lee had said nothing about them. As far as Hill was concerned, Longstreet had gone too far in criticizing his men in public. A negative side of Hill now came into view. He was the epitome of an antebellum Southern planter. "Of a very high strung sensitive nature," a member of his staff felt, Hill was extremely jealous of his personal honor and quick to react to any aspersion.

On July 12, Hill hotly fired off a terse message to Lee: "I have the honor to request that I may be relieved from the command of Major-General Longstreet."

Longstreet read the message as it passed through his office and endorsed it just as tersely: "Respectfully forwarded. If it is convenient to exchange the troops, or to exchange the commander, I see no particular reason why Maj. Gen. A. P. Hill should not be gratified."[50]

Later in the day, when the staff officer asked for a routine report, he received the acid response "Maj. Gen. Hill declines to hold further communication with Maj. Sorrel."

Sorrel took the message to Longstreet. "Write him again," the burly general snarled, "and say that the note was written at my command and must be answered satisfactorily."

This Sorrel did. Hill returned the note unanswered. Longstreet then wrote Hill directly. Again Hill ignored the communiqué. Longstreet thereupon ordered Sorrel to place Hill under arrest.

The aide arrived at Hill's headquarters tent in full military regalia. Hill arose as he entered, coldly returned the salute, uttered no word as Sorrel announced the arrest order, saluted again and stood stiffly as Sorrel departed. J. R. Anderson assumed temporary command of the Light Division.

An exchange of scathing letters followed between Hill and Longstreet. Then Hill challenged Longstreet to a duel. Arrangements were under way for the confrontation when Lee interceded. Precisely what the commanding general did is unclear. Sorrel exaggerated when he later wrote that Lee "acted quickly and effectively, using his unvarying tact and great influence. He brought matters, through other friends, to an adjustment honorable to both."[51] In fact, "matters" thereafter between Longstreet and Hill were at best coldly courteous.

While Hill remained confined to quarters, a new Federal army under Gen. John Pope left the environs of Washington and moved into north-central Virginia. Jackson's division quickly shifted to Gordonsville to protect that strategic railroad junction and to keep an eye on Pope. The Union commander's bombastic announcements began infuriating Virginians. "If pompous and pretentious proclamations could make a soldier," a Richmond newspaper stated,

"Julius Caesar would be a baby in the hands of Gen. Pope. The man is simply a compound of vulgar self-conceit, impudence and brutality."[52]

By the third week of July, Pope's strength had climbed to 50,000 men. Lee recognized that another division had to go to Jackson to help block the Union threat. Whom to send was the question. Longstreet was the ranking major general, yet he was needed at Richmond. The man next in seniority as well as ability was Hill. The Virginian was too good a commander to keep in arrest. Military expediency dictated that he be returned to the field. This Lee did on July 26. Two directives quickly followed from Lee. First were orders for Hill and his 10,000 troops to proceed at once for duty with Jackson's command at Gordonsville. Second was a letter to Jackson which contained the interesting statement: "A. P. Hill you will find I think a good officer with whom you can consult and by advising with your division commanders as to your movements much trouble will be saved you in arranging details as they can act more intelligently."[53]

In his impeccably courteous way, Lee was telling Jackson that Hill was a team man but sensitive to military protocol and etiquette; and that Jackson should keep Hill and all his generals regularly informed as to what he was doing.

Jackson would ignore the suggestions. The result was one of the Civil War's most heated and damaging feuds.

Hill's Victory
at Cedar Mountain

In midafternoon on July 27 the Light Division began entraining for the vital railhead at Gordonsville. Hill departed from Richmond three nights later with the final elements of his command.[1] He took Dolly, Netty, and Russie with him. The war had brought husband and wife closer. With no family at all in Virginia, Dolly insisted on being with her husband—even in the field. The occasional snide remarks about her presence in the army seem not to have bothered Dolly unduly. She and Hill loved each other intensely, and she wished to be at his side whenever possible.

Hill's feelings at being transferred to Jackson probably included resentment. Jackson's failure to be on time, Hill believed, was the major factor in the Confederate defeat at Mechanicsville. On the following day, at Gaines's Mill, Hill committed his brigades to battle on the assumption that Jackson would appear in support. Again Jackson offered no help—until late in the day, when the Light Division lay battered. Incredibly, the same situation occurred a third time just days later at Frayser's Farm, when Jackson did nothing to assist in that hard-fought struggle. Thus, Hill came out of the Seven Days convinced that the eccentric and overpublicized Jackson had totally fouled up the most critical campaign of the war to that time.

In addition, Hill was joining Jackson at a time when both men were preoccupied with unpleasant events. Hill had just experienced arrest and had come close to dueling with Longstreet; Jackson was then busy with the court-martial of a brigadier who had failed to meet Jackson's rigid standards in a battle fought four mouths earlier.[2] Neither Jackson nor Hill, in other words, was in any mood for haughtiness on the part of the other.

The Light Division, with Leroy Stafford's Louisiana brigade temporarily swelling its ranks, encamped five miles southeast of Gordonsville. On August 3, Jackson and Hill led a procession of officers to a communion service at Green Springs Church. A cavalry-man observed that "the clanking swords sounded strangely as each man arranged his so as to kneel at the chancel rail." Of great concern to the officers was the military situation, and Jackson was totally mute on the subject. "None of Jackson's old officers ever try to divine his movements," Pender was quick to notice.[3]

Word reached Gordonsville that two undersized Federal divisions commanded by Gen. Nathaniel P. Banks had pushed south toward Culpeper. Jackson resolved to march at once and crush this force before it could be withdrawn or reinforced. On the morning of August 6, Hill's division left camp and baggage behind and started northward to close up with Jackson's other two divisions. The day was extremely hot, and the roads were so dusty that the men could barely see. Hill was at the head of his column when Capt. Charles Blackford, of the 2nd Virginia Cavalry, an old friend, came up beside him. Blackford asked: "Where are we going?"

Hill answered sarcastically: "I suppose we will go to the top of the hill in front of us. That is all I know."[4]

The day's march ended at nine that night. Soldiers bivouacked north of Gordonsville without tents and with hastily cooked rations. The next day's march was even worse. Beginning at eight, the men trudged four abreast "through plantations and by-roads." Dust settled over everything, there seemed to be no air, and the road was like a furnace. "The straggling was deplorable," according to one of Hill's officers, "although hardly anything else was to be expected in such heat as we had."[5] Jackson finally called a halt at midnight, with his divisions on the outskirts of Orange Court House. Exhausted and hungry, the soldiers went to sleep along the road where they stopped.

In the first hours of Thursday, August 8, the major rift between Jackson and Hill began. Not knowing where his tired troops were going, or why, continued to irritate Hill; Jackson meanwhile appeared to grow more reticent each day. When the divisions reached

Orange in the dead of night, Jackson issued instructions for the following day's advance. Richard S. Ewell's division would take the lead; Hill was to follow Ewell; Jackson's own division under Gen. Charles S. Winder would bring up the rear. That was clear enough. However, at some point later in the night, Jackson changed his mind. He directed Ewell to proceed by an alternate route to the west, presumably to lessen congestion on the main road. Hill, next in line in the original order of march, was not told of his change.[6]

He nevertheless carried out his instructions explicitly. Before dawn on the eighth he had his men ready, "with the head of my lead brigade resting near the street down which I understood Ewell to pass." The sun slowly rose, minutes ticked by, but there was no sign of Ewell. Frustration and impatience began gnawing at Hill. He turned to a longtime friend, Chaplain J. William Jones, and complained: "I tell you, I do not know whether we march north, south, east or west, or whether we will march at all. General Jackson simply ordered me to have the division ready to move at dawn. I have been ready ever since, and have no further indication of his plans. That is almost all I ever know of his designs."[7]

After a while, a Confederate brigade passed down the street, then another. Suddenly Hill realized that these were not Ewell's men; it was Winder's division, which was supposed to be third in line and behind him. Perplexed and disgusted, Hill rode forward to ascertain what was happening. Then he learned that Jackson had altered Ewell's route.

Rather than barge into the middle of Winder's column, Hill decided to let that division pass. Winder's wagons followed the infantry, so Hill waited for them to pass too. An angry Jackson now galloped upon the scene. Giving Hill a black look, and in his abrupt manner, he asked why the Light Division was not marching. Hill explained why, in as few words as possible, for he was seething.[8] Jackson then rode off. By the time Hill finally got his brigades in motion, the whole Confederate advance had turned into a farce. Not one unit was anywhere near Culpeper, the objective. The road was clogged with men and wagons; and beyond Barnett's Ford, where Ewell's division converged with Winder's, there was a horrendous traffic jam. Meanwhile, the temperature had zoomed above ninety degrees, causing men to fall out of ranks, gasping for breath. Jackson bitterly called a halt to the escapade. Late in the afternoon he dispatched Maj. Franklin Paxton of his staff to tell Hill to return his division to Orange. This was a directive that Jackson repeatedly denied thereafter.[9]

Ewell that day had marched eight miles to avoid the congestion he encountered; Hill's division had barely covered a mile before retracing its steps; the element of surprise on which Jackson had based his entire offensive was gone; Winder was ill; Ewell was swearing in exasperation; Hill was angry; Jackson was livid; an untold number of soldiers were prostate or dead from sunstroke. It was the worst performance a Jackson force had ever made on a march. And the fault was totally Jackson's. The whole thing might have been avoided if the tight-lipped Jackson had been more communicative with—and more considerate of—his subordinate officers.

Lee's admonition to Jackson a week earlier had done no good. The taciturn Jackson demanded instant obedience. "Obey my orders first and reason about them afterward," he had asserted. Perhaps something in addition to the demand for unquestioning obedience was boiling in Jackson. Was it distrust, jealousy, or longtime dislike of Hill? That the Light Division, which constituted fully half of Jackson's strength, did not receive top priority in Jackson's strategic thinking suggests the likelihood that personal feelings were superseding military expediency. A developing contest was under way between Cromwell and the Cavalier. Seeds of discontent had been sown. Jackson would later officially blame Hill for the foul-up in getting out of Orange.[10] More damaging, Jackson henceforth exhibited real doubt as to whether Hill could perform promptly and skillfully. As for Hill, his opinion of Jackson had only worsened.

After bivouacking his men on the night of the eighth, Hill made a suggestion to the commander. It would be impossible, said Hill, for the Light Division and its artillery to make an advance the next day if the wagon trains still occupied the roads. I volunteer to take my brigades by another route, Hill stated, and I will rejoin the command at any point and at any time you designate. No, Jackson replied curtly. The wagons have been ordered off the road. Hill was to advance as originally scheduled.[11]

Saturday, August 9, began clear and bright. The absence of any breeze foretold another scorching day. Jackson directed Gen. Beverly H. Robertson's cavalry to fan out as tentacles, with the divisions of Ewell and Winder to follow toward Culpeper. Hill, back in Orange, was to catch up with the main force as quickly as he could. That was a challenge "Little Powell" welcomed. Wearing no uniform coat, and with shirt-sleeves rolled up, he got his troops on the road soon after two in the morning. Edward Thomas, now commanding the Georgia brigade, took the lead; Branch, Archer, Pender, Stafford, Field, and Gregg followed in that order. Gregg's brigade halted at the Rapidan with instructions to protect the 1,200 wagons as they filed across the ford.[12]

"The day was remarkably hot and dusty," one of the Tennesseans wrote, and the red dust of the road became suffocating.[13] All morning men staggered from the silent line of march. Early in the afternoon Hill and his soldiers heard the deep boom of cannon six miles away. Word soon drifted through the ranks that Federal cavalry and artillery were disputing Jackson's advance. Once again Jackson did not inform Hill—and half of the army—about what was happening. Instead, Jackson ordered Ewell and Winder into immediate line of battle. Artillerist Willie Pegram was shocked to learn that Jackson ordered his men to open fire "without even waiting long enough to allow the stragglers to catch up with their regiments."[14]

Battle had exploded some five to six miles south of Culpeper. The Confederates had the better position. Imposing Cedar Mountain (sometimes called Slaughter Mountain) was on the right; heavy woods protected the left. In front was open ground sloping into a broad valley of meadows and cornfields through which meandered Cedar Creek. Banks had hastily placed his men in formation along the valley. A Rhode Island officer wrote that the Confederates "hoped to draw us on the heights; we chose to remain in open, plain ground." But not for long.[15]

Quick orders went out from Jackson. Winder's division was to take position astride the Culpeper Road, and Ewell's troops were to proceed to the right over the shoulder of Cedar Mountain. This would be a concave line, but the two divisions were barely connected. Artillery batteries on both sides had wheeled into position and were banging away at close range. Winder was killed while watching the fire, and William B. Taliaferro took command of his division. That was only part of the confusion.

Jackson at Cedar Mountain once more displayed an I-can-do-it-by-myself attitude. Possibly the lethargy of the Seven Days still lingered, or possibly three divisions were more than he could handle at this time. Whatever the reason, he blundered into combat on the road to Culpeper. At five that evening, as he was still attempting to unscramble his lines to attack, Federals swarmed forward in a heavy assault of their own. The whole area ignited in a conflagration of shells, sound, and smoke. A Maine soldier termed it "the most tremendous volleys we had ever heard. Crash succeeded crash; the mighty thump of the shells against the forest trees was not heard for the din of the musketry." Ewell's troops on Cedar Mountain were only weakly assailed. The main Federal thrust came on the Confederate left, with line after line of bluecoats advancing through fields of corn and wheat. Federals swept around Taliaferro's left as heavy numbers pounded his front. The Confederate line began to snap, with part of Jackson's old division becoming (in the words of the general's chief biographer) "an ungovernable mob, breaking rapidly to the rear, and on the very verge of panic."[16]

Meanwhile, Jackson had sent Capt. Charles Blackford rearward to the edge of some woods to inform Hill where to go when he arrived. Blackford peered anxiously down the road for several minutes. Then, to his "infinite relief," up rode Hill at the head of the Light Division. Blackford gave him the message; Hill barked out the order to his brigades, and the men "followed with a shout."[17] He still had no idea of Jackson's battle plan, but he was going where he was needed, and he was taking with him the most powerful element in Jackson's army.

For a moment the smoke of battle seemed to dissipate. Behind the Southern lines, as far as the eye could see, was a long line of dust signifying the approach of Hill and his division. Hill had already sent Thomas and two batteries of artillery to Jubal Early's assistance. Early's brigade had formed to the right of Taliaferro's division, and after the artillerists maneuvered their pieces through another traffic jam of men and wagons, Southern infantry shifted position to protect the guns of Pegram and W. B. Hardy as they unleashed salvos into advancing Federals. The arrival of Thomas's brigade, Early later conceded, "was very timely." The Georgians got behind a fence bordering a cornfield, Early added, "and effectively checked [Federal] progress, strewing the ground with the killed."[18]

It was now six o'clock, and the sun was beginning to set blood-red in the western sky. Jackson and a courier rode anxiously through the woods in search of Hill. They came to open ground and there met Hill, coming up on foot with Branch's brigade right behind him. Jackson sharply informed Hill that he was behind time; then Jackson ordered him to deploy his brigades along the road. Hill, wrote the courier accompanying Jackson, "took the remark in entire good humor, and running back to the servant leading his horse, he vaulted into the saddle and quickly formed his men into line."[19]

Hill sent Branch down the left of the Culpeper Road, at the same time directing Archer and Pender in turn to double-time farther to the left so as to envelop the Federal right. Branch, a former congressman, was an orator of some renown. While his brigade was poised for the signal to attack, he launched into a patriotic oration and was building up steam when into his ranks rode a hatless Jackson. He galloped up to Branch, shouting, "Push forward, General! Push forward!"

The North Carolinians sprang to the attack. A staff officer wrote: "Forward with quick step and then quicker went the whole line after their illustrious leader and then with an irresistible yell they charged over the field, their wild yell mingling with the rattle of their musketry." In truth, their "illustrious leader" was so weak from a siege of diarrhea that he had to sit down every fifty yards or so. Yet, Branch boasted later, "the excitement braced me up."[20]

His Tarheels had advanced no more than a hundred yards when they encountered soldiers in the 27th Virginia of the celebrated Stonewall Brigade fleeing toward the rear. A lieutenant in Branch's brigade recalled: "They met us and broke through our ranks as best they could, producing of course in places considerable disorder, and making with their confusion and the comments and entreaties of their officers who were striving to rally them, a clamor like a bedlam." Branch's men, Hill reported, passed through the broken ranks, "received the enemy's fire, promptly returned it, checked the pursuit, and in turn drove them back and relieved Taliaferro's flank."[21]

Hill—shirt soaked with perspiration and sword in hand—led the climactic assault of his division. He too was caught in the excitement of battle. As his lines moved forward, straggling inevitably occurred. Hill spied a lieutenant among one group of soldiers half-running toward the rear. The general reined his horse in front of the man and angrily shouted, "Who are you, sir, and where are you going?"

The lieutenant feebly replied in a halting voice, "I am going back with my wounded friend."

Hill abruptly leaned over and ripped the bars of rank from the man's collar. Staring him coldly in the eye, Hill snarled: "You are a

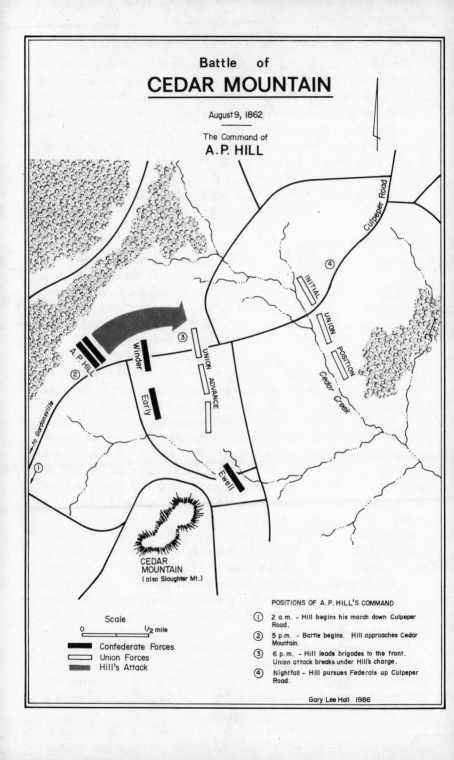

Battle of
CEDAR MOUNTAIN

August 9, 1862

The Command of
A.P. HILL

Culpeper Road

④ INITIAL

UNION POSITION

Cedar Creek

③ UNION ADVANCE

A.P. HILL

② Winder

to Gordonsville

① Early

Ewell

CEDAR
MOUNTAIN
(also Slaughter Mt.)

Scale
0   1/2 mile

■ Confederate Forces
□ Union Forces
▨ Hill's Attack

POSITIONS OF A.P. HILL'S COMMAND

① 2 a.m. – Hill begins his march down Culpeper Road.

② 5 p.m. – Battle begins. Hill approaches Cedar Mountain.

③ 6 p.m. – Hill leads brigades to the front. Union attack breaks under Hill's charge.

④ Nightfall – Hill pursues Federals up Culpeper Road.

Gary Lee Hall 1986

pretty fellow to hold a commission—deserting your colors in the presence of the enemy, and going to the rear with a man who is scarcely badly enough wounded to go himself. I reduce you to the ranks, sir, and if you do not go to the front and do your duty, I'll have you shot as soon as I can spare a file of men for the purpose!"

With that, Hill galloped forward to continue leading his men.[22]

Branch, Archer, and Pender were all advancing against the Federals. Archer's 1,200-man brigade came under concentrated fire and quickly took 135 casualties. Then, wrote one of Hill's Tennessee-ans, "Branch and Archer advanced rapidly, gradually pushing back the Federals, until they reached a wheat-field occupied by their reserve lines. Here an obstinate stand was made, and for a few minutes the battle seemed doubtful, but opportunely Pender threw his brigade upon their right flank. This changed the aspect at once. They hesitated a moment, then broke and fled in confusion from the field."[23] The 10th Maine had been in the assault across the wheat field. It maintained its position for thirty minutes, at a cost of 173 of 461 men engaged. The 5th Connecticut, wrote its historian, "was broken in pieces. . . . Several of its best men were killed; fifty were struck down within two minutes. The wounded crept behind the rocks and wheat-stacks, where some of them were shot again and again."[24]

Maine-born Henry Prince was commanding a brigade when he was captured by some of Hill's men. The Federal general was brought before Hill as minié balls whistled all around. The suave Prince stood stiffly at attention and said to Hill, "General, the fortunes of war have thrown me in your hands."

"Damn the fortunes of war, General!" Hill shouted. "Get to the rear! You are in danger here!"[25]

It was growing dark when, wrote Hill, Federal general Banks "made an attempt to retrieve his fortunes by a cavalry charge." Two squadrons of Pennsylvanians advanced diagonally across the open wheat field. In doing so, they exposed their flank and came under a deadly fire in which, Hill observed, the Yankees "had many saddles emptied and fled in utter confusion."[26]

Jackson was anxious that Banks's forces be driven farther north-ward. He ordered Hill, whose troops were less wearied by battle, to take up the pursuit. Hill passed the word for Early's infantry and William E. Jones's cavalry to accompany him. The Light Division started up the road in the sweltering heat. Hill's men quickly covered a mile and a half in an effort to catch what a Federal admitted was a "terrified mass in their headlong retreat."[27] Hill's pursuit began slowing to a crawl. A full moon provided little light. When Hill approached woods, he had to wait for artillery to come up and shell them. Then the infantry could safely advance only to the next wooded area before halting again for cannon to clear the way. Pegram's battery suffered a brutal thrashing in the process. Making prisoners of demoralized Federals encountered every hundred yards or so consumed more time. Near eleven at night, after receiving word that Federal reinforcements were moving southward from Culpeper, Jackson ordered Hill to cease the chase. The Light Division turned around and marched five miles back to the battlefield to bivouac in fields awash with blood.[28]

Cedar Mountain had been a costly engagement for both sides. Total Federal casualties were 2,381 men. Jackson reported his own losses at 229 killed, 1,047 wounded, and 31 missing, of which 49 dead and 345 injured were from the four brigades Hill had committed to action.[29] But for the Confederates there was more to the contest than casualty lists. Jackson appeared to have had only limited knowledge of the situation before starting the battle and only limited control of its progress. A captain in the 21st Virginia of Jackson's division wrote the day after the battle: "Our whole brigade is cut entirely to pieces and today has no existence as a brigade. The men are Scattered in every direction and fully one half Killed and wounded. The devils flanked us, got to our rear, and cut us up generally." Southern hopes seemed slim during the struggle, a Richmond newspaper stated, but got "renewed vigor when the division of Gen. A. P. Hill came up."[30]

Jackson's orders throughout the day were so garbled and incomplete that the disposition of his large reserve elements was left completely in Hill's care; and Hill may have felt a sense of satisfaction when his men stabilized the line after some of Jackson's supposedly best soldiers ran from the field. Jackson had won a victory, to be sure, but Hill had won the battle for him.

August 10 opened as another scorching day, but at eleven, relief-giving rain began falling. The Light Division buried its dead during the steady downpour. On the twelfth, Hill's division fell back to the Crenshaw farm, midway between Gordonsville and Orange, and made camp. There still were no tents, so the men "slept on the ground, in the woods, or open fields, without regard to the weather."[31]

From the battlefield Hill had acquired a gray stallion, which he named Champ and rode exclusively thereafter. The general established his headquarters tent on the lawn of Howard Place, the palatial home of Col. John Willis. Hill chafed at what had happened to his hometown a few miles up the road. Culpeper had been stripped by Federal occupation, with most of its citizens now destitute. A large number of Confederates seized at Cedar Mountain were incarcerated in the court house, just up the street from his boyhood home. Hill was unusually restless. Although he enjoyed what one officer called "a thorough *entente cordiale*" with his brigade commanders, the unpleasant feelings between Jackson and Hill were becoming a matter of concern to field officers in the Light Division.[32]

McClellan's Army of the Potomac was abandoning the Virginia peninsula and heading back to Washington. Lee thereupon began consolidating his army at Gordonsville so as to give full attention to Pope. Late in the afternoon of August 15, Jackson's force marched northward. The next day the divisions of Taliaferro, Ewell, and Hill reached Mountain Run to the west of Clark's Mountain. They encamped there to await Longstreet's arrival from Richmond with ten brigades. Lee's Army of Northern Virginia was then reunited. The commanding general carefully formulated his strategy. Pope's army stood along the north bank of the Rapidan. Lee resolved to hold him there by putting Longstreet in his front. Jackson in the meantime would cross the Rapidan at Somerville Ford, move rapidly northwest toward the Rappahannock, and then curl in around Pope's dangling right flank. Deception and speed were the principal ingredients in Lee's plan. Jackson was determined to employ both to maximum advantage.

The original order from Lee's headquarters called for Jackson's divisions—with Hill in the lead—to march out "at dawn" on August 20. At the last moment Jackson arbitrarily changed the departure time to "as soon as the moon shall rise." However, either Hill did not get word of Jackson's change (which is likely because both Taliaferro and Ewell mentioned no revision in marching orders), or he considered Lee's directive unalterable save by Lee himself. In any case, Jackson and his staff were up at three o'clock on the twentieth; but when they shortly thereafter reached the line of march, no troops were in sight. Jackson galloped through the darkness to Hill's encampment, where he found the men still asleep, cooking rations, or leisurely packing their gear. To Jackson's gruff demand for an explanation, one of Hill's brigadiers replied that he had received no marching orders for the middle of the night.

Now the whole advance (in Jackson's estimation) was two hours behind schedule. A "much put out" Jackson then ordered the lead brigade onto the road. As an added precaution, he assigned a staff officer to each division to see that the marching orders were obeyed.[33]

Jackson was now convinced that Hill simply could not be trusted to move promptly. He would bear watching. As for Hill, he never gave any explanation for his "failure to march on time." The commander of the Light Division doubtless saw the incident as but another failure by Jackson to maintain simple communications. Moreover, the sensitive Hill bitterly resented Jackson's not only issuing direct orders to one of his brigades but also assigning some inconsequential staff officer to monitor the Light Division's progress.

Hill's men set the pace in front that day as the Confederates crossed the Rapidan. Early the next morning the march resumed. Jackson now tucked Hill between Taliaferro and Ewell. The troops were "in a half starving situation," Pegram noted, but they marched in silence.[34] On the twenty-second, Jackson's force left Beverly Ford and followed country roads and open fields to a bivouac area near the burned bridge at White Sulphur Springs. Rain began pouring late that afternoon. Hill and his staff were fortunate to find cover in the deserted home of Dr. Martin Scott. Jackson established his headquarters nearby in a house surrounded by an attractive worm fence. Gregg's boisterous South Carolinians huddled in the rain a few yards away. That set the stage for an acceleration of Jackson's anger.

The humorless general passed the word at sundown that in kindness to his hosts, the fence around their home was not to be used for firewood or otherwise disturbed. The next morning Jackson surveyed what was left of the fence. He promptly ordered Gregg's regimental colonels all placed under arrest. One of them angrily stated: "We were released upon arrangement with the owner of the farm to pay for the damage done. Five regimental commanders . . . all arrested for a few palings of an ornamental fence taken under such circumstances! And then to be told that there was no discipline in our army!"[35] Opinions of Jackson inside the ranks of the Light Division continued to worsen, as did his opinion of them.

Jackson's disposition, and his attitude toward Hill, did not improve in the hours ahead. Early's brigade had crossed the Rappahannock on a flimsy dam, which became submerged during the night's heavy downpour. That left him isolated and potentially in danger. The early-morning sun on the twenty-third was just starting to burn away rain clouds when Jackson reached the river. He was rain-drenched, and the sight of the impassable bridge over which he had planned to march his divisions put him in an even more foul mood. He waded his horse to the middle of the swollen stream and sat there, motionless, for an hour. At length Hill led his horse out and sought to break the tension by conversation. However, one staff officer observed, Jackson "was so abstracted and rude" that Hill turned around and went back to his division "without any commands or instructions."[36]

The river remained high that Saturday. Engineers arrived and managed to construct a temporary bridge, which permitted the troops of Early and Lawton to recross the Rappahannock early on the twenty-fourth. Meanwhile, Hill had carefully posted his batteries on the hills that loomed over the crossing. At ten that Sunday morning, some seven Federal batteries opened a barrage, which, Hill reported, "continued without intermission until late in the afternoon." The Light Division's guns responded in kind, producing what Kyd Douglas termed "the noisiest artillery duel I ever witnessed." A volunteer member of Hill's staff observed that the Federal artillery "threw a storm of shot & shell at us . . . they must have expended several thousand rounds, & in all, so well sheltered were we, our killed & wounded did not reach 20."[37] Early in the afternoon a heavy column of Federal infantry approached on the road leading to the springs. Hill waited until the Yankees were within easy range, then sent shells ripping into their ranks. The line buckled and started forward again, only to receive another blast from Lindsay Walker's well-placed guns. The Federals thereupon ran from the field, Hill noted with satisfaction.[38]

The batteries of the Light Division held off Union probes as Jackson reached Jeffersonton. There, in the middle of a large field, Lee met with his generals to formulate the next steps in the offensive against Pope. The plan adopted called for Longstreet to mask Jackson, who with his three divisions would move rapidly down a valley formed by the imposing Blue Ridge Mountains to the west and a chain of foothills known as Bull Run Mountains to the east.

Jackson would next cut through Thoroughfare Gap in the Blue Ridge range and swoop down on Pope's rear. The Union army would then be cut off from Washington and caught between the two arms of Lee's army.

The march began at sunrise, August 25, "with the utmost promptitude and without knapsacks." Ewell was in front, Hill in the middle, with the Stonewall division last in line. A private in Hill's 55th Virginia described a portion of the march: "The hot August sun rose, clouds of choking dust enveloped the hurrying column, but on and on the march was pushed without relenting. . . . It was far on in the night when the column stopped, and the weary men dropped beside their stacked muskets and were instantly asleep, without so much as unrolling a blanket. A few hours of much needed repose, and they were shaken up again long before 'crack of dawn,' and limped on in the darkness only half awake. There was no mood for speech, nor breath to spare if there had been—only the shuffling tramp of the marching feet, the steady rumbling of wheels, the creak and rattle and clank of harness and accouterment, with an occasional order, uttered under the breath and always the same: 'Close up! Close up, men!' "[39]

Soldiers gobbled ears of corn from adjacent fields and green apples from nearby trees as the four-abreast ranks snaked down roads, over hills, and through woods. They removed hot and ill-fitting shoes, preferring to walk barefooted in the dust. The three divisions reached Thoroughfare Gap on the twenty-sixth. It was undefended. The Federals had committed a major blunder by not covering their western flank.

Part of Hill's dislike of Jackson stemmed from the latter's depth-less piety. During the evening when the troops passed through Thoroughfare Gap, the division commanders met with Jackson in a rare council of war. Jackson listened to the views of the generals, then announced that he would give his decision the following morning. Hill was too steeled from past experience to expect results from their input; and as he left the headquarters tent, he laughingly said to Ewell: "Well, I suppose Jackson wants time to pray over it."[40]

Jackson broke from tactics found in military texts. He divided his small force into three prongs. Ewell's division marched toward Bristoe Station to burn the railroad bridge over Broad Run, neutralize Pope's main supply line, and protect Jackson's rear. Jeb Stuart's cavalry and two infantry regiments under Isaac Trimble converged

This wartime likeness of Hill, published here for
the first time, was made during his tenure as commander
of the Light Division. The calico shirt was one of
the many sewed by his wife. Note the famous
yellow gauntlets, which are the gloves
Hill was wearing at the time of his death.

(Museum of the Confederacy)

Kitty Morgan, Hill's beloved "Dolly,"
sat for this portrait at the age of eighteen.
Six years later she married the dashing
lieutenant from Virginia.
(Henrietta T. Millns Collection)

Hill as a U.S. Army officer in the 1850s.
Family tradition maintains that Hill had this photograph
made on the eve of his marriage.
(Museum of the Confederacy)

The proud colonel of the
13th Virginia (1861)—
the only known likeness of Hi..
in the full uniform of
a Confederate officer.
(Confederate Veteran)

The second of two flags th..
Dolly Hill made for her
husband's regiment. It
replaced a standard
captured in battle.
(Museum of the Confederacy)

These two photographs of Hill clearly show the physical deterioration that occurred in the 1863–1865 period. To the right, Hill can be seen shortly after his promotion to corps command. The photograph below reveals an obviously unwell general with weak eyes and prematurely graying beard. (Library of Congress)

Frances Russell Hill, the daughter whom the general knew longest, taken near the end of the Civil War. "Russie" inherited her father's clear blue eyes.
(Museum of the Confederacy)

In 1878, Lucy Lee Hill posed for this photograph as a young lady approaching adulthood. The last survivor of the general's immediate family, Lucy always insisted that her father had never received the accolades he deserved.
(Henrietta T. Millns Collection)

Kitty Forsyth—Hill's widow remarried in the
postwar period—at the age of seventy-five.
She remained contemptuous of the "Lost Cause"
that had killed her husband.

(Henrietta T. Millns Collection)

The woods in which Hill was slain are visible in this 1929 photograph, taken from the Boydton Plank Road, down which Hill galloped.
(Petersburg National Battlefield)

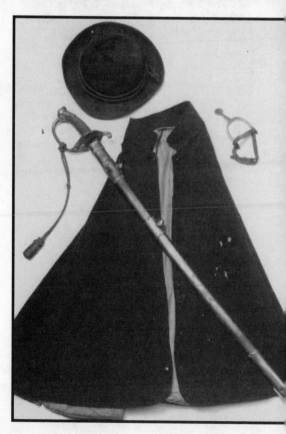

Pictured are four items Hill was wearing when he was killed—his cape, sword, spur, and small crowned hat.
(Museum of the Confederacy)

on Manassas Junction to seize the supplies stockpiled at the depot. The third wing, including Hill's division, remained with Jackson and advanced on the railroad junction.

The bone-jarring marching pace continued to be brutal, despite bleeding feet, lack of water, empty stomachs, fatigue, and the ravages of diarrhea. After averaging three miles per hour in some instances, the divisions halted on the twenty-seventh at Gainesville. They had covered fifty-four miles in thirty-six hours. Jackson had effected one of the great flanking movements of the war. He was behind Pope's army, and only twenty-seven miles from the Northern capital. On the other hand, Jackson had barely 24,000 men; Pope could congregate 80,000 or so Federals—and Lee's army was a good distance away.[41]

Shortly after sunrise on August 27, the Light Division arrived at the railhead. The men could not believe their eyes. It was the Christmas of dreams! On two railroad tracks, stretching for fully half a mile, scores of Union boxcars stood coupled. They were filled with staples and delicacies of every imaginable variety, ranging from champagne, whiskey, coffee, lobster salad, sardines, and corned beef to vegetables, candy, cakes, nuts, fruits, and pickles. Only Trimble's two regiments guarded the bonanza. Hill made no attempt to stop his famished soldiers as they led the way in assaulting the boxcars. Trimble would huffishly note in his official report: "It was with extreme mortification that, in reporting to General A. P. Hill for orders about 10 o'clock, I witnessed an indiscriminate plunder of the public stores, cars and sutlers' houses by the army which had just arrived, in which General Hill's division was conspicuous, setting at defiance the guards I had placed over the stores."[42]

The troops had just begun to feast when an urgent order to "fall in" came down the line. A mile to the north of the junction, a spotlessly clean brigade of four New Jersey regiments under Gen. George Taylor was disembarking from a train. They began marching toward Manassas under the mistaken assumption that only Confederate cavalrymen, not infantry, stood in their front. Union soldiers were "advancing toward us in perfect order over an open plain," one of Hill's men recalled, as Hill brought up four of his batteries.[43] He also ordered the brigades of Pender, Archer, Field, and Thomas to move into support position. This was to be a contest between experienced Confederate cannoneers and inexperienced Federal infantry. With Willie Pegram's guns doing most of the damage, the

Southerners won with ease. Taylor's brigade disintegrated: 135 men killed or wounded, 300 captured, the remainder displaying "disgraceful" conduct when they "retreated rapidly and in disorder along the line of the railroad." Confederate losses were minimal.[44]

It was near noon when Hill's men eagerly made their way back to the railhead to resume their gorging. To their chagrin, Jackson had posted a stronger guard around the stores. The Light Division waited impatiently until Jackson finally issued an order that before the supplies were put to the torch, Confederates could help themselves to as much as they could eat and carry. The hours that followed were never equaled or forgotten in the Army of Northern Virginia. One of Hill's Virginia soldiers described the scene: "It was more than funny to see the ragged, rough, dirty fellows, who had been half living on roasted corn and green apples for days, now drinking Rhine wine, eating lobster salad, potted tongue, cream biscuit, pound cake, canned fruits, and the like; and filling pockets and haversacks with ground coffee, tooth-brushes, condensed milk, silk handkerchiefs."[45] A South Carolinian noted that "fine whiskey and segars circulated freely, elegant lawn and linen handkerchiefs were applied to noses hitherto blown by the thumb and forefinger, and sumptuous underclothing was fitted over limbs sunburnt, sore and vermin-splotched."[46]

The depot was set ablaze at midnight, Hill reported, and the whole area became what a Federal officer two days later called "a scene of desolation and ruin . . . a smouldering mass of ashes."[47] Jackson's location was now indelibly marked. His next task was to find a position that was defensible and close to the line of Lee's expected advance through Thoroughfare Gap. Jackson chose the elevated ground behind the tiny village of Groveton.

That new march, which began at one in the morning on August 28, was seemingly a tangle of confusion. Jackson appeared to be heading for Centreville, farther in Pope's rear, for Hill's division took the road in that direction. Hill's march continued all the way to Centreville, either as a decoy to lure Pope out of position, or because of another failure by Jackson to communicate. Jackson moved his other two divisions west of Bull Run and into the woods at Groveton.

Hill reached "forlorn and pitiful" Centreville at daylight on Thursday the twenty-eighth. Around eight in the morning Jackson at Groveton got a report that Federals were in full retreat on the turnpike toward Washington. He sent a message to Hill: block the fords at Bull Run and hold the line against the enemy. It was two hours before Hill, marching away from Centreville toward Bull Run, got the new directive. By then, his pickets had captured two separate Union couriers with dispatches making it clear that Pope was not retreating. He was concentrating his army at Manassas Junction to overpower Jackson.[48]

The Confederate commander had been wrong in his assumption of Federal movement. Hill knew it. So did his troops, who now could plainly see the dust of "thousands of Yankees" approaching. There was no time, Hill reasoned, to contact Jackson and get new orders. Of course, Hill could have obeyed Jackson's instructions and left the misinformed commander with two-thirds of his force to grapple with the enemy. After all, Jackson insisted on blind obedience. But not this time, Hill concluded. "I deemed it best to push on and join General Jackson," in violation of orders.[49] Hill was correct in his decision. Jackson never made mention of this self-assertiveness on Hill's part, and the silence is proof that it met with Jackson's approval.

Thus, while Pope struck for the Manassas Junction area in the belief that Jackson was still there, two Confederate divisions were hiding in the woods five miles to the west. The other division steadily closed the gap that hot and windy day. Hill kept his men marching at a brisk pace. Thirst soon became acute in the ranks. During a brief rest stop, soldiers in the Light Division dashed over to a well in the front yard of a farm. They eagerly drew several buckets of water, drank with gusto, and began filling their canteens. As they were finishing, the elderly owner of the farm sauntered over and said: "I don't think that water is very good. When the battle was fought here last summer, some dead men were thrown into it, and it has not been cleaned out since."

A North Carolina soldier noted: "You can imagine that those canteens were soon emptied, and some of the men also."[50]

The Light Division crossed Bull Run, soon turned right, and filed into woods alongside the road to Sudley Springs. From that position Hill's men were merely listeners to the roar of battle, which exploded to the right when Jackson, late in the day, ambushed Gen. Rufus King's Federal division. Hill himself and a couple of his batteries got a taste of the fighting. The van of a Union column was sighted moving toward Hill's position. With wry humor the general wrote: "That evening there was a little artillery practice of my batteries on the enemy's infantry." Hill personally directed the first salvo.[51]

The little-known engagement at Groveton would become obscured by the blood bath of the next two days. Yet the August 28 collision was a crippling blow to Jackson's high-level command. Taliaferro fell wounded and was lost for some time; Ewell went down from a bullet wound that cost him a leg. With Winder killed at Cedar Mountain, that left Hill as the only experienced division commander Jackson had.

Uncertainty in command structure was but one problem the Confederates faced that night as they dug earthworks and converted an area into an arena.

Fighting Pope—
and Jackson

When sundown brought an end to the fighting at Groveton, Jackson drew his men back to take advantage of a long flat-topped ridge a mile north of the Warrenton–Centreville road. An unfinished railroad bed ran 500 yards below the crest of the ridge, and most of Jackson's line was within 100 yards of the roadbed. The Confederate front became a tight 3,000 yards, and the three divisions manning it should have been more than enough. Yet losses through battle, straggling, and sickness had reduced Jackson's strength to 18,000 troops at most. In addition, on Jackson's left—"the post of greatest danger" and the one to which Hill was assigned—woods extended right into the Confederate lines.[1] Hence, and in spite of the nighttime hour, Hill stacked his infantry all around the railroad bed. In two ranks along the front were, from left to right, Gregg, Thomas, and Field. Behind them in one solid line comprising half of the division were Archer, Pender, and Branch. Hill's batteries were spaced in an open field in the rear of his dual defenses. Yet so much of the infantry works were in a tangle of trees and brush, Hill conceded, "as to preclude the effective use of much artillery."[2]

Hill put the men to work reinforcing the railroad bed—but not to a natural stopping-point. On the far left he crowded Gregg's South Carolinians at a point where the railroad passed through a stony, brushy knoll that sloped from the north to the railroad and then beyond it toward Bull Run. To Gregg's left was an open field. Gregg posted one of his regiments along the boundary fence as pro-

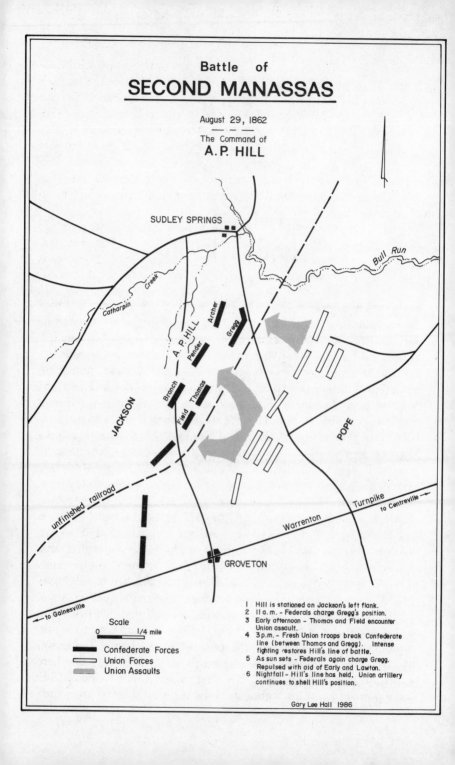

Battle of
SECOND MANASSAS

August 29, 1862

The Command of
A.P. HILL

SUDLEY SPRINGS

Bull Run

Catharpin Creek

A.P. HILL

Archer
Gregg
Pender
Branch
Field Thomas

JACKSON

POPE

unfinished railroad

Turnpike
to Centreville

Warrenton

GROVETON

to Gainesville

Scale

0   1/4 mile

■ Confederate Forces
▢ Union Forces
▨ Union Assaults

1 Hill is stationed on Jackson's left flank.
2 11 a.m. - Federals charge Gregg's position.
3 Early afternoon - Thomas and Field encounter
   Union assault.
4 3 p.m. - Fresh Union troops break Confederate
   line (between Thomas and Gregg). Intense
   fighting restores Hill's line of battle.
5 As sun sets - Federals again charge Gregg.
   Repulsed with aid of Early and Lawton.
6 Nightfall - Hill's line has held. Union artillery
   continues to shell Hill's position.

Gary Lee Hall 1986

tection. The extreme left of Hill's position thus formed an obtuse angle that pointed toward the Union lines. Edward Thomas's Georgians fanned out for battle along the wooded tongue to Gregg's right. However, for some inexplicable reason, Hill left the gap between the two brigades unattended. The opening was about 175 yards wide. Almost as bad, in front of it was a chasm six to ten feet deep, behind which advancing troops were not visible. Hill apparently never saw the gap, and Jackson never checked the line. Its existence was Hill's fault—a blatant oversight by one who should have known better.

Men in the Light Division were not aware of the broken line as they crouched in the predawn darkness, but they were understandably nervous. One of the South Carolinians observed: "Before us was Pope, with at least the bulk of the Federal army, which, of course, we magnified by many thousands; behind us was no base, no subsistence, no reinforcements."[3]

The sun had been up in a clear sky for an hour that Friday (August 29) when the Federals came after Hill. Pope's intent was obvious: to destroy Jackson's wing before the rest of Lee's army under Longstreet reached the field. The Union brigades of Gens. Wladimir Krzyanowski and Alexander Schimmelfennig advanced toward Hill's front; and when the one on the Federal right began swinging toward the northwest, Hill immediately concluded that Pope wanted to turn his left flank. This meant that Gregg's brigade had to play the first vital role. Shortly after eleven, as the two predominantly German brigades moved through woods toward the railroad cut, Gregg responded with the best defense he could make: he attacked.[4]

Two of his regiments recovered from the initial shock of the Federal onslaught and then hit the Union line so severely that its center collapsed. Gregg's troops punched through and, like a wedge, drove the two Union brigades apart. The Federals rallied and, aided by reinforcements, formed a line in the woods. Gregg resumed the attack, and Union soldiers hastily fell back to their kickoff position. By noon, things were about where they had been at dawn, except that dead and wounded soldiers were scattered in the woods and open ground.

Pope was not through, by any means. The morning's action was but an overture to what now erupted. Gen. Carl Schurz's Germans had always been of suspect ability. Now four veteran brigades from the Army of the Potomac moved into action. These troops, commanded by Joseph Hooker and Jesse Reno, were fresh as well as spirited. They crashed through the underbrush toward the railroad bed defended by Hill's other front-line brigades, Thomas and Field. Hill's men, lying down to load and rising only to fire, poured volley after volley into the charging Federals. Musket balls shredded leaves and twigs, ripped branches from trees, and soon ignited the long dry grass between the opposing lines. Uncontrollable fires began to rage, and men sweated and choked in a kind of battle even the Army of Northern Virginia had seldom fought.

Blue and gray lines came together; a wild melee of hand-to-hand fighting spilled out of the woods and over the railroad embankment. Bayonets flashed through the smoke; muskets became clubs; men crowded around colors as lines swayed back and forth. Hill, on foot, moved from sector to sector as he directed the Confederate defense. It was a prickly situation, he admitted. "The most persistent and furious onsets were made by column after column of infantry, accompanied by numerous batteries of artillery."[5]

Now Hooker played his ace: Cuvier Grover's unused brigade. Grover moved his predominantly New England regiments into action with novel tactics. He told his men to advance at a walk until the Confederates fired a volley. Then they were to rush the works, deliver a round of musketry, and continue into the Southern lines.

At three o'clock Grover's troops began to advance in spearlike formation. Covered by underbrush in the woods, they suddenly disappeared from Confederate view by crowding in behind the railroad embankment. They were precisely in front of that wide gap in Hill's line. With a yell, they swarmed over the embankment, fired into the Southern ranks, charged with a rush—and broke completely through Hill's first line. Grover's charge rolled back Gregg and Thomas like swinging doors and placed Gregg's brigade in danger of being trapped.

Gregg desperately pulled the 14th South Carolina out of reserve and sent it against the northern flank of the Union thrust. "The firing was incessant," one of the South Carolinians wrote, and he added: "They seemed determined not to abandon the undertaking; we were resolved never to yield."[6]

On the other side of the 175-yard gap, Ed Thomas rushed the 49th Georgia into the right flank of the Union spearhead. One of Gregg's colonels labeled the fight "the consummation of the grand debate between Massachusetts and South Carolina," but the conflict was a great deal more than that.[7] The fight was close and obstinate, the combatants sometimes delivering an intense crossfire from a distance of no more than ten yards. Hill personally rode into the action and assisted in rallying his shattered line. At one point he sent a staff officer to ascertain how Gen. Maxcy Gregg was doing. "Tell him," Gregg replied, "that our ammunition is exhausted, but rocks are very plentiful, and we will hold our position with them until we can get ammunition."

Hill promptly dispatched his staff to collect ammunition in pockets and haversacks. Then he rode rapidly to Gregg's section of the line. To the men he cried out with that clarion voice of his: "Good for you, boys! Give them the rocks and the bayonets, and hold your position, and I will soon have ammunition and reinforcements for you!"[8]

After a vicious contest lasting close to an hour, Grover's units fell back—or at least three-quarters of them did. The rest were lying motionless on the ground in and around the railroad cut. Hill now played his ace. He sent Pender's brigade in pursuit. It struck Hooker's weary lines with such force as to send them reeling. Yet Pender's enthusiasm carried him so far in pursuit that he came under heavy fire. The brigadier fell wounded and his men took a bloody pounding before retiring to Hill's main position.

By six o'clock every man in Hill's division was on the battle line. The Louisiana brigade was now lending assistance, but the Light Division was the center of attention. "With a heroic courage and obstinacy almost beyond parallel," Hill wrote of his soldiers, they "had met and repulsed six distinct and separate assaults." Lee later praised Hill's men for withstanding the Federal attacks "with their accustomed steadiness."[9] Pope's men seemed now to become dispirited, and the Confederates were near exhaustion. But Pope was still not convinced of defeat.

The sun was beginning to set. Portions of Hill's division were down to one round of ammunition per man, and Federals could be seen massing in the shredded woods for another onslaught. Kyd Douglas of Jackson's staff rode up to Hill for a progress report. Hill instructed Douglas to tell Jackson that he was hard-pressed, but that he would do the best he could. Douglas rode back down the line to Jackson, whose face darkened with apprehension at this report. In sharp tones he snapped at Douglas, "Tell him if they attack again, he must beat them!"

Douglas started off, but Jackson was now so concerned that he trotted after him. In a few moments, Hill came riding up to them. He outlined the situation as Jackson listened quietly. "General," said Jackson, "your men have done nobly. If you are attacked again, you will beat the enemy back."

Jackson had barely finished the sentence when the explosion of musketry came from Hill's front. "Here it comes!" Hill shouted as he reined his horse around and galloped toward his lines. "I'll expect you to beat them!" Jackson shouted after him.[10]

Waves of Federals under Gen. Philip Kearny rolled toward the railroad cut. The struggle rapidly became as fierce as any waged that day. A member of W. G. Crenshaw's battery termed the action "the heaviest musketry firing of the war." Others agreed. Private George C. Parker of the 21st Massachusetts wrote that while his unit awaited its turn to attack, "We saw brigade after brigade go in and come reeling out with half a Regiment, and could hear the terrible rattle of musketry ten times more deadly than cannon." The Light Division artillery sections were also waiting for orders when, wrote one gunner, "the gallant A. P. Hill rode into our battery and said to our captain that the Louisiana brigade, being out of ammunition, was holding the enemy in check with rocks."[11] An Alabamian in Archer's brigade later painted a vivid picture of the intensity of the action: "Three lines of battle, one after another in beautiful order with banners flying, hurled themselves against our men in the cut. The front line was nearly annihilated, but the second came to the rescue and nearly met the same fate. . . . Such a contest with rocks and butt ends of muskets I have never seen or read of before or since. . . . The maddened men, the flying stones, the clubbed muskets, the shouts, yells, smoke, dust, din, and rattle of that scene passes description."[12]

Hill confessed that "this onset" by the Federals "was so fierce and in such force that at first some headway was made." The "headway" came when Kearny's Federals smashed through Hill's front line.[13]

Field's brigade answered Hill's call. "Giving the best 'Rebel Yell' that is in us," the Virginians rushed toward the two heavy Federal divisions making the assault. The Union column lost its momentum when hit. In the ensuing combat, Charlie Field went down, so severely wounded that it would be over a year before he returned to duty. Hill then sent out a general appeal for reinforcements, as seemingly endless lines of Union soldiers slowly pushed the Confederate brigades away from the railroad line. Gregg withdrew his men 300 yards to a ridge overlooking the field. The Carolinian, whose impaired hearing picked up only a portion of the battle's roar, waved a Revolutionary War scimitar over his head and bellowed to his skeletal ranks: "Let us die here, my men! Let us die here!"[14]

At that critical minute, the Virginia and Georgia brigades of Jubal Early and Alexander Lawton double-timed into action from another sector of Jackson's line. They knocked the Federals off balance, Jackson later asserted, and "drove them from the wood and railroad cut with great slaughter." Early continued his advance some 300 yards beyond Hill's main line before Hill directed him to return and assist in the shoring-up of the Confederate defenses.[15] A member of Hill's staff thereupon rode to Jackson, saluted, and announced: "General Hill presents his compliments and says the attack of the enemy was repulsed." Jackson's left had held against overwhelming odds.

A rare smile crept over Jackson's face. "Tell him I knew he would do it!"[16]

One of Hill's artillerymen wrote home: "When the sun went down, their dead were heaped in front of that incomplete railway, and we sighed with relief, for Longstreet could be seen coming into position on our right; the crisis was over . . . but the sun went down *so* slowly." Union cannon furiously shelled the woods and embankment that starry night as Hill's men took turns filing to the rear to fill stomachs and cartridge boxes in preparation for a resumption of the battle at sunrise.[17] Hill himself was mentally and physically exhausted. Cloaking the weariness, however, was a mixture of pride and concern—pride at what his Light Division had done that day, concern at the human cost and at what tomorrow would bring.

Saturday, August 30, began hot and dry. Silence hung heavily over the battlefield all morning, as the two armies stood poised. Pope again miscalculated: not only was the Union commander unaware of Longstreet's exact position with half of the Confederate army, he also concluded late in the morning that Jackson had abandoned the field. He thus made plans for a quick strike forward. As Pope was issuing orders, Hill was surmising that any new Union attack would come against his battered left. So he strengthened Gregg's sector as much as he could.

At two o'clock the assault came suddenly and in heavier force than any of the onslaughts of the previous day. Three thick lines of

Federals emerged from the woods and struck Jackson's position. The attack by Gen. Samuel P. Heintzelman's brigades first struck Jackson's right but rapidly spread to Hill's position. Lt. Wayland Dunaway of the 47th Virginia watched the spectacle from inside Hill's works. "In perfect array," he wrote, the Yankees "kept step as if on dress parade, and bore their banners proudly. I looked for a terrific shock, but before they came to close quarters with us, the Confederate artillery, massed on high ground behind us, opened upon their closed ranks, and wrought such fearful destruction as, I believe, was not dealt in any other battle of the entire war."[18]

Hill, as on the previous day, summoned Pender's brigade to come forward, as well as Field's regiments (now under Col. John M. Brockenbrough). Virginians and North Carolinians charged screaming as Hill's batteries raked the Federal lines at close range. Hill reported that the Union advance "was again checked and eventually repulsed with great loss." An adjutant in Pender's brigade stated more forcefully: "We slaughtered them like hogs. I never saw the like of dead men in all my life."[19]

Pope ordered still another assault. Most of his army was locked in a death struggle with Hill when Longstreet calmly unleashed his half of Lee's force against the completely exposed Federal left flank. Pope's lines staggered from the attack, bent badly, and teetered on the verge of disintegration. Pender, far on the left, scanned the Union position through his binoculars and discerned that the Union line was now at right angles to his own. He promptly notified Hill: "If you will order the division to attack, the thing would be up with them."

Hill agreed. Quick orders went to the brigadiers, and at six o'clock the entire Light Division jumped forward as Hill sent word to Jackson that he was taking the offensive. His brigades advanced en echelon: Branch on the left, Archer to his right, then Thomas, Pender, and Brockenbrough. Gregg's battered brigade brought up the rear to protect the division's left flank.[20]

The oblique direction of Hill's attack produced momentary confusion when a portion of the Light Division collided with two of Longstreet's brigades. Quickly, however, the full Army of Northern Virginia—two solid lines of 50,000 men—swept forward in a five-mile crescent and, said Hill, "drove everything before them."[21] The Union army fell back, half in retreat and half in rout. The 32nd Massachusetts was one of the reserve units that rushed up to help. Its colonel described the stunning scene: "Almost immediately we came upon swarms of stragglers. . . . Then came crowds of wounded men, ambulances, wagons, empty caissons, until at last the road was fairly blocked. . . . Men were running, panting, cursing, and some worn out and exhausted had thrown themselves upon the ground by the roadside utterly indifferent to their fate."[22]

Two armies, one chasing and the other chased, raced through woods and open ground. Archer's troops captured half of a Federal battery, and Pender's men soon bagged the remainder. Brockenbrough displayed his inexperience by leading his men into Taliaferro's division; Branch ran into a pocket of Federal resistance and required help to extricate his brigade. For a half mile the Southerners continued the pursuit. Pope's units began to regain some cohesion; they took a stand on the battlefield of a year earlier and put up a stiff fight as night descended. Both Pender and Archer pushed too far forward and had to shoot their way back to Hill's main position. With darkness came rain, which poured in sheets for most of the night. Hill was oblivious to the weather. "The battle being thus gloriously won," he reported, "my men slept among the dead and dying enemy."[23]

Such a success came at unprecedented cost to the Light Division. Hill's losses in the two-day battle were 199 killed and 1,308 wounded. Gregg's South Carolina brigade bore the brunt of battle. Its casualties were 613 men, including 10 officers dead and 31 others crippled.[24] Frightful indeed was the pounding that Hill's ranks had taken; but they had held their position to the point of exhaustion, then counterattacked when victory was within reach.

Much more could be said of Hill's performance. Second Manassas was his first major defensive action. He incurred his highest losses of the war simply because he was the chief target of two days of Union assaults. He did not allow the heat of battle or enemy breakthroughs to cloud his thinking or to shake his confidence. The manner in which he rushed troops to the right place at the right time was a masterly display of coordination. He drove his men hard and demanded much. Victory was the result. Even the usually restrained Jackson wrote glowingly in his official report: "Assault after assault was made on the left, exhibiting on the part of the enemy great pertinacity and determination, but every advance was met most successfully and gallantly driven back."[25] Nevertheless, marring Hill's near-perfect conduct on the twenty-ninth was that

unmanned gap left in his line. Why it was there was a mystery—
and, incredibly, a similar gap would occur again in another place
less than four months later!

In the killing and mutilation of those two days, Hill twice displayed a human, compassionate quality so much a part of his nature.
A Massachusetts surgeon was captured in the August 29 fighting.
When Hill learned that the physician was voluntarily ministering to
wounded Confederate soldiers, he accorded him full privileges as a
noncombatant. Thereafter, the Union surgeon "was welcomed at
Hill's headquarters as a guest and allowed to roam at his leisure
before being passed through the lines a few days later." Similarly,
Capt. Duncan A. Pell of Gen. Ambrose E. Burnside's staff fell into
Confederate hands. He was brought to Hill, who, remembering his
West Point days with Burnside, treated Pell "with much kindness
and attention." When Pell told Hill that "he would like to see the
fun," Hill personally took him to the front to watch the final stages
of the battle.[26]

Lee was not content with victory at Second Manassas. To destroy
Pope's army was the greater objective. As rain turned the countryside
to mud on the night of August 30–31, Lee formulated the next strategy. He would again launch a sweeping envelopment using Jackson's
wing. Not only did Jackson move faster than Longstreet, but Jackson
was already in position on the Confederate left. By swinging wide to
the north, crossing Bull Run at a ford, and sweeping eastward on
Little River Turnpike, Jackson would come in on Pope's tender
flank at Fairfax Court House.

There were obstacles to the plan. Jackson's divisions were bloody
and fatigued from the Second Manassas fighting. Jackson (in spite
of castigating Hill for doing the same thing) generally marched so
rapidly as to leave scores of stragglers in his wake—which meant
that his already depleted forces would decrease further as they moved.
The bad weather could also be a factor. Lee knew too that the lead
elements of McClellan's Army of the Potomac were now in the
Washington area and might join Pope at any moment. Lee, however,
liked to gamble.

Accordingly, at noon on August 31, with the Light Division in the
lead, Jackson's three divisions started on another flanking pursuit of
Pope. Rain continued intermittently, mud-runs existed where roads
had once been, and the ground everywhere was spongy. Hill's troops
were aching from fatigue when they began the march; wet and

hungry as well, they were anything but a victorious army moving toward final triumph. Nonetheless, Hill was determined to set a pace that would comply with Lee's wishes and Jackson's demands. Inevitably, straggling soon began, and it reached such proportions that Jackson ordered Hill to slacken the pace up front. If Hill in fact slowed down his advance, it was not enough. Jackson would later charge that Hill "permitted the head of his column again to march too rapidly, and allowed a large number of men to straggle from the ranks."[27] However, when Jackson directed Hill to halt and bivouack near Pleasant Valley Baptist Church on the Little River Turnpike, the column had slogged barely ten miles. Rain and mud, rather than Hill's pace, had broken down solidarity in the ranks. Confederates spent the night without cover or food.

Monday, September 1, brought more bad weather—and another battle. The march resumed at daybreak under heavy clouds that gave promise of rain. Soldiers plodded along as much from instinct as from duty. Progress was understandably slow. It took Hill's men and Jackson's other two divisions a half day to advance three miles along the turnpike. Around two-thirty in the afternoon the van of Hill's division collided with Federals at Ox Hill. The fire became so intense that Jackson halted the winding column near Chantilly plantation. Orders came down to the division commanders: turn southward into battle line roughly parallel to the road; Hill would be on the right, Ewell in the center, Jackson's division on the left.[28]

Hill moved to beat the Federals to the punch. He sent the troops of Branch and Brockenbrough "to feel and engage the enemy." These two brigades had just started forward through woods on the far right when the clouds erupted and blinding rain drove directly into the faces of the men. Slowly they advanced across a field and drove the Federals through some woods to the edge of a cornfield. There they confronted the Federal divisions of Kearny and Gen. I. I. Stevens. Branch's men delivered a volley of musketry; the Federals responded; and when much of that return fire came in on Branch's right, the brigadier had fears of being flanked. With Brockenbrough's regiments on his left weathering an onslaught, Branch asked Hill for instructions. The general replied, "Hold your position at bayonet point, if necessary!"[29]

This directive by Hill to use the bayonet was more than mere bravado. The violent rainstorm had drenched muskets. Powder was wet; weapons were useless. Men would have to fight with their bayonets, rocks, or anything else at their disposal. Hill sent an aide to inform Jackson that his ammunition was wet. Jackson replied characteristically and tersely, "Give my compliments to General Hill, and tell him that the Yankee ammunition is as wet as his; to stay where he is."[30]

Branch's 18th North Carolina checked the threat on the far right. Stevens's division now charged across the cornfield. Hill sent Gregg as support for Branch, followed soon after by Thomas. Pender then moved into the battle. Except for Archer's brigade in reserve, Hill had committed the entire Light Division to combat. Stevens's assault was repulsed, and the Federal general was killed by a bullet through the brain as he held a stand of colors. Kearny's division rushed full force into the struggle. "The conflict now raged with great fury," Jackson wrote, "the enemy obstinately and desperately contesting the ground." A Wisconsin officer noted: "The noise of the artillery and musketry intermingling with the roll of very sharp thunder produced a striking effect. The darkness incident to a sky overcast with heavy, rolling clouds, lighted up alternately by flashes of lightning and the flames of artillery, made a scene long to be remembered."[31]

Gunfire continued in the gathering darkness. Suddenly, in a lightning flash, members of the 55th Virginia saw a Union horseman riding swiftly toward them. They called on him to surrender. The rider whirled his steed and frantically started back. The Confederates fired a volley, and the man toppled from his saddle. They found him in the mud, a single bullet hole in the seat of his trousers. It was Kearny.[32]

With the death of that general, the battle subsided. Pope's army faded away in the night, leaving some one hundred loaded wagons as booty for the Light Division. Morale inside the Union ranks was shattered. "The campaign was destined to end in humiliation," a Federal officer later asserted. "The braggart [Pope] who had begun his campaign with . . . silly bluster . . . had been kicked, cuffed, hustled about, knocked down, run over, and trodden upon as rarely happens in the history of war."[33] Hill rode over the field in the darkness, then dismounted at a cabin alongside the road. On the porch lay Kearny's body. Hill looked at the remains of his friend and murmured, "Poor Kearny! He deserved a better death than that."[34]

At the battle of Chantilly, Hill played a pivotal role. He had again coordinated his brigade movements with skill. His losses of 39 killed and 267 wounded seemed slight, given the size of the Federal hosts and the atrocious weather conditions. Federal casualties were twice those figures and included two division commanders dead.[35] The fighting from Cedar Mountain to Chantilly fully established Hill as the premier division leader in the Army of Northern Virginia.

Weariness rather than elation characterized Hill's division after the Manassas campaign. Rations continued to be scarce. The army, one soldier admitted, "presented anything but a prepossessing appearance—the name 'tatterdemalions' right well describing the outer." Lt. W. W. Lenoir of the 37th North Carolina wrote in his diary: "Marching and fighting as continually as we did without time to wash our clothes or our persons, and sleeping on the ground all huddled together, the whole army became lousy." Grumbling about Jackson's demanding ways was also widespread through the ranks. For example, Pender informed his wife that he did not like serving under Jackson, "for he forgets that one ever gets tired, hungry or sleepy."[36] It was Lee who now granted the men little rest.

Despite excruciating pain from a broken hand and sprained wrists incurred in an accidental fall from his horse, Lee resolved on the most daring strategy of the war up to that point: invasion of the North. The decision seemed radical; but the other options—attacking impregnable Washington, remaining in the northern Virginia area totally ravaged by war, retiring southward and giving up everything that had been won that summer—all were disadvantageous. On the positive side, a successful Confederate offensive in the North might induce the Federal government to sue for peace, or bring recognition and assistance from England and France, or at the least secure Maryland for the Confederacy (thereby isolating the Northern capital geographically). Hence, Lee started his army toward the Potomac River crossings near Leesburg.

The march was long and the weather hot. During a rest stop on one of the first days, members of the 14th Tennessee were lounging in the road with their heads on their bedrolls or knapsacks. Soon a group of horsemen galloped into view. When they got closer, the men recognized Generals Lee and Hill, plus members of their staffs. Hill riding a few feet in advance, shouted, "Move out of the road, men!"

Lee quickly interjected: "Never mind, General, we will ride around them. Lie still, men."

The army commander reined his horse to the left, and the entire party rode around the Tennesseeans. Lee's gesture, one of them stated, "was just his way, his consideration for others, especially his soldiers."[37]

At sundown on September 3, the Light Division bivouacked along the road on the north side of Dranesville. Then it was that Hill and Jackson began to go at it again. Jackson was not in a good mood as Lee's army headed northward. "Filled with conscientious scruples," an acquaintance commented, Jackson "was always ready himself to obey orders to the letter and in like manner he required that his subordinates should be similarly obedient." The march was barely under way when Jackson arrested several of the battery commanders for allowing gunners, in violation of orders, to ride on caissons as the army crossed the Potomac. It was widely believed that Jackson "probably put more officers under arrest than all other Confederate generals combined."[38]

According to a somewhat garbled account by usually reliable Jed Hotchkiss, Jackson on the night of September 3 summoned his division commanders to headquarters. He orally informed Hill, Ewell, and Taliaferro that the next day's march was to begin precisely at 4:00 A.M. As insurance, Jackson had the three generals set their watches with his.

Precisely at 4:00 the next morning, Jackson, following custom, rode out personally to ensure that all of his divisions were moving out on time. The commander no doubt wanted to give a critical look at Hill's troops. They were to take the lead, and on two occasions recently their performances had not been up to Jackson's expectations. Now Jackson found Hill's men standing idle. Gregg's brigade had not even broken camp. It was immediately obvious to Jackson that Hill had relayed orders to his brigadiers but failed to ensure that the orders—and the march—had been executed as directed. Jackson gruffly inquired of Gregg why his troops were not on the road. The proud Gregg, resentful of Jackson's attitude, replied in clipped tones that his men were filling their canteens in preparation for the advance.

Just at that moment, Hill rode into the camp. Jackson "mildly" reprimanded him for not being prompt in obedience to orders, Hotchkiss stated. "Hill took this reprimand rather sullenly, his face flushing up, but he said nothing."

Jackson then raised his voice so that both Hill and the partially deaf Gregg could hear and intoned, "There are but few commanders who properly appreciate the value of celerity!"

An impatient Jackson watched the South Carolinians finish filling their canteens. He ordered Gregg, now also upset, to lead his men down the road. Growing more angry by the minute, Jackson sat on his horse and scrutinized Hill's column as it passed. Hill was in the van, but neither he nor his staff seemed to pay any attention to keeping the ranks tight and intact. In fact, Hill appeared to be setting a faster-than-usual pace so that Jackson would not complain again about any foot-dragging on the part of the Light Division. Yet the accelerated pace soon had the division fairly strung out, and straggling became heavy.

Jackson's face was flushed with anger. Soon it was the noon hour, when, by orders, Hill was supposed to halt his men for the customary rest stop. Hill kept the troops marching. The fuming Jackson could take no more. He galloped to the head of the lead brigade and sought out its commander, Gen. Ed Thomas. Jackson told the Georgian to halt his soldiers in accordance with instructions. Thomas gave the order, and his soldiers began lounging alongside the road as Jackson sat quietly on a horse nearby. The noon rest period passed; at Jackson's command, Thomas resumed the march.

Hill meanwhile continued to lead the army's advance. Turning in his saddle a few minutes later, he beheld a fractured line of march and knew that someone had halted without his orders. Angry, Hill rode back to get an explanation for the huge gap now existing in the division's column. "Why did you halt your command without orders?" he demanded of Thomas.

The brigadier pointed to Jackson, dismounted several feet away. "I halted because General Jackson told me to do so," Thomas replied.

Hill was furious. This was the last straw. In his eyes, Jackson never kept his generals properly informed; he had steadfastly refused to divulge his orders or changes in orders to division commanders; he was a stickler and fanatic about the most inconsequential of military matters; he had repeatedly violated military protocol by dealing directly with subordinates rather than going through the normal chain of command. Hill had had all that he could take. He dismounted, stomped up to Jackson, and, presenting the hilt of his sword, sneered, "If you take command of my troops in my presence, take my sword also."

Jackson ignored the offer. "Put up your sword and consider yourself in arrest," he said and galloped off. A short time later, orders passed down the line that Branch was to assume command of the Light Division.[39]

The most brilliant division commander in Lee's army was under arrest for the second time in two months. Worse, Hill was relegated to marching on foot at the rear of his brigades as the Army of Northern Virginia embarked on its most dramatic and dangerous campaign. Between Hill and Jackson was a personal breach that would never heal. Was all of this an omen of disaster about to occur?

Antietam Creek: "A. P. Hill Came Up"

"General Hill marched on foot with the rear guard all the day through Maryland, an old white hat slouched down over his eyes, his coat off and wearing an old flannel shirt, looking as mad as a bull," a North Carolina lieutenant wrote of the September 5 advance by the Confederates.[1] Never had Hill known such humiliation. He was under field arrest and awaiting formal charges. During this indeterminable period he could remain with his troops but he had no authority over them; and if a battle developed, he would be only a spectator from afar. All of this, Hill felt, was the result of Jackson's inflexible and incorrect actions as a commander.

Hill was so enraged that it took him two days to organize his thoughts rationally. On the sixth, he was composed enough to request officially of Jackson a statement of the charges against him. Hill's request was badly timed. Not only was Jackson still angry at Hill, but that morning his horse had reared and thrown him to the ground. Jackson was sore and in pain when Hill's note came before him. He was in no mood for anything. The next day Maj. Frank Paxton of Jackson's staff responded tersely: "Should the interests of the service require your case to be brought before a court martial, a copy of the charges and specifications will be furnished in accordance with army regulations. In the meantime you will remain with your division."[2]

Hill's troops spent a five-day rest period just east of Frederick as they guarded the major approaches from Washington. The men "feasted on nothing but green corn, browned on the ear before fires made of the fences in the neighborhood." A member of Hill's staff added that "a dirtier, more ragged, exhausted set twould be hard to find." Serving under Jackson was a grueling experience, mentally and physically. "Jackson would kill up any army the way he marches," Pender grumbled.[3] Having their commander under arrest only added to the mumbling inside the Light Division.

Lee might have interceded successfully had he not been preoccupied with the northern invasion. His advance was falling short of expectations. Western Maryland was cool if not hostile to the Confederates. The number of Marylanders who flocked to join Lee, wrote one of Gregg's men, could be shown in two figures.[4] McClellan was now back in full command of the Union forces in the East, and he was putting his massive 87,000-man Army of the Potomac in motion toward Frederick. Lee also learned that a sizable Federal garrison at Harper's Ferry, the important entrance into the Shenandoah Valley, had not fallen back into Maryland as expected. Union troops were still at the Ferry, blocking Lee's main line of communication and retreat.

Again, the audacious and unpredictable Lee resolved to divide his forces in the face of numerical superiority. Jackson, in command of three separate but converging columns, was to proceed southwest to Harper's Ferry, capture the garrison, and secure the Shenandoah gateway. He would then rejoin Lee, just west of South Mountain at Boonsboro, eighteen miles north of Harper's Ferry.

The movements began on Wednesday, September 10. Jackson's three divisions, including Hill's, embarked on a fifty-one-mile circuitous march toward Harper's Ferry. In all likelihood, Hill was recovering at that time from an attack of prostatitis, because he was riding in an ambulance at the rear of his troops.[5] Yet he kept abreast of Jackson's movements, and his intuition told him that combat was imminent. Somehow he had to get a reprieve from Jackson. Late on the afternoon of September 10, the division bivouacked near Williamsport. Hill summoned Kyd Douglas of Jackson's staff to his tent. "It is evident that a battle is at hand," Hill stated. "I do not wish anyone else to command my division in an engagement." Displaying neither remorse nor belligerence, Hill told Douglas that he simply wanted to rejoin his troops. All he was asking was that Jackson restore him to command until the present campaign ended. Then, said Hill, he would return to arrest and await Jackson's orders.

Douglas, as eager as the other staff officers to see this affair concluded, rushed to Jackson's headquarters. Jackson listened quietly, then mumbled assent. He needed his best major general in action; discipline would come later. Quick notification went to Branch to return the Light Division to Hill. For the moment, the Hill-Jackson feud would give way to the much larger confrontation between Lee and McClellan.[6]

Once Hill returned to duty, one of his officers stated, his spirits soared. "Donning his coat and sword he mounted his horse and dashed to the front of his troops, and looking like a young eagle in search of his prey, he took command of his division to the delight of all his men."[7]

On the morning of September 11, Jackson crossed the Potomac at Light's Ford and immediately split his command to prevent the Federal forces then at Martinsburg from escaping westward. Hill's division subsequently moved eleven miles directly down the turnpike from Williamsport to Martinsburg. Advised of the Confederate approach, 2,500 Federals under Gen. Julius White fled from Martinsburg on the night of the eleventh, allowing the Southerners to seize the town with its "large quantity of commissary and quartermaster's stores."[8]

Famished soldiers filled stomachs and knapsacks with food before taking to the road again. They marched four miles that day, seventeen the next. Those troops who gave out along the way were loaded into ambulances rather than allowed to straggle. Meanwhile, Federals gathering in a trap at Harper's Ferry were convinced that Hill was moving toward them with 30,000 men (six times the number that Hill actually had).[9]

Jackson was quite familiar with the lay of the land around the Ferry. He knew that Loudoun Heights on the Virginia side of the Potomac and the Maryland Heights across the river dominated the entire region. If Confederates could get batteries in position on those mountains, Harper's Ferry was defenseless. Jackson's column arrived just west of Harper's Ferry at eleven in the morning on the thirteenth. Hill's division began forming battle lines on School House Ridge, immediately west of the main Federal line on Bolivar Heights. Union infantry could be seen in position on the high ground. Some of Hill's troops skirmished with the 9th Vermont and 3rd Maryland (U.S.) throughout the afternoon and into what a Billy Yank called the "inky darkness."[10] Yet for the most part the

Light Division stood in battle line as Jackson patiently awaited the posting of the guns of John G. Walker and Lafayette McLaws on the commanding hills.

The sabbath morning of September 14 passed in an air of expectancy as Hill's men continued to wait. Late in the afternoon Hill received orders from Jackson to "move along the left bank of the Shenandoah and thus turn the enemy's left flank and enter Harper's Ferry." The other Confederate divisions would create diversions. On comparatively shallow Bolivar Heights, Federals were supposedly in a "naturally strong" position, which stretched from the Potomac to the Shenandoah.

Hill shifted his batteries into better position and began shelling the area in his front as Confederate guns barked from Maryland and Loudoun Heights. Along Bolivar Heights, wrote one Confederate, soldiers and civilians alike "were running to and fro like madmen."[11] The 125th New York, a brand-new regiment, was standing in an open field when Hill's cannon let loose their initial salvo. "When the first shell struck," a captain in that unit wrote, "the scampering began. . . . There was an uproar and confusion that baffles the imagination; the infantry, cavalry and artillery gathered up their arms and equipage and stampeded like wildfire. The regiment . . . ran in wild disorder to the nearest ravine for shelter." But there was no escape. Through incredible blundering, a division-size Federal garrison was hopelessly trapped.[12]

As Hill shifted his men obliquely toward the Shenandoah River, he discovered to his amazement an elevation on the Federal left that was occupied by infantry but unsupported by artillery. Hill immediately sent the brigades of Pender, Archer, and Brockenbrough—with Thomas in reserve—to seize the eminence while Gregg and Branch proceeded along the riverbank below and established a foothold on the Federal left and rear.

The whole movement, Hill reported, "was accomplished with but slight resistance." Even Federal general White marveled at the "great spirit" with which Hill's troops advanced. At dusk, Pender led the three brigades under his immediate command to within 150 yards of the Union line. All of the Light Division artillery—nine rifled guns, eight Napoleons, and thirteen short-range pieces—unlimbered 1,000 yards away. Gregg and Branch likewise stood poised on the vulnerable Union flank. "The fate of Harper's Ferry was sealed," Hill wrote succinctly.[13]

Jackson's troops greatly outnumbered the Federals, which was fortunate, for no time existed to conduct any kind of leisurely siege. The garrison had to be overrun at once. Heavy fog lay on the land as Monday, September 15, dawned. Hill, in shirt-sleeves, made one last inspection of his lines. He rode into Gregg's sector and found an impassioned discussion taking place between Gregg and Col. Dixon Barnes of the 12th South Carolina. The courtly Barnes had been arrested by Jackson for a minor breach of orders. He was now begging to be allowed to go into the ranks as a private and fight alongside his men. Gregg was making a reluctant refusal when Hill rode up to where they were standing. Hill asked for an explanation of the matter; after receiving it, he said: "General Gregg, I order you to give Colonel Barnes his sword and put him in command of his regiment."

Hill was wrong in overriding his brigadier, a fellow officer commented, "but the case would stir the heart of a rock."[14]

The fog soon began lifting. A Confederate wrote: "The view was magnificent, presenting such a spectacle as is rarely seen." Morning stillness vanished as the field pieces of the Light Division responded to Hill's command. One of the gunners wrote poetically that "the great circle of artillery opened, all firing to a common center, while the clouds of smoke, rolling up from the tops of the various mountains, and the thunder of the guns reverberating among them, gave the idea of so many volcanoes."[15]

For an hour, Hill noted, "the enemy replied vigorously." Then the Federal fire began to slacken. Hill and Jackson had been watching the action together. Jackson now turned and said grimly: "General Hill, charge and give them the bayonet!"[16] Hill nodded, turned his horse, and raised his hand to a bugler nearby. The musical notes rose above the din of the Confederate artillery fire. Pender's brigade surged forward. Federal fire seemed to pick up again. At that, Hill sent the batteries of Willie Pegram and W. G. Crenshaw to a point within 400 yards of the Union line. They fired a devastating enfilade into the works. Hill's infantry resumed the advance under this artillery cover.

"Rebel batteries frowned from every hill," a Union officer recalled; "five times our own numbers held every avenue of escape. . . . It was now almost madness to resist." A Vermont soldier wrote disgustedly that "when the battle flags of A. P. Hill's long lines began to advance upon us, Colonel [Dixon] Miles's [courage] failed him for the men he had so badly handled." Hill's infantry were but yards from the Union positions when, near nine in the morning, a lone Federal horseman rode out toward them. He was carrying a white flag.[17]

Hill dispatched Lt. "Ham" Chamberlayne of his staff into the Union lines. Colonel Miles, the garrison commander, had been mortally wounded. Chamberlayne thereupon sought out Gen. Julius White, whose troops had entered the Ferry barely in time to be trapped. White and his staff accompanied the Confederate aide into Hill's lines for the formal surrender. The party reached a crest of a hill on the Charles Town turnpike when Hill galloped up from his command. In contrast to White, who was immaculately dressed, the coatless Hill resembled a farmer who had just completed his plowing. White expressed praise for the skill and energy exhibited by the Confederates in the investment of Harper's Ferry. Hill replied courteously, "I would rather take the place twenty times than undertake to hold it once."[18]

The group then rode a little farther down the road to a schoolhouse that Jackson was using as temporary headquarters. When White formally asked for the terms of surrender, Jackson replied: "The surrender must be unconditional, General. Every indulgence can be granted afterward." White acquiesced; Jackson then directed Hill to arrange the terms of capitulation. At ten o'clock Hill and White began drafting the surrender document. "I granted General White the most liberal terms," Hill stated; White agreed.[19] Officers and men were to be paroled and would not serve again in the army until officially exchanged. The officers could retain sidearms and private baggage. All captured Federals could keep blankets and overcoats and would be supplied with two days' rations before departure. Hill even loaned twenty-seven wagons for carrying excess baggage. (He would later complain strongly that the Yankees were inexcusably slow in returning the borrowed wagons.)[20]

Hill then rode into the town. He observed that "there was apparently no organization of any kind. That had ceased to exist." On seeing Harper's Ferry for the first time, another officer noted that the buildings "were now a mass of ruins, and the remainder of the town presented the appearance of a plucked goose." The seizure of the post, however, yielded immense dividends: 12,000 prisoners, 13,000 stand of arms, 73 cannon, 200 wagons, and quartermaster stores too multitudinous to be inventoried. Hill's losses for this harvest had been but 3 men killed and 66 wounded.[21]

Early in the evening of September 15, Jackson informed Lee that he was marching north with most of his command to rendezvous with the army. "As Hill's troops have borne the heaviest part of the engagement, he will be left in command until the prisoners and public property shall be disposed of, unless you direct otherwise."[22] One of Jackson's divisions left at ten that night; the other departed three hours later. Hill's troops continued paroling prisoners, securing stores, and ensuring that the Harper's Ferry "door would be open when or if the Army of Northern Virginia needed to use the Shenandoah Valley passageway.

Pender's and Branch's brigades took charge of the captured Federals. One Billy Yank confessed that "we were most civily treated by the rebels, whom we found to be . . . men like ourselves; only the rebels were not nearly as profane as our men—in fact, they used no profane language at all. They shamed us."[23] There was a startling physical contrast between victor and vanquished: the Confederates were in tatters, while the defeated Federals resembled new troops on parade. Hundreds of Hill's men eagerly donned pieces of new blue uniforms—which would have an advantageous effect in battle two days later. The Confederates also swapped old smoothbore muskets for more accurate Springfield rifle-muskets still packed in crates.[24]

As for the mountain of foodstuffs, it was Manassas Junction all over again. Hill's men gorged themselves with everything from oysters to candy. They stuffed pockets with the widest variety of delicacies; and when there was no more room, they "captured horses roaming at large, on whom to transport our plunder." Hill partook in the bounty to the extent of obtaining a new red flannel shirt.[25]

There was a tender moment in the campaign, as Confederate staff officer Charles Venable observed. Hill and Federal colonel Dixon Miles had been friends back in prewar years. As Dixon lay dying, "he sent messages to his household through Hill and asked that his sword should be sent to his wife." Venable added: "The duties to General Hill, who was every inch a Christian, were held sacred."[26]

On September 16, paroling prisoners and collecting stores continued. It was an uncomfortably humid day, marred for Hill by an unpleasant incident. The general was in his upstairs headquarters in one of the armory's buildings, attending to the parolees. Hill looked up from the paperwork to see standing in front of him a man wearing the worn uniform of a Federal cavalryman. "I am a noncombatant of Loudoun County," he said, "and I would like a pass to return home."

Hill's eyes hardened. "What are you doing with those clothes on?"

"I bought them," the man replied.

"You are lying," Hill snarled. "Get out of here, you damned scoundrel!" Hill came around the desk, grabbed the man by the shoulders, forced him through the doorway to the head of the stairs, and started his downward path with a vigorous kick.[27]

That night, according to a member of the 7th Tennessee in Archer's brigade, "we now congratulated ourselves on the prospect of several days' rest."[28] How mistaken he was, for Lee and McClellan were moving steadily toward one of the bloodiest confrontations in American history.

It had begun at Frederick on September 12, when McClellan was beneficiary of the greatest security leak of the war. One of his soldiers found a copy of Lee's master plan for the movements in Maryland, and McClellan learned an incredible fact: the numerically inferior Southern army was divided into five segments. Three separate columns under Jackson were converging on Harper's Ferry; two other divisions were standing idly in and around Hagerstown; a fifth division was crouched atop South Mountain near Turner's Gap. Worse, the divisions were miles apart from one another and disconnected. McClellan had the rare opportunity to destroy the Army of Northern Virginia piece by piece.

In the hours that followed, however, when McClellan should have been pushing hard to destroy the divided segments of Lee's army, the Union commander vacillated, allowing his indecisiveness to shatter his resolve. Finally he began edging westward. On September 14, the Union army beat its way up South Mountain, slowly overwhelming Harvey Hill's division and Longstreet's reinforcements, thus securing the vital mountain passes near Boonsboro.

Then McClellan threw away momentum. Throughout September 15, the Federal general shadowed the Confederates as Lee marched six miles southward to the village of Sharpsburg in order to make quicker contact with Jackson. On the sixteenth, Jackson's two divisions came up from Harper's Ferry. As McClellan's massive army of 87,000 eased toward Antietam Creek, Lee carefully placed the 25,000 troops he had at hand in a good battle line. A low crescent-shaped ridge extended from northwest to southeast of town. The Confederate left rested on the Potomac River; the right was anchored on Antietam Creek, a sluggish north-south stream too deep for the passage of artillery except via bridges. Lee's forces were still disorganized and off-balance on the sixteenth; McClellan could have successfully attacked at almost any point. Yet McClellan spent that day as he always spent a prebattle period: moving men hither and yon, perfecting his lines—in short, fine-tuning a military machine that never ran at high speed.

Through the night of September 16–17, soldiers blue and gray stood in a light rain and awaited a dawn that would bring combat. The woefully outnumbered Lee needed every man he could put in line. Before dawn he sent a courier to order Hill to proceed to Sharpsburg as quickly as possible. The courier reached Harper's Ferry at six-thirty; half an hour later, the first of Hill's brigades marched out of the town. Four others followed, with Thomas's Georgians left behind to guard the Ferry.[29]

Hill took complete charge of the march. His men bore little resemblance to the soldiers he had led into Harper's Ferry two days earlier. Most of them had discarded gray rags and were wearing parts of new Federal uniforms; they were also freshly fed and equipped. Confederate brigades swung easily onto the road and began marching at a rapid gait. Hill did not take the direct twelve-mile route from the Ferry to Sharpsburg but a seventeen-mile course that carried the troops somewhat westward and over the Potomac at Shepherdstown. The Virginian never explained why he opted for the longer march when time was of the essence. In all likelihood, Hill felt the circuitous approach would be safer and faster because the direct route would probably bring him in contact with Federals before he reached Lee's position.

For hours that hot and humid Wednesday, Hill drove his men at a killing pace toward the distant sound of gunfire along Antietam Creek. He paid no attention to Jackson's routine of fifty minutes' march followed by ten minutes' rest. With the exception of two or possibly three times, when the winding column halted just long enough "to draw breath," one soldier wrote, Hill kept the division in motion. The men in front were constantly urged to maintain a brisk pace, while those in the rear began cursing and spitting as a heavy coat of dust enveloped them. Hill was both merciless and inspiring that day. Clad in his new red flannel shirt, he was everywhere up and down the column, prodding laggards with his sword and repeatedly telling the men that they must push on with all dispatch. General Lee needed them. That was all that mattered.[30]

The march soon became too much for many of the soldiers. Men began dropping out of ranks. Most were exhausted; some were repelled by the sound of battle. Hill came upon a frightened lieutenant who had sought refuge behind a tree. Hill's temper snapped. As he usually did when confronted with cowardice, he all but screamed for the man's sword and, on receiving it, broke it over the lieutenant's shoulder. (With the ordinary soldier, however, Hill could be magnanimous. He once accosted a frightened private who murmured, "I can't stand it, General, I haven't the courage." Hill replied in a calm voice, "Go to the rear, then, before you cause good men to run.")[31]

Near two o'clock the weary troops, holding muskets and cartridge boxes over their heads, began crossing the Potomac at Boteler's Ford. Men were staggering from the column every few steps. Hill's anxiety and his temper were rising. The division wagon train was creeping across the river as Hill hastily watered his horse nearby. The general, as usual, was coatless and without insignia. One of the teamsters began cursing and beating his mules, who wanted only to pause for water. Hill shouted at the man to stop mistreating the animals. The teamster looked at the plainly dressed horseman, told him to mind his own business, and turned away. A moment later, he felt Hill's sword make a welt on his back. He did not have to be told thereafter who his division commander was.[32]

As the wet and tired column trudged up the road toward Sharpsburg and the roar of combat, Hill galloped ahead to report to Lee. He had no idea how critical the situation had become. McClellan's army had pounded Lee's left and center throughout the morning; and although the Confederate line had held, it was battered and bloody. Early in the afternoon, Gen. Ambrose Burnside's IX Corps on the Union left fought its way across Antietam Creek and slowly pushed Gen. Robert Toombs's outmanned Georgia brigade backward. The Federals moved deliberately toward Lee's right, which was bending badly and on the verge of snapping. Lee's chief of staff explained why disaster had become imminent: "Outnumbered at every point, the right [had been] called upon to go to the rescue of the left; the center was reduced to a mere shell in responding to the demands for assistance from the right and left; . . . We had no troops in reserve; every man was engaged."[33] Burnside had only to drive a half mile farther and Federals would sever Lee's single line of retreat. The Civil War, at least in the Eastern theater, would end then and there.

Lee was anxiously looking southward at two-thirty, as seconds seemed to tick the death knoll for his army. Suddenly over a rise appeared a group of officers on frothing horses. It was Hill. He had covered seventeen miles in seven hours by pushing his men relentlessly. No more than 3,000 of the 5,000 men in the Light Division were still with him, and they were back up the road, but they were on the way. At the point when Lee's army was about to break from weariness and despair, through the ranks sped reassuring news: A. P. Hill is coming! Hold the line! Hill is almost here!

A perspiring but elated Hill reined his horse in front of Lee and his staff. The column was advancing rapidly, he said. The Light Division would be on the field shortly. Was there time? Lee wondered. Yet he was so happy to see Hill and to have the promise of fresh troops that the commander forgot his usually controlled emotions and embraced "Little Powell." He then directed Hill to place his men as they arrived in support of Gen. David R. Jones's small division on the far right.[34]

Jones could not even muster 2,000 troops to resist Burnside's concentrated assault. Most of the Confederate brigades were down to regimental size. At three o'clock Federals came over the hill in three lines with the sole intention of smashing the Confederate flank. Lee watched helplessly. Waves of the enemy slowly swept forward, as artillery, musketry, and yells combined to make a deafening sound. At three-forty another advancing line was visible coming in from the south. Lee was shaken. That column would outflank the Confederate right with ease. Lee pointed and asked a young aide to use his telescope and ascertain what troops they were. There was a pause. Then the aide called out, "They are flying the Virginia and Confederate flags!"

"It is A. P. Hill from Harper's Ferry," Lee said with unconcealed relief. Hill's men had arrived in time. The commander then ordered his remaining cannon to open on the Federals so as to provide covering support.[35]

The first of Hill's units to reach the field was David McIntosh's Pee Dee Artillery. For the last few miles to Sharpsburg, the horses had gone at a trot, with twenty-one gunners riding atop the bouncing guns and caissons. McIntosh got three pieces in position and exchanged salvos for a while with several Union batteries. Then the Palmetto battery began firing obliquely into approaching Federal infantry. Hill's main column now loped into sight, weariness forgotten in the anticipation of battle. A Georgian wrote of Hill's troops: "They were in good condition and cheered General Lee as they hurried on. The old general's worried look left him as he noticed the enthusiasm of Hill's Division."[36]

McIntosh's battery received no support from Jones's skeletal units. Nevertheless, it hurled double loads of canister into the attacking Federal lines. Great gaps appeared with each belch of fire, yet the blue wave surged forward. When the first line was only sixty yards from the battery, McIntosh concluded that it was "better to let the guns go and save the men." His artillerists scampered to the rear, and a few seconds later Connecticut troops swarmed triumphantly around the captured pieces.[37]

Hill's high spirits on the march now turned to the calm that came over him in battle. He instantly recognized the military situation, Kyd Douglas wrote, "and without waiting for the rest of the division and without a breathing spell he threw his columns into line and moved against the enemy, taking no note of their numbers."[38] The men were dust-covered and bone-tired; they were spitting cotton from mouths barely capable of producing moisture; but the half of the Light Division that had survived the march leaped into battle with the enthusiasm of a full complement.

After conferring quickly with Jones, Hill directed Pender and Brockenbrough to the right to watch the road that crossed the Antietam near its mouth. To their left soon stretched Gregg, Branch, and Archer, the last-named connecting with Toombs in a cornfield that became an arena. Hill's batteries opened fire as each took a strategic position. "My troops were not in a moment too soon," Hill stated in his official report. At his command, and "with a yell of defiance," three of his brigades swept across the open ground.[39]

Archer was so ill that day that he arrived on the field in an ambulance. Aides helped him into the saddle; and despite a high fever, the slim Marylander led his small (350 men) but compact brigade in a sweeping movement that drove deeply into Burnside's right flank. Archer's troops emerged from a cornfield and burst upon the

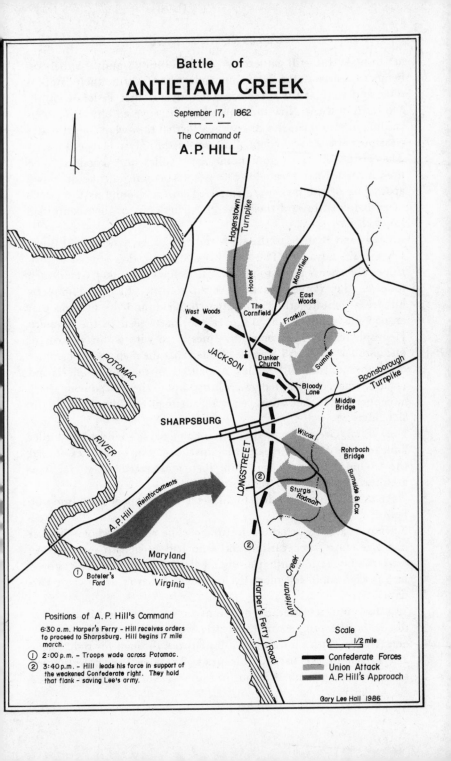

Battle of
ANTIETAM CREEK

September 17, 1862

The Command of
A.P. HILL

Hagerstown Turnpike

Hooker

Mansfield

East Woods

West Woods

The Cornfield

Franklin

JACKSON

Dunker Church

Sumner

POTOMAC

Boonsborough Turnpike

Bloody Lane

Middle Bridge

SHARPSBURG

RIVER

Wilcox

Rohrbach Bridge

LONGSTREET

Burnside & Cox

A.P. Hill Reinforcements

②

Sturgis Rodman

Maryland

②

Boteler's Ford

Virginia

Harper's Ferry Road

Antietam Creek

①

Positions of A.P. Hill's Command

6:30 a.m. Harper's Ferry - Hill receives orders
to proceed to Sharpsburg. Hill begins 17 mile
march.

① 2:00 p.m. - Troops wade across Potomac.

② 3:40 p.m. - Hill leads his force in support of
the weakened Confederate right. They hold
that flank - saving Lee's army.

Scale

0 ____ 1/2 mile

━━━━ Confederate Forces

▨▨▨ Union Attack

▨▨▨ A.P. Hill's Approach

Gary Lee Hall 1986

8th Connecticut, still gathered around McIntosh's guns. In the exuberance of attack, the New Englanders had outrun their support units and were at the three cannon with no other Federals within 500 yards of them. Now they saw some dust-covered blueclad troops rushing toward them and did not realize that they were Confederates wearing portions of Federal uniforms acquired at Harper's Ferry. The Tennesseeans let go a point-blank volley and Toombs's men fired from a different angle. The Connecticut regiment was blown apart: 194 of 350 men were sprawled on the ground as the others raced pell-mell toward their lines.[40] Archer's troops then continued forward.

Gregg and Branch, to the right and rear of Archer, awaited Burnside's main advance. The two brigades bent the Federal thrust, ripped the enemy ranks to pieces with volleys of musketry, and then followed the Yankees as they began retiring. Blue and gray by hundreds came together in a large cornfield, and the fighting that ensued was as vicious as any ever previously seen in the Western Hemisphere. At times opposing lines were within thirty yards of one another; muskets became so heated that the men had to hammer down the ramrods with stones. A member of the 4th Rhode Island recalled that the Confederates burst upon them, "pouring in a sweeping fire as they advanced, and our men fell like sheep at the slaughter."[41]

As usual, Gregg was in the thick of the action. Suddenly a bullet knocked the old gentleman from his horse. An orderly examined the wound area in Gregg's hip, then announced: "General, you aren't wounded, you are only bruised."

At that, Gregg bounded to his feet and limped back into the fight.[42]

Dixon Barnes was not so fortunate. The colonel whom Jackson had arrested a week earlier, and who had begged to serve in the ranks of his 12th South Carolina before Hill personally restored him to command, fell mortally wounded. A hero's death came two days later.[43]

A few minutes after Barnes went down, Lawrence Branch was discussing the progress of the battle with fellow brigadiers Gregg and Archer. With no warning, a bullet tore through his right cheek and came out the back of his head. The dead general slumped silently to the ground. A major in the 33rd North Carolina asserted that Branch's men "almost idolized him. He died as a soldier would wish to die, facing the enemy, in the discharge of his duty."[44]

Hill's successful onslaught took little more than an hour. "Outflanked and staggered by the gallant attack of A. P. Hill's brigades," Longstreet declared, Burnside's assault collapsed. "The tide of the enemy surged back," Hill reported, "and breaking in confusion, passed out of sight" over the ridges to seek shelter along the banks of Antietam Creek.[45] The sun was setting now. Screams of the rebel yell could be heard above the roar of cannon and musketry; men fought amid dead bodies scattered everywhere as McClellan's entire left curled back toward the stream. The fire died down with darkness, and nightfall brought the inevitable moans and screams as wounded men stared at death.

Total Union losses were 12,410 men, including an appalling 2,108 killed. Lee's casualties exceeded 10,316 soldiers, including 1,546 dead. Gen. Isaac P. Rodman's division, which Hill's attack blew apart, suffered 220 dead, 783 wounded, and 70 missing. Hill placed his losses at 63 killed and 283 wounded—figures that were too low. A tabulation by brigades put the losses at 64 killed, 304 wounded, and 6 missing, which is still incredibly small in light of the impact Hill's attack had on the battle. For Hill, the death of Branch was a severe personal blow. "He was my senior brigadier," Hill lamented, "and one to whom I could have intrusted the command of the Division with all confidence."[46]

Hill emerged from the battle of Antietam Creek as the hero of the hour. "Three thousand men, only 2000 of whom had been engaged in the final counterstroke, had saved Lee's army from almost certain destruction," one authority declared. Lee stated in his first official communiqué that Hill "drove the enemy immediately from the position they had taken, and continued the contest until dark, restoring our right, and maintaining our ground."[47] That Hill had unhesitatingly assailed a Federal force of at least twice his numbers, and turned pending defeat for the Confederacy into a stunning victory on the right flank, stamped him anew as the best division commander in the Army of Northern Virginia.

On that Wednesday in western Maryland, Hill had plunged into a battle with little or no reconnaissance simply because he was needed at once. Such boldness saved the army at Antietam Creek. That characteristic of Hill would not always have a positive effect. However, the facts at Sharpsburg were indisputable: he had attacked and routed a vastly superior force, he had averted disaster for Lee, and his timely arrival would keep the Civil War going for another two and a half years. Press accounts in Richmond made no mention of Hill's role at Sharpsburg. Yet Maj. B. W. Frobel's simple statement of praise, "At this time General A. P. Hill came up," would become part of the Southern heritage, given larger prominence when Lee, in the delirium of his final hours, called out clearly: "Tell A. P. Hill he must come up!"[48]

Near midnight on September 17, "as half of Lee's army was hunting the other half" in the postbattle confusion, a major asked Hill if he knew the Burnside whose troops he had so badly manhandled. "Ought to," Hill snorted. "He owes me eight thousand dollars." Burnside had borrowed that sum several years earlier from his West Point chum, and the debt remained unpaid.[49]

The next morning passed with each army warily eying the other. Rain showers marked the afternoon as details of men buried the dead, who were in some places "literally piled in heaps." Lee's army began retiring southward that night. Hill's division, bringing up the rear, "was silently withdrawn" from the line at one in the morning on the nineteenth. Hill expected hourly to have to turn and fight the Yankees, but his men recrossed the Potomac in midmorning— "every wagon and piece of artillery having been safely put on the Virginia shore," Hill boasted. A battery commander in Hill's division noted that each company "gave a cheer as it formed on the south bank of the River and I doubt whether there was a man in the army that did not rejoice that he was out of Maryland."[50]

As the Light Division bivouacked that night five miles south of Shepherdstown, the Federals were making belated pursuit. Four regiments from FitzJohn Porter's corps, covered by seventy cannon positioned on the high ground along the northern bank of the Potomac, crossed the river at Boteler's Ford. They outflanked the artillery train of Gen. William N. Pendleton and captured four cannon as Confederate gunners fled the area. Jackson received word of this development at six-thirty in the morning on the twentieth. He promptly ordered Hill's division—the unit closest to the danger— to backtrack and contest the Federal thrust.[51]

Hill instantly discerned the urgency of the situation. An artillerist in the Light Division commented: "A fighter like General Hill needed no orders when his rear was pressed, and by daylight . . . the tramp of that tireless infantry . . . was heard marching back to the river, the clatter of their canteens, the occasional clanking of a musket butt against a bayonet, and the rambling of the artillery carriages being the only sounds."[52] Hill's men marched so rapidly that they reached the Boteler's Ford area before Porter could get additional Union infantry across to the south bank.

It was not yet nine o'clock when Hill dispersed his 2,000 troops to confront a like number of Union soldiers. The brigades of Pender, Gregg, and Thomas, with Gregg in charge, formed a first line; James H. Lane (temporarily commanding Branch's brigade), Archer, and Brockenbrough, all under Archer, composed a second line. For a moment Hill's ranks stood quietly in a field of corn. In their front, open ground dotted by wheat stacks extended 1,000 yards all the way to the river's edge. Beyond the Potomac, cannon peeked from heavy woods on the opposite bank. A concerned Lee reportedly joined Hill on a slight eminence to watch the action.[53]

At Hill's command, the two lines started forward. Porter's batteries immediately opened on the unprotected ranks. It was a "terrible fire of grape, round shot and shell," one of Gregg's colonels recalled. "Their practice was remarkably fine, bursting shells in the ranks at every tremendous fire of artillery I ever saw, and too much praise cannot be awarded my regiments for their steady, unwavering step." He added: "It was as if each man felt that the fate of the army was centered in himself."[54]

Gregg and Thomas struck the Union line and began pushing it back slowly toward the river bluff. One Union regiment tried to overlap Hill's left. It struck Pender, who detached one regiment to blunt the counterattack while he called on Archer for help. The two Confederate bridges then rushed with a yell and seized a rise of ground that gave them a clear view of the Federals. Then, according to Colonel Lane, the Southerners "poured a deadly fire into the enemy, who fled precipitately and in great confusion to the river."[55]

The main Federal unit engaged was the 118th Pennsylvania. It was a brand-new regiment that had been in the field only twenty days. (The Pennsylvanians were so inexperienced that one company had crossed the Potomac while its captain remained behind to guard the baggage.)[56] Worse, half of the regiment's muskets were defective. The 118th Pennsylvania tried to put up a fight, broke after thirty minutes' action, and fled the field "in an utterly disorganized and demoralized condition." It suffered 269 casualties in this baptismal engagement.[57]

Hill's men now reached the bluff overlooking the Potomac and slammed volley after volley into Yankees frantically trying to recross the river. Some Federals were killed trying to get across an abandoned dam, and their bodies lay hung in the ruins. Other Billy Yanks bobbed lifeless as the swift-moving river carried them downstream toward Harper's Ferry. The one-sided contest was over by mid-morning.

Owing to the horror of the battle's outcome, casualty figures were greatly exaggerated. Jackson reported "an appalling scene of the destruction of human life"; a Confederate infantryman wrote of seeing "the whole river filled with floating corpses and wounded, drowning men"; Hill, obviously giddy from so total a victory, put Union losses at 3,000 dead—a higher fatality than McClellan suffered at Antietam Creek. Actual Federal casualties were 71 killed, 161 wounded, and 131 missing. Hill's losses, mostly from artillery fire, numbered 30 killed and 261 wounded.[58]

Hill closed his battle report on a philosophical note: "This was a wholesome lesson to the enemy, and taught them to know that it may be dangerous sometimes to press a retreating army." The Confederate victory, which Hill engineered, an aide observed, was "a most brilliant thing," and "its effect in stunning the enemy & reassuring our people can scarcely be overestimated." In the exhilaration of victory, however, Hill remained violently contemptuous of any soldier who exhibited "the white feather." A member of the 38th North Carolina wrote home after this engagement that "Sergt. Benneck acted very cowardly & the Genl. thrashed him with his sword on Saturday the 20th and he has not been seen since."[59]

Again little public notice was given to Hill's latest battle exploit. The general was so proud of his soldiers that four days after the Shepherdstown battle he issued a stirring proclamation. "Soldiers of the Light Division: You have done well and I am pleased with you. You have fought in every battle from Mechanicsville to Shepherdstown, and no man can yet say that the Light Division was ever broken. You held the left at Manassas against overwhelming numbers and saved the army. You saved the day at Sharpsburg and Shepherdstown. You were selected to face a storm of round shot, shell, and grape such as I have never before seen. I am proud to say that your services are appreciated by our general, and that you have a reputation in this army which it should be the object of every officer and private to sustain."[60]

This public praise, one of Hill's artillerists wrote, "seemed but a proper and grateful acknowledgement of their services, and served to buoy their spirits and cement more closely their attachment to their commander."[61]

Achieving such success, however, had been an expensive undertaking. To his wife, Dorsey Pender wrote: "You have no idea what a reputation our Division has. It surpasses Jackson's Division both for fighting and discipline. . . . But when I tell you that this Division has lost 9000 killed and wounded since we commenced the Richmond fight at Mechanicsville, you can see what our reputation has cost us." The six brigades in the Light Division numbered barely 4,700 men.[62]

10

Near-Disaster at
Fredericksburg

Hill should have been happy in those last days of September 1862, especially after Dolly and the two children joined him at Camp Branch near Martinsburg. But his anger about the pending charges against him by Jackson smoldered inside him. When he remembered the humiliation of being removed from command and of having to walk at the very rear of his division, the anger blazed. Not even satisfaction over his triumphs at Antietam Creek and Shepherdstown could temper burning resentment. Pride, duty, justice—all were at stake. On the heels of his victories, and with no further campaigning imminent, it was time to resolve the issue. So the contest between the firebrand and the glacier erupted anew.

Barely two days after the Shepherdstown fight, Hill started through channels a polite but forceful letter to Lee. Jackson had arrested him "for neglect of duty," Hill asserted. The serious charges could not remain in limbo. "I respectfully represent that I deem myself to have been treated with injustice and censured and punished at the head of my command and request that a Court of Inquiry be granted me."[1]

Jackson penned a lengthy endorsement to Hill's letter before forwarding it to Lee. He summarized Hill's recent deficiencies, emphasized Hill's failure on several occasions to march promptly as ordered, and described the circumstances surrounding the actual arrest on September 4. Jackson then added an insult: "I found that under his successor, General Branch, my orders were much better carried out."[2]

The papers then went to Lee, who for the first time had to come to grips with the feud. It was difficult. On the one hand, Jackson's authority had to be respected; on the other hand, one of his best fighting generals felt grossly insulted. Indeed, Hill was so incensed that he at least once expressed a wish to take his division to South Carolina for the winter campaign.[3] Lee initially took a low-key approach: the matter, he felt, was not of sufficient import to warrant a court of inquiry. The commanding general returned Hill's request through channels with an annotation: "His [Hill's] attention being now called to what appeared to be a neglect of duty by his commander, but which from an officer of his character could not be intentional and I feel assured will never be repeated, I see no advantage to the service in further investigating this matter nor could it without detriment be done at this time."[4]

Hill was anything but appeased when he read Lee's endorsement. In fact, he became angrier. The highly sensitive Hill interpreted Lee's statement about "what appeared to be a neglect of duty" which "will never be repeated" to mean that Lee found substance in Jackson's charges. On September 30, Hill again asked for a court of inquiry—and this time his language was pointed. "I deny the truth of every allegation made by Maj. Genl. Jackson and am prepared to prove my denial by a number of honorable men. . . . If Genl. Jackson had accorded me the courtesy of asking an explanation of each instance of neglect of duty as it occurred, I think that even he would have been satisfied and the necessity avoided of keeping a black list against me." Hill asserted that either he was not fit to command a division (if Jackson's indictment were true) or else Jackson deserved formal censure for an injustice rendered. Hill then threw in a final blow by referring to Jackson as "the officer who abuses his authority to punish, and then sustains his punishment by making loose charges against an officer who had done and is doing his utmost to make his troops efficient."

Jackson wanted to forget the whole matter. After all, Hill's flawless performance in the past three engagements implied that he had learned his lesson. Yet Hill had virtually issued a challenge. On October 3, Jackson wrote Lee that he did not think a hearing necessary; nevertheless, he was forwarding the formal charges as requested.

Grouped under "Neglect of Duty" were eight specifications, from the crossing of the Rapidan on August 8 to the crossing of the Potomac on September 4. These charges, Jackson felt, belonged more to a court-martial than to a court of inquiry; yet he was disposed to let the matter drop. However, Jackson seemed then to get caught in the fever of the issue as he completed his outline of the charges. Hill's insistence on a hearing at that critical moment in the war, Jackson asserted, was still "another instance of neglecting his duty."[5]

Lee now realized that the situation was close to getting out of hand. One afternoon he went to the Boyd House, the stately brick mansion south of Bunker Hill serving as Jackson's headquarters. Soon an obviously irate Hill rode up the tree-lined drive. A "deeply pained" Lee then sought for several hours to effect a reconciliation between his two generals. At one point he supposedly said, "He who has been the most aggrieved can be the most magnanimous and make the first overtures of peace." Neither officer budged; each refused to drop charges against the other. Instead, one staff officer noted, "the blaze was smothered, but the coals were still there."[6]

Thereafter, only formal communications passed between Hill and Jackson. When they had to meet (which happened as infrequently as the two could arrange it), they saluted stiffly and said as little as possible. Lee meanwhile could only hope that time would prove a soothing medication. He shelved the paperwork relative to the quarrel and turned to the more important task of reorganizing his army.

The necessity of dividing the Army of Northern Virginia into corps for the sake of better control and logistics had become increasingly evident. When President Jefferson Davis asked Lee for suggestions, Lee proposed two corps and nominated Longstreet and Jackson to command them. In the same communiqué Lee stated: "Next to these two officers, I consider General A. P. Hill the best commander with me. He fights his troops well, and takes good care of them."[7] The implication was clear: if anything happened to Longstreet or Jackson, or if a third corps was created, Hill was the front-runner for it, ahead of such other division commanders as McLaws, Anderson, and D. H. Hill.

Longstreet and Jackson were thereupon promoted to lieutenant general. Jackson's new Second Corps consisted of the divisions of Jackson, Ewell, A. P. Hill, and D. H. Hill. This new arrangement had only minimal effect on the ranks of the Light Division. To no one's surprise, the competent Jim Lane received promotion to brigadier and permanent command of Branch's brigade, which he had been leading for weeks. John M. Brockenbrough continued at the head of Field's brigade, but temporarily and as a colonel. The Virginian was attentive and courageous, yet he seemed to lack certain indispensable qualities of a first-rate brigade commander. Hence, promotion was delayed.

At this time also, the redoubtable William H. Palmer joined Hill's staff. Born in Richmond, the twenty-seven-year-old Palmer had enlisted as a private in the 1st Virginia and had risen through the ranks to colonel of that regiment before accepting Hill's offer of staff appointment. Polished, highly organized, and indefatigable, Palmer became Hill's most trusted aide. The other members of Hill's staff were Maj. Richard C. Morgan, Capts. R. H. T. Adams, Francis T. Hill, Conway R. Howard, Robert C. Stanard, R. J. Wingate, and a volunteer aide named Gordon.[8]

The autumn weeks were for the most part a time of rest and refurbishment for everyone. The Bunker Hill area was quiet, open country dotted with rock outcroppings. The wooded areas decreased in direct proportion to the length of time soldiers were encamped nearby. Bunker Hill itself was a scattering of homes at a crossroads ten miles north of Winchester. The two major buildings there were Presbyterian and Episcopal churches—symbolically representing Jackson and Hill, one might suppose. When the Light Division made camp in the area, the men were "badly broken down and scattered," an adjutant wrote. One of Gregg's men was more pointed. The troops "were sun-burnt, gaunt, ragged, scarcely at all shod . . . an emaciated, limping, filthy mass."[9]

Rejuvenation came speedily. Col. Alfred Scales, shortly to join Hill's command, observed: "The air was pure, food was abundant, the naked were clothed and shod, and the rest of the soldier was sweet. The army was recruited in strength, health, hope, and numbers."[10] In an effort to alleviate the ever-present plague of lice and fleas among the soldiers, Hill ordered whole companies at a time to march into the Opequon River. Conscripts, stragglers, and men sufficiently recovered from wounds or sickness entered the regiments in a steady stream. From 4,700 soldiers late in September, the Light Division grew to 9,400 by mid-October. Seven batteries remained with the division; yet Hill had to intercede personally to get the all-but-wiped-out Purcell Battery of Willie Pegram (whom Hill affectionately called "my gallant Captain of the artillery") rebuilt and restored to service. Within a month after reaching Bunker Hill, an infantryman declared, "glad smiles brightened the exchange of greeting, and hearty laughter once more reverberated through the length and breadth of the camp."[11]

Hill likewise enjoyed the calm period, after the confrontation with Jackson reached an uneasy truce. His "three girls" were close by. The troops had presented him with two cherished gifts: a new bronze-colored pipe, so carved that a small hand seemed to be gripping the bowl, and an embroidered tobacco pouch, which thereafter Hill always had on his person. He continued to fraternize regularly with his troops. On more than one occasion, when a rabbit or squirrel chase was in progress in one of the camps, Hill would dismount, join the crowd, and laughingly give chase with his men.[12]

Expeditions and skirmishes were infrequent during the eight-week hiatus in the lower Shenandoah Valley. Late in October, the Light Division moved to Berryville and began a systematic destruction of the Baltimore and Ohio Railroad. Before they quit, the Confederates had torn up over twenty miles of track and had sliced to within four miles of Harper's Ferry, which Federals had reoccupied in the week following Antietam Creek. One Sunday, when Union troops made a stab at Hill's lines, the general held his fire until families could be evacuated from a nearby church service.[13]

On November 3, with Federals occupying Snicker's Gap and Confederates holding Castleman's Ferry at the bottom of the mountain, a short but brisk fight took place. About 1,000 Federals swooped down to seize the ford. Archer, anticipating such a raid, had concealed his troops. The Yankees lumbered into an old-fashioned ambush and caught the fire of the 19th Georgia plus the batteries of Grey Latham and Willie Pegram. "The enemy soon ran away out of sight," Archer stated. While Hill put Federal losses at 200 men, Archer was closer to an accurate figure when he reported 40 dead and wounded Federals left on the field.[14]

Winter struck hard on November 7 when the first snowstorm of the season blanketed the countryside. One of the Tarheel soldiers wrote romantically of the sight: "The sun gleamed out in spots over the scene. . . . The view was spotted like a huge leopard skin, or heaps of iced poundcake with green boughs for dressing." Other soldiers had a different reaction. "My feet are perfectly naked," a Virginian wrote from camp, "and I have to tramp over the frozen snow with bits of old blankets tied over them, which keep constantly coming off."[15]

Hill forcibly occupied Snicker's Gap on the ninth, obtaining in the process 104 prisoners and badly needed supplies.[16] From there, five days later, Hill penned one of the most incendiary letters of his life. He was responding to a personal communiqué from his long-time friend and the army's cavalry chief, Gen. Jeb Stuart. Hill was not well at the time. "Many thanks for your kindness in sending me the letter," he began. "It found me with only one arm useful—the other swollen as big as old Sacketts leg." (The elephantine Delos B. Sackett had been one of Hill's West Point classmates.)

Then Hill let loose a withering blast at Jackson. "I suppose I am to vegitate here all the winter under that crazy old Presbyterian fool. I am like the porcupine—all bristles, and all sticking out too, so I know we shall have a smash up before long. I don't like the complexion here. I think a fatal sin has been committed, provided the Yanks have the sense to take advantage of it, which they don't often do, for they sometimes won't [take] the peach when held to their lips."

Next came a backhanded slap at Jackson's choice for new commander of the Stonewall Brigade, after which Hill returned to his chief nemesis. "How do you like *Paxton* Brig. Gen.! The Almighty will get tired, helping Jackson after awhile, and then he'll get the damndest thrashing—and the shoe pinches, for I should get my share and probably all the blame, for the people will never blame Stonewall for any disaster."[17]

Meanwhile, Union authorities had run out of patience over McClellan's procrastination. Lincoln removed him from command of the Army of the Potomac during the November 7 snowfall. His successor, to the surprise of military men on both sides, was Gen. Ambrose E. Burnside. "Old Burn" was a simple, honest, loyal soldier; he was also, said Federal general John Gibbon, "a man of remarkable enthusiasm with which he was but too apt to be carried away."[18]

When, on the seventeenth, a Richmond newspaper conjectured that the Union army appeared "to be inclining once more to Fredericksburg," it was correct.[19] Burnside's army had been camping around Warrenton, Lee was at Culpeper, and Jackson still was in the Valley. What Burnside had in mind was to steal a day or so on Lee by transferring his army secretly and quickly to the heights of the Rappahannock overlooking Fredericksburg. The Union army would cross the river on pontoons and strike for Richmond—the king in this great chess game of war—while Lee was left grasping at nothing in north-central Virginia.

Burnside actually got a full day's head start. Lee reacted quickly and ordered his men on a forced march to Fredericksburg. Jackson's corps remained in the Valley for several more days before Hill's troops broke camp at two-thirty in the morning on November 22. A Winchester matron watched as Hill's soldiers passed through the town and she was moved with compassion. "They were very destitute, many without shoes, and all without overcoats or gloves, although the weather is freezing. Their poor hands looked so red and cold holding their muskets in the biting wind. . . . One South Carolina regiment I especially noticed, had hands and feet that looked as if they belonged to women, and so cold and red and dirty they were."[20]

By then, the Light Division had climbed in strength to 11,000 troops. In addition, Lt. J. Hampden Chamberlayne informed his mother, "the men are cheerful almost to recklessness, used to hardship, veterans in action & in camp life and becoming regular soldiers. We reckon ourselves up here equal to holding in check 100,000 men, whipping 60,000 and devouring 40,000."[21]

Coincidental with the departure of Jackson's forces for Fredericksburg, Hill was the subject of a front-page "portrait" and story in one of the Confederacy's newspapers. The laudatory write-up ended with the declaration: "Gen. Hill is beloved by his own command, and his name is frequently mentioned with enthusiasm by the troops of other divisions. He is a brave and skillful officer—having made arms not only his profession, but an enthusiastic study, to which he was prompted by the natural tastes and disposition of his mind."[22]

Hill's men crossed the Blue Ridge at Fisher's Gap. Sleet made the rock-hard ground treacherous, and bare feet left bloody tracks along the route. Day after day, from four-thirty in the morning until six-thirty at night, the long lines "wound up and down and around, with glittering arms and accoutrements, like some huge serpent, with silver scales, dragging its torturous folds along." On Wednesday, December 3, Hill's brigades wearily filed into position south of Fredericksburg. They had covered 175 miles in twelve days on wretched roads amid horrible weather.[23] Now they stood a few miles downstream but in front of Burnside, who was still waiting for the needed pontoon boats to arrive.

Jackson's corps spread out as Lee's right half of the line. Hill's division, the connecting link with Longstreet's corps on the left, was in a cold and uncomfortable camp at Yerby's farm five miles south of Fredericksburg. The officers spent much of this time discussing a widespread rumor that Hill was about to be promoted to corps command. They hoped so. If the Light Division was the basis for a new corps, that would get them out from beneath Jackson's autocratic hand. The rumor turned bitter—and so did the weather. A four-inch snowfall on December 4–5 multiplied the misery. Capt. Greenlee Davidson wrote home from the Letcher Artillery: "Many of our soldiers are thinly clothed and without shoes and in addition to this, very few of the infantry have tents. With this freezing weather their sufferings are indescribable."[24]

On December 11, with a slight improvement in the weather, with concentrated Federal artillery fire pounding Fredericksburg from the east bank of the river, and with the long-awaited pontoon boats finally at hand, Burnside forced his way across the Rappahannock. Yankee soldiers proceeded uncharacteristically to sack the town, after which they slowly formed in massive battle formation. Lee expected the main assault to be against his left at Marye's Heights. To strengthen the already strong defenses of that sector, Lee directed that a division from Jackson's corps come up into the line along the railroad on Longstreet's right. Hill's division was closest to the area, so it received the orders. At dawn on Friday the twelfth, Hill moved his brigades into the position that Gen. John B. Hood's men had held before shifting to the left to buttress Longstreet.

Hill's line extended from Longstreet's flank southeast approximately a mile and a half along a wood-covered ridge just high enough to be foreboding. The Richmond, Fredericksburg & Potomac Railroad paralleled the front of the entire line before bending around Prospect Hill at Hamilton's Crossing, where Hill anchored his right. In his front was open, rather flat country. It seemed an ideal battleground for the Confederates; and perhaps because it was such a natural arena, with Lee packing his army into the most solid mass it ever enjoyed, several commanders on the right became overly optmistic and careless.

There is no question but that Hill's mind was not on defense at

Fredericksburg. The blame so often leveled against Hill for troop dispositions should take into account two distractions he faced. One was a continuation of strained relations with Jackson. Contacts and correspondence between the two generals over the past two months had been chillingly formal, despite outward appearances. William H. Palmer of Hill's staff commented that "on the field Jackson and Hill were very polite and no observer could have supposed that serious differences existed between them."[25] The extremely sensitive Hill had difficulty in handling this tension.

Even worse for Hill was a personal blow that came in that second week of December. Little Netty died. His firstborn daughter was a victim of diphtheria.[26] Hill received the news as he marched his troops into front-line position. With that loss, the fiery commander became a grieving father—which could account for the peculiar way in which Hill posted his division for battle.

He put twenty-one cannon under Davidson on the far left and fourteen guns under Walker on the extreme right, which was normal; but then Hill established his headquarters way out on the flank near Davidson's guns. It was almost as if he was trying to get as far away from the action as possible. In addition, his infantry was anything but well positioned. Pender's brigade composed the left, behind Davidson's batteries. To Pender's right was Lane's brigade, 150 yards in advance (Hill said later) because the timber was "jutting out into the low ground, some distance from the main body."[27]

Beyond Lane's right were Archer's men, with two regiments of Brockenbrough's brigade completing the first line. Up on the ridge, along a crude road that Hood's troops had constructed a few days earlier, Hill placed his second line. From left to right it consisted of Thomas's and Gregg's brigades, plus Brockenbrough's other two regiments. Jackson then banked up the divisions of Early, D. H. Hill, and Taliaferro behind Hill. On paper this gave Jackson the awesome firepower of eleven muskets per yard of front line. The Confederate right appeared to be absolutely impregnable.

It was not.

Between Lane and Archer was a huge gap caused by an area of scraggly woods, dense underbrush, and swampy ground that projected into a triangle for several hundred yards toward the enemy. This dense tangle was 200 yards wide at its base along the Confederate line; but Lane's right flank was some 250 yards to the left of this area, while Archer's left was 150 yards from the trees. The gap in

Hill's center, therefore, was close to 600 yards wide. Almost as dangerous, Gregg's brigade was posted a quarter mile behind the gap rather than to the side of it; and the woods between the gap and Gregg's line were so dense as to reduce visibility practically to zero.

Who was to blame for such an alignment? The answer is that a number of generals could have been at fault. One assumes that Hill laid out his line under Jackson's scrutiny. Jackson always took great care with battle positions. He certainly must have watched Hill more closely than usual when the Light Division filed into position at Fredericksburg. Staff officer Robert L. Dabney—who was not present at Fredericksburg—claimed that Jackson in fact saw the gap before the battle and asserted: "The enemy will attack here."[28] This notation was Dabney's postwar imagination at work, for Jackson would not have tolerated so weak a point if he had been aware of it. However, it seems evident that Jackson did not inspect his lines closely on the eve of battle. Thus he becomes culpable, along with Hill.

Lane and perhaps two other officers also knew about the undefended area, and they were apprehensive. Jeb Stuart rode along Hill's line on the afternoon of the twelfth, saw the empty ground, and told a concerned aide that Federals would not get close enough for the gap to be a problem. Hill himself never offered a full explanation. He apparently thought the marshy triangle impassable. An additional rationale has long been offered in Hill's defense: the ever-solicitous general allowed the break in the line because he did not want to subject his troops to the health hazard of cold swampy ground.[29]

Whatever the reasons, the situation was Second Manassas all over again—with a major difference. At Manassas, the gap was near a flank and only 150 yards wide. At Fredericksburg, the unmanned sector was Hill's center and encompassed almost a fourth of his front line.

A cold and biting wind laced through the huddled soldiers as they crouched in the darkness of December 12–13. An hour or so before dawn, the wind slackened. In its place came a fog so thick that visibility was no more than fifty yards. Yet the stirring of at least a portion of Gen. William B. Franklin's 55,000-man wing across the way could clearly be heard. Jackson, Hill, and their staffs gathered on Prospect Hill to wait out the fog. Hill was in his usual attire: black felt hat, calico shirt, wool shell jacket, trousers stuffed into knee-high boots, saber and revolver strapped to his waist. Jackson looked unnatural in a new, elaborate uniform—a recent gift from Stuart.[30]

At ten o'clock the fog lifted. Within minutes, a Union officer noted, "the air was soft, not a cloud in the sky. The sun [lit up] with superb indifference the two armies in battle array." What Hill now saw were massed Federals "covering the whole of my front and extending far to the left toward Fredericksburg." George G. Meade's 4,500 Pennsylvanians, arranged in three battle lines, were massing in front of Hill's sector. The morning sun, a Confederate wrote in awe, caused "leaping reflections from thousands of gleaming bayonets."[31]

Then the blue lines began slowly moving forward, as if on some grand review. Their advance had barely begun when boyish Maj. John Pelham wheeled two cannon from the Stuart horse batteries into a position out on Meade's left flank. At a range of only 400 yards Pelham began raking the Union lines. Federal batteries angrily replied and managed to knock one of Pelham's guns out of commission, but Pelham manned a single gun and continued sending a murderous oblique fire into Meade's division. For an hour the Union assault was at a confused standstill. Pelham retired from the field only when ordered to do so.

Dozens of Federal guns spent the next hour in a furious and unanswered cannonade on Hill's position. Union artillerists were soon convinced that "the rebel guns were in a measure silenced."[32] Shortly after noon, 850 yards away, Meade again advanced in line of battle across the plain. Not a sound came from the Southern lines. On marched the blue ranks for about 200 yards. Inside the Confederate lines, shouts rang out and the forty-seven cannon in Hill's division simultaneously bombarded the Union lines. The columns buckled, then became ragged. A second salvo belched forth, Hill reported, and "shell and canister from our long-silent but now madly aroused batteries plowed through their ranks."[33]

Southern artillery banged away so furiously that the Union advance seemed on the verge of disintegrating; yet the bluecoats recovered and surged forward with more determination and speed. The cannon fire and musketry became ragged as men on both sides fired at will, loading and discharging at their own speed. Yankees were dropping steadily now, and in the woods here and there a Confederate reeled after being hit by blind fire. Suddenly, to Lane in the

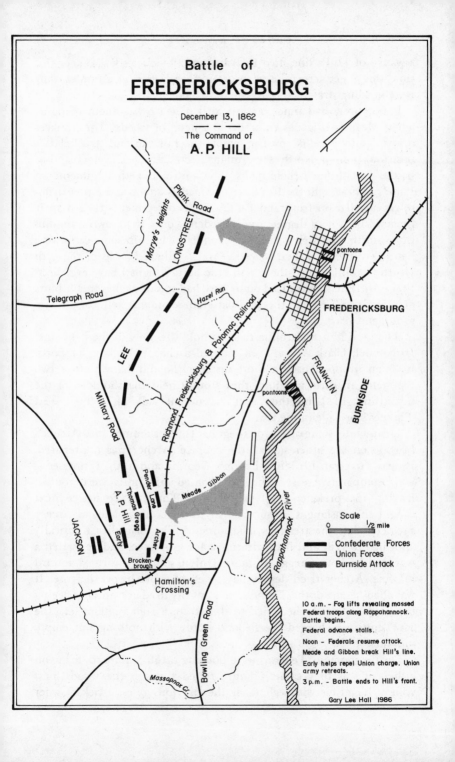

Battle of
FREDERICKSBURG

December 13, 1862

The Command of
A. P. HILL

Plank Road

Marye's Heights

LONGSTREET

Telegraph Road

Hazel Run

FREDERICKSBURG

pontoons

Richmond Fredericksburg & Potomac Railroad

LEE

FRANKLIN

Military Road

BURNSIDE

pontoons

Pender Lane

Meade - Gibbon

Thomas Gregg

A. P. Hill

Rappahannock River

Early

JACKSON

Archer

Brocken-
brough

Hamilton's
Crossing

Bowling Green Road

Massapnax Cr.

Scale

0   1/2 mile

■ Confederate Forces
☐ Union Forces
▨ Burnside Attack

10 a.m. - Fog lifts revealing massed
Federal troops along Rappahannock.
Battle begins.

Federal advance stalls.

Noon - Federals resume attack.

Meade and Gibbon break Hill's line.

Early helps repel Union charge. Union
army retreats.

3 p.m. - Battle ends to Hill's front.

Gary Lee Hall 1986

advance of Hill's line, two facts became obvious: the Yankees this time would get across the open ground, and, as if in a funnel, they were heading straight toward the undefended gap.

Lane barely had time to warn Hill of what was about to occur when Meade's brigades entered the tongue of woods. The Yankees drove Confederate skirmishers across the railroad and struck Hill's position. Lane's North Carolinians were seasoned veterans, but battles had thinned their ranks. The 37th and 28th Regiments on Lane's right caught the full force of Meade's attack and found themselves assailed on front and flank. The two regiments turned their lines a full ninety degrees and "fired not only their own ammunition, but that of their dead and wounded, which in some cases were handed to them by their officers." Maj. William Morris of the 37th North Carolina called the action "the hardest fight I have ever been in. . . . the Enemy advanced on us & we had to use the bayonet & butts of our Guns." Slowly the two battered regiments fell back to regroup and rearm.³⁴

The 33rd North Carolina tried to hold the apex of the bent line. Its colonel, Clark Avery, even ordered a charge. Lacking supports, his men dropped back a short distance. So did Lane's other two regiments in turn, although they stoutly held the shoulder of the breakthrough. Lane then sent an urgent call for help to Ed Thomas's brigade in the rear.

Meanwhile, some of Meade's regiments had slammed into Archer's brigade on the other side of the coppice. Archer was unprepared. Federals overran his left—the 19th Georgia and 14th Tennessee— with comparative ease. The two Confederate units were routed, leaving 160 prisoners in Union hands. The 7th Tennessee next caught the onslaught. It succumbed to uncertainty and, as Archer sneered, "left the trenches in disorder." The brigadier frantically appealed to Hill and Brockenbrough for assistance, and he started a warning back to Gregg. As more Union soldiers swarmed toward his line, Archer tried desperately to effect a patchwork defense. It was chaos. Some of the Tennesseans angrily fired at comrades fleeing the field. While Archer tried to shift troops from right to left, the 1st Tennessee charged the Federal horde with nothing but empty muskets.

For the moment, Federals were pouring through the gap, firing on either side as they came. Gunfire rolled through the woods, new volleys blending with echoes of the previous ones. Black powder smoke in waves rose above the trees, obscuring everything but the area immediately in front of each man. It was well-nigh impossible to think.

Maxcy Gregg knew that his reserve position faced the huge gap in the front line. Yet he seems not to have anticipated any involvement in the battle swelling through the woods. He had directed his men to stack arms. Most of them had taken cover in the woods to avoid Federal shells, which were "screaming through the forest, cutting down giant trees" and adding more volume "to the deafening sound." Suddenly men in Orr's Rifles looked up and saw Federals dashing toward them. The Yankees were as stunned to see the Carolinians. Hasty fire broke out erratically.[35]

Gregg, hard of hearing and confused at this unexpected development, galloped into the area—and mistook the advancing Union line for retreating soldiers from Archer's brigade. He rode over to Orr's Rifles and told the men to cease firing because the troops in their front were Confederates. By this time, the brigade historian acknowledged, "the Rifle regiment was, as a body, broken, slaughtered and swept from the field." Gregg brought other troops into line and bravely jumped into the thick of the fighting. Seconds later, a bullet tore through the brigadier's spine and he tumbled mortally wounded from his horse.[36]

Col. Daniel H. Hamilton of the 1st South Carolina quickly assumed temporary command. The former U.S. marshal for South Carolina calmly rode along the fractured line and told his men "to remain quiet and steady." The Carolinians did not stand "firm as on parade" (Hill's words); on the other hand, Hamilton "threw back the right wing of his regiment and opened a destructive fire" that rapidly ground Meade's attack to a halt.[37]

By now, Federal general John Gibbon's division had entered the battle against Hill's left. Gibbon's men initially bogged down under heavy fire; but when Meade punctured the Southern line, one of Gibbon's brigades rushed forward with a shout, charged across the railroad, and drove the Confederates farther back into the woods, "killing a number with the bayonet and capturing upward of 200 prisoners," a Federal officer claimed. As this fighting raged, Pender came riding down his line amid ricocheting bullets and flying shells. His left arm was hanging limp, blood dripping from his fingers. A bullet had pierced his arm. When aides expressed concern, Pender replied: "Oh, that is a trifle. No bones are broken."[38]

The high point for the Federals had been reached. Meade and Gibbon both had penetrated the Confederate line, but their losses had been high. Now the tables turned.

Thomas's men, under orders from Hill, struggled through undergrowth to the aid of Lane. The Georgians and North Carolinians together began to plug the gap. Yet more aid was needed. It came from Jubal Early. The three brigades of "that gallant old warrior," Hill wrote, "came crashing through the woods at the double-quick." Rebel yells momentarily drowned out the sound of battle, and "the enemy, completely broken, fled in confusion." As Early's men rushed past the South Carolinians' broken ranks, one of them saw Gregg. "The old hero, unable to speak, unable to stand alone, raised himself to his full height by a small tree, and, with cap in hand, waved them forward."[39]

Early's men did not restore the line alone. Bloodied regiments in the brigades of Lane and Archer became rallying points as the Confederates quickly built a connecting line. Thomas's troops were now intertwined with Lane's while Brockenbrough's regiments reinforced Archer's thin line. From left, center, and right, the Southerners began surging back toward the river. Exhausted Union soldiers found themselves in danger of being trapped. Billy Yanks began "running like a herd of buffalo," one observer wrote, while behind them Confederates "came out of the woods like a band of wolves." A New England officer put it more vividly: "As we drew back reluctantly, the rebels followed, in defiance of the batteries protecting our flanks, and swept us again with musketry, and their batteries caught us in the open; shells burst close upon us, and solid shot plunged into our ranks and knocked men, bleeding and senseless, into the mud to die."[40]

By three in the afternoon the battle had ended in Jackson's sector, although the massacre of Burnside's army in Longstreet's front would continue until nightfall. The brigades of the Light Division were in the painful process of putting themselves together again when an order came down from Jackson to prepare for a night assault. "I want to move forward," he said excitedly, "to attack them—drive them into the river yonder!"

The men slowly began forming for a renewal of the battle. Col. Alfred Scales remembered discussing Jackson's plan with Pender, "he in the light of his military education, and I in the light of its common sense and practicability. We both agreed that the order was injudicious and hazardous." Before Jackson's guns could open a preliminary bombardment, close to a hundred Union cannon across the river began blanketing the area with shells. Confederate artillerists sought to make a contest of it, but Jackson ordered them to cease firing. They were wasting ammunition against superior batteries. The attack was canceled. Under cover of darkness, the divisions of Early and Taliaferro relieved Hill. His weary men trudged to the rear.[41]

In the fighting on Lee's right, both sides took heavy losses. Meade reported 1,853 killed, wounded, and missing out of 4,500 engaged. Gibbon put his casualties at 1,267 men. The Light Division suffered 231 killed, 1,474 wounded, and 417 missing—figures that were two-thirds of Jackson's total losses.[42]

Hill's compassion and respect for heroism were evident after the battle. One of the chaplains wrote: "I remember seeing him visiting, as was his custom, his field hospitals, looking after the comfort of his wounded, and with his own hands lifting some of the poor fellows into more comfortable positions." The loss of Gregg weighed especially heavy on him. "A more chivalrous gentleman and gallant soldier never adorned the service which he so loved," Hill stated.[43] He also took an extraordinary step in commending the valor of Union troops in the battle. Two different accounts report that Hill sent laudatory messages through the lines during the flag-of-truce period for burying the dead.[44]

The fact remains, however, that Hill was delinquent at Fredericksburg on two counts.

First was the gap in the line. Hill downgraded it in his report, calling it an "interval" along his front. Jackson used the same word, but in a barbed sense. The Federals pushed forward "before General A. P. Hill closed the interval which he had left between Archer and Lane." Jackson, as supreme commander of the right, was responsible for his front line, but he believed that the gap was the result of misjudgment or negligence on Hill's part. The ever-opinionated Archer was also quick to pass the blame to Hill. To his brother a few days after the battle Archer asserted: "I told Gen. Hill that there was danger of being flanked and it was Genl. Hill himself who told me that Gregg was close enough to the 'Interval' to prevent my being flanked. The Maj. Genl . . . attributes [the breakthrough] to the deafness of Gregg who was ordered to advance when the heavy artillery commenced, & who probably did not hear, either that, or the orders."[45]

A more substantial indictment of Hill is his lack of leadership in the battle. His whereabouts and activities at *any* time during the five-hour engagement are unknown. A rumor even circulated behind the lines that he had been captured during the action.[46] If he provided any direction at all, it is not recorded. The brigade commanders seem to have been left alone to ascertain the situation and to keep one another informed as best they could. Hill's coldness toward Jackson and his grief over Netty's death certainly were impairments but do not excuse his conduct. In no other major battle in which he participated was Hill as inconspicuous as he was at Fredericksburg.

11

"This Slumbering Volcano"

Fredericksburg and its environs struck many soldiers in the last weeks of December as resembling hell itself. Devastation was everywhere. One of Hill's men wrote that from shallow graves on the battlefield, "there were heads, hands and feet sticking up through the dirt, and myriads of worms and insects of various kinds working all over the piles." Another Johnny Reb informed his wife that Fredericksburg "was a beautiful city before the fight but now it is almost a heap of ruins. there was 175 houses burnt and nearly every house was shot with cannon. . . . all together it is a heart rending scene of destruction."[1] Throughout the countryside, barns, churches, and empty structures became homes for untold numbers of helpless refugees. Cold rain or snow almost daily pelted the area. The roads were reduced to such horrible conditions that a Federal pontoon train, hopelessly stuck, had to be set afire to keep it from falling into Confederate hands.[2]

Hill's fatigued brigades struggled through "one continual slush of mud" to a timbered tract eight miles downriver from Fredericksburg. At the site, christened Camp Gregg, the men "grotesquely settled in huts of wood & canvas in various proportions and of every ugly & curious kind." The same writer added that the veterans "all seem in very good heart; indeed they think so little of their hardships and privations as would astonish people in civil life." Hill established his headquarters at a home halfway between Jackson's base at the Corbin mansion and D. H. Hill's quarters at Grace Episcopal Church.[3]

There were occasional respites from weather and weariness as year's end approached. On December 27, pickets on opposite banks of the Rappahannock were indulging in their usual bantering when a Yankee called over and asked the Tarheels in the 37th North Carolina if they had "a sorry corporal" they would be willing to swap for Burnside. If not, the Federal quickly added, their side would trade the general for a run-down horse. That night, Hill was among a large group of officers who attended a Christmas party and "were as merry as if there were no war."[4]

The new year began on a somber note at Camp Gregg. Soldiers were marched to an open field on New Year's afternoon to witness a military execution. Pvt. Patrick McGee of the 1st Virginia in Longstreet's corps was shot to death for desertion, robbery, and perjury. Hill for a short time was president of a First Corps court-martial; and in forwarding the condemnation papers for another soldier, the division commander expressed his feelings clearly about capital punishment, as well as about Longstreet. To the adjutant general of the corps Hill wrote: "I send you over the record in the case of Youngblood whom we have directed to be executed. If the sentence meets the approval of the General, I would suggest that the sentence be published *at once* to the Army, and also that the prisoner be notified *at once* of his fate. . . . Our desire is to promote the efficiency of the service and its proper discipline, and suggestions coming from the Lt. Genl. are always received with pleasure and never regarded as any incursion of our privileges, and I hope no hesitancy will be felt in freely making them."[5]

Tuesday, January 6, was marred by a cold drizzle, which fell most of the day. Nevertheless, at eleven Hill staged a grand review of his division. The 10,000 troops paraded as well as the elements permitted. It was "a most imposing sight," one of Jackson's aides commented. "I doubt not the finest division in the Confederate army, and its gallant little Major General, A. P. Hill, has no superior in any army. The Division is in fine condition and much better clothed than I expected; will whip twice their number of Yankees at any time." However, Hill's men had been doing more constructive things than preparing for a parade. On the following day, the Light Division turned over $10,000 in cash to help the destitute of Fredericksburg.[6]

In long rows of log huts and shanties, the troops quickly settled into routine. The pregnant Dolly and little Russie joined Hill for the winter months. Dolly "delightfully fixed" a home for the family in a small house only a few hundred yards from Hill's headquarters. One of Dolly's brothers described Russie as "in excellent health, very bright & exceedingly pretty." In mid-January, Dolly contracted diphtheria, but the disease ran its course in two weeks without any permanent damage.[7]

The peaceful lull in military operations gave Hill the opportunity to try again to bring the matter with Jackson to a solution. The war of words resumed, and the correspondence grew long and finally bitter. It began on January 8, when Hill reminded Lee of the charges outstanding against him. Hill still wanted a court of inquiry convened as soon as possible. Two of his most important witnesses—Branch and Gregg—were dead, Hill stated, and other officers were leaving the army and would not be available to testify. Hill was so anxious for a hearing that he waived any claim to having officers of equal rank form the court. He would settle for gentlemen of lesser rank.

Lee was understandably concerned at this new petition. Two of his three highest-ranking generals were engaged in a dispute, and the matter was not going to fade away with time as he had hoped. On January 12, Lee replied to Hill. His letter obviously was thoughtfully produced and carefully written. The undertone of Lee's reply was simply that he would like to see the whole matter dropped.

"I do not think that in every case where an officer is arrested there is necessity for a trial by court-martial," Lee wrote, "and I consider yours one in which such a proceeding is unnecessary." Lee then patiently pointed out (as if it were imperative that a professionally trained soldier be reminded of this) that military arrest was often required to maintain authority. A commander had the right to arrest, just as he had the right to release from arrest. That point had been made in Hill's case; nothing more need be done.

Lee concluded by stating the belief that "upon examining the charges in question, I am of the opinion that the interests of the service do not require that they should be tried, and have, therefore, returned them to General Jackson with an endorsement to that effect. I hope you will concur with me that their further prosecution is unnecessary, so far as you are concerned, and will be of no advantage to the service."[8]

If Jackson was aware of Hill's new petition, he made no mention of it. His thoughts at this time were on a loftier plane. While Hill was pondering Lee's response, Jackson was writing his wife: "I trust that, in answer to prayer, our country will soon be blessed with peace. If we were only that obedient people that we should be. I should, with increased confidence, look for a speedy termination of hostilities. Let us pray more."[9]

Hill wrote Lee again near the end of January. His second letter bore marks of legal guidance in the composition. Hill disagreed totally with Lee's rationale. "I beg leave to state that I do not now, nor never have disputed the right of the Superior to arrest any officer under him, and to release him whenever he saw fit to do so; or that he might do so, and prefer no charges, provided the *party arrested consented thereto.*—Otherwise, an engine of tyranny is placed in the hands of commanding officers, to be exercised at their will, or to [their] passions and whims, and against which there is no appeal. In my case the Commanding General, having bypassed the charges preferred against me by Genl. Jackson, without trial, is a rebuke to him, but not as public as was Genl. Jackson's exercise of power towards me.

"The General must acknowledge that if the charges preferred against me by Genl. Jackson were true, that I do not deserve to command a Division in the Army. If they are untrue, then Genl. Jackson deserves a rebuke as serious as [my] arrest. I beg leave most distinctly to disclaim any credit which Genl. Jackson may have given me for the good results of his punishment, as to my better behavior thereafter, and that its only effect has been to cause me to preserve every scrap of paper received from Corps Hd. Qrs. to guard myself against any new eruption from this slumbering volcano."[10]

Name-calling was going too far. Lee had heard enough. The army commander chose not to reply to Hill's letter or to take action on his request. For two months thereafter the matter smoldered. The feud then resumed on a different note. Hill on March 8 submitted his report of the Cedar Mountain campaign. The language was, for Hill, restrained, yet the report was naturally slanted in his favor. Hill went to lengths in explaining his version of the "slow marches" he allegedly made. He then forwarded his account through channels. Jackson took one look at the document and became angry all over again, for Hill had practically accused him of failing to give proper directives for the march to Cedar Mountain.

Now Jackson counterattacked. He dispatched staff officers Frank

Paxton, Sandie Pendleton, and Kyd Douglas to gather all information pertinent to the case. Jackson personally grilled Douglas on events relative to Cedar Mountain. Even Hill was asked to present testimony that might be used against him. In mid-March he wrote Pendleton: "Your note is just received. The order to me on the night of the seventh of Aug., regulating the order of march, was written. I did not preserve it. The order to encamp at Orange Ct. House on the night of the 8th was verbal, and my recollection is that it was from Major Paxton. Of this, however, I am not sure, only that such directions were recd. by me. Of this there is no doubt."[11]

With new data at hand, Jackson appended a very detailed endorsement to Hill's report. It was in essence a point-by-point rebuttal of Hill's statements. The length and painstaking tone of the endorsement make it clear that Jackson had toiled for hours over the draft. When Hill learned of the overly long rebuttal, his anger grew, and it was not always on a mature level. Hill began exhibiting pettiness by overreacting to any unusual expressions of authority on the part of Jackson.

In the second week of March, for example, Jackson's chief of ordnance instructed his counterpart on Hill's staff to perform some minor duty. Hill exploded: it was September 1862, on the march toward Frederick, all over again. Strongly supporting the chain-of-command system, Hill had always insisted that directives to and from subalterns pass over his desk, for informational purposes at least. Now Jackson was ignoring that basic axiom of the military code. Hill quickly made an issue out of whether staff officers had the authority to issue and receive orders without the knowledge of their generals.

"I do not believe," Hill wrote Lee, "that an officer of the Ordnance, Qr. Mr., Commissary, or Medl. Dept. had the right to send an order direct to a subordinate, not under his immediate command, and which order would alter, probably destroy, the entire organization of such Department, that Dept. being under command of another. I conceive that the unity of my command is entirely destroyed, if my superiors can give orders direct to my staff officers, and my knowledge of those orders made entirely dependent upon the will of the staff officer. How can I be justly responsible for the condition of my command, when half my Ordnance train would be taken from me, and I know nothing of it until the Ordnance Officer chose to inform me?"[12]

Lee disagreed with Hill's premise and said so the same day. To abide by such a rigid chain-of-command framework as Hill suggested would create a mountain of red tape. Field commanders should not have to "attend to all the staff operations of their commands in addition to their military operations." Lee stated further: "If any objection to their execution exists, the commanders should apprise their [chiefs of staff], and, if necessary, suspend the execution till sustained." A general's trying to oversee every little detail of command would "be the cause of delay and loss" of at least "half of the advantage" of having a good staff. Lee closed his letter with a pointed statement: "I request, therefore, that all orders from the chiefs of staff departments may be considered as emanating directly from me, and executed accordingly."[13]

Hill stepped up his demands for a hearing on Jackson's charges; Jackson was carefully reworking the text of his charges. (As Douglas put it, "General Jackson was still at it, and Hill still of the same mind.") Then Lee heard that a message copied from a Federal signal line—a message which was supposed to be held in secret until it reached Lee's hand—was being discussed widely in Lane's brigade. Lee asked Jackson to ascertain where the leak occurred and to relieve the officer in question. Jackson ordered his signal officer to investigate. He discovered that Capt. R. H. T. Adams, Hill's communications chief, had leaked the contents of the intercepted message.

Adams did not deny the act. He obeyed only his general's directives, he said, even if General Hill's security measures differed from those of General Jackson. Adams was relieved of command, unknown to Hill, and directed to present himself at once to General Lee. A day or so later, Hill sent a note seething with anger to Jackson's adjutant general. Adams had gone to army headquarters, "and now returns and reports that Genl. Lee is ignorant of any such order [for Adams to report to the commander]. I request to know why Capt. Adams, a most capable and the *most efficient* Signal Officer, was relieved from duty on my staff. I say nothing of the discourtesy of relieving thus summarily an Officer of my Staff, without any explanation to myself."

In a second communiqué that day, Hill all but demanded to know from Lee "how far my authority extends in my own Division." Lee promised to refer the whole matter to Richmond for an opinion from the adjutant general's office.[14]

At this same time, a November 1862 letter from Hill to Sandie

Pendleton mysteriously came to Jackson's attention. In it Hill had stated: "I have received but one order from Maj. Gen. Jackson to Capt. Adams to detail three signal operators to report to Capt. Boswell. This order was received yesterday and obeyed the same day. A copy of the *same order* was received by Capt. Adams direct, not through me, and I directed him to pay no attention to it."[15]

Jackson bristled as he read the communiqué. Five months earlier Hill had committed an insubordinate act; now, in writing, Hill had stated that Jackson's orders would be obeyed in the Light Division only if they passed through Hill himself. This was the last straw. On April 24, Jackson forwarded all materials relative to Hill—reports, correspondence, affidavits, and the official statement of charges—to Lee. At the end of his accompanying letter, Jackson fired the heaviest shot of the entire controversy: "When an officer orders in his command such disregard for the orders of his superiors I am of the opinion that he should be relieved from duty with his command, and I respectfully request that Genl. Hill be relieved from duty in my Corps."

Lee must have sagged momentarily when he read that statement. His best corps commander wanted his best division commander sent elsewhere—right on the eve of another major campaign in Virginia. Whether Lee in time could have succeeded in bringing about a reconciliation is conjectural at best. Too much had been said and done over too long a period for Hill and Jackson to forget their animosities completely.[16]

While the Hill-Jackson quarrel dominated conversation in the Light Division those first four months of 1863, a variety of activities and events marked life in the winter encampment.

The weather was rarely agreeable. "Nothing but mud and water," a Carolina soldier wrote home. "If the Yankees knew as much about it as I do, they would not be so anxious to get here."[17] Late in January, cheers ran up and down the Federal lines. Confederates soon learned the cause: Burnside had been removed from command of the Army of the Potomac. His successor was the North's highly popular Joseph Hooker—a general whom a Richmond newspaper then characterized as "this second edition of the braggart Pope."[18]

Hill's men continued to occupy themselves with letter-writing, "bull sessions," snowball battles, reading, gambling, singing, trading tobacco for coffee with Billy Yanks across the river, and, of course, much daydreaming. A newspaper correspondent assured his readers that "the boys in camp are, to all appearances, well clad, shod and fed, and seem to be as happy as ever men were, all *Twaddle* to the contrary notwithstanding." Religious revivals were in full swing that winter, "with undiminished interest" manifested by large numbers of soldiers. Men in Lane's brigade built a commodious chapel. Unfortunately, not all of the troops treated it with reverence. Chaplain Francis Kennedy of the 28th North Carolina soon reported dejectedly, "The Church has been so mutilated and abused by the soldiers that Genl. A. P. Hill has ordered it to be nailed up and not opened again."[19]

Disease, the ever-present scourge of the Civil War armies, was not as severe that winter as it could have been. Measles and mumps ran through several regiments. Dreaded smallpox broke out in the Light Division early in March; but as soon as an infected soldier was detected, he was rushed to a quarantine hospital. As a result, one of the Virginians stated, smallpox "created some alarm, but with the exception of destroying the beauty of several soldiers no damage was sustained."[20]

By April an officer in the South Carolina brigade could boast that the troops were physically and mentally strong. "Notwithstanding hunger and cold, the men gained flesh and strength, and, for the most part, recovered from the complaints of the last summer." In spite of a rash of desertions, common to winter quarters, the Light Division had 799 officers and 10,601 soldiers ready for action when the spring campaign began.[21]

Hill himself had much to do throughout this period—in addition to carrying on the running controversy with Jackson—but he was able to spend considerable time with his family. One officer described Dolly that winter as "a very pleasant lady, though not at all pretty." That Mrs. Hill was in the first stages of another pregnancy may have had something to do with the negative impression. Despite the feud with Jackson ("the old humbug," Pender called him), Hill appears to have maintained a warm disposition toward others. A Tarheel soldier assigned to his staff as a clerk recalled that "General Hill and staff were very nice, kind and pleasant."[22]

The division commander made a number of trips to Richmond while the army encamped south of Fredericksburg. "Quite a pleasant" diversion came to Hill in mid-February when the Virginia House of Delegates recognized him as an honorary member. The Speaker of the House stated at the ceremony in the capitol building:

"General Hill, It is with sincere pleasure that I communicate to you the passage of a resolution inviting you to a privileged seat in this House. It is an honor of no ordinary import. It is no mere formal reception of one who has won fame for himself and honor for his state. No words can adequately express the sentiment of abounding gratitude this House entertains . . . and this House, in extending its hospitable courtesies to the chieftains of the army, is proud in recognizing you as one of them, who, though young in years, have already won for yourself the fame and performed the deeds of a veteran."

Hill thanked the members of the House of Delegates for the honor accorded him and added: "The knowledge that what little I have done in the service of my country is appreciated by the legislature of my native state is sufficient to nerve my arm in the future. I shall endeavor to merit the appreciation so generously bestowed." The general then endured what a reporter called "an ordeal of introductions and hand-shaking" by grateful political leaders."[23]

In the middle of that winter recess, rumors circulated that "some of the politicians" in Richmond were trying to have Hill transferred to the Army of Tennessee. Hill paid little attention to the reports. From Richmond he sent a quick note to his sister: "I shall leave for camp on Thursday next—unless sent West, which there is some talk of doing. Russie is charming."[24]

Hill spent much of this time in writing official reports. Interestingly, he did not prepare them in chronological order. On February 25, he submitted a detailed narrative of operations in the August 20–November 5, 1862, period. Three days later came the report of the Seven Days campaign. On March 8 (as noted earlier), Hill started his summary of the Cedar Mountain action through channels.

Three personnel changes on the command level also occupied his attention in late winter. His brother-in-law, Maj. Richard C. Morgan, left the division staff and went to Kentucky to join his now-famous brother, John Hunt Morgan, whose cavalry exploits were the talk of that border state. There was some personal pleasure in Morgan's departure from the Light Division staff. "I think the General will be very glad to get rid of him," Pender declared. "He sees what weak men he has around him and regrets it too." Less than a week later, Hill named Col. William H. Palmer as chief of staff.[25]

The second appointment carried more impact. Col. John Brockenbrough had failed to measure up as a brigade leader. Hill was so disappointed in the Virginian's performance at Fredericksburg that he did not mention Brockenbrough in his official report.[26] A change in command had to be made. On March 5, therefore, Brig. Gen. Henry Heth was ordered to take charge of the Field-Brockenbrough brigade. Nurtured in the same Virginia background, Hill and Heth had been boyhood companions and West Point classmates, and Hill had been a groomsman in 1857 at Heth's wedding. Heth had gone on to achieve a solid record as Lee's quartermaster general in the early days of Virginia's mobilization for war. Lee looked on him almost from the perspective of a patron. Tradition has it that Heth was the only officer whom Lee called by first name.

When he joined the Light Division, Heth was thirty-seven, of medium height, with a bushy mustache and an engaging manner. He was by then "a strongly opinionated man," his biographer has stated, "not always objective in his appraisal of others, but . . . he candidly admitted his own weaknesses and manfully resisted the temptation to take himself too seriously." Hill would find Heth a brave officer who never put self-preservation above duty; but while Heth may have possessed "a fierce loyalty to his subordinates," that same intensity did not always apply to superiors. Although they remained lifelong friends, Hill and Heth would establish no closeness in their military relationships. Perhaps the two fundamentally dissimilar men knew each other too well.[27]

Securing a replacement for the slain Gregg required care. Gregg had been an inspiring general and the men of his brigade were as proud as they were valiant. A mediocre commander would not suffice. Hill had a natural successor in mind, and President Davis gave his approval. Before the war Samuel McGowan had been a prosperous attorney, state legislator, and acting major general of the South Carolina militia. He exuded the air of the gentleman he was. As colonel of the 14th South Carolina in Gregg's brigade, McGowan was perceptive, prompt, and energetic. He was then forty-three, with dark hair swept to one side, intense eyes, and cropped beard. Hill had been watching McGowan ever since the Seven Days campaign. Loud cheers ran through the camps of the South Carolinians at the announcement of his promotion to brigadier general.

As spring approached, Hill became eager for a resumption of military activity. The fight with Jackson had made him tense as well as quick-tempered. Hill half convinced himself that there would not be as much campaigning in 1863 as in the previous year.

Nonetheless, he blurted out on one occasion that he would burn down Washington if he could reach the Northern capital.[28]

Meanwhile, on the northern side of the Rappahannock, handsome and gregarious Gen. Joseph Hooker had spent the period from February to April reconstructing the Federal army, elevating morale from rock-bottom level, and devising an almost perfect plan of attack. Hooker had no intention of butting heads with Lee, as Burnside had done. Instead, his 10,000 cavalry would sweep around the Confederate flank, cut railroads and communication lines, and isolate Lee from Richmond. Hooker next would leave a third of his men—40,000 troops under Gen. John Sedgwick—at Fredericksburg to assail Lee's front. Then Hooker, with about 70,000 Federals, would march upstream, cross the Rappahannock and Rapidan rivers, and curl around the unprotected Confederate left flank. With Longstreet and two divisions campaigning in southeastern Virginia, and Harvey Hill with part of his division combatting a new threat in North Carolina, Lee's reduced forces would also be caught in a mammoth vise.

On April 25, the sun broke through after ten days of rain. As the ground began rapidly to dry, stirrings in the Union camps across the Rappahannock were audible and visible. Federal musketry and cannon fire upriver over the next three days were unmistakable proof that at least a large part of Hooker's army was in motion. Concern spread through the Southern ranks. Where the Yankees were going, and for what purpose, were unknown. One thing was certain: it was time to get ready for battle.

Lee ordered Jackson to place his divisions in front of Fredericksburg and to be prepared for any movement. Hill thereupon was directed to return to the Hamilton's Crossing area and to put the Light Division along the military road behind the ridge where Gregg had waited during the Fredericksburg fight. The twenty-five-mile trek was arduous. For sixteen hours on "a dull, drizzling, uncomfortable" April 29, the men plodded toward the Fredericksburg works. Lt. Chamberlayne of Hill's artillery wrote that "the march was through mud, mud, & cold north east rain, no sleep, no food." Men fell asleep while marching and stumbled headfirst into the mire. The next day, while Federals were reporting Hill to be in the Shenandoah Valley en route to attacking Winchester, the men of the Light Division were drenched by rain as they huddled in muddy trenches at Hamilton's Crossing.[29]

Thanks to Jeb Stuart's vigilance on the Confederate flanks, Lee knew by April 30 that Sedgwick's presence at Fredericksburg was a bluff—that the real threat was to the west in the tangled confusion of the Wilderness. This rough and gloomy woodland, twelve miles long and six miles deep, lay silent along the southern bank of the Rappahannock and the Rapidan. It was a foreboding tract of stunted pines, saplings, dense underbrush, and dark little streams that seemed to begin and end nowhere. A man in the Wilderness could generally see no more than twenty yards. The few winding roads through it were akin to trails through a jungle. It was, in short, no place for an army to be. It was the very place where Hooker had halted his columns. Lee detached Jubal Early and 9,000 troops to hold the heights behind Fredericksburg while he led the rest of his army westward to take advantage of Hooker's tactical mistake.

Crossroads at Chancellorsville

Friday morning, May 1, 1863, dawned clear and beautiful. One of McGowan's soldiers noted that clover fields were in bloom, bees were humming, birds singing, "and all nature seemed to be awaking to joyous and glorious life." The march from Hamilton's Crossing began at four in the morning. Soldiers speculated on their destination and the likelihood of battle as the column wound its way to Salem Church, rested there for two hours, then resumed the march.[1]

Four miles from the crossroads junction known as Chancellorsville, Lee halted the advance. Unsubstantiated reports had Hooker withdrawing back into the Wilderness and consolidating his forces along the Chancellorsville plateau. Hill, Jackson, and Lee conferred over maps for a few minutes, after which Hill sent the brigades of Heth, Lane, and McGowan to feel their way forward up the Orange Turnpike to the crossroads.

Heth's skirmishers made contact quickly and became hotly engaged. Jackson summoned Hill to ride forward with him.[2] In the gathering twilight the two generals reached the front of Hill's line. Skirmishing was heavier. Hill dismounted to check troop dispositions. A Palmetto soldier recalled seeing Hill. "Little Powell" was at an angle in the road, "standing with several officers around him. He was holding the reins of his horse's bridle in his left hand, was talking rapidly, and at the same time gesticulating vigorously with his right hand. We passed near enough to him to note his earnest manner. . . . I remember that his appearance and manner inspired me with confidence, for he impressed me with the conviction that he was a man whose spirit was rising as dangers gathered and thickened, that he meant business, and that he was going to win."[3]

To test the strength of the Federal position, two of McGowan's regiments punched forward en masse. The Carolinians ran into heavy fire and dashed back to cover at the edge of a woods. Jackson ordered Hill to cease the advance and to maintain his present position. Darkness fell with the Light Division poised inside the Wilderness. Hill established his headquarters along the Orange Plank Road east of Jackson's bivouac and waited for Lee's next move.[4]

The army commander by then had determined on the most desperate gamble of his military career. It was obvious to Lee that Hooker had lost both his confidence and his nerve. Lee could now take charge of events. Stuart had brought word that Hooker's right flank, three miles west of Chancellorsville, was dangling "in the air" without any support. Even though Lee had left part of his army to confront Sedgwick, the Confederate leader decided to divide his forces again so as to assail that vulnerable Union flank. Lee, with but 14,000 troops, would occupy the attention of Hooker and half of the Army of the Potomac; Jackson would take 28,000 men (in addition to cavalry screening the column) on a roundabout fourteen-mile march so as to come in on Hooker from the west. Success would depend on Jackson's swiftness and on Hooker's blindness to the division of the Confederate army for a time into three pieces.

Hill got little sleep on the night of May 1–2, for Jackson ordered the troops to begin the long march at 4:30 A.M. Yet the lead elements did not debouch on the road until around seven. Since the Light Division was third in line behind the divisions of Robert E. Rodes and Raleigh E. Colston, Hill had to wait most of the morning. That Saturday he was clad "in his simple 'fighting jacket' and old slouched hat, with no badge of rank save that which God had written on his noble face." He, Lee, Pender, and several other generals sat together on their horses, oblivious to the bullets that occasionally whistled through the area. It was close to eleven when Hill galloped to the head of his division and led the men down the winding road behind Jackson's other troops.[5]

A member of the Richmond Howitzers watched in admiration as the Light Division passed. "Hill's superb troops seemed to be resolved that [Jackson] should not be compelled to wait even a moment for them. They were in light marching order, and I thought I had never seen anything equal to the swinging, silent stride with which they fairly devoured the ground. . . . All was silent as the grave, save the muffled and almost synchronous tread of the thousands of feet in the soft road, and the low clatter or jingle of accoutrements."[6] At Catharine Furnace, where Jackson's column turned southward for a short distance, Federals from Hooker's center attacked under the impression that Jackson was retreating. The 23rd Georgia put up a gallant fight by itself for a time. Archer and Thomas heard the firing to the rear, and Archer turned the two brigades back to help. The Federal thrust was eventually blunted.

The rest of the march was unimpeded but wearying. The sun, beating down from a cloudless sky, got hotter as the hours passed. A soldier in the South Carolina brigade remembered that "the roads were, fortunately, just wet enough to be easy to the feet and free from dust . . . but we suffered for water." He also admitted that marching through the dense, unbroken wilderness, "most of us became completely lost." Hill's brigades trudged some ten miles before resting in the road for a two-hour period. Then the division resumed "its swaying, panther-like step" and continued the circuitous journey until it arrived at the Orange Turnpike. The long column turned eastward for a mile and halted around four o'clock. The march had been "a very fatiguing one," stated a North Carolina captain, but the men had "held up remarkably well and were in very fine spirits."[7]

Jackson had done it! With seventy infantry regiments, cavalry, artillery, and wagon trains, he had marched across the face of three Union army corps with but one momentary challenge. Now he stood massed on the unsuspecting flank and rear of Hooker's army. Yet in spite of the marching feat, Jackson found that getting his vast force spread out in battle array amid dense woods and thick under-growth was cumbersome and time-consuming. Rodes slowly fanned out his men in a battle front two miles long. It took another half hour for Colston to position his brigades behind those of Rodes. To the rear of Colston, Hill was working feverishly to get at least part of his division into a third line of attack. Meanwhile, the sun was beginning to set, Jackson was getting impatient, and the Light Division—as the rear element of the incredibly long column—was strung out all over the route when Jackson was hoping that it would be a solid battle line.

Pender's brigade soon came up and by Hill's order took a position to the north of the turnpike in support of Jackson's left. Heth arrived next and formed his men on Pender's left. Lane was back up the road a distance, McGowan was farther back, while Thomas and Archer were double-timing miles down the Brock Road after assisting in the fight at Catharine Furnace.

At five-fifteen, with but two-thirds of his force at hand, Jackson unleashed the attack. It caught the Federals totally off guard. Some musket shots in the thicket, a broken line of skirmishers, and then the Billy Yanks beheld "a solid wall of gray bearing down upon them like an irresistible avalanche."[8] Rodes's men drove straight through the disorganized Union line, and Colston's wave broke over the few pockets of resistance that developed. Hooker's right flank evaporated in the most thorough stampede of the war. A Pennsylvania soldier angrily noted that an entire Federal corps "rolled rearward, a helpless, crazed mob, intent on nothing but personal safety." For three miles in the face of Jackson's onslaught, this "insanely terrified horde struggled back in awful and unmanly fright."[9] Behind Rodes and Colston, Hill rode up and down the turnpike, occasionally galloping off on either side of the road as he continued trying to get his division concentrated in fighting order.

Lost in the glory of Jackson's greatest flank attack is the fact that it was rather badly organized and somewhat mismanaged. Rodes swept ahead with Colston only 150 yards behind him; as a result, when a segment of Rodes's line slowed down from obstacles or fatigue, a portion of Colston's line bumped into it. Further, Hill's brigades were still deploying when the assault began and were of no use in the first stage of the battle. All too quickly the sharpness of Jackson's offensive broke down.

Success even added to the disintegration. The Federals collapsed so precipitously that Confederate brigades accelerated their advance; and in the gathering gloom and bewilderment of the Wilderness, Jackson's first two lines became hopelessly ensnarled. Units swerved erratically; cohesion gave way to confusion. By seven-thirty Jackson's powerful assault had lost most of its momentum. Rodes's advance had all but ground to a halt. The Federal rout, in the meantime, had run its course. An improvised but strong Union defensive line was taking shape as the firing slackened appreciably.[10]

Available to Jackson was one reserve: the Light Division. Four of Hill's six brigades were nearby. An officer in Rodes's line felt exuberant when his men cleared some woods and he looked back up the road. "A. P. Hill's troops [were] coming up in line of battle—their ranks intact—their alignment as perfect as if on dress parade, their battle flags well advanced to the front, and the sun, now sinking to rest, making their bayonets and rifles shine like polished silver."[11]

"All seemed quiet" when Jackson sent an order for Hill to move to the front "as quickly as possible." Jackson's idea was to send Hill on a moonlight advance along the turnpike and up the roads leading northeasterly so as to cut the Federal line of retreat across U.S. Ford at the Rappahannock. Hill's division commenced deploying carefully in front as the troops of Rodes and Colston withdrew to re-form. According to the Second Corps signal officer, Jackson was sitting on his horse in the road a half mile from Chancellorsville. He "manifested great impatience to get Hill's troops into line and ready to move promptly, and to accomplish this he sent the members of his staff with orders to Hill and other general officers to hurry up the movement."[12]

Jim Lane spearheaded Hill's advance by leading his Tarheel regiments straight down the turnpike. Simultaneously, Col. Stapleton Crutchfield opened fire with a cluster of Confederate cannon. Federal guns immediately replied with a blanketing fire that sent Lane's men scurrying off the road into the woods. Hill rode into the area moments later and dispatched Palmer to ascertain why Lane was not moving forward more promptly. If our guns ceased firing, Lane suggested to Hill, the Federals would likely do the same and the North Carolinians would be able to continue their advance. Hill ordered Crutchfield's gunners to stop shooting. The artillery duel quickly died away, and Hill directed Lane "to push forward vigorously."[13]

The long-bearded Lane began arranging his regiments for battle. He shook out the entire 33rd North Carolina as skirmishers along both sides of the Plank Road. On the right, adjacent to the road, he placed the 37th North Carolina. The 7th Regiment was on the extreme right. Immediately to the left of the road was the 18th North Carolina, with the 28th beyond it. These dispositions constricted Lane's line into a compact half-mile battle front. Nothing was between the Tarheels and the Federal lines except those dense woods, brambles, and creepers. Lane cautioned his troops to be alert and to "fire on the first men they saw coming" toward them.

It was now eight-thirty and a full moon was peeking through the trees. Lane rode back to find Hill and obtain further instructions.

Just as he reached the Plank Road, Lane saw a figure riding slowly down the road. It was Jackson. The Carolinian informed Jackson that he was looking for Hill to determine if he should advance his brigade or await further orders. "Push right ahead, Lane," Jackson stated with urgency in his voice.[14]

A shirt-sleeved Hill then rode down the Plank Road with several members of his staff. He halted a few yards behind Jackson to continue directing the placement of his brigades. Then he rode up to the corps commander. The calm that had marked Jackson all that trying day was gone. He was now excited: he sensed the kill if pressure against the Federals could be maintained. Jackson returned Hill's salute and asked, "How long before you will be ready to advance?"

"In a few minutes," Hill replied, "as soon as I can finish relieving General Rodes."

"Do you know the road from Chancellorsville to the United States Ford?" Jackson next asked.

Hill paused a second. "I have not traveled over it for many years."

Jackson then turned in the saddle to his young engineering officer. "Captain Boswell, report to General Hill." Then Jackson looked hard at Hill and exclaimed: "Press them, General Hill! Press them and cut them off from the United States Ford!"[15]

At nine-fifteen the Light Division began groping through the dark unknown. Jackson and his staff rode behind the 18th North Carolina during its slow advance, then passed through its lines. They met several of the regimental officers out front. "General," one of them asked, "don't you think this is the wrong place for you?"

"The danger is all over! The enemy is routed!" Jackson shouted. "Go back and tell A. P. Hill to press right on!"[16]

Jackson and his aides rode into the woods; Hill, accompanied by a contingent from his staff, trotted off in the same direction, in sight of Jackson some twenty-five yards distant. The two parties felt their way through the forest for perhaps a quarter mile. Commands of Federal officers, and the ring of axes biting into wood to be used for barricades, grew louder. Hill's chief engineer, Capt. Conway Howard, actually rode into a Union battery and was taken prisoner. Hill had now ascertained the location of the Federal line in his front. He turned his horse and started back to the Confederate position. Off to the side he could hear Jackson doing the same.

The sharp crack of a musket broke the silence. Then a volley of rifle fire from nervous Southerners rolled through the woods. Confederate musketry triggered Union artillery, and a salvo of shells ripped through the trees and ricocheted up the road. Hill and Jackson were now together, their entourage numbering more than a score of horsemen. The party veered away from the turnpike, riders seeking cover as they proceeded rapidly through the darkness toward their lines. Both sides were now picking up the fire and exchanging hurried shots. In that excited atmosphere, Capt. Alfred Tolar of the 18th North Carolina recalled, "the tramp of thirty horsemen advancing through a heavy forest at a rapid gait seemed to the average infantryman like a brigade of cavalry."

Hill galloped in front of the other riders and sought to make a safe avenue of return in the hundred yards they yet had to go. "Cease firing! Cease firing!" he called out to Lane's men. Maj. John D. Barry of the 18th North Carolina was as edgy as his men. He knew that Federal cavalry were roaming the woods, and he had no intention of being deceived. "Who gave that order?" he bellowed. "It's a lie! Pour it into them, boys!"[17]

Only twenty yards separated foot soldiers from mounted officers when a solid sheet of musketry exploded from the Tarheel unit. In a second the Hill-Jackson party ceased to exist, amid a turmoil of anguished shrieks, piercing cries, animals pitching, men falling to the ground, other riders reeling in the saddle as mounts bolted in every direction. Several of the horsemen were killed by the volley, and fourteen dead horses were later found in the area. Somehow Hill missed being shot. At the close-range fire, he instinctively leaped from his horse and lay face down on the ground for a few seconds. He then remounted hastily and rode toward Lane's position with a cry half in anger and half in shock: "You have shot my friends! You have destroyed my staff!" He came upon one of his favorite aides, nineteen-year-old Capt. Murray Forbes Taylor, who was pinned beneath his dead horse. Hill was in the process of extricating Taylor when a courier dashed up and announced in a trembling voice that Jackson lay seriously wounded some fifty yards away.

"Help yourself," Hill said to the half-freed Taylor. "I must go to General Jackson." Then, as an afterthought, Hill stated in a hushed voice, "Don't tell the troops about the General."[18]

Hill raced to the site where two staff officers were bending over Jackson, who was lying at the foot of a pine tree. He had been shot an indeterminate number of times. At the sight of the bleeding general, Hill's animosity toward him momentarily vanished. He had

criticized Jackson, belittled him, sought to have him publicly reprimanded. Now, with the chieftain down, genuine concern and respect
took the place of hostility. Hill knelt beside Jackson, expressed "great
regret" at his wounding, and murmured almost helplessly: "I have
been trying to make the men cease firing." Hill then asked Jackson
if the wound were painful.

"Very painful," Jackson replied in a steady voice. "I think my arm
is broken."

Hill carefully removed Jackson's gauntlets, which were blood-
soaked. Then he took off the general's saber and belt. Next, in a
characteristic display of compassion, Hill sat down on the ground
and cradled Jackson's head in his lap while he gently tore open
Jackson's left sleeve and tried with handkerchiefs to stem the
hemorrhaging. At one point Hill glanced up and ordered Capt.
Benjamin W. Leigh of his staff to secure a surgeon as well as an
ambulance. Capt. R. H. T. Adams, a center of controversy in the
Hill-Jackson feud, bent over and offered his flask of brandy. The
pious Jackson hesitated, then drank a small swallow.

Leigh soon returned with Dr. Richard R. Barr, an assistant surgeon
in Pender's brigade. Jackson did not know him and whispered in-
quiringly to Hill, "Is he a skilled surgeon?" Hill replied that he stood
high in his brigade. Besides, Hill added, nothing was going to be
done of a drastic nature until Jackson's personal physician, Dr.
Hunter McGuire, arrived. "Very good," Jackson said.

Barr prepared a tourniquet for Jackson's badly damaged left arm.
Other ministrations could not be made at that place and time. The
anxious party said little as they waited for an ambulance.[19]

How perilous the situation was quickly became apparent. Captain
Adams heard strange noises in the woods. He left Hill and Jackson
and rode fifteen or twenty yards to investigate. Hill suddenly heard
his signal officer shout: "Halt! Surrender! Fire on them if they don't
surrender!"

Hill looked up and saw two Federal soldiers, standing a few yards
away and looking at the Confederates in bewilderment. In a soft
voice Hill told two kneeling orderlies to arrest the enemy soldiers.
The Billy Yanks dropped their weapons without resistance. Their
presence made it imperative to secure this exposed position where
Jackson lay. Hill eased out from under the general. "I will try to
keep your accident from the knowledge of the troops," he said.

"Thank you," Jackson replied.[20]

It was the last communication between the two commanders.

Hill was now in temporary charge of Jackson's corps. On foot, and with pistol drawn, he rapidly made his way to Heth's position and superintended some adjustments in the line for an expected Union assault. Hill had turned and was starting back to the spot where Jackson lay when a quick burst of artillery fire came from across the way. Searing pain shot across the back of his legs below the knee. A shell fragment had ripped off his boot tops. Hill reached down to feel for blood. He could detect none, yet both legs were so numbed that he could barely stand. He limped for a few steps, but the pain in one leg forced him to sit down on the stump of a large oak. Upon removing the boot, he saw blood on the underclothing.[21]

Word reached Hill that his chief of staff had also been injured. Colonel Palmer was speeding to join Hill when his horse was killed, and Palmer was thrown to the ground so violently that his right arm was dislocated from the socket. He would be lost to Hill for months.[22] In a little while, Hill slowly mounted his horse. He rode to the front, one foot sticking out of the stirrup. Notwithstanding intense pain, he oversaw the disposition of Pender's brigade on Lane's left, with Thomas taking position to the left of Pender. Captain Taylor rejoined Hill and asked if he had been wounded. "Yes," Hill replied, "I have been shot in the calf of the leg. I fear the wound is serious enough to incapacitate me from continuing in command."[23]

Jeb Stuart would have to take charge of Jackson's corps. Hill summoned Adams and sent him out the Ely's Ford Road to find the cavalry leader. Sometime near ten-thirty, Stuart wrote, Adams "reached me post-haste" with Hill's "urgent demand for me to come and take command as quickly as possible." A five-mile gallop brought Stuart to the Chancellorsville lines. Jackson had by then been taken to a safe place, but Hill was still present. He formally turned over command to Stuart and was borne to the rear on a litter.[24]

The Confederate attack of May 2 inflicted heavy losses on the Federal army and bent Hooker's line almost to the breaking point. Nevertheless, Hooker had a solid opportunity to turn defeat into victory the following day. On May 3 the Union army at Chancellorsville still greatly outnumbered the Confederates, two Federal corps had not yet been engaged, and Hooker stood squarely between the forces of Jackson and Lee. A Federal counterattack in strength all but certainly would have been successful. It never occurred.

Sunday the third began with a cool mist hovering at ground level. It was only with effort that Hill could walk, yet he painfully made his way back to the front to be in a position for "advising in all the important operations of the corps." Stuart was glad to have him nearby, but he did not need Hill's strategic advice. Hooker provided the Confederates with a grand opportunity by abandoning the high ground at Hazel Grove, one of the few clearings in the Wilderness where artillery could operate effectively. Stuart promptly crowned Hazel Grove with guns, which blasted the Union defense simultaneously with massive assaults by Southern infantry.

The Confederates attacked in three lines, the Light Division (under Heth) constituting the second wave. Despite Hill's absence, the division performed with the heroism one expects of a veteran unit. The battle line was one and a quarter miles wide. Some 150 yards in front was a strong Federal position of logs and brush. "The breastworks were charged and carried," Heth reported, "the men never hesitating for a moment, driving the enemy before them and pursuing him until a second line was reached, which was in like manner broken." A brutal fire poured into the division from both flanks. Orderliness began to distintegrate. As Hill's division slowly inched forward amid gunfire, a widening gap developed between Archer's left and McGowan's right.

Federals soon poured toward it in a counterassault. "After a desperate and prolonged fight, without supports or a piece of artillery to aid them, but on their part subjected to heavy artillery fire of from ten to twelve pieces, these gallant brigades fell back in order to the breastworks from which the enemy had been driven," Heth stated proudly. The brigades of Lane and McGowan, along with the 40th and 47th Virginia, charged through the woods. "I cannot conceive of any body of men," Heth declared, "ever being subjected to a more galling fire than this force." This attack broke the Union line, but concentrated fire soon drove the Confederates back to the protection of their lines.[25]

Hill's brigades hammered the Federal positions throughout the morning. For hours fighting was intense. Confederates never cut off the Federals from U.S. Ford, as Jackson had wished, but they mauled Hooker's army every foot of the way toward the crossing. That night men in the Light Division beheld a frightful scene. Flames from uncontrollable fires had spread through the undergrowth and over entrenchments. Wounded and dead soldiers on both sides were cremated. A South Carolina officer later noted that "it was pitiful to see the charred bodies, hugging the trees, or with hands outstretched, as if to ward off the flames."[26]

For the next couple of days, while Lee sent part of his army back toward Fredericksburg to blunt an advance by Sedgwick's wing of the Union army, Hill's division maintained its position in the woods near the Chancellorsville crossroads. Hill himself was carried from place to place in an ambulance wagon as he did what he could to assist Stuart. "I was very grateful," wrote Stuart, "for circumstances might have arisen making his presence necessary."[27] In midafternoon of the fifth, rain began falling in torrents. Under cover of darkness and the downpour, the Union army fell back across the Rappahannock. The Chancellorsville campaign was history.

Hill joined Lee and Stuart at dawn on May 6 and asked to return to command. Lee quickly gave consent and Hill took charge of the Second Corps. His legs were still tender and sore, but he was able to ride. Throughout that rainy day, Hill shifted his men and wagons back toward the Orange Turnpike. The next day Confederate soldiers wearily trudged eastward to their camps around Fredericksburg. Hill established his headquarters at the home of Col. William Proctor Smith. For a few days, a Carolinian wrote, the men "all took a holiday . . . as a little, bright island in a sea of strife."[28]

The human toll in the battle had been horrifying. Hooker's army suffered more than 17,000 losses. An officer in the 14th Connecticut acknowledged: "They have beaten us fairly; beaten us all to pieces; beaten us so easily."[29] Lee's casualties were 12,821 men; 416 of the dead and 2,171 of the wounded were in Hill's division. Among the fatalities was battery commander Greenlee Davidson, one of three brothers who would die in the war. The 55th Virginia lost 140 of 300 engaged. Every officer above the rank of lieutenant in that regiment was killed or disabled.[30]

On May 8 Hill submitted what he called "a very imperfect sketch of our operations" at Chancellorsville.[31] The report was strangely silent about Jackson's wounding and value. In all likelihood, Hill was so busy with details relative to corps command that he entrusted his official summary to a member of his staff.

Bulletins from nearby Guiney's Station on Jackson's condition became ominous. Pneumonia followed the amputation of the general's left arm. Jackson lapsed into delirium. In his final hours he blurted out: "Order A. P. Hill to prepare for action! Pass the infantry to the front immediately! Tell Major Hawks . . ." The devout Jackson had always hoped to die on the sabbath. In midafternoon of Sunday, May 10, the great soldier received his wish to "cross over the river and rest under the shade of the trees."[32]

Whatever grief Hill felt he kept to himself. He spent that Sunday immersed in administrative details relative to Jackson's corps, pausing only long enough that night to exclaim to artillery captain Willie Pegram over what a smashing victory Chancellorsville had been. The next morning Pegram wrote his sister: "There is quite a gloom over the army today, at the news of Jackson's death. We never knew how much we all loved him until he died. His death will not have the effect of making our troops fight any worse. . . . Every one here looks to A. P. Hill as the man to fill his place, & after he once gets a shew, the enemy will fear him as much as they ever feared Jackson."[33]

For the next two weeks at Fredericksburg, the chief topic of conversation around mess tables and campfires was who would succeed Jackson. As speculation continued, jealousies and bitterness toward Hill developed—especially among Jackson's disciples. "He behaved very coarsely to all the members of Jackson's staff," one of them charged. Kyd Douglas commented that it was grievous to notice that "A. P. Hill had not forgotten or forgiven." Cartographer Jed Hotchkiss informed his wife that while Hill was a good military leader, he was not a "Man of God" and did not wear the "Sword of the Lord and of Gideon." (In other words, Hill was not Jackson.) In mid-May, Dorsey Pender told his family of a gross fabrication against Hill. "Some designing person is trying to injure Gen. Hill by saying that [Jackson] frequently said that he wanted Ewell to have his Corps. After it became apparent that he would die, he was delirious most if not all of the time. It is strange what a jealousy exists towards A. P. Hill and his Division, and for what cause I cannot see, unless it is because he and it have been so successful. I hope to stick to him for he sticks to me."[34]

Meanwhile, Lee was carefully weighing his options in the matter of a new corps commander. He had six candidates to succeed the fallen Jackson: A. P. Hill, Richard Ewell, D. H. Hill, Richard H. Anderson, Lafayette McLaws, and John B. Hood. Hill was the front-runner. "I think upon the whole," Lee stated in a letter to Jefferson Davis, that Hill "is the best soldier of his grade with me."

On the other hand, the man who had been closest to Jackson, beginning with the 1862 Valley campaign, was "Baldy Dick" Ewell.

He was now able to walk for the first time since losing a leg heroically at Groveton the previous August. Lee thought him "an honest, brave soldier, who has always done his duty well." Many in the Second Corps regarded Ewell as the "logical successor" to Jackson.[35]

Anxious days became weeks. Then, on May 23, came an announcement from headquarters: Ewell had been promoted to command of the Second Corps. Disappointment was keen among Hill's followers. Yet it was short-lived. On the morning of the next day, Hill was summoned to Lee's tent. A brief but friendly exchange opened the conversation, for Lee had deep respect for his division chief and Hill openly admired the commanding general. Lee soon came to the point. For some time he had thought that his two corps were unwieldy. Reorganizing the army into three corps would promote better cohesion and efficiency and perhaps make Jackson's death less acute. Lee wanted Hill to command the Third Corps. The position entailed promotion to lieutenant general; and since authorities in Richmond had already approved the plan, the assignment would take effect immediately.[36]

Hill had no reservations about the new post. He welcomed additional responsibilities, and he was excited at the prospect of being thereafter one of the three generals in whom Lee had most confidence. The other two corps commanders were old acquaintances. With Ewell he had always enjoyed good relations. The situation with Longstreet was not as cordial. They had feuded openly a year ago, and Longstreet still sniped at Hill—and others—in official reports. Hill's natural courtesy would be tested anew.

The appointment of Hill to corps command sparked negative reaction from some quarters. Generals Longstreet and Porter Alexander complained that other field officers were more qualified, and that Hill had been chosen primarily because he was a Virginian.[37] No evidence supports those statements. Granted, Hill had never commanded more than one division in prolonged action; but neither had anyone else under consideration. The overriding issue in this matter was Lee's feelings; and if the army commander did not feel a special affinity for Hill at this point in the war, he certainly felt comfortable with him. President Jefferson Davis also took offense at the charge that Hill's Virginia heritage was a determining factor. In a postwar letter the president stated that "there had been complaints in certain quarters that Virginia was getting more than her share of the promotions. But the truth was that A. P. Hill was so clearly entitled to the place, both on account of his ability as a soldier and the meritorious services he had rendered, that General Lee did not hesitate to recommend him, and I did not hesitate to make the appointment."[38]

Hill's promotion to corps command did not cause any lessening of his tough standards of discipline. On the day after his advancement, he received through channels an official report that the 58th Virginia had lost its colors while hastily retreating after incurring heavy losses. Hill rejected the colonel's request for a new flag. He brusquely endorsed the report: "I am constrained to recommend to the general commanding that the regiment not be allowed to carry a color until it has redeemed its own by capturing one in battle."[39]

Such concern over regimental behavior was the stuff of which excellent brigadiers and fighting division commanders were made. Lieutenant generals in charge of corps had of necessity to focus on the bigger picture. They were expected to give more attention to planning and organization—with correspondingly less involvement in combat leadership.

Hill would never quite master that transition.

Gettysburg:
The First Day

In the last days of May 1863, while Federals reported Hill en route to assist in the lifting of the siege of Vicksburg, Miss., Dolly Hill joined her husband at Fredericksburg.[1] The thirty-seven-year-old lieutenant general had regrettably little time for his pregnant wife, however. He had to organize a new army corps, and do it quickly.

Hill faced a larger task than simply commanding three times more men. Within Lee's organizational structure, a corps was a physically complete army unto itself. It comprised three infantry divisions and five battalions of artillery. The corps had its own quartermasters' stores, ordnance, wagon trains, medical facilities, and other support services. As military units, the corps in Lee's army related to one another only through army headquarters. The commanding general could, of course, shift the divisions of a corps at his discretion. Yet rarely did Lee make such intrusions in the chain of command. He was content to have his lieutenant generals take all responsibility for the condition, disposition, and performance of every man from the newest recruit to the most experienced major general.

The Third Corps was composed of the Light Division, a new division to be organized, and Richard H. Anderson's division from Longstreet's corps. Anderson's division, intact and seasoned, required no alterations. Its battle-hardened brigades were under proven generals: William Mahone, Edward A. Perry, Carnot Posey, Cadmus M. Wilcox, and Ambrose R. Wright. Some observers believed that the troops of the division were better than its leader. That was an unfair conclusion. Anderson was a quiet, colorless, but well-liked professional soldier from South Carolina. He had served so long under Longstreet that he was accustomed to "Old Pete's" slow, methodical ways. Hill's tendency on occasion to leap before he looked initially disturbed Anderson, but the self-effacing general kept silent —on that and all other matters. "His capacity and intelligence were excellent," Longstreet's chief of staff wrote, "but it was hard to get him to use them."[2]

Hill's first priority, as he saw it, was to find a successor to lead the beloved Light Division. He had personally molded that unit into the most famous division in Confederate service. Hill's intense desire to preserve its "pride in its name . . . its 'shoulder to shoulder feeling,' and good feelings between the different brigades" was understandable. Hill carefully pondered the matter of his successor. The problem, in his view, was seniority in rank versus proven ability. He then wrote a lengthy letter to Lee. Heth and Pender were the two obvious choices for major general, Hill stated. Heth, the senior brigadier was a "most excellent officer and gallant soldier." On the other hand, "Gen. Pender has fought with the Division in every battle, has been four times wounded and *never* left the *field*, has risen by death and wounds from fifth Brigadier to be its senior, has the best drilled and disciplined Brigade in the Division, and more than all, possesses the unbounded confidence of the Division."

What Hill proposed was, in his mind, a logical compromise: take two brigades (Archer's and Heth's) from the oversized Light Division, unite them with two other brigades, and give them as a division to Heth; the remaining four brigades (Pender's, Lane's, McGowan's, and Thomas's) would then constitute the Light Division, under Pender. Lee agreed without hesitation, and the necessary orders were issued.[3]

This arrangement was orderly in some respects, problematical in others. The four best brigades in the corps, all from Hill's old division, were kept together and placed under the best division commander. The other two brigades from the Light Division were linked with two brigades that were strangers to the Army of Northern Virginia. One was a North Carolina brigade under suave James J. Pettigrew, the most educated of all Confederate generals; the other was the Mississippi brigade of Joseph Davis, the president's nephew. It too was untested; and while Davis was a congenial and conscientious officer, he had never led troops in battle. At the head of the division was Henry Heth, who had been with Lee's army exactly three months. It would have been more equitable if three brigades from Hill's division had been used as a base for each of the two constructed divisions.

Hill's corps was a veritable maze of units. There were thirteen brigades from eight different states. Half of them had never worked with the other half, and only eight of the brigades were under seasoned leaders. Hill was going to have to treat the corps with meticulous care for it to gain maturity with a minimum of trauma. Time was needed, but in the late spring of 1863 the Confederacy had little of that to spare.

Fortunately, Hill's artillery components were superb. Col. Lindsay Walker was in charge of the corp's twenty batteries. Hill and Walker had worked together for a year and genuinely respected each other; and when Hill gave Walker a free rein in the handling of the seventy-five guns, Walker fulfilled every expectation in his quiet, efficient way. Three of the battalion commanders were among the best in the Confederate armies. William T. Poague, a Washington College graduate, seemed always to be in the thick of action and performing gallantly. South Carolina artillerist David Gregg McIntosh, "a man of superior intellect, educated, dignified, and rather reserved," was as experienced as he was capable. McIntosh's brother-in-law, Willie Pegram, was a shy scholar who had left the University of Virginia to go to war. During battle, his spectacles were invariably beclouded by artillery smoke. As a result, he often resembled a philosopher musing over the world's problems as he cleaned his glasses and directed cannon fire.[4]

The personal staff that Hill assembled late in May remained with him thereafter. It consisted of Lt. Col. William H. Palmer, chief of staff; Maj. W. Norborne Starke, assistant adjutant general; Capts. Murray Forbes Taylor and Francis T. Hill, aides; Maj. R. J. Wingate, inspector general; Capt. Richard H. T. Adams, chief signal officer; Maj. E. Baptist Hill, chief commissary; Capt. William S. P. Mayo, assistant commissary; Maj. James G. Field, chief quartermaster; Capt. Henry M. Field, assistant quartermaster; Dr. John W. Powell, chief surgeon; Dr. Francis L. Frost, assistant surgeon; Sgt. George W. Tucker, chief of couriers.[5]

Some resentment over assignments to command in Hill's corps was inevitable. Archer thought he should have been named a division commander. The strong-willed Marylander reacted noticeably when he was bypassed. Pender wrote his wife: "I fear my promotion has caused Archer to be cool towards me. His manner the last time we met was not as cordial as heretofore, and he seemed very much embittered and rather down on Gen. Hill and I suppose because I will not join him in the latter, he will grow cool towards me."[6]

The army commander was aging noticeably at this time, but he was in a joyful mood. He firmly believed that "the Army of Northern Virginia, as it then existed, could accomplish anything."[7] Formal reviews seemed to Lee one of the best ways to inspect the new divisions, so a number of such ceremonies occupied the last days of May. Hill accompanied Lee and other generals on at least three reviews. At one of them, Lee happily began riding "at a sweeping gallop." A large entourage of riders sought to keep pace; by the end of the ride, however, only Hill among the generals had kept up with Lee.

Hill had a narrow escape on the final day of May. He rode out to inspect several of the Rappahannock crossings. As usual, he was wearing a calico shirt and shapeless hat. At the last stop he led his horse into the river before galloping back through the woods to his headquarters. A short while later, a Confederate picket shouted across the Rappahannock: "I say, Yanks, why didn't you shoot General Hill? He stood right here half an hour ago."

Federals hollered back just as good-naturedly that they had seen a man pass along their front; but supposing that he was merely the officer of the guard, they paid him no mind.[8]

By early June, the Confederate army had refurbished itself and was better equipped and in better spirits "than at any period prior or subsequent." One of Hill's surgeons predicted that Lee's forces would "fight better than they have ever done, if such a thing is possible."[9] Such optimism played a part in Lee's decision to launch a second invasion of the North. The continuing hope of securing foreign recognition and aid for the Southern cause underlay the invasion plan. Other factors were the need to do something to reverse the blue tide pressing the beleaguered Confederacy at every point; the desire to get the war out of Virginia, at least for a while; and the opportunity to gather needed supplies from the lush Pennsylvania countryside. Finally there was always the possibility of capturing Washington and bringing the war to an end.

On June 3, Lee boldly began withdrawing most of his army from the front of Hooker's numerically superior forces. Longstreet and Ewell were to head west toward the Valley. Hill would remain in the lines at Fredericksburg, Lee informed him, "making such disposition as will be best calculated to deceive the enemy, and keep him in ignorance of any change in the disposition of [my] army." Should Hooker strike across the river, Hill was to fall back along the Richmond, Fredericksburg & Potomac Railroad. Should the Federals disappear from Hill's front, he was to give pursuit and keep Lee informed. The last paragraph in the directive to Hill clearly reflected Lee's confidence in his new corps commander. "You are desired to open any official communications sent to me, and if necessary act upon them, according to the dictates of your good judgment."[10]

The lead elements of Ewell's corps were barely out of sight when Federals opened a furious artillery bombardment of Hill's position, spliced a pontoon bridge over the Rappahannock, and sent a contingent of troops to the west bank of the river. Hill naturally became concerned. The country was brushy and woody; by June, honeysuckle and its cousins had reduced visibility to zero. Hill's new corps was all that stood between the mighty Army of the Potomac and Richmond. Hill's task was to guard a twenty-mile front despite these problems.

As Lee halted his westward advance, Hill promptly shifted Heth's division closer to Fredericksburg and the major river crossings. Hill was finally able to convince his wife that she had to go to the rear. The pregnant Dolly, growing larger and more dependent each day, had lingered imprudently, Pender wrote to his beloved Fanny. "I know you are too good a wife to have given me as much anxiety and trouble as she gave the General."[11]

By the afternoon of June 6, no more Federals had crossed the river. Hooker had merely been probing, Lee concluded, and Hill's corps could handle the situation. The Confederate westward advance thereupon resumed. For the next four days, from his headquarters on Howison's Hill, the new lieutenant general conducted demonstrations to keep Hooker off balance. "With uncanny vigilance," one writer asserted, Hill "prevented any communications between the two sides of the river, capturing the scouts who had been sent out by Hooker to ascertain Lee's movements." One of McGowan's men wrote contemptuously that the Yankees during this period did not engage "in anything more hostile than music and cheering, or, on one or two occasions, such a bold display of pickets as to require a few shells at our hands."[12]

Lee's plan of march into the North was a bit complicated, but sound. Longstreet would remain at Culpeper to give aid to Hill, should Hooker lunge southward. Ewell, with a brigade from Stuart paving the way, would move rapidly northward through the Shenandoah Valley, cross the Potomac, and advance through Maryland into Pennsylvania. Then Longstreet would also start northward. While Longstreet acted as a screen, Hill would move westward from Fredericksburg and follow in Ewell's footsteps. Longstreet's corps would bring up the rear as the whole army carried the war onto Northern soil.

Hooker, meanwhile, had sought to obtain permission for a new drive on Richmond, but an uneasy Federal government had prevented it. Not until June 13—a full ten days after Lee's army started for the Valley—did Hooker realize that Lee had stolen a march on him. That night the Federals began withdrawing from the Fredericksburg ridges they had occupied for months. Lee had outmaneuvered Hooker as convincingly as he had outfought him at Chancellorsville.

"Yankees have recrossed the river and disappeared, save their pickets," Hill reported. He deduced correctly that Hooker was belatedly in pursuit of Lee. Therefore, on the fourteenth, Hill started his divisions to rejoin the main body of the army. Anderson took the lead; Heth was to follow the next day; Pender would depart Fredericksburg when it was certain that the area was no longer in danger from Federals. Optimism prevailed in Hill's ranks. "What a fine appearance the regiment made as it marched out from its bivouac," a member of the 26th North Carolina remembered. "The men beaming . . . ; the colors flying, and the drums beating; everything seemed propitious of success."[13]

Toughened by hardships and hunger, exposure and danger, Hill's troops were welded together—in spite of the newness of corps organization—into an emotionally compact unit. They continued the march for mile after mile, day after day, through heat and through rain; and they did it with a minimum of complaints and only brief spurts of straggling.

The route of march passed first through the battlefield of Chancellorsville, where the two armies had grappled six weeks earlier.

Each man was left to his own thoughts as he viewed torn woods, dead horses, and half-buried dead. Late on June 17, Hill reached his hometown. Culpeper retained little of its prewar beauty. So "mutilated by barbaric invasion" and "devastated by pestilence and famine" was the town, a newspaperman wrote, that "sack cloth and ashes fill the place of wine and scarlet." From Culpeper, the Third Corps crossed the Blue Ridge Mountains at Chester's Gap. The columns strained under oppressive heat. "The powers of the troops were taxed beyond endurance," one of Mahone's Virginians wrote. "Men were falling from sunstrokes."[14]

At ten in the morning on June 20, the head of the column reached Front Royal and created "an immense sensation. Children all went over to see the troops—bad to worse." Two miles north of Front Royal, the two forks of the Shenandoah River merged to form the main stream. A pontoon bridge had been built to permit the army to cross. Passage was restricted, and soon thousands of men were sprawled over nearby fields and woods as they waited their turn. Large numbers of bats blanketed one clearing. As they began darting here and there close to the ground, soldiers struck at them with sticks and muskets. Hill and his staff rode into the area, saw the excitement, and dismounted. Quickly they "entered into the sport with as much zest as the boys. The General laughed immoderately at the performance of the soldiers and laid aside all the graver cares of war."[15]

Lee joined the Third Corps as it wound its way past Berryville and Shepherdstown toward the river that divided Union from Confederacy. On the morning of June 23, with the Potomac before them, Hill issued a proclamation to the corps: "We will move at 2 o'clock to cross the Potomac and conquer a glorious peace on their own soil!" Col. Abner Perrin of the 14th South Carolina responded in a sense when he wrote: "I do not suppose that any army ever marched into an enemies country with greater confidence in its ability to [conquer] and with more reasonable grounds for that confidence."[16]

Even an outsider could sense the confident feelings of the troops. Lt. Col. Arthur J. L. Fremantle of the British army had journeyed to America to observe the Civil War. He caught up with the Confederate army at this point, and he was impressed when he saw Pender's division leading Hill's corps on the march. "The soldiers of this Division are a remarkably fine body of men, and looked quite seasoned and ready for any work. Their clothing is serviceable

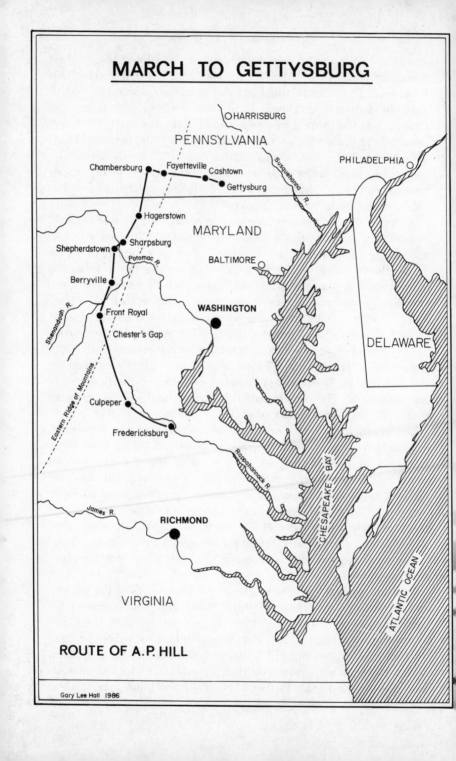

. . . but there is the usual utter absence of uniformity as to colour and shape of their garments and hats; grey of all shades, and brown clothing, with felt hats predominate."[17]

Pender's old brigade got its new commander the same day, when newly promoted Alfred M. Scales joined the march. Scales, in his mid-thirties, was an attorney and former U.S. congressman who had enlisted as a private and risen rapidly to a level befitting his talents. A regimental band serenaded him that evening, and "Gen. Scales made a happy speech."[18]

Rain was falling again on June 24 when Hill and Longstreet went to Lee's headquarters for a conference. As the three men were talking, young Leighton Parks, whom Lee had met on the Maryland invasion the previous year, came to the tent with a bucket of raspberries as a present. Lee picked up the lad, kissed him, and insisted that Parks join them for lunch. Lee sat the boy on his knee and played with him until Hill demanded equal privilege. Then Longstreet, his family wiped out by yellow fever a year earlier, asked for the same pleasure. When it was time to return to matters of war, a smiling Hill ordered a horse brought up for the lad. Parks was too small to mount, whereupon Lee placed him in the saddle. "Give him time," Lee said laughingly, "and he'll do for the cavalry yet!"[19]

The next day Hill's men arrived in the rain at Hagerstown. Hill, "looking ready for a fight," an Alabamian noted, galloped into the center of town to meet Lee. Since Chancellorsville, one of Hill's persistent concerns was the absence of Willie Pegram. The young artillery wizard had been at home in Virginia trying to overcome a fever. Now, on June 25, as Lee and Hill walked their horses through a large gathering of curious Hagerstown citizens, the army commander turned to Hill. "I have good news for you," Lee said. "Major Pegram is up."

Hill smiled. "Yes, that *is* good news."[20]

Later in the day Hill and Longstreet caught up with Ewell's Second Corps, and on the twenty-sixth the Confederate army advanced for the first time into Pennsylvania. Gen. Carnot Posey of Anderson's division informed his wife that "every effort is used to check any depravations. No houses or barns are burnt, no women & children turned out of doors. . . . So you see we are not barbarians nor do we imitate the infamous example of our enemy."[21]

Lee, using the easternmost range of mountains as a screen, continued the northward advance. At Chambersburg, Hill turned his corps eastward for four miles and encamped near Fayetteville. While the men were settling down to rest after marching 157 miles in twelve days, Gen. Isaac Trimble (who had been traveling with Ewell) went to see Lee. The Marylander suggested that a brigade be sent to occupy Baltimore, an unexpected move Trimble felt would "rouse Maryland and thus embarrass the enemy." Lee apparently saw some merit in this wild plan and asked Hill, "the only corps commander near," if he could spare a brigade. Hill thought the idea preposterous; he replied that giving up a brigade would "reduce his force too much." The suggestion was abandoned.[22]

Lee's orders of June 28 have always engendered some confusion, at least that portion pertaining to Hill. The overall plan was for Ewell to drive on Harrisburg, with Longstreet in support. Hill was to move "in the footsteps" of Early's division of the Second Corps, "cross the Susquehanna downstream from Harrisburg, and seize the railroad between Harrisburg and Philadelphia." Late that night, however, Lee received a report that the Union army (now under Gen. George G. Meade) was closing in faster from the southeast than he had thought. An anxious Lee changed the schedule: Ewell was ordered back to the main body; the eastward advances of Longstreet and Hill were cut back; the Confederate army was to concentrate east of the mountains as quickly as possible.[23]

That night Dorsey Pender wrote his wife. "I never saw troops march as ours do; they will go 15 or 20 miles a day without leaving a straggler and hoop and yell on all occasions." For this, all the credit should go to the corps commander. "Genl. Hill thus far has managed the march of his Corps and I think will give as much satisfaction as Lt. Gen'l. as he did [as] Maj. Gen'l." This was to be Pender's last letter.[24]

It was raining again on Monday the twenty-ninth. Hill's corps headed eastward on what amounted to a reconnaissance in force. Hill cautiously pushed his troops through the pass of South Mountain. The men were unusually well-equipped with arms, and they enjoyed the novel sensation of having full stomachs. Heth's division, under orders from Hill, marched to Cashtown. Pender was to follow on the thirtieth, with Anderson's division to proceed to the village the next day.

Cashtown is situated at one of the few gaps in the Pennsylvania mountains. It was important as well because several roads led from it, and one of them snaked eight miles to another community, called

Gettysburg. Nestled in farm country, Gettysburg was a town where no fewer than ten major roads converged. Two educational institutions and a shoe factory were there, and a railroad had been started west of town.

With Pender's division at hand, Heth gave permission for Pettigrew's large brigade to proceed to Gettysburg, "search the town for supplies (especially shoes), and return the same day." The long march over the hard macadam roads of the North had played havoc with the scraggly foot coverings of Lee's men. Clothing was becoming more ragged each day. Heth was among those affected. In Cashtown he obtained a new hat. It was too big, but an aide stuffed papers inside the hat band until it fit.[25]

A number of writers have questioned the propriety of Heth's order. He was sending 2,400 men on a sixteen-mile round-trip in debilitating humidity to look for supplies in a town through which Jubal Early's men had passed four days earlier. And sending a brigade into the unknown without cavalry support was, at the least, foolhardy.

Stuart's whereabouts at this stage of the campaign was unknown and critical. His cavalry were supposed to be the eyes and ears of Lee's army. Yet after Lee crossed the Potomac, Stuart took off on a deep raid around the Union rear. This reduced the Confederate army to the status of a blindfolded giant groping in enemy territory. Lee tried to make light of the predicament. "The enemy is a long time finding us. If he does not succeed soon, we must go in search of him."[26] Nevertheless, the commander was apprehensive.

Pettigrew never got any shoes at Gettysburg. On the western outskirts of town, his North Carolinians bumped into Federal cavalry. Sounds back in Gettysburg suggested Union infantry as well. Pettigrew knew that Lee did not want to bring on a battle until the Confederate army was consolidated. So he withdrew and rode back to Cashtown to inform Heth that Federals of undetermined strength were in Gettysburg.

Heth was listening to Pettigrew's report when Hill joined them. Hill quickly dismissed Pettigrew's concerns. "The only force at Gettysburg is cavalry," he said, "probably a detachment of observation. I am just from General Lee, and the information he has from his scouts corroborates what I have received from mine—that is, the enemy are still at Middleburg and have not yet struck their tents."

Heth said, "If there is no objection, then I will take my division tomorrow and go to Gettysburg and get those shoes!"

"None in the world," Hill replied without hesitation.

Pettigrew still feared the worst. Capt. Louis G. Young of his staff had closely observed Federal movements around Gettysburg. Pettigrew summoned Young to the conference with the hope that his testimony as to Union numbers might be more convincing. Young emphasized that the Federal movements were those of well-trained soldiers, not home guard. Hill was not persuaded. "I still cannot believe that any portion of the Army of the Potomac is up," he declared. Then he added: "I hope that it is, for this is the place I want it to be."[27]

Hill then ordered Anderson's division to start to Cashtown at dawn. He duly informed Lee of the situation and stated his intention "to advance the next morning and discover what is in my front."[28]

Lee was not overly concerned at Hill's report because he had received word from an informant that Meade's army was still some distance to the south. This was true of the main body, but both Lee and Hill were unaware of two factors. First, while there were "only some Federal cavalry" in Gettysburg on June 30, those horsemen were two tough, full brigades under Gen. John Buford, and they were armed to the man with breech-loading carbines, which meant that they could fire fourteen rounds per minute, while Confederates would be lucky to get off three shots in the same time. Second, the collision between Pettigrew and Buford had caused Meade to accelerate his army's march. By the morning of July 1, the lead elements of the Army of the Potomac were filing through Gettysburg to the heights immediately west of town.

July 1 marked the start of one of the most famous and most costly battles in all of history. Hill began the battle under a handicap: he was ill. The malady could have been upset stomach, diarrhea, simple exhaustion, or a flare-up of the old prostate problem. Whatever the illness, Hill was confined to his cot for the first part of the morning, and he looked "very delicate" to many who saw him. By his own admission, he was unwell the entire day.[29]

Hill's corps came alive that Wednesday as a predawn shower settled the dust. Heth was under orders from Hill to be ready to march at 5:00 A.M.; and by an unusual directive from the corps commander, each man who wanted an issue of whiskey at that early hour was to receive one. Hill's final instructions to Heth were succinct and to the point: "Do not bring on an engagement." Yet both generals still believed that nothing but some cavalry and local militia were inside Gettysburg.[30]

The caprices that plagued Henry Heth's career showed themselves in the first movements of the day. His division of 7,500 men was unevenly divided among four brigades. Rather than place his strongest brigades in the lead, Heth simply determined the order of march based on where the troops had bivouacked along the road the previous night. Thus, the brigades of Archer and Davis took the lead. They were the worst choices. Barely 1,000 Alabama and Tennessee veterans composed Archer's battered brigade, and its commander on July 1 was sick with fever. As for Davis's Mississippians, two of its regiments were spanking new for combat, and its brigadier was going into battle for the first time as well. Behind them were the troops of Pettigrew and Brockenbrough, with Pegram's artillery in support. An hour behind them, Hill also sent Pender's division of 6,000 Confederates as a backup, if needed. McIntosh's artillery battalion accompanied Pender's division.

In an orthodox pattern on each side of the road, the lead brigades sent out skirmishers in three lines. Men hopped over fences, darted through underbrush, and disappeared momentarily in woods as they led Heth's division eastward. "Birds were singing their joyous notes," one of Hill's Tarheels observed, "and thousands of hearts were beating high with hope."[31]

The day was now clear and becoming hot, and by ten o'clock the Southerners had covered five miles. Heth's first two brigades came to an eminence within sight of Gettysburg. A battery of six Federal guns began raking the Confederates. Men broke and sought cover. Quickly, Pegram unlimbered his twenty-gun battalion along the fence-lined road and returned the fire. The Federal artillery did not increase in volume. Heth, too eager to succeed in his first demonstration as a division commander, concluded on his own that only a thin screen of Federal cavalry stood in front. He then compounded his error by ordering the troops of Archer and Davis down the wooded slope toward Willoughby Run. The half-mile battle line, wrote Heth, was "to make a forced reconnaissance, and determine in what force the enemy were."[32]

Archer's men, on the right of the road, climbed a fence and crossed a little stream with no opportunity to get much-desired water. The Confederates then rushed through woods—straight into a sheet of musketry on both front and flank. Too late they recognized the Federals as members of the celebrated Iron Brigade of Gen. John F. Reynolds's I Corps. They were veteran infantry, not cavalry or militia, and they were in strength. Now under a crossfire on the flank as well, Archer's troops ran pell-mell out of the woods, downhill, and across the brook. A momentary traffic jam occurred. Federals closed in and overran the whole brigade. Archer, "in pathetic exhaustion" and mad as a hornet, was among the seventy-five men captured.[33]

The immaculately dressed brigadier was being led to the rear when up rode a former West Point classmate, Gen. Abner Doubleday.

"Good morning, Archer," Doubleday exulted. "How are you? I am glad to see you."

Archer shot back: "Well, I am not glad to see you by a damned sight!"

Doubleday straightened in the saddle, turned to an officer and said: "Take him to the rear. Take him to the rear."[34]

Over on the left side of the road, Davis's Mississippians advanced with Archer's men and outflanked the Union right. Their first volleys of musketry were accurate and telling. The front line of the Federals fell apart. Davis's green troops then sprang forward across open ground and, despite fire from a Union battery, sent blue lines reeling backward. Federal cannon now opened on the brigade with fire accurate enough for the Confederates to seek protection. The untutored Davis learned of a deep cut in the unfinished railroad nearby. His two regiments on the right dashed to the cover of the cut. That was another mistake. Now Federal infantry swarmed back, got to the edge and, from above, began to fire into Southerners trapped in the earthen ditch. The 6th Wisconsin began enfilading from the east end of the cut. Davis's men broke and ran back toward their lines. Over 200 of his 1,500 men were captured in the railroad cut, in addition to other casualties.[35]

With unintended humor, Heth later reported: "The enemy had now been felt, and found to be in heavy force in and around Gettysburg." Heth now did what he should have done in the beginning: he stood poised and awaited orders from Hill. He hastily brought up

Pettigrew and Brockenbrough; and with what was left of Archer's brigade, Heth built a new line in a wooded ravine in anticipation of Pender's arrival. McIntosh's batteries lumbered onto the field, set up behind Heth, and, with Pegram's guns, shelled the Federal position for two hours. Pegram later reported firing an incredible 400 rounds in the course of the day.[36]

Back in Cashtown, Hill had spent half the morning hours trying to regain his strength. The sound of gunfire to the east was unsettling for him. As Hill pondered the situation, Lee and his staff made their way down the crowded pike into the village. Lee had been riding leisurely with Longstreet farther up the road when he heard firing in the direction of Gettysburg. Now the sound was heavy and continuous, which indicated a severe engagement. Although Lee was outwardly calm, he too felt Hill's anxiety and excitement.

From Hill's paleness and slow movements, it was evident that Lee's corps commander was not well. After an expression of solicitude, Lee asked the reason for all the gunfire. Hill replied that he was not sure, because Heth had been instructed to ascertain what force was at Gettysburg and, if he found infantry opposed to him, to report the fact at once, without forcing an engagement. I will investigate myself, Hill said.

Painfully, he mounted his horse and started eastward on the Gettysburg road. His face was ashen, but direct action was for Hill a stimulant. Unlike Lee, he wanted a general engagement; and now that it had come, Hill was freed of the restraints of being a corps administrator. He was going to direct troops in battle again. Hill soon joined Pender's division, pushing its way eastward through a stream of stragglers and wounded men. Lee was a few minutes behind him.[37]

The two generals met with Heth amid Pegram's batteries on a ridge just west of Willoughby's Run. When they learned what had happened earlier in the morning, Hill immediately ordered Pender to form his brigades behind Heth and to prepare for an assault. Lee reiterated that he did not want to initiate full battle until more of his army was up and more information about the enemy's strength was known. So Lee and Hill waited, and watched the continuing long-range artillery duel.

One humorous incident broke the tension for a moment. The 16th North Carolina was lying in reserve near Pegram's guns. When a

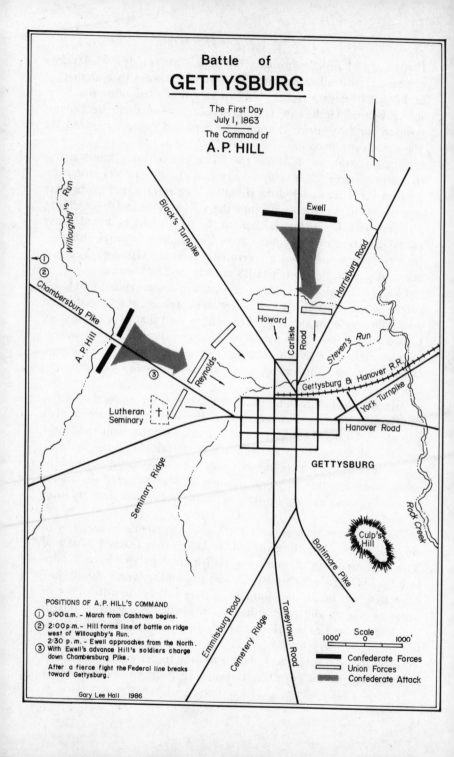

Battle of
GETTYSBURG

The First Day
July 1, 1863

The Command of
A. P. HILL

Willoughby's Run

Black's Turnpike

Ewell

Chambersburg Pike

Harrisburg Road

A. P. Hill

① ②

③

Howard

Carlisle Road

Steven's Run

Reynolds

Gettysburg & Hanover R.R.

York Turnpike

Lutheran Seminary

Hanover Road

Seminary Ridge

GETTYSBURG

Culp's Hill

Rock Creek

POSITIONS OF A.P. HILL'S COMMAND

① 5:00 a.m. – March from Cashtown begins.

② 2:00 p.m. – Hill forms line of battle on ridge west of Willoughby's Run.

2:30 p.m. – Ewell approaches from the North.

③ With Ewell's advance Hill's soldiers charge down Chambersburg Pike.

After a fierce fight the Federal line breaks toward Gettysburg.

Gary Lee Hall 1986

Emmitsburg Road

Cemetery Ridge

Taneytown Road

Baltimore Pike

Scale
1000'   0   1000'

■ Confederate Forces
□ Union Forces
▨ Confederate Attack

Federal shell exploded nearby, a fragment scratched a captain's head and produced blood. The officer darted for the rear, shouting: "I'm dead! I'm dead!"

The regimental colonel calmly beckoned to two stretcher-bearers. "Go and take that dead man off—if you can catch him."[38]

Around two-thirty, the Federal right flank began giving way toward Gettysburg. The reason for this became joyfully evident a few minutes later: Ewell and the Second Corps were coming in on Hill's left. They quickly formed a right angle with the Third Corps and plowed into the Federal flank. For a while Billy Yanks gallantly maintained two-thirds of their position. Heth rushed up and asked permission to join in with this attack by Robert E. Rodes's division. "No," Lee replied. "I am not prepared to bring on a general engagement today. General Longstreet is not up."[39]

All of a sudden, Lee saw something that changed his mind. Rodes's brigades were pressing the Federals. This meant that the battle had now become general, and the whole Federal line seemed about to give way. Good fortune so often blessed the Army of Northern Virginia at dark moments. Now occurred such an instance. Less than half of Lee's army was on the field, but a two-pronged attack from north and west could be Second Manassas all over again! Hill, who rode up at that moment, received quick orders: commit Heth and Pender to battle.[40]

Heth's men, in a solid line, swept over fields where they had been defeated in piecemeal fashion earlier. Firing as they advanced, and yelling like demons, the Southerners soon encountered an equally strong blue line. This area—two parallel ridges with open land, wheat fields, patches of woods, and fences running everywhere—became the stage for a stand-up fight involving thousands of infantrymen. A private in the 26th North Carolina observed: "Never was a grander sight beheld. The lines extended more than a mile, all distinctly visible to us. . . . The roar of artillery, the crack of musketry and the shouts of the combatants, added grandeur and solemnity to the scene."[41]

Pettigrew's men charged into the famous Iron Brigade and a sister unit. One of those Billy Yanks wrote that "as soon as the Confederates had reached within a few yards of the top of the ridge, the men arose and delivered their fire directly in their faces, staggering them and bringing them to a stand, and from that moment the musketry rattle and artillery fire kept up such a constant roar as would bewilder men under any other circumstances." In the 26th North Carolina, eleven color-bearers and youthful Col. Henry Burgwyn were killed. In places, opposing sides were pouring volleys into each other at no more than twenty yards.[42]

Slowly, grudgingly, the first Union line withdrew, and soon the second line seemed ready to give way. The Confederates were succeeding, but they were taking heavy losses. At that critical moment, a bullet struck Heth in the head and he toppled unconscious from the saddle. He appeared dead. In reality, the paper stuffing in the oversize hat he was wearing slowed down the bullet to no more than impact velocity. Even though Heth remained "insensible for some hours," paper wadding had saved his life.[43]

Although Pettigrew temporarily assumed command of Heth's division, that unit had fought itself into weariness. Hill, closely watching the action, now turned to Pender's men. They had double-timed much of the distance from Cashtown to Gettysburg, only to wait impatiently under fire for hours before given their chance. Pender's troops made a well-ordered advance through the ranks of Heth's "much exhausted and greatly reduced" division. Colonel Perrin, commanding the South Carolina brigade, wrote: "The poor fellows could scarcely raise a cheer for us as we passed. . . . We continued to advance under a most terrible shelling & musketry fire for two miles & without firing a gun until we came upon the enemies strong position."[44]

Pender's troops charged into the mouths of Federal cannon. A Union artillery officer remarked that his guns were "cutting great gaps in the front line of the enemy. But still they came on, the gaps being closed by regiments from the second line, and this again filled by a third column which was coming over the hill. Never have I seen such a charge. Not a man seemed to falter. Lee may well be proud of his infantry."[45]

Scales's brigade formed the extreme left of the attack. It held its fire, marched through a storm of musketry, and advanced toward McPherson Ridge. The effort was a disaster. "Only a squad here and there marked the place where regiments had rested," Scales (himself wounded) reported. The brigade's 500 casualties included every field officer.

Still the Confederates pressed the attack. The color-bearer of the 13th North Carolina suddenly had his right arm torn from the socket by an artillery shell. The youth hardly paused, but shifted the flag to the other arm and bounded ahead with the shout "Forward, forward!" The Federal lines, assailed on two sides, broke. Union soldiers in increasing numbers dashed toward the rear. Perrin's brigade had lost half its strength in the fighting, but two of its regiments pursued Federals into Gettysburg itself as "a broad tumultuous stream of panic-stricken men" fled down the road. Of the 16,000 Federals who had gone into battle in front of Gettysburg that morning, according to one of their number, "scarcely five-thousand remained with their colors."[46]

It was after four o'clock. Hill—as well as Lee—wondered where the main body of the Union army was. "The want of cavalry had been and was again seriously felt," Hill remarked. As a pause developed in the battle, Hill formed his brigades back on Seminary Ridge. Lee joined him there, and the two generals watched retreating Federals form on the hills to the south behind the town. Hill thought that "the rout of the enemy was complete."[47] Lee knew better: the Federals were falling back to regroup along a more defensible line.

Enough daylight remained for one more lunge that might bring total victory. Lee asked Hill if his men could advance from their present position across the town valley and seize the opposite hills. At no time in the Civil War did anyone ever question Hill's pugnacity; but he was also one of the most solicitous commanders where the condition of his men was concerned. The divisions of Heth and Pender had taken frightful losses. Those still in line had been marching and fighting since five that morning. In addition, they were almost out of ammunition and no replenishment was in sight. Anderson's division was still miles from the battlefield and would not get up before dark. No, sir, Hill replied to Lee, my men have had all they can take for one day.

Lee then turned to Ewell and suggested that the Second Corps seize the Cemetery Ridge area before the Union army arrived in force and made a stand. Lee's failure to give a direct order and Ewell's decision not to push forward constitute one of the war's most controversial incidents.

With nightfall, a merciful quiet settled over the battlefield. Hill's men on Seminary Ridge could clearly hear Federals across the way fortifying their lines, and the rumble of artillery and tramp of infantry through the dark hours gave unmistakable proof that most of Meade's army was now on the field. Nevertheless, Lee had no intention of disengaging from the contest. "Gentlemen," he said to Hill and Longstreet, "we will attack the enemy in the morning as early as practicable."[48]

Hill's role in the July 1 fighting at Gettysburg was pivotal; and in the postwar debates among former Confederates over who was responsible for Southern defeat in the battle (no Southerner dared admit that the superiority of the Union army had anything to do with it), Hill received his share of condemnation. Much of it is undeserved. Partisan ranger John S. Mosby concluded that "great injustice" had been done in accusing his idol, Jeb Stuart, of dereliction at Gettysburg, and he sought to set the record straight. His book, however, is so prejudiced against everyone else that the text becomes hysterical in places. Over thirty pages concentrate on Hill's "failures." And even Harry Heth, trying to shift weighty responsibility from his own shoulders, speculated after the war "whether if Stonewall Jackson had been in command of Hill's corps" on July 1, "a different result would have been obtained."[49]

The ever-critical Jed Hotchkiss, Jackson's map maker, charged that Hill "should have awaited the concentration of Lee's army," and that Hill's impetuosity led directly to "the fierce combat" at Gettysburg. Gen. Porter Alexander soundly criticized Hill in his memoirs. "Hill's movement was made of his own motion. . . . Lee's orders were to avoid bringing on an action." The heavy losses that the Second and Third Corps took on the first day, a Virginia artillerist added, "reflected upon the tactical skill of their commanding officers."[50]

In this postwar quest for scapegoats, Hill's critics ignored a number of facts, plus a telling statement. The latter came from Lee. "It had not been intended to fight a general battle at such a distance from our base," he wrote in a long memorandum to President Davis, "but finding ourselves unexpectedly confronted by the Federal army, it became a matter of difficulty to withdraw through the mountains with our large trains." Moreover, said Lee, collecting needed supplies in the face of the enemy was dangerous. "A battle thus became, in a measure, unavoidable."[51]

Overlooked as well is that success, not defeat, crowned Hill's efforts that first day at Gettysburg. Hill thought his actions on July 1 "a brilliant victory," which resulted "in the almost total annihilation of the First Corps of the enemy." Victory was not so overwhelming, but

Hill's men were prominent in inflicting 2,450 casualties among the 8,200 Federals engaged.[52]

Viewed against the alternatives he faced, Hill's actions were sound if not commendable. For example, he could have remained poised at Cashtown. To have done so would have blocked the passage of Longstreet's corps and brought two-thirds of Lee's army to a standstill deep in enemy territory. Hill received no specific instructions for July 1 principally because Lee stood greatly in need of information and put Hill in charge of an eastern probe to provide more data as to the Federals' whereabouts.

Hill was constrained by the knowledge that Lee did not wish to bring on a general engagement. This led him to dispatch only a brigade on June 30 and only a division on July 1. As an afterthought, because he was always concerned for the safety of his troops, Hill on July 1 ordered Pender to follow Heth at a respectable distance and Anderson to stand in readiness; this would normally be considered good preparedness. Hill's critics assert, however, that sending so many men to reconnoiter to the east caused a massive collision that precipitated a major battle, with terrible consequences for the Confederacy. Hindsight has rarely worked more accurately.

On the night of June 30, Hill dutifully informed Lee that he intended to make a probe toward Gettysburg at dawn. Hill also warned Heth not to seek a full-scale battle. So confident was Hill that all would be well that on the morning of July 1 he planned to go with Pender's division (second in line of march), rather than ride with the lead elements of the Third Corps. Hill did become culpable once Heth became locked in combat. Maj. David McIntosh was correct in his analysis that Hill "was too sturdy a fighter, unwilling to give ground, and he must have thought the alternative in the face of increasing numbers, was between a vigorous offensive and abandoning his ground."[53]

Bystander to Defeat

Around six in the morning on Thursday, July 2—a day that promised early to be sultry and humid—Hill ordered Anderson's division to relieve Heth's battered brigades at the front. Then he rode over to Lee's headquarters on Seminary Ridge. The two generals presented a contrast to an officer standing nearby. Lee wore a uniform coat buttoned to the throat and was "the best looking man in the universe." Hill was wearing one of his calico shirts and appeared "rather slender." Soon Longstreet, "fat and full," joined them for a discussion of the day's planned attack. At one point Lee sat on a fallen tree and placed a map in his lap. Hill and Longstreet stood on either side, and the three generals intently studied the chart. Soon they saluted and started off on foot in different directions.[1]

Hill's line was the center of a slowly curving arc. Ewell's men, on the left, faced south and southwest. On Ewell's right was Pender's division, which extended along Seminary Ridge until it linked with Anderson's men on the far right. They were spread out facing the center of the Union army. Longstreet's corps was to be on Hill's right, "in a line nearly at right angles" to the Third Corps.[2]

The battle strategy that Lee developed for that day called for Longstreet to assail the Federal left by advancing diagonally up the Emmitsburg Road. Hill's corps was to "cooperate" in the assault. Pender would make a demonstration in his front and exploit any advantage he encountered. Anderson's division, which still had not been tested in Pennsylvania, was to hold until Longstreet's attack reached its sector. At that point, Anderson's troops were to assist the First Corps. As Hill understood Lee's plan, "I was to co-operate with [Longstreet] with such of my brigades from the right as could join in with his troops in the attack."[3] Heth's division, under Pettigrew, was to be held in reserve because of losses suffered the previous day.

Hill meticulously checked troop dispositions and ensured that fifty-five cannon were strategically placed along the lines. Then he took a position to await a resumption of the battle. He waited and waited, as the temperature soared above eighty-five degrees. The idle hours of morning passed with Longstreet slowly moving into position. At one point a more concerned Lee looked toward the Union lines and said to no one in particular: "I wonder where General Longstreet can be."[4] For Hill, the agonizing delay must have provoked memories of Mechanicsville and Frayser's Farm, when opportunity was lost for want of promptness. Hill's enthusiasm waned with the hours of inactivity, which may have been a major factor in his lackadaisical performance that day.

Lee's entourage of staff officers and foreign observers soon joined Hill on the eastern edge of Seminary Ridge opposite the Codori house. The air was stifling. Hill asked an aide for some water. The man returned, bearing "some dirty stuff in a pail, with an apology that no good water was to be had within a mile." Did the general wish to wait for better water?

"Oh, no," Hill replied. "That will do very well," and he drank long from the bucket.[5]

Occasionally, Lee and Hill had brief conversations. Most of the time the two generals sat on tree stumps or under shade trees and said nothing. Into that tension soon rode Jeb Stuart, reporting for duty. Lee raised his arm and exclaimed with unconcealed irritation: "General Stuart, where have you been? For three days not one word from you!" Whatever reply Stuart made was unimportant at the moment.[6]

Near four in the afternoon, the sound that Lee had awaited all day finally came: Longstreet's batteries opened fire like some mammoth thunderstorm to the south. Hill promptly notified his artillery chief: "General Longstreet is about to attack the enemy's left. Watch his movements and aid him as much as possible." The guns of the Third Corps soon joined in the bombardment. Presently Hood's division of the First Corps charged across the open ground and disappeared in rapidly accumulating battle smoke. McLaw's division followed suit an hour later. Hill rode along part of his front during this early stage of the fighting. As the struggle intensified, he demonstrated that the previous day's illness was gone by climbing a tree to observe Longstreet's attack from a better vantage point.[7]

Longstreet's men drove hard, but by six o'clock the attack had snarled in a wheat field near Anderson's right flank. It was time for Hill's troops to enter the contest. Anderson's division sprang into action—and everything quickly became a mess. It was Hill's understanding that Anderson would be under Longstreet's control during the action, while Longstreet assumed that Hill would direct his own support. Anderson therefore independently attacked the left-center of the Union lines hastily formed in a peach orchard.[8]

His brigades had to sweep 1,400 yards across uncovered ground. They reached the Emmitsburg Road with a loud shout and surged forward toward a swale along Plum Road. But the brigades were not utilizing strength by attacking en masse. They moved en echelon, each unit individually pivoting, with brigade commanders giving what directions they could according to the dictates of the moment. Federal fire quickened as Confederates started up an incline. Wilcox's Alabamians drove hard for a spot a mile north of Little Round Top. Col. David Lang's small brigade of Floridians backed them up, with Ambrose Wright's Georgians advancing on the left.

Now Federals came from behind their works in assaults of their own. Wilcox's men met the first successfully, then fell back when a Union brigade struck his right front. The Floridians and Georgians fought with equal valor, also without support. It was a standoff battle that faded away with daylight. According to Wright, "The enemy rushed to his abandoned guns as soon as we began to retire, and poured a severe fire of grape and canister into our thinned ranks as we retired slowly down the slope into the valley below." Hill noted that when the units received no support, "the ground so hardly won had to be given up, and the brigades occupied their former positions in line of battle."[9]

Just at sundown Hill received news that caused his spirits to sag. His best division commander and close friend, Dorsey Pender, was grievously wounded. Pender had been riding down his line to prepare his Light Division for attack. He was oblivious to Federal shells exploding in the area. Suddenly a shell fragment tore through his thigh. The wound was crippling, and it was the kind of injury that often did not respond well to the treatments of that day. Hill voiced his concern to Pender and, at the same time, directed Pettigrew to assume command of the Light Division.

The second day's fighting at Gettysburg came to an end with little accomplished. Anderson's three brigades of 4,100 men had lost 1,561 killed, wounded, and missing. Cadmus Wilcox seethed with anger for years over the loss of so many (577) of his Alabamians. "I am quite certain," he wrote Lee after the war, "that Gen'l A. never saw a foot of the ground on which his three brigades fought on the 2nd of July. I may be wrong [about] Gen'l A., but I always believed that he was too indifferent to his duties at Gettysburg."[10]

Left to his own devices in his first battle under Hill, Anderson was indecisive and sloppy in his actions. Even one of his privates saw that the division's advance "lacked concert of movement" and resulted in "a large sacrifice" of life.[11] Anderson did not even send in all of his brigades, as Hill desired. Mahone's Virginians never saw action, for reasons still not clear.

Hill's leadership on July 2 also left something to be desired. Assigned to a cooperative role, he seemed never to get caught up in the fever of battle. Maybe it was the fact that the one division in his corps with which he was totally unfamiliar in combat was making the attack. Perhaps, in spite of the surface cordiality between Hill and Longstreet, mutual resentment still smoldered, so that neither made any attempt to clarify the responsibility for Anderson's division. In addition, Hill could have ordered Heth's division, or Pender's, to enter the action. Possibly Hill, remembering the carnage of the previous day, when he had attacked without specific instructions, decided to do nothing without directives from Lee.

If Hill displayed weakness in coordination, however, so did Lee. The army commander was the only one who could have reorganized the Confederate movements once the fighting began. Had Lee wanted Hill's entire corps to cooperate fully with Longstreet, he could have ordered it forward. The second day's struggle at Gettysburg was, in essence, a series of errors on the part of all the Confederate leaders.

By midevening, breezes had blown away the gunsmoke, and the stars shown brightly. Hill rode again to Lee's headquarters, where he shook hands with a number of Stuart's officers, now on the scene. Lee was busy in his tent, but Hill's voice carried to him. With an affection that was unusually warm—almost fatherly—Lee came out, made his way through a group of officers, grasped Hill by the hand, and said: "It is all well, General. Everything is well."[12]

Robert E. Lee was not himself at Gettysburg. The absence of cavalry, Lee's unfamiliarity with the ground, and his location between the Union army and South Mountain all inhibited his mobility. A debilitating attack of diarrhea also hampered Lee, and evidence continues to point toward coronary problems as well. Lee in Pennsylvania abandoned the great turning movements that had brought him victory after victory. The one time he had previously used a head-on assault—at Malvern Hill—had been so disastrous that it should have taught him an unforgettable lesson. At Gettysburg, however, he fought as he had never fought: a relentless hammering of a superior enemy. The first day brought only limited success: the second day brought even less. Lee's resolve was unshaken. He determined to renew the battle on the third day.

Longstreet argued (insubordinately, at times) against a continuation of the struggle. The burly corps commander repeated the obvious: the Confederates were attacking larger numbers on ground of the enemy's own choosing. It would be much better for the Army of Northern Virginia to withdraw, pick a strong defensive position, and force Meade to come to it. Lee listened patiently, quietly refused to reconsider, and, late on the night of July 2, formulated his battle plan.

The center of the Union line would be the target. Longstreet's corps was in the best condition to make the assault, but Lee probably reasoned that Longstreet's lack of faith in the plan made it dangerous to entrust the attack solely to his men. Lack of confidence is half of defeat, says an old military axiom. Hence, Lee directed the divisions of McLaws and Hood (the latter under the indifferent Evander Law) to remain where they were. The lone division of Maj. Gen. George E. Pickett from the First Corps would be in the attack, with Heth's division (under Pettigrew) substituting for McLaws, and Pender's division taking the place of Law. It appears that Lee selected the units simply because of their position in the line. The lack of veteran leadership at the head of Pender's two brigades gave Lee concern. He solved this problem by ordering Maj. Gen. Isaac Trimble, then without a command, to take charge of the two units.

On the surface, this shifting gave Longstreet 11,900 men—substantially the same strength he had with Hood and McLaws. However, the force was unbalanced and disorganized. Forty-seven depleted regiments were involved. Pickett's fifteen regiments were all Virginians and had seen no serious action since Antietam Creek ten months earlier. Trimble's ten regiments were North Carolinians and as valiant as any units contributed to the cause by the Old North State. Two of Pettigrew's brigades were small and under the command of colonels. One of them, led by Col. Robert M. Mayo, was simply in no condition to make an assault. Pettigrew's remaining brigades were Davis's Mississippians, still bleeding from the wounds of July 1, and Pettigrew's own badly mauled Tarheel regiments. In fact, half of Pettigrew's division had been cut down in the first day's fighting, so that only 4,300 men were ready for duty on the third day.

The raggedness did not end there. Nine brigades were to attack, two were to be in support, and the eleven were to converge in their assault from three different directions. The one division that was to go in as a unit—Pettigrew's—was at the moment the weakest in Lee's army.

Friday, July 3, was beautifully clear, with bright fields and a fair landscape at first giving little hint of the intrusion of war. On Lee's left, Ewell waged a three-hour artillery duel with Union batteries before sending Confederate infantry attacking up the east side of Cemetery Hill. Ewell's men gained temporary control of some Federal works. However, coordination floundered and the breakthrough proved disastrous. The early-morning hours passed on the rest of the field with two giant titans staring menacingly at one another. Lee, Longstreet, and Hill met late in the morning in front of Pettigrew's division to discuss battle details. Lee repeated the general battle plan. In contrast to Longstreet, Hill enthusiastically endorsed the assault idea and begged Lee to let him commit the entire Third Corps to the action. "No," replied Lee. "What remains of your corps will be my only reserve, and it will be needed if General Longstreet fails." On the other hand, should the assault succeed, Hill again was to send in Anderson's division as a support for Longstreet.[13]

After Hill and Longstreet received orders from Lee on the partial merger of their two corps, they strolled away a short distance and sat down on a fallen log. The conversation they had was calm and somewhat lengthy as the two men reached agreement on the disposition of the troops. Hill then rode off to his corps, announced the forthcoming action, and told the brigade commanders to take their instructions thereafter from Longstreet. Hill and Longstreet had parted without even a shake of hands, and they exchanged no communication the remainder of the day. Hill assumed that Longstreet was to be in command of all the brigades involved in the attack. Longstreet appears somehow to have concluded that Hill would have a degree of control over his own units. Thus, neither man really took charge.

Pettigrew's four brigades were to compose the front line. Trimble's two brigades were to form to the right and rear. This deployment made the second line shorter than the first, but no one caught the error. To the right of Pettigrew and Trimble, Pickett placed his three brigades in two lines. Wilcox's brigade from Anderson's division took position as a flank guard. The infantry were ordered to remain out of sight until Confederate artillery could silence the Federal batteries across the way. Then the two wings were to charge in converging lines toward a small clump of trees in the center of Cemetery Ridge a mile away.

The only action in Hill's front that morning was a local affair involving the Bliss house and barn between the lines in Pettigrew's front. The two buildings had changed hands several times over the past twenty-four hours. A Federal regiment (14th Connecticut) came out to remove the two nuisances by setting them afire. Several Federal cannon provided support. Hill galloped up to Capt. Joseph Graham of his artillery. "Can you reach the enemy from here?" Hill asked.

Graham answered affirmatively. Hill thereupon ordered him to open on the position with six guns. "In less time than it takes to tell," one cannoneer remembered, 100 guns were involved in a half-hour duel that wasted a lot of ammunition for both sides. With the two buildings ablaze by Federal orders, uneasy silence settled again over the field.[14] Lee, Hill, and Longstreet then made a final inspection of the swelling open ground over which the Pickett-Pettigrew assault was to be made.

At one o'clock Longstreet fired two signal guns. Moments later, both sides erupted in a cannonade involving perhaps as many as 250 guns. Men crouched low and hugged the ground as shells whistled and exploded around them. Smoke rolled over the scene of action and concealed everything from sight. "For two hours," a Federal colonel noted, "the roar was continuous and loud as that from the falls of Niagara." One of Hill's soldiers wrote: "The very earth shook beneath our feet, and the hills and rocks seemed to reel like a drunken man. . . . the shrieking of shells, the crash of falling timber, the fragments of rock flying through the air . . . the splash of bursting shrapnel, and the fierce neighing of wounded artillery horses, made a picture terribly grand and sublime."[15] The battle area then grew quiet again.

Somewhere around three in the afternoon the Confederate brigades moved out of the woods and started the journey across open ground to Cemetery Ridge. The traditional picture of the Pickett-Pettigrew charge is of a 1,000-yard-wide line marching forward with "the deliberation and accuracy of men in drill."[16] It was not that way at all. The two wings started separately, with the advance of most of Pettigrew's division ragged and uncertain from the start. Confederate artillery was of little help. The batteries were lined up along Seminary Ridge, which actually falls away from Cemetery Ridge as it goes northward. Neither Longstreet nor Hill did anything to coordinate the attack, strengthen its support, or create a diversion. The infantry was left alone to attempt the impossible.

Six brigades of 10,000 men were in the front line. The second line, three brigades of 5,000 troops, was shorter and followed 200 yards to the rear. Wilcox's brigade was posted behind the right of the column. Both of its flanks dangled in the air. Federal artillery opened a concentrated fire on the unprotected Confederates. "Great gaps are made every second in their ranks," a Union officer wrote, "but the gray soldiers close up to the centre and the color-bearers jump to the front, shaking and waving the 'Stars and Bars.' " Yet "the men are dropping like leaves in autumn."[17]

The Confederate line began arcing forward, the right and left being more advanced than the center. A veritable storm of artillery fire and musketry was ripping through the Confederate ranks. Three horses were killed beneath Pettigrew during the charge; he was leading his men forward on foot when he was struck in the hand by grapeshot.[18] Trimble received so severe a leg injury that the limb was later amputated. Col. James K. Marshall, who assumed command of Pettigrew's troops, was knocked from his horse by a shell blast. Somewhat unsteady, Marshall remounted his horse and was shot dead a few seconds later.

For about fifteen minutes, lines on the Confederate left sent "a close and unremitting fire" into each other. Mayo's Virginia brigade, assailed on two sides, broke to the rear in near-panic. Davis's Mississippians soon followed suit. Now devastated by the storm of gunfire tearing through its line, Pettigrew's division faltered and began to fall back. This forced Trimble's men to do likewise. Wilcox, meanwhile, had failed to move forward to the support of Pickett, who was encountering equal disaster. Federals now began overlapping Pettigrew's left. Simultaneously, as Hill watched helplessly from the rear, Pettigrew's division—and Pickett's as well—simply crumbled away as infantry and artillery fire poured in from three sides. Those Confederates who raced back across the field were "terribly punished as they did so," an Englishman observed. Even Hill acknowledged that these survivors "fell back in disorder."[19]

As the injured Trimble passed Hill on the way to the rear, he shouted, "If hell can't be taken by the troops I had the honor to command today, it can't be done at all!" For those who lived to tell about it, the assault of July 3 *was* hell. Total Confederate losses exceeded 60 percent of those engaged. The 26th North Carolina, which first took a beating on July 1, now numbered 82 men. The 47th North Carolina could barely muster 100 troops. At day's end the 38th North Carolina consisted of 40 men, commanded by a lieutenant. Pender's division lost 12 of 15 field officers. Not a company in the brigade had more than one officer. One of them, Lt. W. H. Blount, wrote his sweetheart that night, "I think it was the will of Heaven that we should fail."[20]

One of the most persistent questions about July 3 is why Lee chose Longstreet to direct the climactic assault at Gettysburg. Granted, Longstreet was the most experienced corps commander; yet he had also been dilatory and sullen throughout the first two days of combat. In addition, almost two-thirds of the troops in the Pickett-Pettigrew charge were Hill's men, and Hill himself had openly voiced an eagerness for the attack. Hill could not have changed the outcome of the assault, but he would have exercised more care and control over its execution had the responsibility been his.

The battle formation of the attacking force was the weakest in the history of the Army of Northern Virginia. Lee appears to have given no thought to reinforcements. He left the details of the actual attack to Longstreet and Hill, and neither of these old antagonists took control. Longstreet would not, and Hill, assuming Longstreet to be in charge of the offensive, could not. Thus Hill's men became a sort of orphan force, left to tag along as best they could.

Added to this was the fact that Hill's corps had taken heavy losses on the first day at Gettysburg. By July 3, the leadership at brigade and division level was too new, overall control too loose, demands too

great, to weather the murderous fire encountered during that unprotected advance on Cemetery Ridge. Once Mayo's brigade on the far
left gave way before an enfilade fire, a domino-effect disintegration
followed.

Hill's inability to provide personal and inspiring leadership was a
final factor. Promotion to corps command had in essence separated
him from the ranks—he had to watch while others participated. It
was not a natural role for Hill; he never handled it well, and it
brought him more frustration than fulfillment. Painful to him as
well was the slaughter of his units at Gettysburg. Third Corps losses
in its first campaign were 1,554 killed, 4,362 wounded, and 1,755
missing—a total of 7,671 men.[21]

After sundown on July 3, Lee conferred with Ewell and Longstreet. Then he rode over to Hill's headquarters, a common wall
tent pitched on the E. Pitzer farm alongside the Cashtown road. The
army must return to Virginia, Lee acknowledged. Unless Meade
renewed the battle on the morrow, Hill would lead the retreat. Lee
had spent the whole of a week issuing disastrous discretionary orders
for the advance. Now, on the withdrawal, he would be absolutely
precise. The two generals sat on camp stools and carefully studied
a map by the light of a single candle. Lee traced the route to be used
with his finger. Hill for the most part listened silently and nodded
agreement. Around one in the morning Lee wearily mounted his
gray horse and started back down the line. Hill lay on his cot and
tried to get a few hours' sleep.[22]

15

Ebb Tide at
Bristoe Station

Quietness prevailed the next morning. As the hours passed, the clouds thickened. Rain began at one that Saturday and poured the remainder of the day. At dark, Hill's infantry formed in roads and began inching westward behind the wagon trains. Longstreet was second in line, with Ewell composing the rear. The Potomac—and safety—were forty miles to the south. As cavalry fanned out in front and on flanks, Hill was to cross the mountains above Fairfield and prepare defenses while awaiting the other two corps. Thereafter the troops of Ewell and Hill would alternate in the lead and in the rear.

A defeated army in retreat requires skilled leadership. Hill, now relieved of uncertainty caused by imprecise orders, performed his duties on the march with high competence. Weather conditions presented a problem. Rain turned roads into "a universal quagmire." A Virginian in Hill's corps wrote of the after-dark trek: "We were up to our knees in mud and water all night. It was impossible to preserve the company organization in such darkness and difficult marching. The men would halloo out the names of their companies in order to keep together." In addition, scores of wagons, ambulances, cannon, and caissons were all jammed into one seemingly inextricable mass on the roads and adjacent fields, and hundreds of men stumbled about in the storm with no place to go. It was, to one soldier, "a vast moving panorama of misery."[1]

Such was not the case, however, with Lane's brigade and other lead units in Hill's corps. As rumors flashed through the Union camps that Hill was among the fatalities at Gettysburg, the corps commander was reconstructing good spirits and high morale as his columns wound southward.[2] Chaplain James Sheeran of the 14th Louisiana was startled on the dismal march when a new contingent of troops came into view. "At length the loud laughter of the men, comprising the head of A. P. Hill's column, advancing, banished every indication of sleep. . . . They fought hard . . . and were now falling back and wading to their knees in mud and mire. They were as cheerful a body of men as I ever saw; and to hear them, you would think they were going to a party of pleasure instead of retreating from a hard fought battle." Lee, riding with Hill, must have been impressed.[3]

Hill reached Hagerstown on July 7 and lay in line of battle there for six days while a pontoon bridge was being readied. Lee, Hill, and Longstreet meticulously prepared a defensive line on the heights between Hagerstown and Williamsport, in the expectation that Meade would press hard in pursuit. Hill's troops by then were so exhausted that soldiers had no hesitation about lying down in mud to sleep.[4]

On July 13, again acting as the army's rear guard, the Third Corps moved in the direction of the pontoon bridge at Falling Waters. Rain was coming down in sheets again. The routes to the Potomac crossing lay over narrow farm roads, which were soon churned into all-but-impassable mire, often ten inches deep. On into the night the columns struggled, hungry and weary. Lightning occasionally arced through the sky, causing one soldier to shout in disgust: "Hell is not a half-mile from here!"[5]

The weather cleared about daylight and a heavy mist hung over the Potomac Valley. Heth and Pettigrew were one and a half miles from the river when Hill halted the two divisions and ordered Heth to form them in line of battle on either side of the road and facing northward across an open expanse. Heth did so; but in the belief that Southern cavalry were screening his front, he posted no skirmishers. His troops, thoroughly fatigued by the all-night march, stacked arms, ignored mud and sunlight, and were soon sound asleep.

At eleven, Hill directed Heth to start Pettigrew's division toward the river crossing. Heth's men were to follow "as speedily as possible." Suddenly a squadron of some fifty horsemen emerged from the woods a half mile away. Heth, Pettigrew, and their staffs watched the mounted troops. Assuming them to be the Confederate screen, Heth called out: "They are our cavalry! Do not fire on them!"[6]

The riders nonchalantly advanced to within 175 yards of Heth's line. Just as they were recognized as Union cavalry (a contingent of the 6th Michigan), the horsemen broke into a gallop. They charged into the Southerners, according to a surprised Johnny Reb, "cutting and thrusting with their Sabres, and firing on us with their pistols, and shouting: 'Surrender, you damned Rebels!'" Pandemonium erupted, a South Carolina officer admitted. "Some men recovered their arms in time to fire upon them, some ran away, some fought with empty pieces, some even had recourse to stones." One soldier went into action swinging a fence rail; another unhorsed a rider with an ax.[7]

Repulsing the Federals took only three or four minutes, but the brief affair had tragic consequences. Pettigrew, his smashed hand heavily bandaged, tried to mount his horse and was thrown. He jumped up from the ground, reached into his coat and got a revolver, and rushed toward a Federal trooper. The man turned and shot Pettigrew in the stomach. As the Confederate general slumped critically wounded to the ground, one of his men killed the Yankee with a rock. This one-sided action at Falling Waters produced casualties of 39 Federals and 2 Confederates.[8]

The rest of Hill's corps filed unchallenged across the Potomac into Virginia. Lee was back on home ground, but his army hardly resembled the confident force of three weeks earlier. A lieutenant in Pettigrew's brigade wrote that the unit went north with "3500 men, strong, healthy and in fine spirits." It returned to Virginia "with about 500 broken down, half famished men." Another soldier commented that "hundreds had no shoes, Thousands were as ragged as they could be—some with the bottoms of their pants in long frazzles; others with the knees out, others out at the elbows, and their hair sticking through holes in their hats." Hill's corps in particular struck one officer as being "in a terrible condition."[9]

On July 16, Hill's men reached Mill Creek, west of Bunker Hill, and encamped. Rations were very scarce, so several cavalrymen went out on their own to "obtain" supplies. Pickets stopped them and refused to let them pass out of the lines. At that moment, up rode Hill, inspecting his positions. The cavalrymen explained their predicament to the general. "I am very sorry for you," Hill replied, "but

I can do nothing. You are not in my corps. You must apply to General Stuart for passes." Then, seeing the disappointment on their faces, Hill smiled and added: "I'll tell you what you ought to do: flank them."

With that, the horsemen walked up to the pickets, allowed as how the general had given them permission to pass, and walked out of the lines. The sentries, having seen them talking to Hill, let them pass. "Well," said Hill, watching the scene and laughing, "that is the coolest and boldest flank movement I ever saw!"[10]

Two personal losses then struck in rapid order. Early on the morning of July 17, Johnston Pettigrew died at Bunker Hill, in the brick mansion that Jackson had used as headquarters the previous autumn. A clerk on Hill's staff wrote of the thirty-five-year-old North Carolinian: "How we all loved him! A Noble, gallant soldier and gentleman." Hill termed him "the gallant and accomplished Pettigrew." The next day, a few hours after the amputation of his leg, Dorsey Pender died in a Staunton hospital. Hill was sorrowful. "No man fell during [the] bloody battle of Gettysburg more regretted than he, nor around whose youthful brow were clustered brighter rays of hope." One of Pender's regimental colonels later wrote: "He was young and handsome, brave and skillful, prompt to decide and yet when decided, more prompt to execute. He was known, admired and trusted by his superior officers, beyond any of his age in the service."[11]

Hill would miss Pender sorely in the months ahead; but like all good generals, Hill had to put his personal feelings behind him and concentrate on getting his corps back in shape. On July 10, the army started for Culpeper. Hill's troops, behind Longstreet's, crossed the Blue Ridge at Chester Gap. Hill left Wright's brigade to guard the pass at Manassas Gap. On the twenty-third, Hill reported, "an overwhelming force of the enemy" attacked the Georgians. The brigade "heroically met the onset and held [its] ground furiously," noted a correspondent. Elements of Ewell's corps then arrived, "changed the fortune of the day and put a speedy end to the conflict."[12]

The following day Federal cavalry under Gen. George Custer sought to impede Hill's movements. Hill dismissed the encounter by reporting: "The enemy was soon put to flight in confusion, and no more annoyance occurred on the march." On July 26, Hill arrived at his hometown. In the eyes of one soldier, Culpeper was now "a dingy, dirty-looking place" where the main buildings had been used as military hospitals for so long that they "were rapidly tumbling to pieces." Hill relished the pleasure of a week's visit with his pregnant wife, daughter, Russie, and the few others of his family remaining in Culpeper.[13]

One afternoon Hill was enjoying refreshments at the home of his brother, Maj. Baptist Hill. The Reverend John A. Broadus, a boyhood chum and a highly esteemed army missionary, entered the parlor. Hill greeted his longtime friend warmly, and Broadus was immediately struck by Hill's lack of pretension in spite of his status in Lee's army. "He was very cordial," Broadus noted of Hill. "His duties have not puffed him up, but have only sobered him."[14]

In the first week of August, Hill was ordered to shift the corps to Orange Court House, fifteen miles to the south. That new encampment, a mile outside the town, became home for almost three months, time needed for rest and restoration. The entire Third Corps had practically to be rebuilt in those late summer months. More than 625 horses, two-thirds of the animals in Hill's command, had been lost in the Gettysburg campaign; and those horses still with the guns were "for the most part totally unserviceable."[15]

With only 11,207 men present on duty, Hill's corps was then the smallest of the three in the Army of Northern Virginia. The desperate need for leadership in Hill's old Light Division was indicative of the army's deteriorating condition. Of the original brigadiers, Branch was dead, Gregg was dead, Pender was dead, Archer was a prisoner of war, and Field was incapacitated. Only Thomas remained at the head of his brigade. Hill moved quickly to improve matters in his beloved division by appointing plain-looking, heavy-set, but highly competent Cadmus M. Wilcox to succeed Pender as division commander. Wilcox was a forty-year-old bachelor, a professional soldier who had been at West Point with Hill, McClellan, and Pickett. He was six feet tall and customarily wore a short round jacket and battered straw hat. Wilcox was not a deep thinker, but he was a tough fighter who, once a military objective had been fixed, drove toward that point unswervingly. Although Hill liked Wilcox personally, he maintained the same distance from him as from other officers.

Hill did not believe that military forces should be idle. While Lee began a system of furloughs for the men, Hill industriously supervised daily drill and regular inspections. Beef, bacon, potatoes, flour, vegetables, and such delicacies as apples and blackberries became plentiful. New recruits, conscripts, and men released from hospitals arrived in camp, as did "a great deal of clothing and shoes."[16] Morale began to improve. Brigade commander Scales reflected the new spirit when he wrote his wife: "Matters in the brigade look more promising now. I feel more cheerful about the command." Another officer would recall that "our elastic spirits revived from the depression of July, and satisfaction with the present and confidence of the future were almost unanimously expressed."[17]

Troop reviews became regular sights around Orange. Late in August, Hill reviewed the divisions of Anderson, Heth, and Wilcox. A newspaperman informed his readers: "The respective brigades were in excellent condition and presented an imposing illustration of the 'pomp and circumstance of glorious war.' " At noon on September 12, Lee arrived with his daughters for another review of the Third Corps. One of Hill's men observed that "the scene was graced by the presence of ladies from surrounding country, and many officers' wives who generally flocked like gentle doves to the army when war's wild alarms had for a time subsided." Lee sat on his horse atop a slight elevation, with Hill just behind him. "As [Lee's] veterans passed in review, and he surveyed their ranks marching with steady step, the great soldier's face seemed to light up with admiration for the men whose confidence and affection he knew he possessed."[18]

One other morale-builder was much in evidence. Shortly after the Confederate army had settled down at Orange, Lee had issued a proclamation that concluded: "God is our only refuge and strength. Let us humble ourselves before him." In the weeks that followed, a full-blown religious revival swept through the army camps. The Third Corps participated fully in this awakening: at least two regiments experienced over sixty converts each in a single week. A member of Perrin's brigade remembered that "the most ordinary preachers drew large congregations; scarcely a day passed without a sermon; there was not a night, but the sound of prayer and hymn-singing was heard." At scores of nightly assemblies, songs of praise ascended heavenward with the smoke of campfires. One soldier in the 8th Alabama fervently wrote home: "Probably when we fear and love God, we will be blessed with peace. He can close this war whenever he chooses to do so."[19]

Even amid large-scale professions of faith, Hill remained an undemonstrative Episcopalian who generally went to church on Sunday and attended other services only when convenient. Mrs. Hill's postwar assertion that her husband was a constant and fervent worshipper was wishful thinking on her part (although Hill would dutifully accompany his wife to any religious gathering she wished to attend). Hill was also loyal to such friends in the clergy as John Broadus and J. William Jones. On one occasion, Hill and Dolly joined General and Mrs. Scales at a church service in Scales's brigade because Broadus was preaching. The missionary wrote home afterward with obvious satisfaction: "Hill made some fuss over me, introducing, etc., and inviting me to come and stay with him and preach at his headquarters."[20]

Not all was of a pleasant nature at the Orange encampment, however. Blazing sunlight on tents and lean-tos brought daytime misery, sickness increased as the army remained immobile, and Lee had to make examples of a number of soldiers convicted of desertion. Lane's North Carolinians were especially embarrassed when nine members of their brigade were shot to death by firing squads during the month of September. Scales explained the value of such public executions when he told his wife matter-of-factly: "We have in this Division shot 15 or 20 men for desertion & more will be shot yet it has had a fine effect in hurrying up those who are absent without leave."[21]

With only the Rapidan separating portions of the two armies during this period, fraternization became commonplace. A North Carolina lieutenant wrote the homefolk that "our pickets talk & change papers, our camps are in sight of each other & we see as many Yanks as we wish to." Meanwhile, Meade remained indisposed to advance on Lee. The Confederate lines were too strong. Any attempt to cross the Rapidan, Meade informed Washington authorities, "would result in a considerable sacrifice."[22] The stalemate began to change in mid-September. Longstreet went to Tennessee with two divisions to reinforce Gen. Braxton Bragg's hard-pressed army. (Widespread rumor also had Hill en route to Chattanooga.)[23] Two corps in the Union army likewise left Virginia on new assignments. These reductions brought the opposing armies almost to numerical equality—whereupon Lee again determined to take the offensive.

Hill was ready for action. On the one hand, the three-month lull had been healthy; his corps had increased by almost 50 percent and now numbered 16,300 men. Yet the weeks of inactivity had made Hill restless and fidgety. Each day he looked at the devastation of his north-central Virginia homeland and wished for revenge. Additionally, Hill was not happy over his controlled performance at Gettysburg. He wanted another opportunity to demonstrate tactical prowess as a corps commander, and this new campaign could well be that chance. He enjoyed a quick visit behind the lines with Dolly and Russie before the army departed. The love Dolly and her husband shared is evident in a note she sent to a friend: "Powell has been with me since Saturday night. He leaves me this afternoon. You know how badly I must feel. However I am going to stand it like a soldier for I should be thankful to have him anytime."[24]

Meade's army was encamped north of Culpeper, with two Federal corps stretching to the Rapidan. The best way to remove the menace from Virginia, Lee reasoned, was to turn Meade's right, force him into retreat, and then assault the Federals as they were withdrawing toward Washington. Lee was so plagued by rheumatism on October 8 that he could not mount a horse. In spite of the pain, he reviewed his strategy at length with Hill and Ewell. At sunrise the next morning Confederate columns were marching northward through fields and over country roads. An officer later described the inspiring spectacle: "The weather was magnificent, and the crimson foliage of the wood rivalled the tint of the red battle-flags, fluttering above the long glittering hedge of bayonets."[25]

The only roads at Lee's disposal led to Warrenton. Hence, he made that town his objective point. On October 11, after two days of swinging around Cedar Mountain, Hill's gray and dusty troops entered Culpeper. It was deserted. The day before, Meade had learned that at least Hill's corps of Lee's army was marching to turn his flank.[26] Meade rapidly began falling back from Culpeper along the Orange & Alexandria Railroad. Suddenly the situation was a repeat of August 1862: a Union army frantically retreating, a Confederate army in hot pursuit.

Lee reached Warrenton with Ewell on the afternoon of the thirteenth. Hill, having traveled by a more circuitous route, arrived near sundown. No further advance could be undertaken that day because the Confederate army was being supplied by wagon trains, which were creeping behind the infantry. As it was, several of Hill's regiments went at least two days without rations.[27]

Complaints were few, however. A young soldier declared: "We were convinced that Meade was unwilling to face us, and we, therefore, anticipated a pleasant affair, if we should succeed in catching him."[28] Men cheered in anticipation of finishing the Union army once and for all. Stuart reported to Lee after dark that Federals were hastily burning stores at Warrenton Junction, due east of Warrenton. Lee saw a good chance now of cutting the Federal line at Bristoe Station or some other point on the railroad.

Before dawn on Wednesday the fourteenth, Hill had his men marching over familiar ground. The troops advanced down two roads to Auburn Mills, then turned left to Greenwich, where they found campfires still ablaze. Hill veered eastward for Bristoe Station. He was both enthusiastic and impatient that morning. Part of the Federal army was close at hand. Hill sensed the kill, if he could make quick contact and strike promptly. However, the Federals had the jump and were ahead of him. They were using the best roads, which meant that the gap between the two hosts would likely widen as the marching hours passed. For much of the morning, an anxious Hill rode near the head of the column and occasionally galloped forward in hopes of catching sight of the Yankees.

Heth's division was in the lead; it had undergone major reorganization since Gettysburg. Joe Davis still commanded the Mississippi brigade, but only three of its four regiments were present. Now at the head of the Field-Brockenbrough brigade was Gen. Henry Harrison Walker. An 1853 graduate of West Point, "Mud" Walker had risen to brigadier after "gallant and meritorious" service in the 40th Virginia. A large mustache was Walker's only striking feature. Outside his brigade he was not well known. Pettigrew's brigade was now under William W. Kirkland, who had served two years as colonel of the 21st North Carolina. Kirkland had proven himself "a splendid fighter and superb soldier," and during his short stay with Hill he was "very courteous and agreeable." Rounding out Heth's division was a brigade new to the army. It consisted of the 15th, 27th, 46th, and 48th North Carolina and was under the command of John R. Cooke, a thirty-year-old civil engineer by training and a brother-in-law of Jeb Stuart. Cooke was so young in appearance that his soldiers initially called him "that boy." Yet seven battle wounds had earned him promotion to brigadier. His skill and daring, a newspaper stated, "are only equalled by his modesty."[29]

Discarded Federal knapsacks, overcoats, and the like littered the roadside that Wednesday morning and gave a lift to already high Southern spirits. Hill rode forward and reined to a halt on the crest of a plateau overlooking Bristoe Station, Broad Run, and the surrounding plain. Beyond the waist-deep run, out of reach, heavy columns of Federals were slogging northward toward Manassas

Junction. However, sprawled in the valley immediately in front of Hill was Federal general William H. French's III Corps—thousands of unsuspecting soldiers cluttered in a mass as they awaited their turn at the ford across Broad Run. A Tarheel declared that "the whole face of the earth in that vast plain seemed covered with Yankees. I never saw so many of them at one time during the war."[30]

Not since Chancellorsville had an opportunity like this existed for the Confederates! "No time must be lost," said Hill. An attack must get under way at once!

Broad Run was a swift-moving north-south stream above Bristoe Station. Hill was coming in from the west, and the run was directly in his front. His intention was to unleash Heth in a battle line across the plain and over the run, creating confusion and destruction as he went. Heth's orders were to send three of his brigades forward, with the fourth held in reserve. At the same time, Poague's battalion of artillery was brought up to the hilltop and ordered to open on the enemy. The first salvo, Hill reported, caught the Federals "completely by surprise," and they "retired in the utmost confusion." Poague confirmed this. "Such scampering and skedaddling was hardly ever seen."[31]

Ewell's men, approaching rapidly from several miles away, heard the first shots fired. "Hill is into them!" Ewell's troops shouted joyfully. At this point, however, Hill had already made two mistakes that would cost him dearly. He failed to take the time to reconnoiter the whole area in front of him; and in his eagerness to take advantage of hordes of Federals standing around defenselessly, Hill, the corps commander, reverted to his role as division leader. In essence, he took command of Heth's division while virtually ignoring the divisions of Wilcox and Anderson, then converging on the scene.

Heth began making his dispositions. Walker's Virginians were formed on the left of the main east-west road to Bristoe Station. Kirkland constituted the center. To his right, Cooke's men double-timed into position. This was their first battle under Hill, and they were anxious to make a good impression. Yet Hill was growing more impatient by the minute. Poague's artillery fire was hastening, not impeding, the Federal withdrawal. Heth had only two of his brigades in line when Hill told him to attack immediately, lest the Federals escape. Heth gave the signal as Hill moved to the right of an elevated clump of woods to watch the action.[32]

Just as he took his position, something caught Hill's eye. Not all of the Federals were fleeing. Some were standing on the west bank of Broad Run, in a line parallel to the railroad. Worst, they were on Heth's right and would be in his rear when Heth's brigades advanced across the stream. How many were there? What was their intention? Hill sent word to Heth to halt the advance. Now Hill had to return to high command and involve the two-thirds of the Third Corps he had ignored earlier. He sent a second courier galloping across the field to warn Cooke that his right might be in some danger. A third messenger from Hill rode back to find Anderson and have him rush up McIntosh's guns plus two infantry brigades.

Cooke's men had moved into a clearing when the order to halt came. Now he began to encounter gunfire from his right—from the direction of a railroad cut almost perpendicular to the battle route. Cooke shook loose two companies from his 27th North Carolina on the extreme right to ascertain the Federal strength. The colonel of the regiment soon informed Cooke that Federals in large numbers were behind the embankment. With that news Cooke rode up to Heth. The enemy will take me in flank if I move forward, he said. Heth relayed the information to Hill. Back came Hill's reply: McIntosh's guns have taken position on high ground, and the lead elements of Anderson's troops are in sight. That is adequate protection for the right. Proceed with the advance.

An unhappy Cooke acknowledged the order by stating: "Well, I will advance, and if they flank me, I will face my men about and cut my way out!"[33]

Following the ten-minute halt, Kirkland and Cooke resumed the offensive. One of the North Carolinians described the 800 yards that lay before them. "The space between us and the railroad was a barren, open field, descending with a gradual declivity to the railroad embankment. Across and beyond the railroad about 300 yards, upon a considerable elevation, were extensive woods and thickets; here the enemy had posted their artillery. In front of these woods, and on the face of the hill descending to the railroad embankment, was posted what we supposed was the enemy's skirmish line."[34]

Hill and other Confederates were convinced that only a Federal detachment was behind the embankment. They were all wrong. Over 3,000 men in Gen. G. K. Warren's II Corps were in position to deliver a crossfire. Put more bluntly, three entrenched Northern divisions calmly awaited two Southern brigades in one of the neatest traps arranged in the Civil War.

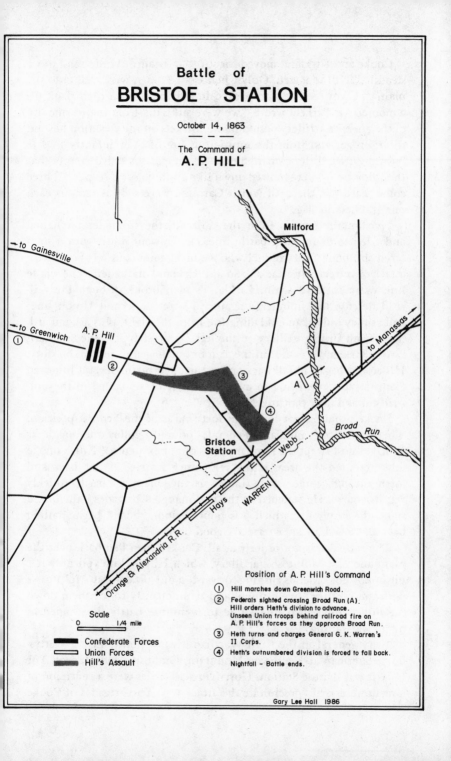

Battle of
BRISTOE STATION

October 14, 1863

— — —

The Command of
A. P. HILL

to Gainesville →

to Greenwich →

A. P. Hill

Milford

to Manassas →

Bristoe Station

Webb

Broad Run

A

Hays WARREN

Orange & Alexandria R.R.

Scale

0   1/4 mile

■ Confederate Forces
▢ Union Forces
▨ Hill's Assault

Position of A. P. Hill's Command

①   Hill marches down Greenwich Road.

②   Federals sighted crossing Broad Run (A).
Hill orders Heth's division to advance.
Unseen Union troops behind railroad fire on
A. P. Hill's forces as they approach Broad Run.

③   Heth turns and charges General G. K. Warren's
II Corps.

④   Heth's outnumbered division is forced to fall back.

Nightfall – Battle ends.

Gary Lee Hall 1986

Cooke and Kirkland moved forward "in beautiful order and quite steadily," Hill reported. Only when Cooke's men were well onto the plain did they see Federals packed in a firing line on their flank. In a moment, a Tarheel wrote, "we were suffering from the terrific fire of the enemy's artillery posted in the thickets on the elevation beyond the railroad, and from the murderous fire of their infantry in safe position behind the embankment." A compatriot stated simply that their first lines "were mowed down like grain before a reaper." Three color-bearers in the 27th North Carolina were shot as soon as each one grabbed the flag.[35]

Five hundred yards from the railroad, the Confederates halted and tried to maintain a battle line. Cooke went down with a shattered shinbone. The colonel who assumed command was faced with attack or retreat. He attacked. So did Kirkland on the left. The whole line swept forward again. Kirkland's men broke through the railroad defense but foundered against a stronger second Union line; and as they did so, an enfilading fire from the right, plus a bombardment from Union artillery on the left, began stripping the Southern ranks. Kirkland was shot in the arm but managed to remain on duty. His troops began to fall back across the open plain. Several hundred Confederates, unwilling to expose themselves, remained in the railroad cut and were captured.[36]

Cooke's soldiers got to within forty yards of the Federal position. Then, from front and flank, Federals "poured a volley into our ranks which almost swept the remnant of us out of existence." Battle smoke now obscured the area. Hill, "very much worried," rode back and forth through some scrub timber as the one-sided battle quickly ran its course. He watched as the two mangled brigades, "unable to stand the heavy fire which was poured upon them," began falling back in what Hill later termed "good order."[37]

The retreat was not orderly at all. Cooke's men fled back over the plain and past McIntosh's artillery, which Hill had inexplicably left unsupported. Federals rushing forward in pursuit overran McIntosh's position, captured five cannon, and triumphantly rolled them down the hill to their own lines. The forty-minute battle thus ended as night was falling.[38]

Every general in the Civil War had his low point: Lee at Gettysburg, Sherman at Kennesaw Mountain, Grant at Cold Harbor. For Hill, it was Bristoe Station. Horrifying casualties were a reflection of how unnecessarily precipitate the attack was. The brigades of Cooke and Kirkland had been battered. The former lost 700 men, the latter, 602. The 27th North Carolina, which caught the full force of the enfilading fire, suffered 290 casualties of 416 engaged—thirty-three of its thirty-six officers were killed, wounded, or captured.[39] Hill's total losses were 1,378, or roughly one man lost every two seconds of the engagement.

Harsh personal criticism assailed the Third Corps commander. "Hill is a fool & woeful blunderer," wrote one of Jackson's former staff officers. Other comments were equally sharp: "unpardonable mismanagement" . . . "slaughter pen" . . . "a gross blunder on the part of our corps general" . . . "bloody massacre." A Richmond newspaper levied a sarcastic blast: "It is certainly a little singular, and a fact calling for explanation, that a pursuing army should have its artillery captured by a retreating adversary."[40]

Hill neither hedged nor rationalized. To his credit, he took complete blame for the disaster. He filed his official report promptly; and in a confession truly remarkable in Civil War communiqués, Hill closed with the statement: "I am convinced that I made the attack too hastily, and at the same time that a delay of half an hour, and there would have been no enemy attack. In that event I believe I should equally have blamed myself for not attacking at once."

Secretary of War James Seddon endorsed the report with the observation: "The disaster at Bristoe Station seems due to the gallant but over-hasty pressing of the enemy." Jefferson Davis read Hill's account and passed a blunt judgment: "There was a want of vigilance."[41]

The "grievous blow" at Bristoe Station "affected brave Hill deeply," an acquaintance wrote, and "General Lee was no less melancholy." As rain fell on the fifteenth, Federals retreated "in great haste" because of a report that Hill was about to strike again. That morning Lee rode over the battlefield with Hill. The two men viewed the torn ground, with bodies still strewn around the now-abandoned railroad cut. Hill desperately explained what had happened and repeatedly apologized. Lee, with obvious disappointment, silently looked over the scene as raindrops fell from his hat brim. "Well, well, General," he finally said, "bury these poor men, and let us say no more about it." The two officers then rode slowly from the field.[42]

Habitually overlooked because of the debacle at Bristoe Station is the campaign itself. Lee had forced the Army of the Potomac into retreat; he had caused the destruction of tons of Union materiel, wrecked miles of the vital Union-held Orange & Alexandria Railroad, and inflicted 2,292 casualties (which included 1,400 men captured).[43] Bristoe Station was the one setback in an otherwise successful operation.

The overall accomplishment meant little to Hill. Bristoe Station would be the nightmare he would never forget. That battle came five months after his introduction to corps command—five months that raised questions about Hill's competence at that level. He was a splendid organizer, with intuitive judgment about good subalterns. Because he was magnetic and attractive, he had the affection of his staff, the respect of his officers, and the admiration of his men. Instilling confidence and high morale was easy for Hill. But after Bristoe Station he was no longer the spirited, hard-driving man who had carried the Light Division to fame.

What changed Hill was a combination of things. The larger responsibility of corps command was not appealing to him. Staying clear of combat, as he was forced by rank to do, was counter to his nature and talents. The attacks of prostatitis were becoming more frequent and more crippling. Most damaging of all, perhaps, Hill lacked the breadth of vision and wisdom to be superb at the head of a corps. Too often narrow and impetuous in his thinking, he did not have Jackson's deep confidence or Longstreet's unshakable calm. Unrivaled as a division commander, Hill simply did not—or could not—adjust as well to the next step up the military ladder.

A South Carolina sergeant who served under Hill for practically the entire war described part of the change that came over Hill in the summer and autumn of 1863: "The great responsibilities of the lieutenent generalcy seemed to have told upon his naturally buoyant spirits, and there was ever a gravity about him that he maintained until the day of his death." The sergeant added that "he had ceased to be the inspiring Hill of the old Light Division."[44]

Pleasant Family
Diversions

Following the Bristoe Station debacle, Lee made a quick assessment of the situation. Autumn was rapidly passing, and with it the warm weather. If he continued to push Meade, the Union army—like a turtle retreating into its shell—would simply fall back to the defensive stronghold at Washington. In addition, the Confederate supply lines were already overextended; Southern soldiers were badly in need, especially of shoes. "Thousands were barefooted, thousands with fragments of shoes, & all without overcoats, blankets or warm clothing," Lee noted.

He therefore broke off the offensive. After Hill's men struggled through days of steady rain to destroy the Orange & Alexandria Railroad from Bristoe to the Rappahannock bridge, the Army of Northern Virginia encamped along the south bank of the river. The temperature plunged, and soldiers huddled around campfires with clothes frozen to their bodies.[1]

Hill was in an understandably low mood, which may explain why he hurt the feelings of some admiring Culpeper friends. A prominent citizen came to offer him a sixty-man contingent of local troops as a personal bodyguard. The county's most distinguished soldier deserved such pomp and honor, the man said. Hill rejected the offer in rather blunt terms. "I have no use for an escort. Besides, sir, I think that your sixty able-bodied men could render better service to the country by joining the ranks of some infantry regiment than by acting as bodyguard to any general."[2]

The uncomfortable surroundings along the Rappahannock nurtured two rumors about Hill that spread through both armies. One series of reports had Hill under arrest for the mismanaged attack at Bristoe Station. More persistent was the rumor that Hill and his corps were being transferred to Tennessee. Some of his troops even began packing their gear in anticipation. Neither assertion was true, but together they gave an aura of loneliness to Hill. Wearing a long black cape to ward off the chill, he was seen daily making solitary rides through his camps.[3]

His spirits momentarily lifted on November 1, when word came from Richmond that Dolly had given birth to a daughter. In honor of Hill's sister and the man he most admired, this third girl was named Lucy Lee. Soldiers in Hill's corps affectionately built a rough-hewn cradle and presented it to the family.[4]

On the afternoon of November 7, Hill's corps was put on alert for a possible major Federal movement. It came at nightfall, when Gen. John Sedgwick's corps routed Ewell's bridgehead at Rappahannock Station and took 2,000 prisoners. Lee was shocked at this lunge southward by Meade's army, but he quickly recovered. His forces must fall back. The ensuing withdrawal was surprisingly unmolested, and Hill's troops were soon in earthworks on the south bank of the Rapidan.

Meade, under pressure from Washington to do something before the onset of winter, devised a plan to make maximum use of Federal numerical superiority. His army would force its way across the Rapidan and move east of one of the Rapidan's tributaries, Mine Run. By slipping around Lee's right flank, Meade hoped to draw the Confederate army out into open country. There Federal numbers would tell in stand-up combat.

Confederate cavalry discovered the Federal thrust in its opening stages. Lee promptly placed Ewell's corps in secure entrenchments behind Mine Run, which, with densely wooded banks and marshy bottomland, was a formidable position. Hill's corps, now up to 19,000 men, was encamped along a thirteen-mile sector extending from Ewell's left at Clark's Mountain westward to Liberty Mills. While the Confederates reinforced their lines day by day, weather delays and man-made blunders hampered Meade's advance. The Federals for a time seemed stalled. One day Captain Poague asked Hill what he thought the Union army would do. "I don't know," Hill replied, "but I wish they would show their hand and give us a chance at them!" Poague concluded from this remark that Hill "was hoping to get even with them for the Bristoe affair."[5]

On November 24, President Davis arrived for a two-day visit to Lee's army. One of Hill's bands serenaded the chief executive upon his arrival, and Davis addressed a large gathering of men in the Third Corps. The following day, in cold rain, the president reviewed Hill's divisions and was lavish in his compliments.[6]

Lee had no grand plan for stopping Meade, but he was thinking offensively. If the Federals advanced far enough, Lee intended to move out of his earthworks, march eastward, and assail the Union army on unfortified ground. Jubal Early, at the head of the Second Corps in place of the incapacitated Ewell, commanded the right of Lee's line and was closest to Meade's route of march. On November 26 the Union army forded the Rapidan. Hill was ordered later that day to advance on the Orange Plank Road and form on Early's right as the Confederate army slowly began swinging around and facing east.

The next day, a mile and a half east of Mine Run, the head of Hill's troops met Stuart's cavalry retiring before the van of the Army of the Potomac. First Hill and then Lee rode out to get personal looks at the "stiff fight" taking place. It was obvious now that Meade's whole army was in motion. Hill deployed Heth's division in support of Stuart. The Federal advance was checked as continuing rain turned roads "into ditches and bogs." Lee ordered the army to withdraw behind Mine Run and the imposing earthworks. The Federals also fell back to high ground east of the rain-swollen stream. By nightfall, with Hill pointing the way, Anderson's division had linked with the Second Corps. Lee's lines were solid.[7]

Throughout the following day, Hill's men sent mud and dirt flying as they strengthened their fortifications. Lee inspected the lines in the afternoon, accompanied (said an officer) "by Hill, in his drooping hat, simple but cordial." Although Federals could clearly be seen massing on the opposite heights, Hill reported confidently: "We were ready to receive them."[8]

November 29 and 30 passed with both armies merely continuing to jockey for position. On the morning of Sunday the twenty-ninth, Lee, Hill, and their staffs were making another inspection of the defenses. The entourage came to a spot where a group of soldiers, huddled together against the cold, were engaged in a prayer service. Lee halted and dismounted; the other riders did the same. The officers removed their hats and stood silently until the prayers were concluded. As they remounted, a staff officer noticed that Hill appeared "thoughtful, almost to the point of tenderness."[9]

On the night of the thirtieth, as an "icy wind raged over the open face of the field . . . piercing the very bones," Lee held a council of war. Meade now seemed averse to fighting. Hence, said Lee, the Confederates would launch their own offensive. Hill's corps was directed to move out of its breastworks under cover of night, take a position on Meade's left and rear, then attack at daylight. Anderson and Wilcox speedily got their divisions into position, then sat in the cold darkness and awaited the sunrise. December 1 dawned. The Confederates rushed forward—and found only unattended camp-fires and the debris of a departing army. Meade had backed away from what a Billy Yank called "one of the greatest battles that was never fought." A Richmond newspaper chortled: "A mountain in labor, and behold at parturition a mouse is brought forth. Meade has marched up the hill and then marched down again."[10]

Hill pressed forward in pursuit and "picked up some 200 prisoners and a few muskets" before rejoining Lee.[11] The army then slowly made its way southward toward winter quarters. From Bristoe Station to Mine Run, Lee had suffered close to 4,300 casualties. Nothing had been accomplished but holding Meade at bay. The 1863 autumn campaign was a bungled, disjointed operation for both armies. It was time to call a halt and begin anew in the spring.

The Confederates went back to their old camps along the Rapidan. Hill established his headquarters tents in a grove of pine and cedars at the southern base of Clark's Mountain. As for his troops, a correspondent reported that they were "returning to camp and very much to their old quarters. The commissary and quartermaster wagons line the roads daily, conveying supplies to the different camps, and the men are busying themselves in fitting up comfortable quarters for the winter. The religious services which were broken up by the stir of the past week have been resumed, and these meetings are nightly attended by eager crowds, who make the woods resound with praise of the Most High." On December 6, Hill joined Lee, Stuart, and other military dignitaries for services at the Episcopal church in Orange.[12]

A thank-you note was Hill's major activity the next day. After returning to the south side of the Rapidan, Hill received a large pair of silver spurs from a group of "young country women" near Columbia, S.C. In their presentation letter the ladies announced a vow never to marry anyone but a Southern soldier. Hill directed his reply to their spokesman.

"My Dear Miss Mary: The very handsome pair of spurs so kindly presented to me by yourself and young friends have been received, and I thank you most heartily for the token of good will and of the esteem in which you hold services incident to my position. If I have done aught to win these spurs, the gallant soldiers of your own native State are entitled partly to the credit. They have never faltered when the charge was sounded. The noble, steadfast devotion of the few in the field should cull a blush of shame to the cheeks of those who are fattening at home upon the distress of their country. At all events, mete out to them the punishment you threaten and never let them know the cheer of the domestic fireside, or be smiled upon by 'Heaven's last, best gift'—women.

"When these cruel wars are over, Miss Mary, I shall be reminded of Columbia, and I hope spurred to a visit in that direction to meet my kind friends. Please remember me affectionately to your young friends, and give to each a kiss for me, which I will repay to you with interest when we meet. Very affectionately, your friend, A. P. Hill."[13]

Hill found time a few days later to send a hasty letter to his sister Lute. "I hope this note will not reach you all in a grumbling humor because we did not swallow Gen. Meade and his whole army. We are content to have gained a bloodless victory, which has had almost as bad an effect on the Yankees as if we had slain a hecatomb of men to our glory and we have had so much fighting that, like Napoleon's veterans, we are content to be let alone for a breathing space. . . . Meade seems to be going into Winter Qrs. in Culpeper, and I suppose we will do the same somewhere in this region. Dolly is already anxious to come up, and old Mr. Graham has asked me to bring her to his home."[14] Mrs. Hill and the two children apparently joined Hill in camp a few days later.

With food and other supplies in greater abundance, Christmas of that year was happy for the troops. In fact, when the 13th North Carolina of Scales's brigade fell heir to a sizable quantity of whiskey, some of its members proceeded to get first boisterous and then belligerent. The Carolinians started a fight with Richmond's Irish Battalion, after which they demolished two sutlers' quarters. The next morning, some three dozen Tarheels awakened in the guardhouse.[15]

The troops settled into the quiet of winter camp, but courts-martial were active for weeks at a time. Occasionally a volley of musketry could be heard as some firing squad carried out a death sentence. Four soldiers in one of Hill's North Carolina brigade were executed at one time for desertion.

On January 7, 1864, Hill, with Generals Stuart and John B. Gordon, left the front and journeyed to Richmond to welcome Gen. John Hunt Morgan. Hill's brother-in-law had acquired an almost legenddary reputation as a Kentucky cavalryman, and just weeks before, Morgan had escaped from a Federal prison in Ohio. Now he was being accorded a hero's welcome in the Confederate capital.

Snow blanketed Richmond as the generals, and Mrs. Hill, checked into the Ballard House. Morgan arrived by train later that evening. At noon the following day a formal reception was held in front of City Hall. Generals Hill, Stuart, Gordon, Simon B. Buckner, and Edward Johnson each attracted attention. Morgan spoke briefly to the large crowd. "When the cheering had somewhat subsided," a newspaper reported, "calls were made for Gen. A. P. Hill, who came forward and bowed to the multitude and then retired." Hill for some reason was unable to speak. "Stuart did," a bystander remembered, "with all his voice."[16]

Hill and Morgan made a visit on Saturday the ninth to Libby Prison. They conversed amiably with a number of Federal prisoners of war, especially those from Kentucky. Capt. George R. Lodge of the 53rd Illinois carefully scrutinized the two Confederate generals as they passed through his sector of the prison. The Illinoisan praised Morgan's appearance and manner, then wrote: "Hill is about my size, sandy whiskers and red face. Rather an ordinary-looking man, except his eye and that is keen, flashing, and very intelligent."[17]

On Sunday, General and Mrs. Morgan, the Hills, and several staff officers attended morning prayer service at St. Paul's Episcopal Church. That evening, declining invitations to the next day's scheduled visit to the Virginia legislature and a ball at the Ballard House, Hill returned to camp and resumed command of his corps. (Richard Anderson had been in charge during his absence.)[18] Hill's pleasant, courteous manner made him well liked in Richmond, even though he took part in the social life reluctantly. Given a choice, he much preferred to stay at home with his wife and infant daughters.

Dolly, Russie, and Lucy spent the winter with Hill at Mayhurst, the three-story Orange County home of the Col. John Willis family. The twenty-room mansion offered spacious accommodations for the Hills, and the general had his headquarters tent pitched in the front yard. Lee was a frequent visitor to the estate, and he and Hill became even closer friends in those quiet wintry months. While rumors continued to circulate that Hill was on his way to duty in Tennessee, Lee was informing President Davis that he was willing to part with any of his generals except Hill.[19]

Hill had few close friendships, but he treasured those he had, even at a cost to his reputation. This was the case with Henry Heth. Gettysburg, and even more so, Falling Waters and Bristoe Station, had raised questions as to Heth's competence for division command. He sought to shore up his reputation that winter by journeying to Richmond with written testimonials from colleagues. One such letter was from Hill, who wrote: "Having been informed that it was possible some misapprehensions existed in regard to your management of your Division at Gettysburg, Falling Waters and Bristow, it is but simple justice to you that I say, your conduct in all those occasions met with my approbation." Hill repeated that the responsibility for Bristoe Station was exclusively his. "At Bristow the attack was ordered by me, and most gallantly made by your Division. Another Corps of the enemy coming up on your right was unforeseen, as I had supposed that other troops were taking care of them."[20]

Hill submitted his detailed report of the Mine Run campaign during this period, but he also found time to send chatty letters to acquaintances and kinsmen. To one friend he wrote: "The rumor of a review runs counter to my own knowledge. I have not thought of such a thing, because it would be simply impossible just now, without great trouble and long marching to some of the troops. . . . Dolly and the children are well, and Dolly sends her love and wants to know what success you all have met with 'spearing' out a boarding place for her. Please recollect when you write to me that 'Jeff's portraits' are somewhat plenty here, and I don't give you any right to treat me as if you and I were 'business' correspondents."[21]

In unusually lighthearted fashion Hill wrote an influential Richmonder: "The promotions for my staff have not yet been recd., but I live in hope, and provided the millenium does not estop all proceedings, suppose even this will right in the *long* run.

"We have no fault to find with the amount of water lately issued to this army, the ration of which has been full to overflowing. I cannot say so much for the other component parts, equally necessary, and much more acceptable when dry.

"I hope the Ambulatory Corps is all right. 'Long may they move!' If that dry parchment, which encloses all that is earthly of our

Richelieu, were in a little more danger of stopping some whistling minnie, he would be a little more amenable to the ministering of prices of such an organization."[22]

One of Hill's most intriguing notes in the winter of 1863–1864 was to his brother-in-law and former staff officer Richard Morgan, then a prisoner of war at Fort Delaware. After telling Morgan that his sister and the children were well, and that Russie was "very much petted and spoiled," Hill then made an inquiry about the prison commandant. "Ask Gen. Schoepf if he was ever in the Coast Survey office."[23]

Inside Hill's camps, the winter months brought varying activities and feelings. "The troops were not regularly well supplied with good and sufficient rations," Wilcox recalled, "nor was their clothing of the best; their *morale* was, nevertheless, excellent."[24] A major reason for high morale amid adversity was another religious revival, which swept through Lee's army in those idle months. Several meeting-houses were erected. Cold weather could not chill the religious interest manifested by the soldiers. A lieutenant in the 47th North Carolina happily proclaimed to the homefolk: "We are having a glorious time. God is pouring out his spirit upon us. We have nightly meetings, and many of our brave defenders are flocking to the altar asking what must they do to be saved."[25]

Hill's firm discipline was in evidence several times that winter when desertions increased sharply. The corps commander sent at least eight convicted soldiers before firing squads in a one-month period. There were other somber aspects of camp life. Enough skirmishes with Federals occurred to keep the men always on the alert. The camps also became more dismal with the passage of time. By February, no trees were in sight; and getting firewood (if it could be found at all) necessitated a walk of a half mile or more.

Unusual events began to break the monotony of camp life late in March. After some twelve inches of snow fell in one day, the brigades of Cooke and Kirkland "joined battle." The horror of Bristoe Station was forgotten as those two units waged a combat of snowballs. For several hours hundreds of men fought back and forth across a large field. One participant closed his account of the affair with the observation: "there was more laughing and hollowing than ever I heard at one time."[26]

Gov. Zebulon B. Vance visited the winter camps and made at least two appearances in Hill's predominantly North Carolina corps.

Vance made "a tolerably good speech" to a large audience that included Generals Lee, Hill, and Rodes. Yet, noted one Tarheel
colonel, the address "had too little seriousness & too much buffoonery
in it for a Gov. on so solemn an occasion." On April 1, another
crowd turned out to hear Vance speak in the Third Corps. It poured
rain, and Vance sent word that he was too hoarse to speak. Drenched
soldiers hooted "April Fool!" as they trudged back to their shelters.[27]

The Confederates were aware that Gen. Ulysses S. Grant was the
new general-in-chief of the Union armies. They were not overly impressed by this latest general from the West. Neither was anyone else
on seeing Grant for the first time. The victor at Fort Donelson,
Shiloh, Vicksburg, and Chattanooga was of average height, kept
a cigar clamped in the corner of his mouth, dressed plainly, and
generally had a scrubby look about him; he seemed to be a loner,
deaf to the applause that followed wherever he went.

Hill must have felt deep resentment when Grant, on March 26,
established supreme army headquarters at Culpeper, Hill's hometown. In the weeks that followed, a quiet preparation began to stir
Lee's army to wakefulness. Ordnance officers and quartermasters
scurried to and fro; medical detachments stockpiled supplies; aux-
iliary units increased their activities. Generals' wives soon began
departing for the rear. Once more Dolly Hill remained with her
husband as long as possible, but this time out of necessity. General
Scales explained: "Mrs Hill is not satisfied with remaining here
after all the ladies had been ordered away & all the others had left,
but [she] said she had no home & she had as well make Orange her
home as any where else. At the opening of the campaign she expects
to go to Lexington, Va."[28]

Hill and his wife shared a particularly enjoyable event before
saying goodbye again. On May 1, a clear and warm Sunday, the
Reverend Richard Davis of St. Thomas Episcopal Church baptized
Lucy Hill in a ceremony at Mayhurst. General Lee was godfather
and held the infant in his arms throughout most of the service.[29]
For Hill's friends, this occasion should have been a happy ending
to the five-month encampment. It was not, for anyone who had
watched Hill closely that winter. Dolly was surely aware of the
situation; Lee doubtless saw it; division commanders and staff officers too must have been privy to it.

Hill was not well, and his condition seemed to be worsening.

January and February had been difficult months for him physically. For a period in March, he had had to relinquish corps command because he was "quite sick and incapacitated." On April 11, a horsemanship tournament was held at Heth's headquarters. Hill had agreed to serve as chief judge, but when the riders gathered for the event, Hill was so ill that he had to resign the judgeship and watch the tournament from the sideline.[30] By then, his walk was noticeably slow, his cheeks were becoming pronouncedly sunken, and a weary, sad haze seemed at times to cover those once-flashing hazel eyes.

In truth, the prostatitis that had occasionally plagued Hill for almost twenty years was becoming more severe. The disease, then untreatable, had many symptoms. Urination was frequent but slight and extremely painful because the swollen prostate gland often pinched the urinary tube. Nephritis was beginning to impair the kidneys. The prostate condition had also produced urethral strictures, which themselves lead to infection and further discomfort. Fever and chills could accompany the urinary discomfort. At times it was agonizing to sit and impossible to ride. Adequate sleep was out of the question since the brain would keep sending urination messages to which the body could not adequately respond. Such a condition would trigger fatigue and, at times, depression.

This was the status of Hill's health as April became May; and in the months that followed, the prostatitis would intensify and develop into another life-threatening condition.

Lee was also not in the best of health at this time, and the army's high command was shaky. Things were not the same as they had been ten months ago at Gettysburg. Longstreet had gone to Tennessee back in September, helped Bragg win a victory at Chickamauga, and then failed in a semi-independent operation against Knoxville. He returned to Virginia embittered. Ewell was still incapacitated, mentally as well as physically, from the loss of a leg. Early, Ewell's senior lieutenant and principal substitute, was now showing an arrogance that would increase with the ensuing years. That left Hill, who seemed basically unchanged, but who still had not established a reputation as a corps commander.

Instability in command likewise characterized Hill's corps. Cadmus Wilcox was going into his first major battle as a division leader with four seasoned brigade commanders (Lane, McGowan, Scales, and Thomas), but the other division was not in such good shape. Heth had learned the responsibilities of a major general. Yet while

Joe Davis now had brigade experience, the other three brigadiers were new to the division. Cooke and Kirkland had led brigades in the Bristoe Station disaster; the fourth general, Henry Walker, had demonstrated to date only promise. Hill displayed no concern about any of this. Unbridled confidence in his men led Hill to conclude that the ability of the soldiers would more than compensate for the inexperience of the generals.

On Monday, May 2, Hill felt good as he rode to the top of Clark's Mountain and joined Lee, Longstreet, and Ewell for a council of war. Lee studied the gently rolling country below him for a while, then announced his belief that the Federal army would move against his right and cross the Rapidan at Germanna or Ely's Ford. Corps commanders should have their troops in readiness, Lee said. The Confederate army would move when Grant did.

It would have been infinitely better had Lee begun consolidating his forces immediately. His army was sprawled over a vast area. Hill, with 22,000 men, was encamped around Orange Court House, some twenty-five miles to the southwest of the Wilderness. Ewell's 17,000 troops were ten miles nearer the Wilderness, but they were scattered from Rapidan Station to Verdiersville. Longstreet's corps, 10,000 infantry strong, was at Gordonsville, forty-two miles from where Lee thought Grant would move. The Union commander had about 119,000 troops; Lee could perhaps muster 62,000 infantry, artillery, and cavalry—if everyone got up into position in time.

Shortly after midnight of May 3–4, the Union army began crossing the Rapidan. The 1864 campaign was under way. Lee reacted quickly when he received the long-awaited signal from Clark's Mountain that Grant's army was in motion. Orders had gone to Hill earlier for the men to cook rations, pack gear, and prepare to march. Hill was ready; he had even strengthened his ranks by releasing all soldiers under arrest and undergoing court-martial sentences.[31]

It was one in the afternoon on the fourth when 14,500 soldiers representing two-thirds of Hill's corps started on the Orange Plank Road toward the Wilderness. Anderson's division remained behind as rear guard for the wagon trains. It was to rejoin the corps the next day. Heth's division was the lead element of Hill's march, with Wilcox's troops tightly behind Heth. Ewell's Second Corps was advancing along the Orange Turnpike. The Plank Road roughly paralleled the turnpike at varying distances and then intersected with it just to the west of Chancellorsville. Lee was aware that only two of his three corps were at hand. As he rode eastward alongside Hill, Lee sent instructions to Ewell—moving along the easier and less winding turnpike—not to trigger a general engagement until Longstreet had made the time-consuming march from Gordonsville.[32]

Hill's command by that stage of the war was so shabbily dressed in such a variety of clothes that the men looked like anything but soldiers. Yet they swung down the road at a determined pace and with light hearts. "Marse Bob is going for them this time!" men shouted at one another. A Virginia artillerist, who like everyone else knew the odds against the Confederates, later noted: "These lunatics were sweeping along to that appallingly unequal fight, cracking jokes, laughing, and with not the least idea in the world of anything else but victory. . . . It was the grandest moral exhibition I ever saw!"[33]

It had not yet begun to grow dark when Lee called a halt to the march. He and Hill pitched their tents in a roadside grove near a hamlet with the grandiose name New Verdiersville (the soldiers promptly dubbed it My Dearsville.) At the wooded site, Hill's men were twelve miles from where they had started. More important, they were about as close to the Wilderness as was the Federal column. The Wilderness was where Lee wanted to make contact. There, amid impenetrable thickets and on inadequate roads, Grant's superior numbers would count for less, his supremacy in artillery would be nullified because there were few places where cannon could be used, and the 4,000 wagons moving with the Union army would be a cumbersome handicap.

Lee's plan, if successful, would enable the Confederates to cut the Army of the Potomac in two, hold its halves divided and entangled in the Wilderness, and then drive what they did not destroy or capture back over the Rapidan. This was precisely what Lee had done to Hooker a year earlier.

At dawn on a radiant May 5, Hill started his two divisions in motion toward the Federals. Stuart and some of his cavalry were fanned out ahead, watching for any enemy troops. Hill's men marched through familiar surroundings, for the road over which they traveled was the same route they had followed in the Mine Run campaign. Lee soon rode up and joined Hill on the eastward advance. At a steady and rapid pace the columns passed the now-somber Mine Run earthworks and continued toward the ominous woodland that was the Wilderness.

Wilderness
and Sickness

Near eleven in the morning that Thursday, May 5, a courier from Ewell dashed up to Lee. Ewell had pushed ahead and sighted the Federal army. It was advancing southeastward and was now in the Wilderness. Lee sent the courier back to Ewell with a repeat of earlier instructions to regulate his advance with Hill's and to avoid a general engagement until Longstreet joined the army. Unknowingly, however, both Lee and Grant were in a helpless situation: once the two armies made contact, fighting would explode regardless of any timetable.

That contact came when Federals spotted Ewell and launched an attack along the Orange Turnpike. Ewell responded with an assault of his own. Thus commenced a battle that would last until the end of the war, with the two armies locked in almost daily combat until Appomattox mercifully brought it all to an end.

The sound of firing in Hill's front around noon sent the general galloping forward. Near the road junction at Parker's Store, a small body of Federal cavalry had struck Hill's column in flank. The Pennsylvania and New York horsemen, armed with rapid-firing Spencer carbines, maintained a spirited fight for a short while until Cooke's brigade (under Hill's orders) sent them disappearing back into the thickets. Kirkland's regiments took the lead as a tactical problem came into existence.[1] The roads on which Ewell and Hill were marching had by now diverged to three miles apart. The distance between the two Confederate corps was widening, with an attendant loss of communication. Hill's left and Ewell's right were no longer in contact.

Hill kept his soldiers moving along the Plank Road toward the Brock Road, four miles away. That junction—two dusty roads intersecting deep in an almost impenetrable labyrinth of trees and underbrush—would become vital to the whole Wilderness campaign. Union general Winfield S. Hancock's II Corps was already marching south of the intersection. If Hill's Confederates could occupy the junction, Hill could sweep north on the Brock Road and hit the left flank of Gen. G. K. Warren's V Corps, which was attacking Ewell. Warren could be destroyed or forced back across the Rapidan— whereupon Lee could turn all of his attention to Hancock, then isolated farther south of the road junction.

Meade also realized the importance of the Brock Road intersection. He rushed Gen. George Getty's 6,000-man division from John Sedgwick's VI Corps toward the crossing; at the same time he ordered Hancock to backtrack with all haste to Getty's support. Getty reached the junction with the Plank Road and threw up breastworks. Hancock's troops began arriving at two o'clock.

A mile and a half west of the intersection, the head of Hill's column had halted at an opening on high ground. The place was the Widow Tapp's farm. In that no-man's-land it was one of the few clearings where stood deserted houses or barns, reached only by unused and overgrown farm roads. It afforded a view of the enemy massing to the north, and it also enabled Hill to post Poague's battalion of artillery on the western edge of the clearing and in line with Hill's infantry.

Near three o'clock Lee and Stuart joined Hill on a shaded knoll just to the north of the little farmhouse. The three generals seated themselves to study the terrain while Heth's full division came up into battle line. Apprehension gripped the party. Ewell was already engaged with undetermined numbers of Federals; other Federals were massed in unknown strength in front of Hill; the gap between Hill and Ewell remained open and critical.

A few minutes later, Lee suddenly rose and shouted to his chief of staff to bring up troops. Out of a pine thicket across the clearing, a line of Union soldiers was moving. They were within 200 yards— easy musket range. Stuart rose cautiously to his feet. Hill, beginning to show unmistakable signs of illness, remained seated and gazed defiantly at the enemy. Then, across the way, came a shouted command

and the Federals inexplicably moved back into the pines. One of the North's grandest opportunities of the war was unknowingly lost.[2]

Heth's brigades had pushed ahead beyond the Tapp farm to within a mile of the Brock Road. The Southerners advanced cautiously, knowing full well that Federals were close in their front. Now the Confederates closed up and began forming a battle line perpendicular to the Plank Road. Cooke's brigade straddled the road; Davis was on his left, Walker to the right. Kirkland was immediately behind Cooke in reserve. Most of Hill's artillery, and all of his supply wagons, were two miles back at Parker's Store.

As Hill oversaw the deployment of his veteran units, Lee dispatched Wilcox's division northward in an attempt to link with Ewell and make a solid front of Lee's two wings. Wilcox had advanced several hundred yards when, around four o'clock, Federals poured through the woods in a furious assault on Heth. Hancock was coming at Hill with the three full divisions of Getty, David B. Birney, and Gershom Mott. Heth caught the entire onslaught as some 30,000 Federals concentrated on Heth's 6,700 Confederates.

Hill's first reaction was to mass sixteen guns under Poague and McIntosh in the large field at the Tapp farm. A staff officer pointed out to him that no adequate road existed for withdrawing the guns, should the infantry line snap.

"I know this," Hill replied with a tinge of irritation. "In battle the guns must take their chances of capture. They will help to hold the line if such an emergency occurs."[3]

Getty's Federal brigades had worked themselves to within 100 yards of Heth's line before the attack began. Thus, the Union assault was a short punch to the center while Birney and Mott poured in on the flanks. It produced a battle as intense as it was blinding. A Pennsylvania officer remarked that "the noise of the musketry, multiplied and re-echoed by the thick woods, was often frightful, and many a stout heart which had passed unshrinkingly through the dangers of well-fought fields quailed before the leaden blast which cut and stripped the young pines as if a cyclone had swept over them. . . . It was a fearful experience."[4]

Only smoke and sound guided the aim of the soldiers on both sides. Volleys of musketry were fired at unseen targets four feet from the ground. We halted, one Union soldier wrote, "returned the fire, and then dropped down, to get cover from the hail-storm of bullets. The enemy did the same. Again the lines were ordered to advance; but when the men rose, so many were at once shot down that it became plain that to advance was simply destruction. The men dropped again. They could not advance, but there was no thought of retreat."[5]

With fresh brigades of Federals streaming in on Heth, Lee had to abandon thoughts of linking Hill with Ewell. Wilcox's division was then easing northward somewhat at right angles to both the Plank Road and Heth. Lee ordered it to the support of Heth's crippled lines. McGowan's brigade constituted Wilcox's right and was at the northern edge of the Tapp farm. Before moving out, the South Carolinians decided to have a brief prayer service. "It was one of the most impressive scenes I ever witnessed," a Palmetto soldier remembered. "On the left thundered the dull battle; on the right the sharp crack of rifles gradually swelled to equal importance; above was the blue, placid heavens; around us a varied landscape of forest and fields, green with the earliest foliage of spring; and here knelt hirsute and browned veterans shriving for another struggle with death."[6]

The brigades of McGowan and Scales then rushed screaming into the woods and immediately collided head-on with Federals delivering an assault of their own. Instantly, wrote a Tarheel soldier, "the whole Wilderness roared like fire in a canebrake." McGowan's brigade never lost momentum, Wilcox reported. It "swept through the Wilderness like a tornado, driving everything before it—far in advance of the line—and had to be recalled." It returned triumphantly into line with 200 prisoners and the knowledge that its determination had caused a Federal line to break "in a disgraceful manner."[7]

In spite of the momentary setback, the Federal attacks against Hill's lines continued. A second onslaught drove through the woods and recoiled under concentrated musketry; then came a third, a fourth, a fifth. Scales's brigade managed to close a gap in Heth's line. Thomas marched up with his Georgians and formed on the left, where Kirkland's North Carolinians were in the midst of a hornet's nest of the enemy. Quickly Thomas sent his men driving into a Federal turning column—and the Georgians promptly received a slicing flank fire. Soon Thomas's men were fighting at right angles to one another, and, in some places, back to back. Visibility was twenty yards at most.

A veritable free-for-all on a gigantic scale ensued as both sides fought for control of a simple road junction buried in thick woods. "There are but one or two square miles upon this continent that

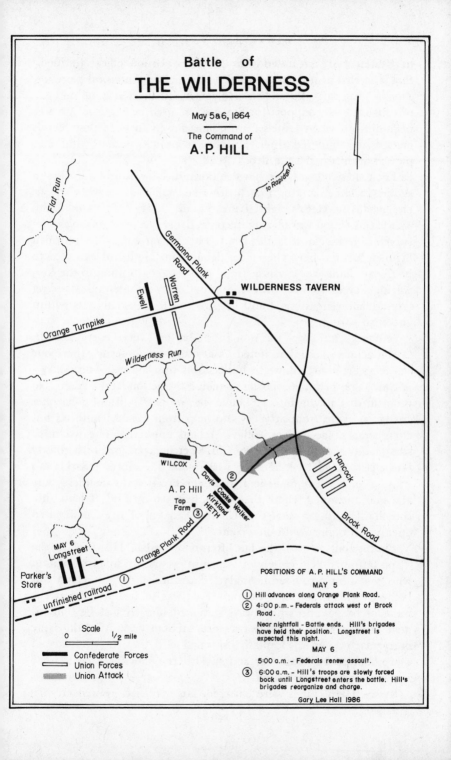

Battle of
THE WILDERNESS

May 5 a 6, 1864

The Command of
A.P. HILL

to Rapidan R.

Flat Run

Germanna Plank Road

Warren

Ewell

WILDERNESS TAVERN

Orange Turnpike

Wilderness Run

WILCOX

A. P. Hill

Tap Farm

Davis
Cooke
Kirkland
Walker
HETH

Hancock

Brock Road

MAY 6
Longstreet

Parker's Store

unfinished railroad

Orange Plank Road

Scale

0   1/2 mile

━━━ Confederate Forces

▭ Union Forces

▨ Union Attack

POSITIONS OF A.P. HILL'S COMMAND

MAY 5

① Hill advances along Orange Plank Road.

② 4:00 p.m. - Federals attack west of Brock Road.

Near nightfall - Battle ends. Hill's brigades have held their position. Longstreet is expected this night.

MAY 6

5:00 a.m. - Federals renew assault.

③ 6:00 a.m. - Hill's troops are slowly forced back until Longstreet enters the battle. Hill's brigades reorganize and charge.

Gary Lee Hall 1986

have been more saturated with blood," a Union officer testified.[8] Hill himself was now in the thick of the fighting, physical pain and a rising fever notwithstanding. He personally directed Lane to commit his men as a support for Scales's fractured ranks. The sun was beginning to set as Lane's Carolinians moved forward past Heth's dented and huddled lines. Scales's troops got second wind and pushed again toward the Brock Road.

The Lane-Scales advance bogged down in swampy ground. All of a sudden, a large flanking force of two Federal brigades wheeled out and made for Heth's right. Lane put up the best fight he could. While this action was blazing uncontrollably, Federals in waves continued to beat against Heth's front. The line on which Heth formed his men had not been chosen for defense, for Heth had expected to be the assailant. Yet it was a strong position, conforming to the low, waving ridges between the morasses, offering splendid standing ground, and remaining almost invisible until the enemy was within 40 or 50 yards.

Hancock's full corps was now in the battle. Every Federal assault, a Massachusetts chaplain noted, "was into an ambuscade, where our soldiers were mowed down by bullets from unseen lines of musketry." A New York *Tribune* reporter watching the action later wrote: "No room in that jungle for manoeuvering; no possibility of a bayonet charge; no help from artillery; no help from cavalry; nothing but close, square, face-to-face volleys of fatal musketry. The wounded stream out, and fresh troops pour in. Stretchers pass out with ghastly burdens, and go back reeking with blood for more."[9] Kirkland's brigade used a line of Federal dead for breastworks. Soldiers blue and gray remained where they were, firing away, and at least subconsciously wishing what Col. Charles Venable of Lee's staff stated openly: "If night would only come."[10]

Throughout most of the late-afternoon combat, Hill back at the Tapp farm had kept closely informed of events. An infantry captain who saw him wrote admiringly: "Surrounded by his staff, this beloved general, whose custom it ever was to feel in person the pulse of battle, and who always stationed himself just beyond his men in action, sat, a stately presence, anxiously awaiting the issue of events." When the captain informed Hill that his company of sharpshooters was ready for action, Hill responded: "Face the fire and go in where it is hottest!"[11]

By six, Heth's lines were battered. His men had poured an estimated 100,000 bullets into massed Federals in the course of a ten-minute period. Yet the Yankees were still assaulting in force. To add to the weight of Hancock's attacks on Heth's front and right, Gen. James Wadsworth's division of the V Corps was moving through the woods toward Heth's left. Thomas's men double-timed past Hill and moved to buttress Davis's Mississippians on the left. Then Lane's Tarheels, the largest brigade in Hill's corps, loped past and filed to the right to reinforce Walker. Hill had now committed every unit he had to battle. The general, anxiety so acute that he was oblivious to personal safety, galloped up and down the line amid flying bullets to encourage the troops to maximum effort.

The Federal line vacillated and, in some places, began falling back in the face of Confederate reinforcements. Heth grew so excited at this repulse of the Yankees that he ordered a local counterattack without informing Hill. The assault "proved to be a mistake," he later admitted. "I should have left well enough alone." His men bullied their way almost to the Brock Road before reeling back with skeletal ranks and the shock of defeat.[12]

It was now after seven and rapidly growing dark. Six different attacks had been made on Hill's lines, but the final crisis still faced him. A courier dashed up to Hill: Wadsworth's division was driving straight for the gap between Hill's left and Ewell's right. Hill knew without checking that every regiment he had was engaged. To pull one loose would jeopardize the whole battle line. The only unit available to him was Maj. A. S. Van de Graaff's 5th Alabama Battalion: 125 men who were at the moment guarding prisoners.

Hill put them in a skirmish line, told them to rush through the bushes and woods screaming the rebel yell at the top of their voices, and to give every indication that they were the lead elements of several brigades. The Alabamians bravely did as they were told. This handful of soldiers crashed through the underbrush, fired their muskets rapidly, and screamed themselves hoarse. Wadsworth's division had gotten lost earlier in the day and then had been pounded in battle before getting lost a second time. When this new Confederate attack came toward them at nightfall, the Federals stopped in their tracks, threw up earthworks, and called it a day.[13]

Collecting the dead was out of the question, and the woods in places had caught fire from the hours of fighting. Smoke drifted over the lines, bearing the fragrance of burning pine and the stench of burning flesh. Hill's 15,000 Confederates had somehow held back

40,000 equally determined Federals. His "successful resistance to so formidable a battle array" was deserving of high praise, one of Lee's artillery commanders asserted. "Hill did not stand on the defensive but made repeated dashes upon the line of the enemy. . . . He conducted the engagement with great spirit and aggressiveness, repeatedly broke Hancock's line of battle, and compelled him to use his reserves in propping it up."[14] A North Carolinian in Hill's corps saw it differently. The day's conflict had been "a butchery pure and simple." That was certainly true in some areas of the battleground. For example, the 55th North Carolina went into action with 340 men, of whom 34 were killed and 167 wounded. Directly in their front lay 157 dead Federals.[15]

The two armies did not pull apart at day's end. They simply stopped fighting where they were, with remnants of regiments and brigades facing in every direction all over the Wilderness and nobody quite knowing where friends or enemies might be. Lt. Col. William L. Davidson of the 7th North Carolina crept to a small stream for water and was quickly captured. A few moments later, Lt. Col. Clark B. Baldwin of the 1st Massachusetts sneaked to the same stream for the same purpose and just as quickly fell into Confederate hands.

Most of the troops lay quiet, poised and tense in the darkness. No one dared speak above a whisper. On one part of the line, footsteps became audible. Soon could be heard the clang-clang-clang of empty canteens banging against each other. Then up to the line walked a soldier, several canteens hung around his neck; in a normal voice he asked, "Can any of you fellas tell a man whar he can git some water?"

Instantly the woods exploded in an exchange of musketry. Men leaped to their feet, officers shouted, and a battle momentarily began. Quiet slowly descended anew over the area.[16]

A graver problem existed back at Third Corps headquarters: Hill's strength was failing him.

That day had been his most brilliant as a corps commander. Directing units into battle was what he did best, and in the Wilderness he had maneuvered his lines so skillfully that his troops had held back vastly superior numbers. Yet when that Thursday's fighting ended and excitement faded with sunset, the numbing pain Hill had felt all day became overpowering. He was feverish, cold, and bone-tired; everything in his groin hurt; he needed desperately to relieve himself, but the exertion produced only more discomfort.

By nine o'clock he welcomed the chance to sit down and rest. He pulled up a camp stool next to one of Poague's guns in Widow Tapp's field and, pale and weak, stared into the small campfire in front of him. His lines were in disorderly and hence dangerous condition, but Hill was too ill to concentrate.

Lee was already devising strategy for tomorrow's battle. Closing the gap between Ewell and Hill was paramount. Therefore, Hill was to sidle to the left and link with Ewell; Longstreet would come up behind Hill by midnight and take his place in line. At dawn, with his divisions and that of Anderson, Longstreet would attack the Union left while Ewell pressed hard against Grant's right. Heth and Wilcox were delighted to learn that reinforcements were on the way. According to one of Heth's men, the two divisions "lay in the shape of a semicircle, exhausted and bleeding, with but little order or distinctive organization."[17] Only yards separated their disjointed lines from those of untold thousands of Federals.

If Hill ever wrote an official report of the Wilderness campaign, it has been lost. Thus, who gave the order for those lines to remain as they were through the night has never been firmly established. Heth's postwar writings have been the traditional source of information on why the lines were not readjusted. That source is unreliable. Heth seems to have penned his account to absolve himself of any responsibility and to shift any blame away from Lee.

It is true that Heth and Wilcox went to Hill to express concern over the disarray of their lines and to seek permission to adjust their divisions for a probable Union attack at daylight. Hill said no. Reorganizing lines at night, in a heavily wooded area such as the Wilderness, and only yards from the enemy lines, was all but impossible. Pulling back any portion of the Southern line would mean abandoning Confederate wounded in the area. In response to Heth's first visit and plea, Hill added: "Longstreet will be up in a few hours. He will form in your front. I don't propose that your division shall do any fighting tomorrow. The men have been marching and fighting all day and are tired. I do not wish them disturbed." Hill is also quoted as saying that evening (with weariness in his voice): "Let the tired men sleep." Heth was not impressed.

Three times, Heth said, he went to Hill in an attempt to get his lines strengthened. The third attempt supposedly ended with the sick Hill shouting: "Damn it, Heth, I don't want to hear any more about it! I don't want them disturbed!" Heth later stated that he rode away from that brief conference "agitated by an anxiety such as he had never felt before or afterwards." He subsequently wrote, in a feeble attempt to temper his accusation: "The only excuse I can make for Hill is that he was sick." So apprehensive was Heth, he asserted, that he then went over Hill's head and sought to take his case to Lee. For two hours he rode back and forth in a vain search for the army commander. He then spent the remainder of the night pacing to and fro behind his lines in frustration.[18]

Heth's whole story is a dramatic one, to be sure, but it does not fit known facts.

Colonel Palmer, who was with Hill throughout the evening of May 5–6, vividly remembered Hill telling both Heth and Wilcox: "General Lee's orders are to let the men rest as they are." Wilcox went from his conference with Hill to see Lee—and found him. Lee reassured Wilcox that Longstreet "will be up, and the two divisions that have been so actively engaged will be relieved before day." Wilcox was so relieved by this news that he said nothing further of the irregular lines.[19]

Heth's story of a vain two-hour search for Lee is unbelievable. Lee's headquarters were conspicuous just a few hundred yards behind Heth's own lines, and the commander was in his tent all evening. Further, of all the accounts written of the unadjusted lines on May 5–6, only Heth's omits any reference to the major point: Longstreet was expected to be up and in place before daylight.

In addition, and contrary again to Heth's account, Hill did not dismiss the matter after their third conference. Hill remained anxious over the state of his lines—so much so that shortly after midnight he painfully made his way to Lee's tent to ascertain Longstreet's whereabouts. There was no news, but Lee repeated instructions that Hill let his men remain in line where they were. There is no reason to doubt that Lee made such a statement. From the breaking of camp in Orange County, Hill had been under Lee's directives because the army commander was always with the Third Corps.

Hill and Palmer returned to corps headquarters near one in the morning. Hill, as usual, was convinced that a fellow general would arrive on time. His staff did not share his optimism. "We could not sleep," Palmer recalled. "We knew that at the first blush of the morning the turning attack on our right would open with overwhelming numbers, and, unsupported, the men must give way."[20]

Around four, on a day that promised to be hot, Hill arose from his cot. He had had little more than two hours' sleep; the pain in his side and lower back were all but unbearable. (A London *Herald* correspondent reported that by May 6 Hill's illness "had unfitted him for the service.")²¹ But greater concerns faced the corps commander. He had expected Longstreet to be up and in line. Instead, the First Corps had just reached Parker's Store, two miles to the rear. Its tardiness now made Hill's disjointed lines dangerously vulnerable.

Hill gingerly mounted his horse as dawn came and, with his staff, began riding northward to inspect the interval between his left and Ewell's right. Palmer was left behind to maintain corps headquarters. It was five o'clock. Hill had barely disappeared from view when Longstreet came riding easily across the clearing. Palmer, who had known the burly Carolinian for several years, joyfully grasped his hand and exclaimed: "Ah, General, we have been looking for you since twelve o'clock last night."

Longstreet ignored the statement. "My troops are not up," he began. "I have ridden ahead . . ."

At that moment, his voice was drowned by an explosion of musketry in the woods along Hill's entire battle front. The Federals were attacking again!²²

The crash of rifle fire rolled from one end of the Union II Corps to the other. Hancock had the solidarity any general likes in battle. His troops were packed along a one-mile front; they were coming out of the rising sun, the glare adding to the obscurity of the Wilderness; and Wadsworth's division of the V Corps was poised on the right to lend its strength in the assault.

Heth and Wilcox were strangely unprepared for the dawn attack. Instead of being aroused a couple of hours in advance of daylight, the men had done nothing more than hope that Longstreet would get there in time. He did not. Now thirteen Union brigades, in indeterminable numbers, and striking in front and on both flanks, were swarming against the Confederates. For a half hour, Heth and Wilcox fought with everything they had. Bullets severed branches from tree trunks and saplings were cut down by musketry. Bloody remnants of uniforms hung on tree limbs as gruesome ornaments of battle.

Hill's men fought singly, in groups, and everywhere with desperation. The veterans knew how to load and fire rapidly, then fall back to a new and better position. So they slowly began giving ground, fighting bitterly as they did. No order intruded; they were fighting instinctively, and bravely, against a horde of the enemy stomping through the undergrowth. Hundreds, then thousands, of Confederates picked up speed as they retired toward the Tapp farm. Before six in the morning, Hill's situation had gone from dangerous to critical.

Longstreet had just ridden from view up the Plank Road to hasten his men forward when Hill galloped in from the north. He had started back to the Widow Tapp headquarters at the first sound of gunfire. Summoning Palmer, Hill then rode down the Plank Road toward the battle. Some of Wilcox's men were already falling back on the road and in the woods. Instantly, Palmer recalled, "the road was crowded with the enemy moving forward." Lee would report immediately after the battle that the Federal attack "created some confusion." In reality, three brigades of Wilcox's division, and all of Heth's units, were "driven more or less rapidly, crowded together in hopeless disorder, and only to be wondered at, when any of them attempted to make a stand."[23]

An "excited and chagrined" Hill galloped back and forth along the road in an effort to stop the growing disorder of his troops. Lee was doing the same, using language that was uncharacteristically sharp. Soon Lee found himself in the midst of McGowan's veteran South Carolina brigade. "My God, General McGowan!" he shouted. "Is this the splendid brigade of yours running like a flock of geese?"

"General," McGowan yelled back in defiance, "those men are not whipped! They only want a place to form, and they will fight as well as they ever did!"

Lee turned anxiously, searching in vain for Longstreet's troops. Wilcox rode up, conspicuous on his white horse, and asked for instructions. With anxiety and despair in his voice, Lee replied: "Longstreet must be here! Go bring him here!" Wilcox raced up the Plank Road as the Army of Northern Virginia faced the worst crisis it had known since that 1862 afternoon at Antietam Creek.[24]

By this time, Union general John Gibbon later wrote, "the roar of musketry was incessant and prolonged. . . . The whole forest was now one mass of flame."[25] Yet the Union assault was losing its punch. Wadsworth's division of 2,000 troops had swept in on Hill's left at too severe an angle. Those Federals bumped into Birney's division, forcing it to swerve to the left. Brigade formations began disintegrating; a colossal traffic jam of thousands of blue soldiers in the dense woods dissolved all alignment. In some places Federals were a dozen ranks deep; in other places, wide empty gaps existed.

The Confederate cannon had been standing silent in the clearing of the Tapp farm since the previous day. Now Hill, on his own initiative, directed Palmer to have Lt. Col. William Poague load his guns with double charges and fire obliquely across the road and over the heads of the retreating Confederates. Palmer hesitated. Wounded Southerners were scattered on the ground in the path of the Federal advance. Should the artillery not wait a few minutes?

"This cannot be delayed!" Hill shouted over the noise of battle. "The guns must open fire!"[26]

Poague's cannon roared. Bursting canister chewed gaps in the massed ranks of Federals in the road little more than two hundred yards away. As the blue line stumbled to a momentary halt, Poague sent another salvo ripping through the ranks, then another. A Federal force began inching toward Poague's unprotected flank. Hill by now had dismounted, and the former artillery officer was helping to man one of the guns.[27]

The conflict had reached a decisive point at the edge of the clearing. A Union corps stood poised to attack; a Confederate artillery battalion stood alone against it. At that high moment of confusion and excitement, a handful of Confederates came running eastward down the Plank Road. They were Texans, lead elements of the First Corps. Longstreet had at last arrived!

A Richmond cannoneer would later write: "Like a fine lady at a party, Longstreet was often late in his arrival at the ball, but he always made a sensation . . . with the grand old First Corps, sweeping behind him, as his train."[28] On this May 6, at barely seven in the morning, Longstreet's fourteen fresh brigades passed through the remnants of Hill's lines and reached the loosely arranged Federal battlefront. Psychology now entered the fray. Hancock's men had reached the edge of victory—one final push was all that was needed. Now fresh Confederates by the hundreds appeared out of nowhere and were attacking furiously. Initiative passed from Union to Confederate hands, while uncertainty and anxiety moved in the opposite direction.

Longstreet's men drove into the Union left and center, then began pressing back Hancock's lines toward the Brock Road. Hill meanwhile reorganized the fractured brigades of Heth and Wilcox.

The dawn Union attack had driven them back some 1,000 yards. (Confederate writers insisted it was only 300 yards; Union estimates ranged up to one and one-half miles.)[29] Hill then led the two divisions northward for another attempt at plugging the gap between his lines and Ewell's.

Hill set a brisk pace. Soon he and his staff were considerably in front of the Confederate column. Midway between the Plank Road and the old turnpike, they reached the Chewning farm. At the end of the clearing stood the abandoned house and several outbuildings. It was unusually quiet. Hill dismounted to ease the pain in his lower back and to study the lay of the land. He sat down on a box and gazed intently at the line of woods to the west.

So absorbed did Hill become with the topography that he did not see the solid line of Federal infantry behind him until the bluecoats began tearing away a fence in their path. When Hill turned around, capture—or death—was a scant 100 yards away.

Keeping his eyes on the Federals, Hill said calmly to his staff: "Mount, walk your horses, and don't look back."

The group did as it was told, the riders moving nonchalantly across the clearing and into the safety of the woods. (Later in the day, a Federal prisoner told Palmer that they had mistaken the horsemen for "farmers riding from the house.")[30] This was the second time in two days that Hill had narrowly escaped falling into Federal hands. Of more importance to him, however, was the information he received from prisoners that the Federal line was the van of Ambrose Burnside's IX Corps. The three Federal divisions were making their way slowly toward the space in Lee's center.

Hill dispatched Palmer back to Lee to see if one of the brigades in Anderson's division, which was temporarily under Longstreet's control, could be rushed toward the gap. Lee assented and with Palmer rode rapidly to Longstreet. "General Hill wants one of Anderson's brigades," Lee stated with a quick salute.

Longstreet, cocky in the belief that his arrival was saving the army, replied cheerily: "Certainly, Colonel. Which one will you take?"

"The leading one," Palmer snorted, with a mixture of impatience and irritation.[31]

A lull now occurred in the battle as both armies adjusted lines in anticipation of whatever the next stage would be. As Hill shored up his left, Longstreet massed four brigades on the extreme right. Hancock's men were still trying to regain cohesion when Longstreet's troops late in the morning struck the Federal flank. The Union line, in Hancock's laconic words, rolled up "like a wet blanket."[32]

Hill similarly counterattacked in his sector. Union soldiers, from behind strongly built breastworks of logs, waged a desperate contest with Confederates charging en masse through woods now catching fire from the intense volleys of musketry. In all of the chaos, and within a short distance of where Jackson had fallen a year earlier, Longstreet too was accidentally wounded by his own men. The heavy-set commander went down with a bullet wound through the throat and shoulder. Some Confederates carried a portion of the Federal works but could not hold them. To the north, Gen. John B. Gordon of Ewell's corps made a belated assault that netted 600 prisoners but failed to break Grant's right.

At day's end, the scene in the Wilderness was as gruesome as any in the entire war. A square mile of land to the west of the Brock Road looked like an image of hell. Dead soldiers lay sprawled in the bushes and against trees. Exhausted men were staggering in every direction, blindly seeking refuge of some sort. The wounded screamed and moaned for help as woods set afire by musketry burned slowly toward forms too maimed to move to safety.

Both armies spent the night of May 6–7 closing gaps and strengthening works so as to present the strongest possible defensive posture the next morning. Experienced soldiers knew that if an attack came, it would most likely occur at dawn, so weary but tense troops squinted with bloodshot eyes as the first rays of light pierced through the woods. Skirmishers resumed dueling; but as the minutes ticked into hours, it became evident that the opposing armies were too battered and too tired to resume the contest.

Two days of fighting had produced horrifying losses. Grant's casualties were about 16,000 killed, wounded, and missing; Lee had lost in excess of 11,400 men, some 7,000 of those casualties from Hill's corps. McGowan's South Carolina brigade, for example, had taken a fearful beating in the Wilderness: 55 killed, 383 wounded, and 43 missing.[33] And the two armies were about where they had been when the battle first began.

In recent years Hill has been singled out as the one most responsible for the near-disaster on May 6. Immediately after the war, however, Longstreet was considered the culprit. His slowness in coming to action at Second Manassas and Gettysburg had set a pattern that Longstreet seemed to repeat in the Wilderness. Mutterings against the First Corps commander would have been louder but for his wounding in the battle.[34]

Hill's physical condition worsened throughout an overcast and rainy Saturday, May 7. He made a morning visit to Davis's Mississippi brigade, which had fought gallantly the preceding day. Hill expressed his thanks, wrote Palmer, "with earnestness and emotion." The general then returned to his new headquarters: an abandoned farmhouse between the Plank Road and the turnpike. Lee joined him that afternoon after a check of Ewell's position. Hill and the army commander sat for a while on the front porch. Palmer then came down from the attic observation post. Federal artillery was moving off to the right, he reported. Grant appeared to be in motion toward the crossroad junction at Spotsylvania.[35]

Lee ordered Anderson, commanding Longstreet's corps, to withdraw from the line after dark and give pursuit to the southeast. Hill and Ewell were to follow Anderson when the situation in their separate fronts appeared to permit it. It was after ten at night before Hill's corps was able to begin its march. Through rain showers and over muddy roads, Hill led his men southward. Day broke damp and foggy; the sun came out in midmorning and created steamy heat.

That was all Hill could take. Now unable to ride a horse, pain coursing through his body at every step, high fever beclouding concentration, he no longer could lead effectively. Soldiers who saw Hill on May 8 described him as "very sick" . . . "too sick for the field" . . . "seriously indisposed" . . . "too feeble to continue." Hill dutifully sent a message to Lee: he was so ill that he must relinquish command. Lee reluctantly accepted the request and placed Jubal Early in temporary command of the Third Corps.[36] Early was untested as a corps commander and unpopular with most soldiers. At the head of Anderson's division was Gen. William Mahone, who likewise was inexperienced at that level.

This unproven leadership was one reason why Hill refused to leave the army in spite of his incapacitation. He ordered one of the ambulances converted into a mobile bed, and lying in the back of the wagon, he followed his corps to Spotsylvania. "Such was his anxiety to be near his troops," an admirer stated.[37]

Lee won the race to Spotsylvania and began forming a line to the north and west of the village. It was in the shape of an inverted V and, when completed, its flanks would anchor on the steep banks of small and shallow streams. The Third Corps reached the area in midafternoon of the ninth. It set to work constructing breastworks to the right of Ewell's corps and to the east of Spotsylvania.

Meanwhile, Grant was probing here and there for a weak spot in Lee's position. Hill's men were barely into their earth-moving labors when Federals were reported moving in some force on the extreme left of the Confederate army. Lee hastily directed Early to send one of his divisions to the threatened region and to dispatch a second division the next morning to combat any enemy troops that might have crossed the Po River.

On the morning of the tenth, Heth sent his division into battle along the Shady Grove Road. A newspaperman declared, "Heth's men were glad of an opportunity to prove to all that the temporary confusion into which they were thrown at the Wilderness was the result of an accident rather than a lack of spirit." The contest gave early indication of developing into an all-day battle. Yet the Federals retired after a few minutes' fighting. Heth gave pursuit. Around two in the afternoon the enemy made a stand in a field near the river; according to a Billy Yank, "a prettier field [was] rarely to be found in that land of tangle and swamps."[38]

Heth attacked twice, was twice repulsed, attacked a third time, and slowly forced the stubbornly resisting Federals across the river. "Our men," an observer boasted, "drove them back some three or four miles, and out of their lines of breastworks, capturing one piece of artillery, one caisson, and some one hundred and fifty prisoners." Hancock likewise reported inflicting heavy casualties—"our front" being "strewn with their dead and wounded," he stated.[39] In this action Gen. Henry Walker was so badly wounded that a foot had to be amputated. The Field-Brockenbrough-Mayo-Walker brigade was thus in need of another brigadier.

Heth's men returned to their works on the right of Lee's line and, buoyed by congratulatory messages from both Lee and Hill, spent a drizzly May 11 crouched in wet trenches. The two armies now stood face to face, "lashing their sides and glaring upon each other like lions about to engage in mortal combat," a correspondent noted. The Confederate line was an arc five to seven miles long. In its center was a large salient that projected north for three-fourths of a mile. The country in its immediate front was open; the Confederate fortifications inside its edge were a strong combination of logs and dirt. Hill's corps of 13,000 men occupied a one-and-one-half-mile position along the right side of the salient. The troops were hungry, weary, and unwashed after almost ten days of constant service, but they were ready to do battle, if necessary.[40]

Steady rain began near sundown. That evening Lee rode a mile south of Spotsylvania to a church that Heth was using as headquarters. A number of generals were there, including Hill, who remained unfit for field duty. The main topic of conversation was the Federal movements of the past week. A staff officer remarked that Grant was throwing his men into battle like a butcher.

Lee disagreed. "I think General Grant has managed his affairs remarkably well up to the present time," he said with little emotion. Then, turning to Heth, Lee stated: "I wish you to have everything in readiness to pull out at a moment's notice. We must attack these people if they retreat."

The pale but still-aggressive Hill spoke up. "General Lee, let them continue to attack our breastworks. We can stand that very well." Heth seconded the thought.

Lee changed the subject. Yet a few minutes later, as Lee rose to depart, the commander said wearily: "This army cannot stand a siege. We must end this business on the battlefield, not in a fortified place."[41]

Shortly after four-thirty the next morning, with a wet and chilly fog at ground level, massed Federals charged the northwest face of the salient. Some of the most vicious fighting of the entire war took place at that "Bloody Angle," as it came to be called. Men of blue and gray slugged it out in the rain for almost twenty hours. For hundreds of yards along the line, only the width of the earthworks separated the two battling armies. Dead men fell on top of wounded men; some soldiers were trampled under the muck of mud and blood. All day and into the night, Confederates grimly held most of their positions while Federals continued to attack with fierce determination and while Lee's engineers frantically completed a new line a mile to the rear. It was past midnight when the exhausted survivors of the assaults staggered back to the new position.

On the other (eastern) side of the salient that wet and incalculably bloody Thursday, the issue also hung in doubt for hours. Hill remained "sick in his ambulance" all day. He recognized that Early was in command of his corps. Nevertheless, he got as close to the firing line as his wagon could get, "lending the aid of his personality to Gen. Early."[42]

Hill's soldiers were involved in three different assaults that day.

Shortly after dawn, Burnside's IX Corps advanced en masse into Hill's sector. The Federal assault met with no success against Wilcox, whose division constituted the left and center of Hill's line. Confederate artillery simply tore the attacking columns to pieces as they appeared in the open. However, on the extreme Southern right, Billy Yanks in Robert Potter's division swept Lane's brigade from a section of trenches and captured two cannon along with several score men. The highly competent Lane had foreseen possible disaster, so he had broken back half of his North Carolina brigade to protect his flank. These two regiments were ready when the shock of Potter's onslaught came, and their enfilade fire brought the Federals to an uncertain pause. By the time Union brigadiers got their men moving again, Wilcox had rushed parts of Scales's and Thomas's brigades to Lane's support. This force drove the remainder of Burnside's men from the field. Among the Union casualties were some 300 men taken prisoner.[43]

With a lull in the fighting on the east side of the salient, Early dispatched the brigades of Perrin, Nathaniel Harris, and McGowan to assist Ewell's hard-pressed troops at the "Bloody Angle." In misty rain these troops went slipping and stumbling through churned mud and fought their way to the apex of the salient. Perrin was shot dead from his horse and McGowan went down with a severe arm wound as the three brigades were swallowed up in the chaos of the battle.

The fighting on the Confederate right in the afternoon was as fierce as that in the morning. Lee resolved to try to relieve the pressure on his left by having Heth launch an attack against Grant's left. The brigades of Lane and David Weisiger (who succeeded Walker) had just moved out into a clump of oaks on the far right when Burnside's divisions struck again. Federals charged into a Bristoe Station–like trap: the guns of Poague and Pegram blasted the columns at point-blank range while the infantry of Lane and Weisiger fired into the exposed flank. Burnside's advance dissolved with heavy losses.

Far into the night the battle for the Spotsylvania salient roared. When men were incapable of fighting any longer, the holocaust slowly ended. More than 10,000 men on both sides had been killed, wounded, or captured. The next morning, with rain still falling, one of Hill's South Carolinians observed that "the ground was literally covered with the dead and dying, and the water that rippled along the trenches from incessant rain, ran red with the blood of the slain."[44] The rain continued through May 14 as troops on both sides strengthened their positions amid constant skirmish fire.

Sunday, May 15, broke clear and pleasant. For the first time in ten days there was peace between the lines. Hill, still ashen and weak, made an attempt at resuming command of his corps, but it quickly became obvious—at least to Lee—that Hill was mentally not up to the task. Hill dispatched Ambrose Wright's Georgia brigade to seize a commanding hill alongside the Po near Snell's Bridge. Hill watched as Wright so badly mismanaged the affair that Nathaniel Harris's brigade had to be sent to complete the task. By the time Lee reached the scene, Hill was furious. The corps commander vowed to haul Wright before a court of inquiry at the first opportunity. Lee, speaking in even terms, then gave Hill what amounted to a lecture.

"These men are not an army; they are citizens defending their country. General Wright is not a soldier; he is a lawyer. I cannot do many things that I could do with a trained army. The soldiers know their duties better than the general officers do, and they have fought magnificently." Lee pointed out that a commander had to do the best he could with what he had. "You understand all of this," he said to Hill, "but if you humiliated General Wright, the people of Georgia would not understand. Besides, whom would you put in his place? You'll have to do what I do. When a man makes a mistake, I call him to my tent, talk to him, and use the authority of my position to make him do the right thing the next time."[45]

As rain started again on the sixteenth, Hill suffered a relapse. His personal physician, Dr. John W. Powell, wrote to members of the Hill family, urging them to try to persuade Hill to accept a sick furlough in order to regain his health. Hill refused all entreaties and insisted on following in his ambulance wherever the Third Corps went. "I cannot leave my command," he stated, "and just as soon as possible, I shall take charge of my brave fellows again."[46]

North Anna to Petersburg

On May 20, Grant abandoned the Spotsylvania line and again shifted to the southeast. Lee had no choice but to do the same. He would fall back to the North Anna River. That would give him a new line for defending both the Virginia Central Railroad and its crossing with the Richmond, Fredericksburg & Potomac Railroad at Hanover Junction. The major problem of such a move was that the North Anna was only twenty-five miles from Richmond, the North's principal objective.

Lee made his dispositions on the afternoon of the twenty-first at the Southworth house, on the right bank of the Po. He was conferring with several generals when up rode Hill. "Little Powell" sat his horse as gracefully as of old, and he cheerily exchanged greetings with a number of officers. The two-week bout with illness had seemingly (though not actually) run its course. I am ready to resume command, Hill eagerly told Lee. The army commander quickly issued orders to that effect. Perhaps Hill should have waited several days longer, for his handling of his troops in the next forty-eight hours was not that of a man physically at his best. At this same time, Lee himself was ailing. He was exhausted from the nervous strain and hard physical life of the current campaign. His own health was now beginning to break. Col. Walter H. Taylor of his staff confided in a letter home that Lee "could attend to nothing except what was absolutely necessary for him to know and act upon."[1]

Hill's brigades left the salient on the night of Saturday the twenty-first with immense relief. "There was thousands that was not buried," a Confederate explained, "and the stench was so bad at Spotsylvania Court House that we could not stand it for you might see hundreds of men laying on the ground rotting." Through the night, and until noon on the twenty-second, Hill's men "tramped rapidly forward through the heat and dust with a will and spirit that speak their own commendation."[2] The thirty-mile march ended when the divisions bivouacked in the woods at Anderson's Station, on the Virginia Central line just to the west of Hanover Junction. Officers and men were exhausted as they formed a line on the left of Lee's new defensive position.

Three miles northwest of Anderson's Station was a North Anna crossing known as Jericho Mills. Most of the countryside was open and cultivated, but near the gristmill ford, heavy woods blocked the river from view. Inexplicably, no Confederate outpost had been placed there. Warren's V Corps discovered the undefended crossing on the twenty-third. By noon Federals had established a beachhead on the south side, and engineers constructed a pontoon bridge across the waist-deep stream.

Early in the afternoon, Hill notified Lee that probing artillery fire from the vicinity of Jericho Mills "had caused some excitement at corps headquarters." Lee, too ill to ride a horse, climbed into a carriage and proceeded two miles westward to a rise where one of his batteries was taking position. For a while, through a telescope, he watched the Federals cross the river. Then Lee turned and said to a courier: "Go back and tell General Hill to leave his men in camp. This is nothing but a feint. The enemy is preparing to cross [the North Anna] farther down."[3]

Hill was not convinced. He ordered Wilcox to make a reconnaissance toward Jericho Mills while the Third Corps began turning ninety degrees so as to be perpendicular to the railroad. Around three in the afternoon Wilcox discovered that Federals in force were across the North Anna and moving southward through woods. He rode swiftly and reported to Hill. A segment of Grant's army was isolated on the south side of the river, Hill concluded. This was a grand opportunity! Advance and attack, he told Wilcox. Shortly thereafter—no one knows exactly when—Hill sent Heth's division to support Wilcox.

Wilcox moved with commendable dispatch. He got his brigades out of camp and on the road in columns of four. The men marched two miles beside the railroad before forming a line of battle to the north. By then it was six o'clock. All four divisions of Warren's corps were across the North Anna. Wilcox, like Hill, was unaware of the Federal strength. He arranged the old Light Division with Thomas, McGowan, and Lane left to right in the front line. Scales formed behind Thomas to swerve around the Federal right if Thomas could overlap that flank.

Once in battle deployment, the Confederates started northward. Thomas was in woods most of the way. McGowan and Lane had to cross 200 yards of open ground and traverse a boggy bottom before moving up to a thick wood where the Federals were presumed to be. The attack began briskly. Thomas and McGowan struck and routed the Federals in their front. A Union soldier conceded that "taken unawares, and unable to withstand the shock, the Iron Brigade fell back pell-mell towards the river, and the heavy columns of the enemy were precipitated upon the Bucktail Brigade, a great portion of which also gave way and joined in the disorderly retreat."[4]

As quickly as Wilcox's attack gained momentum, however, it fell apart. Of course, four brigades were going to run into trouble attacking four divisions, but trouble came even before Federal numbers began to tell. General Ed Thomas was mounted and encouraging his Georgians forward, "as if he was in a fox chase," when an oblique fire tore into their ranks. The Georgians began falling back at the moment their opponents did. That left McGowan's left flank dangling in the air. Scales meanwhile had begun his turning movement —which left him similarly exposed as Thomas's men withdrew. Scales made contact with the Federal flank, but for unexplained reasons did not attack in force.

On the far right, Lane's regiments dashed across a large field and plunged into the woods directly into a fusillade of gunshots from a commanding ridge. Lane candidly informed Wilcox that his North Carolina brigade was breaking apart. "It is not so," Wilcox replied. "Push on."

Lane did so, which now left McGowan's other flank exposed; and within minutes, the 37th North Carolina broke to the rear. Soldiers in Lane's other regiments bleated like sheep at their fleeing comrades. Yet Lane's attack had ground to a halt.[5]

Nightfall, and a heavy rainstorm soaking the field, brought an end to the piecemeal fighting, but Heth and Wilcox were at each other before the gunfire subsided. Wilcox claimed that he saw Heth's men leisurely marching along the railroad behind him but never saw them in battle. Heth bitterly denied the charges.[6] Each side had lost about 650 men. This proved, among other things, that Warren, with superior numbers, had hardly fought a sterling battle either—despite the fact that this was the only engagement between Spotsylvania and Petersburg in which Union soldiers had the advantage of remaining behind works and receiving the attack of the enemy.

On the other hand, perhaps the Southerners had been on defense too much in recent weeks and had momentarily lost the knack of making a cohesive assault. After Lee's statement that the Federal movement at Jericho Mills was a feint, Hill cannot be faulted for sending only one division on his own initiative to investigate. Indeed, rarely is so large a unit as a division sent on a reconnaissance. An accusing finger can be pointed at the Confederate cavalry, however, for failing to report the status of the Jericho Mills crossing, and at Wilcox, for his subsequent disjointed attack. How much difference Hill would have made had he been on the field and personally directing the action is conjectural. He spent the afternoon of the twenty-third with the bulk of his corps—as a good corps commander is supposed to do.

Lee forgot that principle when he rode to Hill's headquarters on the morning of May 24. An intestinal complaint now all but prostrated Lee. Whether he could remain in the field was questionable. He was in pain and testy when he greeted Hill that morning. Hill had just reported his losses when Lee, in a rare display of anger, blurted: "Why did you not do as Jackson would have done—thrown your whole force upon those people and driven them back?"[7]

Hill could easily have pointed out that in sending a lone division to probe for an unseen enemy, he had done precisely what Lee did when he dispatched Heth toward the Brock Road in the Wilderness. Lee's outburst was more an expression of his own weakened condition than a judgment of what Hill did or did not do. Hill's affection for Lee was reverential, and he could sympathize with his physical suffering. So, as always, Hill made no reply.

The worst frustration for Lee in May 1864 was the realization that for the first time in the war he had lost the initiative to the Army of the Potomac. The Union army could pause in Lee's front and prepare for a new offensive without fearing a sudden attack. At the North Anna position, Lee had placed his forces in another inverted V position, and he had strengthened his line with 8,500 soldiers from the heretofore scattered commands of Pickett, Robert

F. Hoke, and John C. Breckinridge. It was not enough. The attrition of war had sapped too much manpower and vitality from the Army of Northern Virginia. The spirit was there; the muscle was not. So Lee, instead of driving into one of the two Federal wings along the North Anna, continued on the defensive. He had been reduced to counterpunching. Thereafter, Lee could only moan helplessly: "We must strike them a blow. We must never let them pass us again. We must strike them a blow."[8]

On May 26, Grant gave up the attempt to make a due-south thrust at Richmond via the North Anna. The Union army broke camp and sidled again to the southeast. Lee set his army in motion the next day. Ewell took the lead, followed by Anderson with the First Corps. Hill's corps constituted the rear guard and departed from the river entrenchments after dark. Heavy rains had put large stretches of the roads under water. Soldiers waded for miles in the darkness, falling into mudholes as they struggled to keep afoot. Yet by such forced marches Lee by May 29 had once more gotten between Grant and Richmond.

Hill's new line extended westward from Totopotomy Creek almost to the Virginia Central Railroad. He was on the far left, with his headquarters near the Shady Grove Church road. As the army briefly rested that Sunday, the highly opinionated Col. Samuel Walkup of the 48th North Carolina voiced disgust anew. He had written a week earlier that "Lee is outwitted by Grant." Now, on the twenty-ninth, Walkup vented his anger toward Hill. He wrote in his diary, after spending the day at Hill's headquarters: "He is a proud, haughty, old maidish son, and selfish looking misanthrope and loves to be a tyrant and vixenish, snaps and snarls at everybody."[9]

Shortly after sunrise on the thirtieth, Federals began withdrawing from Hill's front and moving toward the Confederate right. Hill was disappointed. "I have a good line and would like to fight it," he told Lee.[10] It became clear as the day progressed, however, that Grant was striking for the Chickahominy River, which would put the Union army less than ten miles from Richmond. Heavy skirmishing and deadly artillery exchanges marked the routes of the two armies as they jockeyed for position between the Totopotomy and Chickahominy.

Lee on June 1 sought to deter Grant's movement with an attack by Anderson and Hoke from the Confederate right. It failed badly. Later that stiflingly hot afternoon, portions of the Union army assaulted Hill's lines on the far left. Charging Federals got to within twenty yards of the positions manned by the brigades of Cooke and Kirkland. Hill's artillery then opened with double charges of canister. "It looked to me," wrote a cannoneer, "as if the flame from our gun ran half way down their line. We fired *seventeen* rounds of canister into that column and its advance was stopped." A captain in the 47th North Carolina recalled that before the infantry companies fired a round, "the enemy was completely broken and routed, a large number of them killed and wounded. Our loss was almost nothing as the enemy, depending on giving us the bayonet, withheld their fire, until they were repulsed." Some 100 Federals were also captured in the action. The troops of Breckinridge and William Mahone also cleared the ground in their front at sundown and took almost 150 prisoners.[11]

That night, as Grant continued shifting eastward, Lee transferred Breckinridge and two divisions of Hill's corps to defend the right flank. Confederates marched through the sultry night and into the afternoon of June 2 before they dislodged Federals from, and occupied, the strong position on Turkey Hill. Thirst was severe in the ranks. In addition, the Confederates had had nothing akin to a full meal for a week. Hill was on the field, giving encouragement and reassurances to his men.[12]

Two armies faced each other in an almost straight battle line which ran six miles. The Federals faced west; the Confederates, east. The southern flank of both rested on the Chickahominy River. Throughout the hot morning of June 2, Confederates strengthened their position. Most of Lee's works were in thick woods. Moreover, a newspaperman observed, "they are intricate, zig-zagged lines within lines, lines protecting flanks of lines, lines built to enfilade opposing lines . . . works within works and works outside works, each laid out with some definite design."[13]

The Confederate defenses were a rather strange lineup. Heth was on the far left, with cavalry covering his flank. Mahone and Wilcox were on the far right. Thus, the Third Corps occupied the flanks, while the First Corps (temporarily under Anderson) and the Second Corps (temporarily under Early) formed the main line.

Before rain began falling in the afternoon, Grant made several testing stabs at the Confederate lines. Lee was convinced, however, that the main Union assault would come against his right-center near Cold Harbor. The place was neither a harbor nor a town; it was simply a point where five roads met, and that made it strategic for both armies. Intermittent downpours continued into the night, turning trenches into quagmires and creating such confusion that one of Hill's couriers rode straight into the Union lines by mistake. Yet through the dark hours some 50,000 Federals massed in preparation for assailing 30,000 Confederates. Hill had established his headquarters on a hill between the Gaines homes and Gaines's Mill, where he had demonstrated great fighting prowess a long two years ago.[14]

Dawn, June 3, came slowly because of drizzling rain and a heavy fog, which hung over the low, uneven ground. Three Federal corps stood ready to attack half of Anderson's corps and two-thirds of Hill's. Hancock's II Corps faced the extreme Confederate right; Horatio G. Wright's VI was to Hancock's right; William F. Smith's XVIII was next to Wright. Promptly at four-thirty that Friday morning, there was a roar of cheers, followed by a crash of musketry and the loudest artillery bombardment the Confederate capital had ever heard. Another great battle for Richmond had begun.

Grant was guilty of several major mistakes at Cold Harbor. The first was a failure to reconnoiter. Thus, when his three corps jumped off to the attack, they knew nothing of terrain or of Confederate positions and strength. Initially, Hancock's corps moved gallantly forward in double line of attack. Federals overran a salient in front of Hill and Breckinridge, quickly making prisoners of 300 Confederates, but this Union success was short-lived.

Mahone rushed the Florida brigade of Joseph Finegan into the breach. Breckinridge did the same with the 2nd Maryland Battalion. The salient was retaken after some 200 Federals had been killed.

Hill's artillery and infantry now were sending such a concentrated fire into the ranks of the II Corps that Hancock's soldiers instinctively swerved to the left. Wright's corps, in the Union center of this attack, went straight ahead. Smith, on the right, bore off to his right because of rough ground and a severe flank fire. The farther the Union troops advanced, the more separated the three corps became.

From one end of Lee's line to the other, the battle raged. "Their columns seemed unending!" one of Hill's artillerists later wrote. "Up and down our battle line the fierce musketry . . . [was] crashing and rolling like the sound of a heavy hail on a tin roof, magnified a thousand times, with the cannon pealing out in the midst of it like claps of thunder. Our line, far as the eye could reach, was ablaze with fire; and into that furious storm of death, the blue columns were swiftly urging their way." In many places, scarcely more than thirty yards from Hill's lines, desperate Federal soldiers scraped dirt loose with bayonets and tin plates so as to cover themselves in shallow depressions in an attempt to escape being shot.[15]

Thirty minutes into the unequal contest, Lee sent a courier to determine how well Hill was holding his end of the line. Hill rode forward with the courier to an open expanse and pointed to where Union dead were literally piled in heaps. "Tell General Lee," he stated, "it is the same all along my front." Indeed it was. Hancock's assaults against Hill had cost the Union general 2,000 men in less than two hours' fighting.[16]

There never was any concert to the Federal attacks. The result was predictable: Union assaults came in layers, with Confederates peeling back each one in turn. On Heth's front, elements of Burnside's IX Corps tried to break the Southern line. One charge after another came to grief. An officer in the 48th North Carolina of Cooke's brigade described the climactic moments of Burnside's efforts. "One line would fire and fall down, another step over, fire and fall down, each line getting nearer us, until they got within sixty or seventy-five yards of some portions of our line, but finding themselves cut to pieces so badly, they fell back in a little disorder. Our men seemed to rise all at once, with a rebel yell, and poured lead into them. . . . The old field in front of us was almost covered with their dead."[17]

The battle of Cold Harbor quickly became a massacre. A Union brigadier wrote of his men: "They did all that was possible; but the impossible was asked of them." At twelve-thirty, Grant brought a merciful halt to the fighting. Over 7,000 Union soldiers lay dead or wounded as a hot sun baked the steaming ground. Confederate losses totaled barely 1,500 men. Lee had gained one of the most clear-cut victories of the Civil War.[18]

Until June 12, Hill's men crouched in stifling, filthy trenches near Cold Harbor. It was an extremely unpleasant existence after a month-long campaign. "Our boys are tired and worsed out," a Tarheel soldier wrote home.[19] For several days after the battle, both armies remained on the alert, so that whenever a head appeared above the works even for an instant, it became the target for scores of gunshots. Water was scarce and food all but nonexistent. Dust began to thicken owing to the absence of rain. Worst of all, hundreds of wounded men died unattended between the lines; and their remains, along with those slain on June 3, contaminated the air to an overpowering degree. Not until June 7 did Grant finally consent to a two-hour truce for removing the wounded. By then it was unnecessary. Everyone on the field was dead. The bodies had decomposed so badly that no attempt was made to remove the corpses. Remains were buried where they lay.

Breckinridge's division pulled out of the line the same day and started west to meet a new Union threat in the Shenandoah Valley. Hill spread his troops into the vacated works and then consolidated his corps by shifting Heth's division from the far left to a position behind Hill's line. Hill notified Lee when the new dispositions had been completed. The commander's long acknowledgment contained a sad but true commentary on the plight of the Army of Northern Virginia. "I have little fear of your ability to maintain your position if our men do as they generally do. The time has arrived, in my opinion, when something more is necessary than adhering to lines and defensive positions. We shall be obliged to go out and prevent the enemy from selecting such positions as he chooses. If he is allowed to continue that course we shall at last be obliged to take refuge behind the works of Richmond and stand a siege, which would be but a work of time."[20]

Grant had resolved on precisely that offensive. On the morning of June 13, Lee received the shocking news that the Union lines were empty. Grant's army had slipped away in the night, either down the peninsula or toward the James River. With Early's corps en route to the Valley, Lee immediately sent Hill and Anderson in pursuit of Grant. The day was hot and dry, but Hill's columns marched with a sense of urgency. They skirted White Oak Swamp and, in late afternoon, made contact with Federals on the Charles City road. Hill lost 80 to 90 men in driving the enemy back to the east.[21] Lee had managed—barely—to cover the eastern approaches to Richmond.

In reality, Grant was leading the Union army across the James River. He could no longer maintain a position northeast of Richmond because he was too vulnerable to attack. Moreover, another assault on Lee would doubtless bring a new round of heavy losses, and the North was already reacting loudly to Grant's casualty lists. Once south of the James, Grant believed, he could besiege Lee in front and south of the capital.

The target of the Union army now became Petersburg, situated some twenty-two miles south of Richmond. It was a fortress for the Confederate capital. Three railroads and a dozen highways all converged on Petersburg. The James River Canal was just to the north, the navigable James River immediately to the east. Of paramount importance was the fact that this town of 18,000 residents was in a sense the gateway to the capital itself. If Petersburg fell, Richmond was doomed.

Lee was still not convinced of Grant's intentions, and lack of cavalry inhibited up-to-date knowledge of Federal movements. On the morning of the fourteenth, Lee ordered some of Hill's infantry to push out from their bivouac on the 1862 Frayser's Farm battlefield. Hill moved his troops forward with skirmish lines spread out on either side of the roads fanning northward from Malvern Hill. Lee joined Hill, Heth, Wilcox, Hoke, and Scales at a clearing. Together, the generals watched as two of Hill's brigades fought a spirited skirmish through much of the day.[22]

Although Hill's men were holding their own against Union pressure, unhealthy conditions were taking a severe toll. Exposure, poor rations, humid weather, impure water, general filth, lack of rest—all led to outbreaks of diarrhea, dysentery, typhoid fever, and other diseases. Nevertheless, on the morning of June 15, Hill pushed his men farther to the southeast. He reported Federal cavalry in his front, but the ease with which the Confederates advanced indicated that no Federals in strength were behind the screen of horsemen. At sundown that day, Hill informed Lee: "I have taken a new line, with my left resting so as to cover the White Oak Swamp bridge, with a regiment and battery on the other side, and my right covering the Willis Church road. The line is a very defensible one."[23]

Lee was awakened at two in the morning on the sixteenth and told that at least half of the Union corps had crossed the James and was striking for Petersburg. The divisions of Pickett and Anderson were quickly ordered southward, with two more divisions to follow. Hill received orders to continue shielding Richmond from a possible northside attack. His front extended from Malvern Hill to Riddell's Shop. Hill had 15,000 infantry, a few artillery, and two undersized cavalry brigades. His strength was less than a Union corps, and the whereabouts of three enemy corps at the moment were unknown.

Rarely had Lee been in a more precarious situation. He had fewer than 30,000 soldiers to confront an army more than three times his strength. Half of the Confederates were south of the James, the other half north of the river. The two opposing forces were now in a race for Petersburg, defended only by a hodgepodge force under Gen. P. G. T. Beauregard. On the sixteenth, Hancock and Burnside flung their corps at the Petersburg works, to no avail. They renewed the assaults on the seventeenth, but failed again with heavy losses. Hill attended a church service at Lee's headquarters that day, after which the two generals conferred at length. At three in the morning on the eighteenth, with no Federals remaining in his front, Hill started his men to the Chaffin's Bluff crossing. The march was long and trying, but Hill drove the men relentlessly. Their presence could mean the salvation of Petersburg, for Beauregard had advised Lee that he could not hold the city any longer without reinforcements.[24]

Hill paused at Chaffin's Bluff for two hours, then before daybreak started his weary troops across a pontoon bridge. Throughout the morning and early afternoon of June 18, Hill's troops marched furiously along the Petersburg pike, fighting thirst and spitting dust. "Regiments melted down to the dimensions of companies," a South Carolina soldier observed, "and many companies had hardly a single representative left. A brigade could stretch for miles."[25]

Under a baking sun, Hill led his men for twenty miles. Straggling was widespread, but sounds of Federals attacking Petersburg a third day spurred the columns southward. In midafternoon, Hill's corps reached the city. The first of the regiments to enter Petersburg was the 12th Virginia, composed in the main of Petersburg men. Families and servants rushed joyfully into the streets to greet this half of Lee's army.[26] Hill's men felt no elation when they struggled to a halt on the right of the Confederate defenses. Perspiration streamed from head to toe, bleary eyes gazed from taut faces, and hair was so covered with dirt that the ranks looked like a gathering of aged veterans.

Once again the Army of Northern Virginia and the Army of the Potomac confronted each other in battle array. Hill was not optimistic about the situation when he reached Petersburg. Holding the line with impoverished men against such vastly superior numbers seemed impossible.[27] Yet this had no deterring effect on the iron will of "Little Powell." He would continue giving everything his health would permit. With that resolve, Hill entered his longest—and his last—campaign.

19

The Besieged
Strike Back

For nine and one-half long, agonizing months the siege lasted. Grant concentrated men and material in unprecedented quantities against Lee; he extended his lines, utilized artillery bombardments, hurled his troops into battle at one point after another, and even attempted to mine the enemy position. The Confederate line held, confounding expectations. It was one of the most valorous defenses in modern warfare; "and the record of the series of brilliant operations on our right in the siege of Petersburg," Lee's chief of staff wrote, "may be said to be a diary of the command of A. P. Hill."[1] The arrival of Hill's corps on June 18 enabled Lee to extend his line in an arc to the Weldon Railroad south of Petersburg. Lee saw the futility of trying to maintain control of that rail line indefinitely—despite its links with Wilmington, N.C., and Charleston, S.C.—since the northern end of the line was but three miles from Federal positions. What Lee wanted to do was hold the Weldon Railroad until the summer and autumn crops could be harvested and shipped to the front.

June 19 was the sabbath. Hill and Lee attended an Episcopal church service in the morning and were warmly greeted by a grateful congregation. A matron at the service noted: "General A. P. Hill knelt beside [Lee]. He is a small man, but has a very military bearing, and a countenance pleasing but inexpressibly sad." Hill was not well that day. He spent the night in an ambulance, but he got little rest. At three o'clock he was awakened and informed that a new, unorganized brigade was reporting for duty. Hill curbed his exasperation, calmly refused to accept the unit as it was, and wearily returned to bed.[2]

The Union assaults of June 15–18 against Petersburg had cost Grant 10,000 men. He now determined on what he thought would be a less costly strategy. He began entrenching the bulk of his army. At the same time, he launched a two-pronged stab in an effort to sever the Weldon Railroad. Gen. James H. Wilson with 6,000 cavalry was to cut the line farther south and then advance northward. The II Corps (under Gen. David B. Birney, Hancock being temporarily down from an old wound) and the VI Corps of Horatio Wright moved to the left to get astride the railroad while turning Lee's right flank.

Lee sent his own cavalry to confront Wilson, and Hill dispatched the divisions of Mahone and Wilcox to block the Union infantry. Hill patiently spent a hot June 21 waiting for an opportunity to strike. The opportunity came the following day, when the two Union corps became separated as they moved through the woods west of Jerusalem Plank Road. It was then that William Mahone emerged as the most daring of Hill's division commanders.

Born 1826 in Southampton County, Va., Mahone had graduated from Virginia Military Institute and become a successful railroad president. He commanded the 6th Virginia in the war's first stages and rose to brigadier in the autumn of 1861. There he had remained, and by early 1864 Mahone was widely regarded as a disappointment. He was a mixture of negative things: self-assertive and uncommunicative, with an ego totally out of proportion to his size.

Mahone was five feet five inches tall and weighed less than one hundred pounds. His feet were so long and narrow that when shoe sizes came into being, it took a custom-made 9AAAA shoe to fit him. A long trailing coat accentuated his shortness, and the flowing triangular beard and wide-brimmed hat he habitually wore made him look like a poorly costumed villain in some comic opera. His headquarters sounded like a barnyard. Because of dyspepsia, Mahone subsisted on milk and eggs. Hence, a cow and a flock of chickens were always near his tent. "Billy" Mahone was an odd little man, and he was one of the few generals in the Civil War whose star did not shine until late in the conflict.

This thirty-seven-year-old brigadier was very familiar with the area west of the Jerusalem Plank Road because he had surveyed it when building his Norfolk & Petersburg Railroad. Thus, when the two Federal corps paused in the midst of a tangled wilderness to await orders, Mahone proposed taking three brigades of Anderson's old division and striking Birney's II Corps in flank. Lee and Hill gave ready consent, whereupon Mahone formed the brigades of J. C. C. Sanders, Wright, and Weisiger in battle array. Hill personally led them forward through a ravine that Mahone had recommended using. The ravine not only screened the Confederates from the view of Federals but also brought them within yards of Birney's flank. Around five in the evening, Hill gave the command to attack.

Birney's men were totally unsuspecting when (wrote Pegram's adjutant, Gordon McCabe), "with a wild yell which rang out shrill and fierce through the gloomy pines, Mahone's men burst upon the flank—a pealing volley, which roared along the whole front—a stream of wasting fire, under which the adverse left fell as one man—and the bronzed veterans swept forward, shrivelling up Barlow's division as lightning shrivels the dead leaves of autumn." This was another of those fiery, savage attacks for which Hill was famous. The impact on the II Corps caused the VI Corps to stop dead in its tracks. The onslaught was "more than a surprise," a Pennsylvanian wrote. "It was an astonishment."[3]

Gen. Francis C. Barlow was washing his feet in a nearby stream when Mahone overran his division in front and flank. Barlow's men were rolled back upon Gershom Mott's division, and both retreated with heavy losses. "This was a case," a Union soldier commented, "of run or be gobbled."[4] The collapse of Barlow and Mott exposed John Gibbon's left, and Hill's men promptly slammed into it.

So sudden was the onslaught that Gibbon's men were "caught enjoying their dinner." The Confederates burst upon them, "fighting hand to hand with bayonets, butts of muskets, swords and pistols." Within minutes, a large segment of Gibbon's line surrendered. The 15th Massachusetts was captured almost intact. The remainder of the Union division was "thrown back in disorder." Gibbon lost 317 killed and wounded, plus an astounding 1,406 men taken prisoner.[5]

Mahone's troops drove the routed II Corps to within three hundred yards of the Plank Road before stopping to regroup. Even more might have been accomplished had Wilcox lent expected cooperation. But Wilcox's orders had seemed to him contrary to Mahone's plan, so he had moved off to the right on what Mahone called "a wild goose chase" and was of no help in the contest.[6]

The Jerusalem Plank Road fight was a late-afternoon affair that was short and one-sided. Grant, thoroughly disgusted, labeled it "a stampede." Mahone shattered two Federal divisions, inflicted 3,000 casualties, seized four guns and eight regimental flags, all with minimum losses. The Union army was filling now with conscripts and raw recruits—men incapable of maintaining the army's high quality. The 1,700 Federals captured on June 22 represented more prisoners than the II Corps had lost at Antietam Creek, Fredericksburg, and Chancellorsville combined. A Union adjutant general termed the battle "the most humiliating episode in the experience of the Second Corps." The Confederates, on the other hand, had demonstrated that despite their thin and weary ranks, they were still capable of waging furious battle. The Petersburg *Express* called the affair "one of the most brilliant of the war," and Mahone became the man of the hour.[7]

Having taught Grant a painful lesson, Hill collected his wounded after dark and retired to his old position. On June 23 the II Corps reoccupied its former positions—more carefully. Hill turned Mahone loose again on a probe of the Union left. Joseph Finegan's little Florida brigade pierced the Union line and took 600 prisoners, Hill reported to Lee. Yet, he added, "it was so hot, the undergrowth so thick, and the enemy retiring all this time, our men did not press forward. Indeed, could not [move] sufficiently fast to get up with their main body." Hill called a halt to the operations the next day because Mahone's men had been in the field without sleep for forty-eight hours.[8]

The siege of Petersburg now began in earnest. Every hill and rise of ground became a fort or site for an artillery battery. The opposing lines snaked over the countryside in parallel fashion, sometimes no more than 400 feet apart. Both lines were invincible, so long as the defenders remained alert.

It became a hellish existence for soldiers on both sides, especially the 18,800 men in Hill's half of the Army of Northern Virginia. Those gaunt ragamuffins spent week after week digging earthworks as they lengthened and maintained the lines southeast of Petersburg. The monotony was broken at intervals by operations to prevent Federal infantry from wrecking sections of the Weldon Railroad. Most of the time, however, the troops lived, suffered, and died in a vast maze of trenches, forts, redoubts, and tunnels.

Skirmishing and sharpshooting were constant as well as deadly.

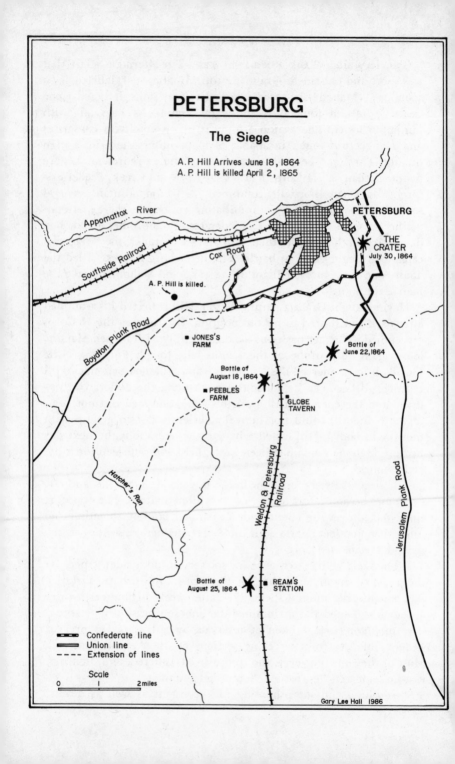

Federal bombardments were regular and nerve-racking. Yet, one of Hill's men stated, "we suffered less from the enemy than from the heat, filth and bad fare." The temperature soared several times above one hundred degrees that first month of the siege. Clouds of impalpable dust hung everywhere. Sickness became widespread.[9]

Throughout the first two weeks of July, rumors again abounded in Federal communiqués that Hill had left the Petersburg lines for duty elsewhere.[10] Northern newspapers were asserting that if the Confederates would come out of their works, Grant would give battle. Lee was at Hill's headquarters when he read such a story. He looked up and replied: "I hope that General Grant is of the same way of thinking. There is nothing I desire now more than a 'fair field fight.' If Grant will meet me on equal ground, I will give him two to one odds." Willie Pegram, who heard the statement, commented: "That was very strong for the old General."[11]

With the army immobilized at Petersburg, Lee and Hill were seeing each other frequently. "Marse Robert" was genuinely fond of the warm and courtly Virginian and came to have greater admiration for him as Hill's passion for the Confederate cause seemed to grow with the ebbing of his strength. Hill was at his tactical best in those months of besiegement. Sustaining the morale of soldiers, keeping them in fighting trim, leading them in successful counterattacks against superior numbers, maintaining composure, and exuding confidence—these continued to be Hill's principal assets, in spite of declining health, which he could not always conceal.

On July 19 the first rain in six weeks fell. "It brings relief from heat and dust, and in a large measure from the flies, which have been very troublesome," a soldier wrote home.[12] A week later, rumor was confirmed that the Union II Corps had recrossed the James and seemed headed for Richmond. Lee countered by sending Anderson's corps, Heth's division, and a large contingent of cavalry to the north. The result of those transfers was to leave the Petersburg line greatly weakened. In front of the city remained only the divisions of Hoke and Bushrod R. Johnson from Beauregard's command, Mahone's division, and part of Wilcox's—18,000 troops at best.

A Richmond editor speculated at this time: "The rumor that Grant is mining Petersburg is nonsensical. . . . It is more likely that he would attempt to undermine Lee's positions, whilst keeping up a great clatter with bomb-shells in Petersburg."[13]

That was precisely what Grant was doing.

Some men in the Union army were not enthusiastic about a siege and felt that, with a little ingenuity, Petersburg could be taken by direct assault. Among this group were coal miners in the 48th Pennsylvania. They were posted opposite an elevated sector called Elliott's Salient. The area, near Cemetery Hill and old Blandford Church, was a somewhat weak point in the Southern line, and closer to the Federal works than almost any other part of the front. In the earthen works Hill had posted a four-gun battery, with veteran South Carolina regiments stationed on either side. Hill also sought to compensate for the salient's weakness by erecting a second line immediately to the rear. As an added precaution, in late July he ordered the construction of a third line.

The 48th Pennsylvania, part of Burnside's IX Corps, found itself facing the salient. One day Lt. Col. Henry Pleasants, a mining engineer by profession, overheard one of his soldiers snarl: "We could blow that damned fort out of existence if we could run a mine shaft under it."[14] From this seed of an idea grew a battle plan. The Pennsylvanians would dig a long gallery from behind their lines to a point beneath the Confederate battery at Elliott's Salient. A large amount of explosive powder would be placed in the end of the tunnel. When the powder was detonated, Federal troops in strength would rush through the gap in the Confederate lines, seize Petersburg, and possibly end the war.

For the better part of a month, 400 miners dug steadily. An increase in skirmish fire made Lee suspicious that a tunnel was under construction. He ordered his engineers to countermine. They sank four shafts around the salient but missed the gallery. The Federals completed the 511-foot shaft by digging 30-foot lateral galleries at the end so that the tunnel was T-shaped. Into those arms were placed 320 kegs containing 8,000 pounds of gunpowder. After sandbagging the powder to direct the force of the explosion upward, the miners spliced together two fuses.

All was ready by the night of July 29. Two divisions would make the attack. The first would rush through the broken line; the second, a large, all-black, untested division, would ride the momentum of the first line. Lee, meanwhile, was convinced that something unusual was pending. He ordered his men to be "ready to move at a moment's warning."[15] Yet the Confederates, who had been listening to unfounded rumors for a month, were not ready.

At 4:45 A.M., July 30, the largest explosion of the war began as a deep, muffled thud. A New York artilleryman described what happened next: "While the earth rocks with a swaying motion like that which precedes the earthquake, a huge black mass suddenly shoots up two hundred feet in the air from the left of Elliott's salient. Seams of fire were glistening from its dark sides, flashes of light rise above it on the sky, and the whole mass of earth, broken timbers, military equipments, and human bodies hangs so like a huge monster over our heads."[16]

"Hell has broken loose over there!" shouted another Union cannoneer.[17] He was correct. The blast destroyed two of Richard G. Pegram's guns and virtually wiped out four companies of the 18th South Carolina and five companies of the 22nd South Carolina. A gaping hole 170 feet long, 70 feet wide, and 30 feet deep suddenly stood in the middle of Hill's line. Smoke billowing skyward clearly marked the spot.

It was such an awesome sight that thousands of Federal soldiers poised to attack stood paralyzed for several minutes. A covering artillery bombardment by 110 guns and 54 mortars finally jolted the infantry into advancing.

Hill was awake that Saturday morning and resting on his cot at corps headquarters when the explosion occurred. He leaped to his feet, took a quick look at the smoke swirling in the sky, and started for his horse. "I am going to Mahone's division!" he shouted at Palmer. "I will take his troops—all that can be spared—to the point of explosion!" Directing Palmer to attend to matters at headquarters, Hill mounted his iron-gray stallion, Champ, and galloped off to Mahone's camp, four miles southwest of the salient.[18]

Lee received word of the explosion shortly after six. He at once dispatched an aide, Col. Charles Venable, to bring up two of Mahone's brigades, "for time was too precious to observe military etiquette and send the order through Hill." Although Hill was a stickler for protocol, he fully agreed this time with Lee's assessment. The two brigades were to pull out of the line as unobtrusively as possible (to prevent Federals from attacking there) and rush to Hill's line in the rear of the explosion site. Lee then rode to Hill's headquarters, only to learn from Palmer that Hill had gone to expedite Mahone.[19]

The division commander needed no prodding. Mahone had the brigades of Weisiger and Wright formed in line when Hill arrived. Hill ordered Willie Pegram to accompany Mahone with the light batteries of Thomas A. Brander and Thomas Ellett. Minutes later, this force was moving rapidly northward.

Hill rode ahead and found Lee at Bushrod Johnson's headquarters. The two generals passed into the lines, sat down on stumps near the Rives salient, and discussed what next needed to be done. No time could be lost. Federals were already swarming in and around the crater. The shirt-sleeved Hill, paying no attention to bullets whistling through the air, and too concerned to rely on couriers, galloped back to hasten Mahone's two brigades to the front.[20] However, Hill's efforts would have been in vain had not the Federal attack ground to a momentry halt largely out of curiosity.

As one after another Union brigade rushed to the crater, Billy Yanks began milling around the yawning chasm. Hundreds of soldiers jumped into the crater for a closer inspection. Soon brigades and regiments were inextricably confused. The two division commanders, James H. Ledlie and Edward Ferrero, were little more than by-standers behind the Union works as their 15,000 troops became a leaderless mass of humanity.

While this lull was developing, Hill carefully led the two brigades up a hidden ravine 200 yards west of the crater. Mahone then put his old brigade, barely 800 men under David Weisiger, in line of battle. It was not a moment too soon, for Union troops now were spilling over the crater and, in large numbers, starting across open ground. Mahone gave orders for his brigade to advance, but the men were not to fire until they were on the enemy. At that, the Virginians gave a loud rebel yell and surged out onto the open ground.

Battle flags swayed as Confederate infantry in a ragged line advanced across rising ground. To the rear, their cannon roared angrily. Mahone's attack front was too short to cover the Federal position, and it went somewhat obliquely to the left of the crater. In any event, the Virginians raced forward until they were within ten yards of the Union line. Then they stopped and sent a volley of musketry ripping into the Federals. Seconds later, the Confederates rushed into the blue masses with slashing bayonets and swinging muskets. For ten minutes the fighting was a turmoil of hand-to-hand, one-on-one combat. The 6th Virginia lost 88 of 98 soldiers, including every man in Norfolk's Company F. Then the Federals broke toward the rear, and Weisiger's men secured the area to the north of the crater (as well as hundreds of discarded Federal muskets).[21]

Wright's Georgia brigade now prepared to attack. At ten-thirty it advanced with the intention of storming the crater. However, it came under such a heavy artillery fire that its line veered to the left, and it reached the works already occupied by Weisiger. The Federals still held the crater and a section of Hill's line on either side of it; the day was getting hotter by the hour; Mahone's troops were running low on ammunition. One more effort had to be made.

Mahone summoned his third brigade, Sanders's Alabamians. As they came to the edge of the woods around eleven, Mahone carefully placed them in battle line. Capt. John C. Featherston was aligning his ranks when a powder-begrimed and ragged Confederate came up and asked to be part of the assault. He had been in one of the South Carolina regiments that had been torn apart by the explosion. "How high did they blow you?" Featherstone asked.

"I don't know," the man replied with a straight face, "but as I was going up I met the company commissary officer coming down and he said, 'I will try to have breakfast ready by the time you get down.' "[22]

The Alabamians listened to simple instructions from Mahone. They were to stay low as they moved up the grade. When they could see the enemy, they were to rush toward them and not stop until they reached the crater. They *had* to be successful if the day was to be saved. Then the command "Forward!" rang out, and the 628 Alabama soldiers advanced briskly toward the crater.

Artillery on both sides were now firing at a deafening level. Sanders's men, once in the open, came under a withering barrage. Yet steadily, straight ahead, they moved. A final dash, and they were in the crater area. Clubbed muskets, bayonets, fists and feet, all were part of a frenzied fight that lasted only a few moments before thousands of Federals began running pell-mell across the field toward their own lines.

Not all of the Billy Yanks left the crater, however, and what ensued was one of the ugliest episodes of the Civil War.

Willie Pegram later confessed: "A few of our men were wounded by the negroes, which exasperated them very much. . . . As soon as we got upon them, they threw down their arms to surrender, but were not allowed to do so." A field officer in the 61st Virginia openly admitted: "I never felt more like fighting in my life. Our comrades had been slaughtered in a most inhuman and brutal manner, and black slaves were trampling over their mangled and bleeding forms. Revenge must have fired every heart and strung every arm with nerves of steel for the herculean task of blood."[23]

Mahone's ordnance officer recalled that when the Confederates reached the edge of the crater and beheld scores of Federals floundering in the loose earth of the chasm, "the whole line delivered a deadly volley, and then used the bayonet with fearful effect upon the confused, disorganized mass of whites and blacks who filled the ditch below. . . . The slaughter was frightful, and the work of vengeance may have exceeded the proper limit."[24]

Some Federals were spared. A member of the 8th Alabama in Sanders's brigade proudly wrote home: "Our Brigade is said to have made the grandest charge of the war, capturing three stands of colors & five hundred Yankees & negroes."[25]

At 3:25 P.M. a relieved Lee wired Richmond: "We have retaken the salient and driven the enemy back to his lines with loss." The battle of the crater had cost Grant 4,000 men. Lee stated of the enemy that "there were upwards of 500 of his dead unburied in the trenches, among them officers & blacks. He suffered severely." Confederate losses were 1,500, of which 278 fatalities resulted from the explosion.[26]

Once again, a frontal assault by Grant against Hill had failed. To be sure, Hill had narrowly escaped disaster, but he had done so through the fighting prowess he had instilled in the Third Corps. Yet Hill neither sought nor accepted any credit for the success at the crater. He was quite willing for Mahone to receive the accolades. Toward that end, Hill issued congratulatory orders which read: "Anderson's division, commanded by Brigadier-General William Mahone, has so distinguished itself by its successes during the present campaign as to merit the especial mention of the corps commander, and he tenders to the division, its officers and men, his thanks for the gallantry displayed by them, whether attacking or attacked."

Hill added, somewhat exaggerating Union losses: "Thirty-one stand of colors, fifteen pieces of artillery, and four thousand prisoners, are the proud mementoes which signalize the division's valor and entitle it to the admiration and gratitude of our country."[27]

The next morning, Lee held church services at his headquarters. Lee and Hill sat together as Rev.-Gen. William N. Pendleton conducted morning prayer. Concentration during the service was broken

by a small dog, which took turns rubbing itself against Lee and Hill
—to the delight of both officers.²⁸

By the afternoon of the thirty-first, unburied Federal dead, plus
Confederates blown to pieces in the explosion, were rotting under
the July sun. A truce went into effect at 6:00 A.M. the next day, and
for four hours men of blue and gray buried bodies with no exchange
of conversation. "Seven hundred of the enemy's dead were buried
or turned over to him for burial," Lee reported. Hill, wearing long
gauntlets, a slouch hat, and round jacket, "silently watched from the
top of the earthworks."²⁹

Both sides now dug in for a long siege. East and south of Petersburg, where Hill was posted and where most of the fighting would
occur, the ground flattened out. Country roads wound around an
occasional swamp. When large numbers of trees were felled for
trench supports and campfires, the whole region became an open
expanse of sandy soil, with only a small patch of woods here and
there. The two armies constructed intricate systems of trenches, each
side having at least two main lines of embankments plus many
traverses. Sharpshooters kept a keen lookout for unwary targets.
Troops stretched blankets, parts of tents, and tree branches over
their rifle pits to ward off the sun's rays. The heat was intense, and
clouds of dust rose at the slightest provocation. "We would long for
a breeze to fan away the stifling heat," one soldier observed, "and,
when the breeze came, for a calm, that eyes, ears and nostrils might
be freed from the smothering cloud."³⁰

Rations on the Confederate side were scarce and vile. "We were
fed on wretched bacon, wormy peas, and corn-meal," a South
Carolina officer recalled. The Southern nation was now too hard-
pressed to correct the situation. When Hill complained bitterly of
"spoilt meat" being distributed to his men, a clerk in the C.S. Subsistence Department could only respond in a memo to the meat
distributors: "Make an allowance for what is absolutely unfit for
use."³¹

As a natural byproduct, desertion slowly became a principal
enemy. On August 12, Hill reported the desertions of 25 men from
the 9th Alabama, 10 from a Maryland battery, and 6 from other
regiments. Yet Hill labored hard to keep his corps in fighting trim,
despite all obstacles. He was at least partially successful, for in mid-
August an inspecting officer gave Heth's divisions high marks after

making a thorough examination of the brigade camps. Hill was also pleased when several of his premier brigadiers, wounded earlier in the campaign, began returning to duty. McGowan, Archer, Kirkland, and Lane all resumed brigade command in August.[32]

Grant had no intention of sitting in a trench and waiting for Lee's army to evaporate. The Union commander determined to keep Lee off balance and under pressure with surprise attacks north of the James along the Richmond front, while at the same time extending the Union left to the west. The latter movement would force Lee to stretch his thin lines around the lower half of Petersburg in order to protect the two railroads that still connected the city with the south. That portion of the line was critical to Lee's defenses. Thus, wrote Colonel Palmer, "at Petersburg the post of danger and ceaseless vigilance was the right. Other troops might rest; Hill's corps was ever on the move, repelling advances on the right."[33]

The first move in Grant's new strategy of encirclement occurred in the August 17–22 period. It was another—and this time successful—attempt to secure the upper part of the Weldon Railroad. On Wednesday morning, August 17, Warren's V Corps marched three miles to the west and occupied more than a mile of track in the vicinity of Globe Tavern. The Federals then began moving northward along the railroad toward Petersburg. The route carried them into unfamiliar and heavily wooded country, where they bivouacked.

Hill reacted quickly to this Federal thrust. He pulled Heth's division out of reserve and sent it, along with Brander's battery, to blunt Warren's advance. Heth attacked in the afternoon of the eighteenth with three brigades. "We drove the enemy back easily," one of Heth's men stated, "and advanced several hundred yards. On the enemy threatening our flanks, we fell back to the line from whence we had first driven them. The enemy attempted to charge us, but a few well-directed volleys drove them back."[34]

In the final stage of the fighting, Lee and Hill rode onto the field. Lee waved his hand toward the north and said to Hill: "I think if you will send a force through those woods and strike them on their flank, you will find that flank in the air. At the same time that this force attacks, let General Heth attack as he did [today]."[35]

Accordingly, Hill ordered Mahone's division and Pegram's artillery battalion to join Heth and Brander for a renewal of the offensive on the nineteenth. Heavy rain showers began falling shortly after noon that day. Near four in the afternoon Hill sent Heth's division "yelling like demons" against the Federal left. Heth first struck the Federals in a cornfield. "With a cheer," a Petersburg newspaper reported, "the Confederate troops bounded forward and swept over all obstruction, pressing the Yankees back with severe loss into their second line; and, charging forward, forced them thence with an equal lack of ceremony." Heth's division had carried two Federal positions while firing less than 1,000 shots.[36]

Mahone had swung through the woods to try to turn the Federal right flank. Just as his men advanced, however, the Federal division driven back by Heth came running straight into Mahone's ranks. The Confederates rounded up some 1,800 prisoners and led them to the rear. Hill then re-formed two of Mahone's brigades and sent them charging again toward Warren's line. By this time, elements of Burnside's IX Corps had arrived to support Warren. The Confederate assault got nowhere.

Just before dark, Hill ordered Heth forward on a second attempt to roll up the Union left. That attack also failed. Nightfall ended the battle, after which Hill informed Beauregard: "The blow struck them has been a very severe one, and I regretted my weakness prevented me from following it up as I would like to have done."[37]

Federals still held the Weldon Railroad. August 20 was relatively quiet. As rain fell, sometimes heavily, Warren fortified his position while Hill planned a new attack to pry the enemy away from the railroad. On the next day, a stormy Sunday, Hill sought to break the Union works stretched across the railroad by a concentrated artillery fire from Pegram's thirty guns, but Warren's troops, protected by earthworks, suffered little damage. Mahone then assaulted through woodland and thick undergrowth with six small brigades. The late-morning onslaught was vigorous but in vain. Union artillery shredded the attacking lines. The 61st Virginia lost 77 of 200 soldiers in a matter of minutes.

In the course of the attack, through a misunderstanding on the part of Hill and Mahone, Gen. Johnson Hagood's brigade got in advance of the charge. Without supports, it rushed through a cornfield and straight into a re-entrant in the Federal lines. Caught in that U-shaped sector, 400 of Hagood's men were captured as the remainder fought their way out under a heavy fire. Six color-bearers were killed in the action. "The corn-stalks," a Pennsylvania soldier noted, "were cut off by the bullets as if with a knife."[38]

One Union report asserted that Hill died in the action from a bullet wound in the side.[39]

Mahone made a quick reconnaissance and, with the assent of both Lee and Hill, rounded up two more brigades for a final assault on Warren's lines. However, it was dark and pouring rain by the time the two units were in position. The attack was canceled. This four-day fight for the Weldon Railroad had cost Grant 4,455 of 20,000 men engaged. Lee's losses were put at 1,600 of 14,000 on the field.[40] Grant could afford such casualties; Lee could not.

The Union army's hold on the Weldon Railroad was now too firm to be broken. Confederates simply could not pay the price in casualties to recover the upper part of the rail line. Henceforth, incoming supplies for Lee on the line had to be unloaded twenty miles south of Petersburg and brought into the city by wagon.

Even as Hill was flailing Warren's men, another Union thrust was occurring to the south. On the morning of August 21, the Union II Corps, which had been north of the James, returned to the lines in front of Petersburg. The Yankees were footsore and fatigued, but "Hancock the Superb" was back at their head. Grant ordered two full but inexperienced divisions to take a position south of and adjacent to Warren's line on the Weldon Railroad. In the next three days, Hancock's troops tore up about six miles of track around Reams's Station.

Wade Hampton's cavalry discovered Hancock's presence. Lee thereupon sent Hill to meet this latest threat. This time, Lee made sure that there were sufficient troops. Seven infantry brigades from Hill's corps, two divisions of cavalry, and much of Pegram's artillery battalion quietly left the Petersburg lines on the afternoon of the twenty-fourth and approached Reams's Station from the west. "Do all in your power to punish the enemy," Lee told Hill.[41]

Through a gross error on someone's part, the Union earthworks were extremely vulnerable. They had been hastily dug, badly constructed, and poorly positioned by cavalry two months earlier. The line resembled a horizontal U, the works meandering west across the railroad, abruptly turning south for 1,200 yards, then cutting east for 1,000 yards. Instead of utilizing the railroad cut, the rifle pits were 30 or 40 yards to the west of it and were no more than three feet in height. Thick pine woods, which offered concealment to an attacking force, were only 75 yards distant. Nevertheless, Hancock placed his troops in the works after hearing that Hill was approaching. John Gibbon's division (with David M. Gregg as cavalry support) was on the left, Nelson A. Miles's division on the right. Hill's forces outnumbered Hancock by about two to one as they bivouacked at Armstrong's Mill, eight miles south of Petersburg.[42]

The next morning, with Hampton's cavalry clearing the way, Hill's column advanced east through wooded country. By now Hill knew that Hancock's troops were behind feeble works and entirely separated from Warren's V Corps farther up the railroad. After a quick reconnaissance, Hill set his battle plan. Hampton's cavalry and two of McGowan's South Carolina regiments would swing around through wooded country and strike Hancock's left from the south. As Hancock leaned toward the point of conflict, Hill's remaining infantry—utilizing woods and underbrush—would assail the Union right. Twelve cannon, under Pegram and masked by trees, moved up almost to musket range of Hancock's center so as to be able to use a reverse fire on the bent Union lines.

Hill had not been well for several days. Shortly after noon that August 25, as he was completing his battle arrangements, the pain in his kidneys and prostate gland became so severe that he had to lie down on the ground, "directly in front of the Union intrenchments." He entrusted the first attack to Wilcox.[43] At two o'clock Wilcox sent George T. Anderson's Georgians and Scales's North Carolinians against the Union right. The brigades made two separate assaults. Both were repulsed, although some of the Southerners got to within three yards of Miles's works.

In midafternoon, Hill tried to take personal control of operations, and he was visible in the activities for a short period. Yet "still being indisposed" at five o'clock, he directed Heth to oversee a second major Confederate assault. The three North Carolina brigades of Lane, Cooke, and William MacRae massed in the woods opposite Hancock's right. As they were doing so, Pegram—"his face aglow with the light of battle," a North Carolinian noted—opened fire obliquely from the right. A Union soldier admitted that the cannonade "scattered our breastworks like kindling wood, and cut off the trees about us as if they were pipe-stems."[44] Pegram's fire "not only swept the whole space enclosed by the intrenchments west of the railroad," a New York gunner recalled, "but took portions of General Gibbon's line upon the left and rear in reverse."[45]

The Confederate bombardment slackened at five-forty because the infantry of Lane, Cooke, and MacRae were sweeping forward. Scales,

Anderson, and three regiments of McGowan were in their left rear as reserves. The Confederates charged 200 yards through felled trees, abatis, and slashings, rushed up and over the earthworks, and began a wild hand-to-hand fight with the Union defenders. "In a moment of panic our troops gave way," a Federal colonel wrote. Soldiers "either threw themselves upon the ground in surrender, or fled across the railroad." Miles desperately called on other units for help. Yet "these regiments remained like a covey of partridges until flushed and captured almost *en masse.*"[46]

Hancock frantically sought to shore up his right by calling in troops from the left. As he did so, however, Hampton's dismounted cavalry and two of McGowan's regiments overran the Union lines on that flank. Federal general Gibbon wrote later that his "whole division seemed suddenly to go to pieces." The entire Union line was disintegrating. Hancock could only watch the disaster unfold. As it did, the gallant Pennsylvanian turned to an aide and exclaimed, "I pray God I may never leave the field!"[47] Yet he did, because there was nothing else he could do to save his men. Darkness was settling over the land as the Union columns slowly retraced their steps.

"Never in the history of the Second Corps had such an exhibition of incapacity and cowardice been given," a Union soldier asserted.[48] Of 2,700 casualties, 2,150 had surrendered on the field. (Mahone's ordnance officer stated, "I thought that we had captured their whole army for I had never seen so many prisoners in a battle before.") In addition, the Union army had lost 9 cannon, 3,100 small arms, and 32 horses. Gibbon was so humiliated by the rout at Reams's Station that he submitted his resignation from the army. Fortunately for the Union cause, it was not accepted.[49]

Hill's losses of 720 men seemed minor in comparison with what had been achieved. The health of the general appeared to improve dramatically as his troops swept over the Union lines with shouts of victory. Just at that moment, Hill received word that Federal cavalry were in his rear. He immediately gathered together his staff, couriers, and all other men he could find, and with Brander's battery, he pushed to the spot that was supposedly threatened. Only a handful of enemy horsemen were there. A few shells from Brander's guns put them to flight. That night Hill brought off his wounded, buried his dead, and proudly returned to Petersburg. "The sabre and the bayonet have shaken hands on the enemy's captured breastworks," he announced.[50]

The South hailed Reams's Station as "one of the most brilliant victories of the war" and a battle in which "the gallant 'tar heels' made short work of it."[51] It was a contest led by the Powell Hill of old: troops marching swiftly, falling on the enemy before he could be reinforced, attacking at the right place with sufficient numbers, hammering to a clear-cut victory. All of this worked at Reams's Station because Hill was operating on the level where he was at his best: division command. He was incapacitated during part of the battle; but the overall scenario was his, and he directed the action with the same deft touch that had brought him into prominence early in the war. The main question for Hill now was whether his health would become a serious impediment.

20

"He Is Now at Rest"

Throughout the remainder of August and the early part of September, as a sporadic bombardment of Petersburg occurred—sometimes reaching a hundred shells per hour—Hill's men strengthened their works while Hill fine-tuned his corps as best he could. In his command were slightly more than 15,400 troops. Conscripts and recruits were not arriving in numbers sufficient to fill gaps caused by battle, sickness, and desertion. Finegan's Florida brigade could not muster 700 men.[1]

The strong segment in Hill's line was Wilcox's division on the left. It contained the remnants of the old Light Division, McGowan's always reliable South Carolina brigade, and a first-rate group of brigadiers. Its commander remained dependable rather than brilliant. In Hill's center, Mahone's five brigades were more and more displaying the hard-hitting characteristics of their major general, with the exception of Wright's Georgia brigade. It was then being led by an incompetent colonel, and Hill considered the unit "almost worthless."[2] Heth's division, on the right, was an all-veteran unit. Now commanding Kirkland's North Carolina brigade was William MacRae, a small, unimpressive-looking brigadier whose high-pitched voice belied his solid fighting qualities. His brigade was one of the best assault units in Lee's army, and its members knew it. It had companions in the brigades of Lane and Cooke, neither of which conceded first place to any other unit. Heth continued to display all of the attributes of a good leader except for luck.

Hill's spirits rose noticeably in September. Headquarters for the Third Corps were at Indiana, the Knight estate on the western edge of Petersburg. Hill's tent was in the front yard. Far more important to him was his success in getting Dolly and the two children comfortably situated directly across the road in a cottage of the estate of James M. Venable. Hill now had his family only fifty yards from his headquarters.

The pessimism he had felt on arriving at Petersburg in mid-June disappeared for a time. Willie Pegram met Hill on a train ride to Richmond and, wrote Pegram, "he laughed very much when I told him that the people of Richmond were expecting Richmond and Petersburg to be evacuated." On another occasion, Hill was proceeding through one of the camps when he saw Chaplain J. William Jones distributing religious tracts to the soldiers. Hill reined his horse, shouted hello to his Culpeper friend, and then added good-naturedly: "Jones, don't you think the boys would prefer hardtack to soft tracts?"[3]

A large crowd of townspeople gathered on September 26 for a divisional review in honor of Lee. One of the brigadiers observed that "General A. P. Hill rode on the staff of the commanding general upon a graceful and beautiful silver grey; and horse and rider showed gallantly." The same writer added, however, that Lee "seemed bored by the ceremonial. . . . Even his horse looked as if he thought it all foolishness."[4]

Days later, Grant sought and achieved a toehold in Lee's lines at Fort Harrison in the Richmond defenses. The attack impelled Lee to bring up forces from Petersburg. Aware of this likelihood, Grant launched a second offensive against the Confederate right. Union objectives were to secure a firmer grasp on the Weldon Railroad and possibly to extend the Federal left far enough to the west to gain possession of both the Boydton Plank Road and the Southside Railroad. Toward those ends, Warren's V Corps and the IX Corps, now under John G. Parke (Burnside having been removed after the debacle at the Crater), advanced toward the network of roads just north of Poplar Springs Church.

Hampton's cavalry intercepted the Union columns halfway to their destination. While the Confederate horsemen dueled with Warren's advance for a day, Hill rushed west with the divisions of Heth and Wilcox. On Friday, September 30, the two sides collided at Jones's Farm. Federal general Robert Potter's division emerged from a wood only 800 yards from the hastily constructed Southern line. Potter ordered a charge. As his men moved forward, Heth and Wilcox attacked simultaneously from northwest and northeast. Each side had twenty-four cannon in position. "Thunder and fire and smoke," a Palmetto soldier wrote, "issued from the opposing hilltops in roaring volumes that rent the air and shook the earth, while shot and shell swept across the field hissing and screaming and crashing into the ranks of the opposing columns as they rushed together."[5]

The whole Confederate line gave a rousing cheer as it struck the Union battle formation. Within seconds, Hill's troops dashed through underbrush and flanked Potter's right. "The only thing to do was run for safety," confessed a Massachusetts soldier. "It became 'Legs versus Liberty,' " another New Englander admitted. Potter's division fled in disorder for a mile, leaving behind enough discarded equipment to make it Christmas in September for needy Confederate soldiers. Hill reported the Union army "severely punished and four hundred prisoners captured."[6]

Under cover of darkness and rain, Warren established a new line near Peeble's Farm. Saturday, October 1, dawned gray, with rain still falling. Hill advanced his divisions to resume the battle. Heth and Wilcox delivered a series of assaults; they bagged hundreds of prisoners as they overran Warren's outer line; but the Federals were in too much strength for Hill to overcome them. Midway through that wet morning, Hill wisely stopped the attacks. He could not break the Union position, Pegram explained, "because of the disparity in numbers. The enemy had one corps & part of another. We had four small infantry brigades besides the cavalry. And such cavalry it is!"[7]

Hill had been able to keep Grant from seizing the Boydton Plank Road and the Southside Railroad. He had inflicted 1,000 casualties and taken 2,000 prisoners at a cost of no more than a third of those numbers. Nevertheless, Grant had extended the Federal line another three miles west of the Weldon Railroad. Lee was forced to do likewise. The Confederate line now became a thirty-five-mile arc from north of Richmond to west of Petersburg—and Lee had only 50,000 troops to man the works. For the first time in the war, the Confederate commander became openly pessimistic. He informed the War Department: "Without some increase of strength, I cannot see how we can escape the natural military consequences of the enemy's numerical superiority. If things thus continue, the most serious consequences must result."[8]

Dwindling manpower henceforth was the major concern. Pegram commented that "while the enemy have had thousands to replace the thousands they have lost, this army has been constantly & gradually diminishing, with no reserve from which to supply the places of those who have fallen." Gen. Bushrod Johnson complained that his division was trying to occupy a line that two and a half divisions had barely managed to maintain.[9] In the second week of October, Lee wrote Hill: "I wish you would see that all the extra duty men in all the departments—wagoners, cooks, clerks, couriers, &c.,—that can possibly be spared be placed in the ranks; that all the reserves, militia, &c., around Petersburg be put in the trenches, and that as many of your old troops as you think it safe to take out be held in readiness for field service. . . . We must drive them back at all costs."[10]

Hill spent most of October attending to routine matters. There were the usual grand reviews of various divisions. At one, a Virginia chaplain got his first closeup look at Hill and had mixed reactions. He described Hill as "a small man, can be scarcely more than 5 ft. 8 in. high, nor weigh more than 125 or 130 lbs; . . . he wears a heavy, long sandy beard; he looks rather weather-beaten; he was dressed very plainly, rode a splendid grey horse and seemed to have perfect control of himself & of his horse in the saddle; he seemed to be very lively and talkative."[11]

Dinner parties offered a brief respite from the drudgery of a siege. Hill and Dolly were at a rather large affair when the conversation turned to the forthcoming presidential election in the North. Hill remarked that he hoped Democratic candidate George McClellan would win, "because if it becomes necessary to surrender, I would prefer to do so to McClellan."[12]

Col. G. Moxley Sorrel departed Longstreet's staff to take a field command in Hill's corps. Sorrel was somewhat apprehensive about the transfer because the July 1862 confrontation between Hill and Longstreet had left Sorrel caught in the middle. Yet, Sorrel wrote after reporting to Hill for duty, "nothing could exceed his kindness in receiving me; it continued all through my service in his corps and I had every evidence of the good feeling of this distinguished officer." Hill's attitude, Sorrel added, "proved him magnanimous and free of petty spite in that [1862] affair, and such was his nature."[13]

Hill lost a longtime brigadier during this period. Gen. James Archer died October 24, only two months after returning to command of his brigade. The rigors of prison life were too much for the Marylander. Hill and Heth both tried to get Pegram promoted to brigadier, but the young artilleryman was regarded as too valuable where he was to be transferred to infantry.[14]

At this same time, President Davis asked Hill for an opinion on the president of one of the military courts. Hill's reply showed his continuing intolerance of incompetence. "For the last month Col. [D. C.] Glenn has been disgracefully drunk, had made a public exhibition of himself in situations which must have lost him the respect of those who saw him or knew of his condition. He has been in charge of the Provost Guard, has been taken to my hospital under charge of a guard and there confined; in fact, Sir, I cannot tell you of the many instances which show that Col. Glenn is unfitted to hold the position he now has."[15]

Late in October, as Hill was battling illness again, Grant tried one more time to cut the Boydton Plank Road and the Southside Railroad. The better part of three Federal corps—43,000 men in all—started west toward Hill's flank. The IX Corps was to strike the western end of the Confederate line and keep Hill occupied; the troops of Hancock and Warren would swing wide around Hatcher's Run and strike for the Southside line.

The Union strategy, grand in design, was badly mismanaged. At nine in the morning on a rainy October 27, Parke's troops struck Hill. They were quickly repulsed. Warren sent a division to turn the Confederate right flank. It promptly got first ensnared and then lost in a swamp. A second division sent by Warren became similarly mired: Hancock meanwhile reached his first stop on schedule, but he had to wait until Warren had extricated his soldiers.

At that point, characteristically, Hill attacked. He was unable to take personal command, but he dispatched Wilcox, Heth, and Hampton's cavalry to take advantage of the Federal confusion. Heth moved speedily and got his force between Hancock and the railroad. When Hancock turned north, he created a gap between himself and Warren. Then he found Confederates blocking his way. Hancock slowed his advance. He lost momentum just as Hill struck.

Hancock found himself assailed on front and flank by Confederate infantry and cavalry. His huge force went on the defensive. Heth sent Mahone in with three brigades. This force smashed through the Union line. "But," wrote Pegram, "it was like one man getting in between four. After making a brilliant dash, capturing a small number of prisoners, killing many and utterly disorganizing the enemy, Gen. Mahone became surrounded, but cut his way out in a very handsome manner."[16]

Hampton's cavalry struck Hancock's left as Mahone pierced the right. Union soldiers retired through woods in disorderly fashion. Fighting was prolonged and intense. Rain added to the misery. One of Hampton's sons was killed and another was seriously wounded. Hancock's main line, heavily manned, held firm until darkness brought an end to the contest. Union forces then abandoned the field, out of ammunition and full of anger. Two Federal corps had been all but routed.

Despite his personal loss, Hampton proposed to renew the offensive at dawn, but Hill was unwilling to leave the Petersburg line so thinly occupied. To have the earthworks empty for any length of time was to invite disaster. The morning of October 28 found both sides in their original lines. "Back at the old spot again, and nothing accomplished!" a Union officer wrote disgustedly. "Two years ago such a failure would have raised a hornets' nest about the ears of the commanding general, but now the country is accustomed to it."[17]

Hill reported 700 Federals captured, in addition to heavy losses inflicted in killed and wounded. Confederate casualties were about 300 men. In a quick congratulatory note to Hill, Lee stated: "I am much gratified at the results obtained, and pleased with the good conduct by the officers and men. You have rendered a valuable service, and I desire to tender to you, and to the officers and men engaged, my thanks for what they have acomplished."[18] This was to be the last major victory for Hill's Third Corps.

Hill's compassion was evident again on October 28, when he sent a short note to cavalry chief Wade Hampton. "My dear General: I take the liberty of writing to you, to express my deep sympathy with you in the end of your noble boy, and my earnest desire, were such a thing possible, to alleviate your grief. Any assistance which I can give you in forwarding your wishes in any way, please do not hesitate to call upon me. With great sympathy, being truly your friend. A. P. Hill."[19]

After an October 30 nighttime probe in which Mahone seized 230 Federals without the loss of a man, the two armies prepared for the advent of winter. The official order for the troops to go into winter quarters came November 12. "The mud has laid an embargo on all field operations," a newspaper explained.[20] For Lee's army, the bleakest winter of the war was about to begin. A Norfolk soldier in Hill's corps wrote: "With slender rations of corn bread and rancid bacon, with scanty clothing, worn out shoes (some were shoeless) and an inadequate supply of fuel, the outlook for the winter was gloomy in the trenches. Indeed, the 'wolf was almost at the door.'" Trenches became wet, filthy, and squalid. Life was a combination of monotony and misery, with occasional intrusions of terror from artillery and mortar fire.[21]

With Hill's health deteriorating slowly but perceptibly, the general and his wife preferred to spend their evenings at the cottage with the children. Occasionally they attended a social function in Petersburg, usually at the home of Gen. and Mrs. Roger A. Pryor. Lee's headquarters at this time was just up the Cox Road from Hill at Edge Hill, the home of William Turnbull. Lee was a regular visitor to the Hill cottage. Dolly wrote her mother on one occasion: "Gen. Lee comes very frequently to see me. He is the best and greatest man on earth, brought me the last time some delicious apples."[22]

At the end of the first week of December, Grant made another attempt to destroy the Weldon Railroad. He sent Warren's V Corps farther south to cut as much of the line as possible. Lee gambled on the theory that this would be Grant's last offensive of the season. Hence, Lee pulled most of Hill's corps from the Petersburg line and sent it to intercept Warren.

The Third Corps dutifully left the trenches on the eighth and struggled south over frozen roads in bitterly cold weather. One of Hill's officers asserted: "In all my experience during the war I do not remember any weather which was so trying to the troops. A high wind and cold rain prevailed when we started on the march of forty miles. To these succeeded hail and sleet which, with execrable roads and worn out shoes made our cup of misery full." Maj. W. S. Dunlop of the South Carolina sharpshooters recalled a night spent in the open amid a sleet storm. "After eating our scant rations and smoking our pipes, we wrapped ourselves in our blankets and gum cloths, and stood, sat or lay around our camp fires in a semi-conscious, half-freezing condition until morning."[23]

The Confederates (at least those who managed to keep up) arrived at Jarratt's, south of Stony Creek, and found sixteen miles of track ripped apart, piles of crossties burning, and bent rails scattered everywhere. Warren's corps was gone, turned back by home-guard batteries, the weather, and the fact that they had only three days' rations.

Hill gave as quick pursuit as he could. Hampton overtook the Federal stragglers and inflicted 100 casualties. Yet Hill's infantry were physically unable to march rapidly and strike a heavy blow. Mutterings could be heard later in Lee's army because Hill did not assail the Federals at some point.[24] Yet that was more wishful thinking than criticism. Like the Army of Northern Virginia, Hill's corps was too weak to display the audacity that had sustained it in previous years.

Once back in Petersburg, Hill penned a chatty letter to his beloved sister. "Dolly and the children are with me, and we are just as comfortable as people can expect to be in these times. The children are growing so rapidly doing so well. Russy is as fat as a butterball and the greatest talker you ever saw. And your little namesake, Lucy Lee, is certainly the sweetest little cherub ever born, gentle and genial as a May morning, and easily managed. . . .

"I have just returned from the hardest trip I have ever had, down the Rail road after Warren. I could not succeed in bringing him to fight, though I marched 40 miles one day and night. We succeeded however in turning him back from Weldon.

"Our army here, as always, is ready to do its duty, and men and officers in good spirits. I suppose now we shall, in addition to Grant, have Sherman on our hands too. Well the Army of Northern Virginia is equal to it, and however much you task [tax] its powers, will always respond, and I hope successfully."[25]

Hill failed to mention that Dolly was pregnant again. The baby was due in late spring.

Capt. William E. Cameron (later a governor of Virginia), remembering Hill at that time, wrote admiringly: "He was constantly on the lines, riding with firm graceful seat, looking every inch a soldier. Like General Lee, he was rarely much attended. One staff officer and a single courier formed his usual escort, and often he made the rounds alone. Of ordinary height, his figure was slight but athletic, his carriage erect, and his dress plainly neat. His expression was grave but gentle, his manner so courteous as almost to lack decision, but was contradicted by rigidity about the mouth and chin, and bright flashing eyes that even in repose told another tale. In moments of excitement he never lost self-control nor composure of demeanor, but his glance was as sharp as an eagle's, and his voice could take a metallic ring."[26]

While Hill still possessed the magnetism and engaging personality that had endeared him to the army, his physical condition was steadily worsening. Protracted urinary and kidney infections had now progressed into uremia. Swollen kidneys, flank pain, inability to urinate, drowsiness from taut nerves and lack of sleep—all were making Hill increasingly lethargic. He occasionally had difficulty in orienting himself. Being attentive and able to carry on a conversation was at times beyond his ability. He was not aware of his exact condition—or of the fact that if untreated, uremia is a fatal ailment.

Hill's incapacitation became noticeable to most people around him. George Tucker, his chief courier, felt that Hill "was an invalid" the last six months of his life. A young officer who met him for the first time that winter was disappointed that the great commander was neither vivacious nor dashing. "General Hill," he commented, "gave the impression of being reticent, or at any rate, uncommunicative. Neither in aspect nor manner of speech did he appear to measure up to his great fighting record." Gen. John B. Gordon, who commanded a portion of Lee's line north of the James, sadly revealed years later that Hill failed to construct a strategic fort he was ordered to build simply because he was too ill to see to the task.[27]

The general's area of responsibility was a long sweeping arc that curved halfway around Petersburg. The entrenchments were as strong as man could make them. Beyond the trenches were abatis, chevaux-de-frise, slashings, all designed to impale any troops who rushed the lines. Life inside the trenches was an ordeal for survival. A North Carolina captain summarized the situation: "Half-clad and half-rationed these brave, devoted men held the lines for nine long months, including one of the most terrible winters that ever spread its white mantle over the earth. Barefooted in the snow, the men stood to their posts on picket, or at the port-holes. Lying in bomb-proofs, so-called, with mud and water to the ankles, and the constant drip, drip of muddy water from above, clothing and blankets saturated, with a fire that only made smoke, these men passed through the winter."[28]

Small wonder that desertion increased. By the end of January, the Tennessee brigade in Hill's corps was down to 300 men. Lee reported of one short period that 56 of Hill's soldiers had left the lines. The commander attributed the runaways to "insufficiency of food and non-payment of the troops." Hill agreed, to a point. "I believe that the ration is insufficient," he wrote on January 24, "yet nevertheless other troops bear without complaint the evils they know we cannot help."[29]

On February 5, Grant broke the winter lull by sending the II and V corps on yet another stab at Lee's right flank. The objective, as before, was the Boydton Plank Road. Federals crossed Hatcher's Run with little opposition and seized a portion of the road. Each side attacked the other on February 6; and in the fighting, while sleet fell, Willie Pegram's brother, Gen. John Pegram, was killed. The Confederate line bent back and would have broken if Hill had not rushed Mahone's division into the fray. Union leaders then concluded that the Plank Road was not as vital as they had thought. The Federals thereupon withdrew a short distance, erected works to guard their newly extended line, and resumed waiting out the passage of winter.

"The hearts of the people & soldiers begin to sink," Colonel Walkup of the 48th North Carolina confided in his diary. "Our prospects getting more gloomy fast." Columbia, Charleston, and Wilmington had fallen. The Confederates had no Atlantic Ocean ports left, and Gen. William T. Sherman's army was advancing north through the Carolinas toward Lee's rear. Petersburg had a "desolate, haunted appearance like some plague had depopulated it."[30]

Meanwhile, the Army of Northern Virginia was slowly evaporating. In the February 15–25 period, there were 586 desertions from the Third Corps. Another 337 desertions occurred in the next ten days. The soldiers who left were mostly from western North Carolina, Lee stated. "It seems that the men are influenced very much by the representatives of their friends at home, who appear to have become very despondent as to our success."[31]

Even if he had been well, Hill could not have stemmed the leakage. Gordon McCabe, Pegram's adjutant, wrote of Hill: "Much he suffered during this last campaign from a grievous malady, yet the vigor of his soul disdained to consider the weakness of his body, and accepting without a murmur the privations of that terrible winter, he remained steadfast to his duty." In truth, for a good part of February, Hill was unable to perform his duties. A member of his staff wrote home on March 3: "Gen. Hill has been exceedingly sick but is now recovering slowly. I am trying to prevail on him to go to Fall Hill and stay, as soon as he is able to move. I would not be much surprised if Mrs. Hill and himself accepted the offer."[32]

The general made every effort to remain in command. It was no use. On March 20, at the urging of his physicians and his commander, Hill agreed to take sick furlough. He, Dolly, and the children went to the Chesterfield County home of an uncle, Col. Henry Hill—but only after Hill had "left strict instructions with his staff to be notified of any threatened movement."[33]

Colonel Hill, a highly esteemed Richmonder, was an officer in the C.S. Paymaster Department. He ensured that his nephew had peace and rest at his estate up the James River from Richmond. A week of such tranquillity restored only a little of Hill's limited strength. On March 29 Hill insisted on accompanying his uncle to his office in Richmond. The general must have noticed the many signs of dilapidation and poverty that war had brought to the Confederate capital. A number of prominent citizens gathered at the paymaster offices to meet and chat with Hill, and the subject arose of the possible evacuation of the capital. Hill abruptly replied that he did not wish to survive the fall of Richmond.[34] Perhaps he was by then resigned to the likelihood that he was not going to get well.

By late March the snow had stopped, the winds had died down, the roads had thawed—and Grant had begun the spring campaign. Actually, Lee initiated the fighting with a desperate March 25 attack on the Federal lines at Fort Stedman. The morning assault ended in disaster, whereupon Grant that afternoon organized a quick strike against Hill's right. Federals overran the picket line near Hatcher's Run. Although the Confederates were able to hold on to their primary positions, the attack cost Hill 800 men captured. Even worse, Grant's position was now dangerously close to Hill's main line of resistance. That line, now twenty-two miles in length, had no more than 11,000 men defending it. Hill's divisions were spread so thin that one of the soldiers told of the pickets being "as far apart as telegraph poles."[35]

Eighteen hours of rain on March 29–30 curtailed large-scale operations. Yet many in Hill's corps regarded this as merely a stay of execution. Colonel Walkup observed in a letter to his wife: "We are expecting an advance here upon our works and fear the Yankees will also come in on our right and rear."[36] There was nothing the Confederates could do. For example, when the 38th North Carolina went out on a regimental reconnaissance, it soon hastened back to the safety of its works—the Carolinians had discovered that the Federal picket line was stronger than the regiment's line of battle.[37]

On Friday morning, March 31, in spite of low, overcast skies, spirits rose in the Third Corps. "Genl. Hill will be back today off sick furlough—which will please us all," a headquarters clerk wrote.[38]

Hill struggled back to duty that morning. He had broken off sick leave because rumors abounded in Richmond that Grant was about to mount an all-out assault on the Petersburg lines. Despite the fact that Hill could barely sit in the saddle, he knew he was needed with the army at its most critical moment. He returned to a Third Corps that was only a shadow of itself. Hill was determined to lead it to the end because it was he who had given it shape and spirit in the beginning.

Saturday, April 1, came in clear and bright, with a brisk wind that dried out the ground noticeably. Hill was in the saddle early that morning. He looked frail and he felt awful; but with his staff and a handful of couriers, Hill spent the daylight hours riding the length of his lines from Fort Gregg to Burgess's Mill. He was suffering the lethargy that uremia often brings. Hill's chief courier, Sgt. George Tucker, recalled: "He passed only a few words with his staff party or those very, very few in the trenches. He seemed lost in contemplation of his immediate position."[39]

Throughout the day, the roar of battle could be heard to the west as Grant sought to drive over and around Lee's extreme right flank. Neither Lee nor Hill knew the outcome of the fighting until late afternoon. Then they learned that George Pickett's lines had been shattered at Five Forks, a vital road junction due west of Hill's right flank at Burgess's Mill. Without being asked, Hill made another yard-by-yard inspection of his entire line. He carefully ensured that all abatis and other obstructions were in place. He checked troop dispositions (the ranks were now so thin that men were standing paces apart in the works), enemy activity across the way, and every remaining detail.

It was dark when Hill, slumped in the saddle, returned to Fort Gregg. He had been on horseback for some fifteen hours; every part of him hurt; his head throbbed from fever and fatigue; his kidneys were sending messages to which the rest of his body could not respond. Hill forced himself to make a final check of Fort Gregg's defenses. Sometime after ten he rode slowly through the night to his headquarters at Indiana. Once he had attended to a small stack of paperwork, Hill walked across the road to the Venable cottage to join his wife and two sleeping daughters.

In reality, the great struggle for Petersburg was at an end. Lee's whole right had been swept away with the Federal breakthrough at Five Forks. It remained only for Grant to deliver the knockout blow at dawn.

The preliminaries began shortly after midnight, when Grant ordered everything on his front to open fire while he massed three huge lines of assault. "The night was extremely dark," a South Carolina officer recalled, "so that we could see the flashes of musketry for a great distance, and could hear the roar that rang along the line for miles."[40] The noise was incessant; the earth trembled from explosions. The skeleton forces of Heth and Wilcox crouched low behind earthworks. The men could not sleep.

Neither could Hill. He lay in bed, seeking relief from pain, exhaustion, fever, and worry. The sound of cannon fire rolled across the sky like waves of thunder. Bright darts of light from Union artillery outlined treetops and the horizon to the east, south, and west. As hard as he tried, Hill could not steer his mind away from the stark reality that all was coming to an end. Even a nap was out of the question. Hill gingerly eased himself out of bed and dressed. For some reason, he donned a white linen shirt that Dolly had recently made for him.[41] Around three in the morning Hill walked across the Cox Road to his headquarters tent. When gunfire flashes permitted, stars were visible. That day—Sunday, April 2—was going to be clear and warm.

The ever-vigilant chief of staff, Colonel Palmer, was waiting for Hill in the yard at Indiana. Any word from Heth or Wilcox? Hill asked. No, replied Palmer, but apparently the Federals had penetrated the line at Rives's Salient on the eastern side of Petersburg. Hill entered his tent. A few minutes later, an orderly brought up Champ, Hill's favorite mount. Like its master, it was weary but steeled to duty. Hill struggled into the saddle. As he eased himself into a sitting posture that he could tolerate, Palmer ran to his side. "General, please let me accompany you," he begged.

"No," Hill answered. "I want you to awaken the staff, get everything in readiness, and have the headquarters wagons hitched up. I am going to General Lee's headquarters and will take Tucker and two couriers. As soon as I have conferred with General Lee, I will return."[42]

Hill left word for Tucker to join him as soon as possible. Then he rode the mile and a half up Cox Road to Lee's camp at Edge Hill. The night was dark and cool; the booming of Federal artillery seemed louder. Each step that Champ took sent a jolt of pain through Hill's body, yet as the general turned off the road and started up the driveway to the Turnbull house, his thoughts were all on the military situation.

Lee had not been able to sleep that night either. When Hill arrived, the commander was lying on his bed partially dressed. Lee looked exhausted; so did Hill. Nevertheless, the two men chatted easily amid the tensions of the moment. Around four o'clock Longstreet arrived at headquarters with the good news that his corps would shortly arrive on the field. The three generals bent over a map as Lee pointed out where he wanted Longstreet's men positioned.

Col. Charles Venable of Lee's staff suddenly rushed into the room. Wagons and soldiers were racing madly down the Cox Road toward Petersburg! he shouted. Federal skirmishers were reported at Gen. Nathaniel Harris's headquarters, less than a half mile from Edge Hill. Lee froze in shock. Harris's quarters were in the rear of the main line; and if the Federals were there, this meant that Grant's soldiers had penetrated the entire Confederate right.

Lee hastily threw a cloak around his shoulders and went out on the front porch. Dawn was approaching, and Lee could see a long line of Federal infantry at the far end of gray fields. He ordered Venable to obtain up-to-date news. Then Lee turned to give Hill orders, but the corps commander was already hobbling rapidly to his tethered horse. The Third Corps's line was severed. He *had* to rally the soldiers. This sudden and unexpected fire in Hill, after weeks of sickness, disturbed Lee. The army leader sent Venable chasing after Hill to tell the general to be careful.[43]

Venable quickly caught up with Hill, Tucker, and courier William H. Jenkins as they were heading southwest. The party reined to a halt. Venable saluted. "The General requests that you not expose yourself," he said.

"I thank General Lee for his consideration," Hill replied. "I am only trying to get in communication with the right."[44] Hill peered quickly through his field glass. Satisfied that all was clear in his front, he, Venable, and the two couriers spurred their horses into a trot.

The Federal infantry attack, which began at 4:45 A.M. just as sunlight was breaking in the east, had swept forward triumphantly. In Hill's sector, the VI Corps broke through the skeletal picket line, "meeting little resistance, and poured their masses over the main defenses, under a heavy fire of artillery and more deadly though less noisy fire of musketry from the parapets."[45] Within an hour, Federals had overrun the Boydton Plank Road and were continuing west toward the Howlett line, the final Confederate position, which Mahone's troops were trying to hold. Yet the Federals were as disorganized in victory as the Confederates were in defeat.

Stragglers from both sides were everywhere. The Union advance disintegrated until it resembled a heavy, broken skirmish line more than a well-ordered battle formation. As Hill rode in from the northeast, he could not and did not know that he was advancing behind the first wave of Union troops. He was approaching their right rear—an area where Federal pickets were fanning out in all directions.

Due south, obliquely away from the Boydton Road, the four horsemen proceeded. To Hill's distress, no Confederate troops could be seen. Soon the general spied Poague's unemployed artillery battalion on a rise of ground. He sent Venable to place the guns where they could open on the enemy. Hill then rode in front for a distance, the two couriers a few steps behind him. They had traveled about 200 yards farther when they came upon two Federal infantrymen. Tucker and Jenkins bolted in front and, with revolvers cocked, called on the Yankees to surrender. They promptly laid down their arms. Tucker turned back to Hill, sitting on his horse, and asked what to do with the two prisoners.

"Jenkins," Hill ordered, "take them to General Lee."

The courier started back with his captives. Hill and Tucker continued riding slowly south. The rising sun was just visible to their left, its rays causing the morning dew to glisten. The route of the two horsemen was across fields, through thickets, and along the outskirts of woods. They soon came into view of a large group of people milling around the huts that had been part of Mahone's winter quarters. Tucker knew that Confederates had abandoned the shanties weeks earlier. "General," he said to Hill, "what troops are those?"

"The enemy's," Hill answered nonchalantly. He continued riding forward without comment. Tucker, becoming increasingly concerned about their purpose, broke the silence again. "Please excuse me, General, but where are we going?"

"Sergeant," Hill said with an earnest tone, "I must go to the right as quickly as possible." Pointing in that direction, Hill added: "We will go up this side of the branch to the woods, which will cover us until reaching the field in rear of General Heth's quarters. I hope to find the road clear at General Heth's."

Tucker made no response, but he rode with his Colt revolver in his hand. He touched his horse and got a little ahead of Hill. The two men crossed the Boydton Plank Road, came to a small woodland, and followed its edge southwestward for about a mile. Not a soldier, Union or Confederate, was in sight. Hill suddenly spoke up: "Sergeant, should anything happen to me, you must go back to General Lee and report it."

They came out of the woods into an open field opposite Heth's line. Massed Federals stood in the road. The two men halted. Hill raised his field glass, looked through it for a moment, and then remarked, "They are there."

"Which way now, General?" Tucker asked.

Hill pointed to a clump of woods 150 yards distant and parallel to the Boydton Road. "We must keep on the right."

Tucker pushed ahead to the edge of the trees, then slowed his horse to a walk. He peered intently through the woods. The trees were thick, and the ground fell away slightly toward a swampy branch. Tucker saw a half dozen or more Federals lurking in the woods. Suddenly two of them ran behind a large tree only yards from the edge of the woodland. Both men aimed their muskets, one man's weapon under the other's.

In that confused moment, Tucker looked to Hill. The general had ridden up on his right. "We must take them," Hill said in a low tone. Possibly he was influenced by the ease with which two other Yankees had been captured a few minutes earlier. In any event, for the first time Hill drew his own revolver while he held the reins of Champ in his left hand. The two riders now were no more than twenty yards from the Federals. "Stay there," Tucker implored Hill. "I'll take them."

The courier advanced a few steps and shouted: "If you fire, you'll be swept to hell! Our men are here! Surrender!"

"Surrender!" cried out Hill, as he reined his horse and leveled his revolver.

Behind the tree were two members of the 138th Pennsylvania. Corp. John W. Mauck, a twenty-nine-year-old carpenter from Bedford County, Pa., looked down at his compatriot, Pvt. Daniel Wolford. "I cannot see it," Mauck whispered. "Let us shoot them." Both men fired.[46]

Wolford's shot missed Tucker. The .58-caliber bullet from Mauck's rifle ran true. Hill never felt the pain of death. The bullet cut off his left thumb in the gauntlet, passed directly through his heart, and ripped out his back. Hill died instantly. The impact of the projectile spun his body around, and he fell face down to the ground.[47]

At the musket fire, Tucker reached out instinctively toward Hill. His fingers closed around the bridle of Hill's horse. Tucker leaned over his mount's neck and, still holding Champ's bridle, wheeled to the left to escape. The courier glanced quickly to the right and "saw my General on the ground, with his limbs extended, motionless."

Tucker galloped to safety. Remembering Hill's last directive to get word to Lee should anything happen to him, Tucker switched over to Hill's superior horse and speedily retraced his route back toward Lee's headquarters. The courier first encountered Longstreet, and he blurted out what had happened. Palmer and other members of Hill's staff rode up. Tucker broke the sad news to them. Palmer and Tucker then rode to army headquarters. They reported to Lee, who was on horseback in the Cox Road in front of the Turnbull house. Lee was handsomely dressed, sword buckled to his waist, and was surrounded by members of his staff. Palmer began telling him of Hill's death, but broke down in tears and motioned to Tucker to finish the account. Lee made no effort to conceal his sorrow. An aide said, "Never shall I forget the look on General Lee's face, as Sergeant Tucker made his report." Tears swelled in Lee's eyes. With a choking voice he said, "He is now at rest, and we who are left are the ones to suffer."[48]

Hours later, the Army of Northern Virginia began its death march to Appomattox.

21

Epilogue

Hill's body was recovered less than a half hour after his death. Members of his staff, and the 5th Alabama Battalion, which was acting as headquarters guard, rushed to the area where Hill had fallen. No Federals were in sight, they apparently having fled after the shooting. The corpse was undisturbed and still warm. The men reverently placed it across the saddle of a horse, and the party began a slow procession back to the Venable cottage.[1]

Meanwhile, Lee had asked Palmer to tell Mrs. Hill. "Break the news to her as gently as possible," Lee said. With all dispatch, Lee added, Palmer should get Mrs. Hill and the children safely to the north side of the Appomattox River.

Palmer rode into the yard of the Venable estate and dismounted in front of the cottage. As the colonel walked up the front steps, he heard a voice singing. It was Dolly, busy with the morning chores that a wife in her seventh month of pregnancy could perform. Palmer knocked on the door. The singing stopped. Dolly opened the door and, at the sight of Palmer, threw up her hands in anguish. "The General is dead!" she screamed. "You would not be here if he had not been killed!"

The chief of staff tried to temper his announcement. "I cannot deceive you at such a moment," he stated. "The General has been shot. Whether fatally or not, I do not know." A few minutes later, soldiers arrived at the cottage with Hill's body.[2]

Palmer would have acted as personal escort for his chieftain except that he received orders to report at once to Longstreet for field duty. Hence, the colonel directed Capt. Frank Hill (the general's nephew) and courier Jenkins to accompany the remains, Mrs. Hill, and the two little girls to a safe place in the Richmond area. The body was laid in the only army wagon that could be found—a dilapidated vehicle with no two wheels alike in appearance or size. Hill's cape covered his face, but Dolly always remembered how conspicuous the wedding ring looked on his mangled left hand. She sat beside her husband's remains, cradling the two daughters in her arms while the wagon swayed, creaked, and bounced on its way toward Richmond.

The family's wish was to bury Hill in Hollywood Cemetery, the capital's "Place of Heroes." Cousins G. Powell Hill and Henry Hill, the latter the son of Col. Henry Hill in the Paymaster Department, met the wagon en route to Richmond. It was dark by the time the party reached the James River across from the city. There the Hills found a capital in chaos. Getting across Mayo's Bridge was impossible because of the flight southward of people from the doomed city. Part of downtown Richmond was in flames; every road leading out of town was packed with soldiers, civilians, wagons, carriages, and horses. The Hill wagon was the only conveyance trying to fight the tide and get into Richmond.

Dolly and the children agreed to go to the Hill home in Chesterfield County (where they had spent part of the winter) and await developments. Around one in the morning on April 3, the two Hill cousins managed to get the wagon across the river and to the paymaster's office at Franklin and 12th streets. The downtown stores were deserted and in shambles as a result of widespread looting. The cousins went from building to building until they found a small plain pine coffin in Blevin's undertaking establishment. Returning to the paymaster's office, they removed the general's gauntlets, washed the dirt from his face, wrapped the body in Hill's army coat, and placed it in the coffin.

No city authorities could be found to give permission for an interment in Hollywood Cemetery, and the Union army was expected to march into Richmond at any hour. The body was returned to the wagon; the Hill cousins recrossed the James before dawn and slowly made their way upriver to the Hill home.[3]

When the wagon was within a mile of the residence, G. Powell Hill went ahead to apprise the family of their coming, in the belief that Dolly and the children had already reached there with the sad news. They had not. The family's second choice for the burial, if Hollywood Cemetery was not possible, was to return the General to Culpeper. Yet as an unusually warm April 3 passed, the impracticability of getting the unembalmed remains to a graveyard a hundred tortuous miles away became more evident.

Mrs. Hill arrived late that day or early the next morning. After a hasty conference the family decided to bury the remains on the estate "and at some future day remove them to his native county and place him by the side of his parents." G. Powell Hill and a family slave, Willis Martin, constructed a rough case for the coffin; and at two o'clock on April 4, with neither religious service nor fanfare, the general was interred in the old Winston family cemetery in the Coalfield area of Chesterfield County.[4]

On June 6, in Culpeper, Dolly gave birth to her fourth child. She had hoped for a son, who could bear her husband's name. It was a daughter. The child was baptized Ann Powell Hill and promptly nicknamed A. P. Dolly returned to her family in Kentucky the following month. From then until her death, according to one of her daughters, she "was very averse to talking of anything connected with the war." A pardon from the federal government in May 1866 did nothing to soften Dolly's bitterness over the struggle that had taken her husband's life.[5]

That the beloved commander of the Third Corps was buried in an obscure private cemetery bothered a number of veterans who had served under Hill. In February 1867, a small group of the general's friends met at Brander & Cook's store in Richmond "to concert measures for the removal of his remains, with the view of giving them a more honorable sepulture" in Hollywood Cemetery. Four men agreed to oversee the movement: Col. William H. Palmer and Capts. John R. Cooke, William Mayo, and J. Hampden Chamberlayne. Palmer eventually secured the somewhat reluctant consent of the family to have Hill's body transferred.

That autumn Palmer went to the Winston cemetery and exhumed the body (which the colonel pronounced "in a good state of preservation"). Hill was reburied in Lot N-35 of Hollywood Cemetery without any religious service and apparently with no immediate family present. A headstone was not erected; rather, the words "Lt.-Gen. A. P. Hill" were cut into the curbing in front of the grave.[6]

Ann Powell Hill died the following year, just short of her third birthday. Funeral services were held at the Morgan family residence, and burial followed in Lexington Cemetery. For months thereafter, Mrs. Hill was reported "in great distress" over the loss.[7]

With her soldier-husband dead, Mrs. Hill dropped his nickname for her and resumed using her given name, Kitty. Her strong-mindedness and independence remained. A number of widows of slain Confederate generals chose not to wed again. Kitty was too embittered by the war, and too full of life, to accept self-imposed martyrdom on behalf of the Southern Confederacy. Around 1870 she married Alexander Forsyth, a Louisville physician and "a courtly gentleman of distinguished appearance." Kitty bore him two daughters: Katrina Roth and Christina Key Forsyth. This third marriage for Kitty was also short-lived. On September 8, 1875, Forsyth died at Hopemont, the Morgan family home. He was buried in Lexington but later reinterred in Louisville.[8]

Kitty and her four daughters continued to live with her mother, Mrs. Henrietta Morgan, at the family home.

Meanwhile, in October 1870, Robert E. Lee had died at Lexington, Va. "Stonewall" Jackson had called for Hill with his dying words. So did Lee. On the morning before he expired, the delirious commander's mind wandered back to the battlefields of the great civil war. He mumbled intermittently; a loud cry occasionally passed his lips. Then, in words plainly heard and understood by everyone in the room, Lee stated emphatically, "Tell Hill he *must* come up." It was the last intelligible thing Lee said until his remark at the moment of death: "Strike the tent."[9]

Virginians at the former Confederate capital had begun immortalizing their heroes in bronze. The first monument, a huge equestrian statue of Lee, was dedicated in 1870; five years later, a similar equestrian statue of Jackson was unveiled on Monument Avenue. Others were merited and needed. In 1879 William E. Cameron wrote a tribute to Hill that closed with the sentiments: "No history of him has yet been written; no stone marks his resting-place in Hollywood Cemetery. If the memories of war are to be perpetuated, not forgotten should he be—that Virginia soldier who never lost a post that duty gave him to defend, and who never failed to crown an attack—if not with success—with the blood-red crown of terrible endeavor."[10]

Veterans' groups were quite active in Richmond during the next decade. In 1887 the Pegram Battalion Association began to pursue the dream of an A. P. Hill monument with the general's remains beneath it. Maj. Thomas Brander, a valorous artillery officer who had become a prominent insurance agent, took the lead in the project. Capt. Thomas Ellett, who also had served under Hill, worked closely with Brander; but the man who made it all come true was Maj. Lewis Ginter.

A former staff officer of Hill's and subsequently one of Richmond's leading developers, Ginter wanted to create a new residential section on the west side of the city and thought it would be appropriate to have a monument to Hill as its centerpiece. That the location would be some distance from Monument Avenue was an advantage, in Ginter's view. He did not envision a huge memorial, one of Richmond's most knowledgeable historians has stated. The major was not anxious to have "a small monument like that for Hill to stand in the glory of Lee's Monument, and . . . the Pegram Battery men preferred for A. P. Hill to stand alone in his glory as he had on many battlefields."[11]

The Hill Monument Association then went to work in earnest. A fund-raising drive brought in a steady stream of donations. The Ginter Real Estate Development Co. donated the intersection of Laburnum Avenue and Hermitage Road. To do the sculpture of Hill, the association hired William L. Sheppard, a local artist of national reputation and a former member of the Richmond Howitzers.

By June 1891, the six-foot base for the statue was ready for Hill's remains. Solemnly, on the afternoon of June 24, a delegation of veterans led by Colonel Palmer went to Hollywood Cemetery with a receptable to exhume what was left of the body. Before the grave could be opened, however, Hill's officers encountered the strong-willed cemetery superintendent, Anthony Bargamin. He refused to allow the remains to be touched unless a letter of permission from the widow was in hand. What Palmer had was a communiqué from Lucy Hill, which stated that both she and her mother freely granted permission. This was not good enough for the circumspect Mr. Bargamin.

At two o'clock on July 1, the delegation of a dozen men appeared again at Hollywood. This time they had the necessary correspondence from Kitty Hill Forsyth. The exhumation took over four hours because the remains were off to one side from the mound of earth, and great care had to be exercised in removing what was there. Funeral director L. T. Christian deposited the remains in an appropriate container. Near sundown, the case was sealed in the receptacle at the base of the uncompleted monument. For the third time, Hill had been buried without any formal ceremony. Thereafter, veterans from the Soldiers' Home took turns guarding the new resting place until the heavier stones of the monument were in place and the vault securely sealed.[12]

In September, as work continued on the monument, Mrs. Henrietta Morgan died in Lexington, Ky. Hill's mother-in-law was eighty-five. All of her six sons had served in the Southern army, and both of her daughters had married Confederate generals (Hill and Basil Duke). Kitty thereafter moved into a house at the corner of West Third Street and Blackburn Avenue in Lexington. There she lived the remainder of her life.[13]

Kitty Forsyth was unable to attend the May 30, 1892, monument unveiling ceremonies in Richmond, but Lucy Hill represented the family. Henry Heth was chief marshal for the festivities, which were deliberately held on Memorial Day. A two-hour parade wound slowly from downtown to the site of the monument. An estimated 15,000 people watched the ceremony. An observer noted that "there has been no such outpouring of all classes since the unveiling of the Lee monument, and certainly the spirit of the occasion was manifest in every face."

Speakers were numerous and tributes were many. Hill's old chaplain spoke emotionally of "the brave and accomplished soldier, the chivalric Virginia gentleman, the devoted patriot, the martyr hero of our dying cause, 'gallant and glorious little Powell Hill.' " In the major address, Gen. James A. Walker presented a long and glowing eulogy. The gist of it lay in one sentence: "Wherever the headquarters flag of A. P. Hill floated, whether at the head of a regiment, a brigade, a division, or a corps, in camp or on the battle-field, it floated with a pace and a confidence born of skill, ability and courage, which infused its confidence and courage into the hearts of all who followed it."[14]

The Hill monument was centrally located and impressive but largely ignored. Twenty years later, when a book appeared listing over a hundred Confederate memorials in the South, the Hill statue was omitted.[15]

With the passing years, death took its natural toll. John Mauck, the Union soldier who killed Hill, died quietly in August 1898 at his Centerville, Pa., home. George Tucker's life ended about the same time. Hill's chief courier had returned to his native Baltimore after the war and become a salesman for a wholesale firm. The fun-loving former cavalryman did not enjoy the postwar years. "Poor Tucker," Palmer stated in a letter, "he became almost a castaway, a drunkard & gave me at times trouble. . . . His family had to earn its own living."[16]

Hill's oldest surviving daughter, Russie, grew into an attractive woman, petite and with the chestnut hair of her parents. "She was a society belle, popular throughout the South," wrote a friend. "She was gifted with much charm and manner, and possessed intellect of extraordinary brilliance." Russie was married twice, first to James Gay of Lexington, Ky., in the 1880s and then in 1895 to Garland Hale of Chicago. On July 19, 1917, Russie died childless in Ashland, Va.[17]

Kitty Hill Forsyth had an unusually long and full life. By 1920 the infirmities of age had severely restricted her movements. The death of her daughter Katrina Forsyth early that year was a blow from which the thrice-widowed lady never recovered. She died March 20 in Lexington at the home of Christina, her other daughter by Alexander Forsyth. Funeral services were held on the afternoon of March 25; over her grave was placed a modest stone with the inscription: "K. Forsyth." For a long time a bush obliterated the marker.[18]

The last member of the general's family to die was his daughter Lucy. On reaching maturity, she moved to Chicago and engaged in literary work for many years. "She was a noted beauty in her youth and her gracious cordiality endears her to friends new and old," an interviewer wrote. In November 1904, at the age of forty-one, Lucy married James McGill. "A prominent planter" of Pulaski, Va., McGill had been a captain of engineers under Lucy's father. The couple settled in Richmond. They were too old to have children. Thus, when Lucy died in 1931, the Hill line died with her.[19]

Just before her death, Lucy Hill McGill made an earnest plea: "I do so want to have justice done my father. It never has been."[20]

She was expressing a belief long held by many of the general's compatriots. Hill has never basked in the glory accorded to most

Confederate generals of equal rank—and dozens of generals of lesser rank. A major reason why historians have ignored Hill for more than a century is the fact that a large cache of the general's papers, stored in an outbuilding of the Hill home in Culpeper, succumbed to the appetites of generations of rats, and this loss repeatedly deterred writers from giving Hill the biographical attention that would have enhanced his reputation. The discovery of a large and previously unknown collection of Hill papers during the course of the research for this book may help to correct the injustice. Hill has long deserved that, for his story is the story of the Southern Confederacy, and his death in the final days of the war was symbolic of the Southern nation's dying hopes.

"Of all the Confederate leaders," Gen. James A. Walker asserted, Hill "was the most genial and lovable in his disposition."[21]

Chaplain J. William Jones wrote of Hill shortly after the Civil War: "And though he knew no tender care, as did Jackson, no weeping friends, as did Stuart, the swift-winged messenger of death left neither wanting. His death groan was lost in the roar of the battle, his death couch moistened with the blood of his comrades, and for his requiem was heard a nation's wail."[22]

The most fitting eulogy to "Little Powell" came from Col. Charles Venable of Lee's staff. "In him fell one of the knightliest Generals of that army of knightly soldiers. On the field he was the very soul of chivalrous gallantry. In moments of the greatest peril his bearing was superb and inspiring in the highest degree. . . . The name of A. P. Hill stands recorded high on the list of those noble sons of Virginia at whose roll-call grateful memory will ever answer: 'Dead on the field of honor for the people they loved so well.' "[23]

Notes

1. STORMY ROAD TO MANHOOD

1 Jedediah Hotchkiss, *Confederate Military History—Virginia* (Atlanta, 1899), 355; John B. Gordon, *Reminiscences of the Civil War* (New York, 1904), 418–19; *Southern Historical Society Papers*, XIX (1891), 178 (cited hereafter as *SHSP*).

2 Powell was instrumental in determining the boundary line between Virginia and Kentucky. His name is embedded securely in geography with a river, valley, and mountain all named for him. Powell was reputed to be "a judge of good tobacco, of good liquor, influential as a politician, jovial and unduly stout." W. H. T. Squires, *The Land of Decision* (Portsmouth, Va., 1931), 205; *Richmond Times-Dispatch*, Oct. 14, 1934.

3 Eva B. Browning to William J. Robertson, Sept. 16, 1931, Ambrose Powell Hill Papers, Virginia Historical Society.

4 *Ibid.*, Oct. 2, 1931; *Richmond Times-Dispatch*, Oct. 14, 1934.

5 Eva B. Browning to William J. Robertson, Nov. 12, 1931, Hill Papers; *The Land We Love*, II (1866–1867), 287–88; *SHSP*, XXVIII (1900), 374. The children of Thomas and Fannie Hill were James, Theophilus, E. Baptist, A. Powell, Margaret, Evelyn, and Lucy.

6 *Souvenir: Hill Monument Unveiling, May 30th 1892* [Richmond, 1892], 15.

7 Z. T. George to William J. Robertson, Sept. 21, 1931, and Eva B. Browning to William J. Robertson, Nov. 12, 1931, Hill Papers; Edward Broadus to William Smith, Feb. 3, 1842, U.S. Military Academy, Cadet Application Papers, 1805–1866, National Archives.

8 *Richmond Times-Dispatch*, Oct. 14, 1934.

9 Hill's file, U.S. Military Academy application papers.

Notes

10 Copy of letter in the Conference Room, Fort A. P. Hill, Va.

11 Eva B. Browning to William J. Robertson, Aug. 25, 1931, Hill Papers; *Richmond Times-Dispatch*, Oct. 14, 1934.

12 Maury, *Recollections*, 22–23.

13 *The Land We Love*, II (1866–1867), 288.

14 Col. Edgar Dudley, in Military Order of the Loyal Legion: New York Commandery (cited hereafter as New York MOLLUS), *Personal Recollection of the War of the Rebellion*, III (1907), 394; George Thornton Fleming, *Life and Letters of Alexander Hays* (Pittsburgh, 1919), 11–12. Cadet Ulysses S. Grant, writing home to a cousin, said of his uniform: "If you were to see me at a distance, the first question you would ask would be, 'is that a Fish or an animal?' " John Y. Simon, ed., *The Papers of Ulysses S. Grant* (Carbondale, Ill., 1967), I, 6.

15 U.S. Military Academy, Monthly Class Reports and Conduct Rolls, 1831–1866, National Archives.

16 Hill to mother, Apr. 3, 1843, Hill Papers.

17 Henry Heth, *The Memoirs of Henry Heth* (Westport, Conn., 1974), 18.

18 *Confederate Veteran*, I (1893), 233.

19 William W. Hassler, *A. P. Hill: Lee's Forgotten General* (Richmond, 1957), 11; G. J. Barker-Benfield, *The Horrors of the Half-Known Life* (New York, 1976), 244; John S. and Robin M. Haller, *The Physician and Sexuality in Victorian America* (Urbana, 1974), 258. Only a decade after the Civil War, the American Public Health Association estimated that one of every 18.5 residents of New York City was infected with syphilis or gonorrhea.

20 U.S. Military Academy, Monthly Class Reports and Conduct Rolls, 1831–1866; Theodor Rosebury, *Microbes and Morals: The Strange Story of Venereal Disease* (New York, 1971), 183; Stewart Brooks, *Civil War Medicine* (Springfield, Ill., 1966), 121.

21 William J. Brown *et al.*, *Syphilis and Other Venereal Diseases* (Cambridge, Mass., 1970), 89–90; Alfred Taliaferro to West Point Superintendent, Mar. 17, 1845, Adjutant's Letters Received (Unregistered, 1845–1852)—Cadet Letters, USMA.

22 Hill to Lt. Irvin McDowell, Mar. 26, 1845, *ibid.*

23 U.S. Military Academy Staff Records, IV (1845–1850), Ser. 14, USMA.

24 Hill to "Georgia," Aug. 1, 1845, Hill Papers.

25 U.S. Military Academy Monthly Class Reports and Conduct Rolls, 1831–1866; Capt. J. A. Thomas to Lt. Irvin McDowell, Sept. 10, 1845, George W. Cullum Collection, USMA; George B. McClellan to sister, May 3, 1846, George Brinton McClellan Papers, Library of Congress.

26 Heth, *Memoirs*, 26.

27 *Ibid.*, 31; Philip Shaw Paludan, *Victims: A True Story of the Civil War* (Knoxville, 1981), 36; U.S. Military Academy, Monthly Class Reports and Conduct Rolls, 1831–1866.

28 Hill to parents, Mar. 16, 1845, Hill Papers.

29 John M. Schofield, *Forty-Six Years in the Army* (New York, 1897), 16.

30 Hill to "Capt.," Aug. 8, 1855, George W. Cullum File Letters, USMA. Hill's assignment-certificate to the U.S. Artillery is in the Museum of the Confederacy, Richmond, Va.

31 Hill to Sec. of War John B. Floyd, Oct. 28, 1858, U.S. Quartermaster Consolidated Correspondence File, National Archives; Hill to family, Oct. 23, 1847, Hill Papers.

32 Hill to family, Oct. 23 and Nov. 8, 1847, Hill Papers.

³³ Percy M. Ashburn, *A History of the Medical Department of the United States Army* (Boston, 1929), 58–59.

³⁴ Hill to family, Jan. 8, 1848, and Hill to father, Feb. 29, 1848, Hill Papers.

2 . LOVE AFFAIRS AND WAR CLOUDS

¹ Hill to father, Apr. 14, 1852, and Eva B. Browning to William J. Robertson, Oct. 2, 1931, Hill Papers; *Richmond Times-Dispatch*, Nov. 4, 1934.

² Hill diary, Oct. 25, 1849–May 15, 1850, Hill Papers.

³ Hill to father, May 5, 1850, *ibid.*

⁴ The first writer to allege that Hill contracted yellow fever was a childhood friend, J. William Jones. See *The Land We Love*, II (1866–1867), 288.

⁵ James Magill (Hill's son-in-law) to Beverly B. Munford, Apr. 20, 1908, Beverly B. Munford Papers, Virginia Historical Society; Hill to E. Baptist Hill, Aug. 16, 1850, Hill Papers.

⁶ U.S. Adjutant General's Office, Letters Sent Relating to Nominations in the Army, 1837–1876, National Archives.

⁷ Hill to Lucy Hill, Sept. 12, 1851, Hill Papers.

⁸ Hill to "Ned," Oct. 8, 1851, *ibid.*

⁹ Hill to Quartermaster General, Nov. 5, 1851, Quartermaster Consolidated Correspondence File.

¹⁰ Hill to father, Feb. 4, 1852, Hill Papers.

¹¹ *Ibid.*, Apr. 14, 1852.

¹² *Ibid.*; Hill to mother, July 6, 1852, *ibid.*

¹³ U.S. Adjutant General's Office, Endorsements, 1851–1870, National Archives; Hill to Lucy Hill, Jan. 23, 1855, Hill Papers; *Richmond Times-Dispatch*, Oct. 21, 1934.

¹⁴ Hill to "Capt.," Aug. 8, 1855, Cullum Collection; Schofield, *Forty-six Years in the Army*, 24; Hill to Lucy Hill, Jan. 25, 1855, Hill Papers.

¹⁵ Schofield, *Forty-Six Years in the Army*, 25–26.

¹⁶ *The Land We Love*, II (1866–1867), 288; Eva B. Browning to William J. Robertson, Nov. 2, 1920, Hill Papers; Hill to "my dear Capt.," Sept. 2 [1858?], Cullum Collection.

¹⁷ *The Land We Love*, II (1866–1867), 288; *SHSP*, XX (1892), 377.

¹⁸ Hill to "Miss Carrie," Apr. 30, 1856, Ambrose Powell Hill Letter, Duke University.

¹⁹ Randolph B. Marcy to daughter, May 28, 1856, McClellan Papers.

²⁰ William Starr Myers, *General George Brinton McClellan* (New York, 1934), 133–34.

²¹ Hill to Randolph B. Marcy, [June?] 1856, McClellan Papers.

²² George B. McClellan to Mrs. R. B. Marcy, July 22, 1856, *ibid.*

²³ Myers, *McClellan*, 134; Eva B. Browning to William J. Robertson, Aug. 25, 1931, Hill Papers.

²⁴ Hassler, *Hill*, 16.

²⁵ Eva B. Browning to William J. Robertson, Nov. 2, 1920, and Lucy H. Magill to William J. Robertson, undated letter, Hill Papers.

²⁶ Calvin McClung to Henrietta Morgan, Aug. 25 and Nov. 1, 1855, letters in possession of Henrietta Millns, Raleigh, N.C.

²⁷ *Richmond Times-Dispatch*, Nov. 4, 1934.

²⁸ All letters cited are in the U.S. Quartermaster Consolidated Correspondence File, National Archives.

29 Hill to George B. McClellan, June 18, 1859, McClellan Papers.

30 Lexington *Kentucky Statesman*, July 26, 1859. Interestingly, two John Hunt Morgan biographers both asserted that the wedding occurred in July 1861. Howard Swiggett, *The Rebel Raider* (Indianapolis, 1934), 25; Cecil Fletcher Holland, *Morgan and His Raiders* (New York, 1942), 38.

31 Lucy Magill to William J. Robertson, Oct. 5, ?, Hill Papers.

32 Woodford B. Hackley, *The Little Fork Rangers: A Sketch of Company "D," Fourth Virginia Cavalry* (Richmond, 1927), 21.

33 William W. Chamberlaine, *Memoirs of the Civil War* (Washington, 1912), 109. The oft-repeated assertion that Hill concealed bitter disappointment at the McClellan-Marcy wedding has no substantiation.

34 Hill to Lucy Hill, Jan. 2, 1861, Hill Papers.

3. THE GENERAL EMERGES

1 *Richmond Enquirer*, June 23, 1861; *Richmond Daily Dispatch*, Mar. 11, 1861.

2 Richmond *Whig*, Apr. 9, 1861; *Richmond Daily Dispatch*, Apr. 17, 1861.

3 *Ibid.*, Apr. 16, 1861; Henry J. Mugler diary-reminiscences, West Virginia University.

4 *Richmond Daily Dispatch*, Apr. 27, 1861; Carrie E. Spencer et al., comps., *A Civil War Marriage in Virginia: Reminiscences and Letters* (Boyce, Va., 1956), 84.

5 James I. Robertson, Jr., ed., *Proceedings of the Advisory Council of the State of Virginia, April 21–June 19, 1861* (Richmond, 1977), 66; *Confederate Veteran*, I (1893), 233.

6 George Cary Eggleston, *A Rebel's Recollections* (New York, 1875), 29–31; Joseph E. Johnston, *Narrative of Military Operations Directed during the Late War between the States* (New York, 1874), 33.

7 *SHSP*, IX (1891), 93.

8 Regimental Order No. 18, regimental letterbook, Hill Papers.

9 Emma C. R. Macon and Reuben C. Macon, *Reminiscences of the Civil War* (n.p., 1911), 141–43, 145.

10 *Richmond Times-Dispatch*, Nov. 4, 1934; *Confederate Veteran*, I (1893), 233.

11 Lucy H. Magill to William J. Robertson, Oct. 5, ?, Hill Papers; unidentified newspaper clipping, *ibid.*

12 Hill to Capt. William S. Parran, May 17, 1861, Campbell Papers, College of William and Mary.

13 After the war, Prince and Hill's other horse, Champ, lived out their lives at the Culpeper home of E. Baptist Hill. *Richmond Times-Dispatch*, Oct. 28, 1934; Eva B. Browning to William J. Robertson, Mar. 14, 1931, Hill Papers.

14 *SHSP*, IX (1891), 93; Johnston, *Narrative of Military Operations*, 22–23.

15 U.S. War Dept., comp., *War of the Rebellion: A Compilation of the Official Records of the Union and Confederate Armies* (Washington, 1880–1901), Ser. I, Vol. II, 130–31; LI, Pt. 2, 139 [cited hereafter as *OR*; unless otherwise cited, all references will be to Ser. I]; *Richmond Examiner*, June 17, 1861.

16 *Richmond Daily Dispatch*, June 25, 1861.

17 *SHSP*, IX (1891), 93–94.

18 Samuel D. Buck, *With the Old Confeds* (Baltimore, 1925), 20; *SHSP*, XX (1892), 379; John S. Barbour to Eva B. Browning, Oct. 2, 1931, Hill Papers.

19 *Richmond Daily Dispatch*, July 12, 1861; Buck, *With the Old Confeds*, 22.

20 *Richmond Daily Dispatch*, July 22 and 28, 1861.

21 Ambrose P. Hill file, "Compiled Service Records of General and Staff Officers, Corps, Division and Brigade Staffs, Non-com. Staffs and Bands," U.S. National Archives.

22 *OR*, II, 478, 982; Buck, *With the Old Confeds*, 23.

23 Johnston, *Narrative of Military Operations*, 36, 58.

24 Randolph H. McKim, *A Soldier's Recollections* (New York, 1910), 46; W. W. Goldsborough, *The Maryland Line in the Confederate Army, 1861–1865* (Baltimore, 1900), 21–22.

25 *Richmond Examiner*, July 27, 1861; Goldsborough, *Maryland Line*, 22–23.

26 *OR*, II, 487; William C. Davis, *Battle at Bull Run* (Baton Rouge, 1977), 225.

27 Eggleston, *A Rebel's Recollections*, 44; Johnston, *Narrative of Military Operations*, 60.

28 Hill file, "Compiled Service Records"; Eva B. Browning to William J. Robertston, Nov. 2, 1931, Hill Papers.

29 *Richmond Daily Dispatch*, Aug. 20, 1861; Thomas C. DeLeon, *Four Years in Rebel Capitals* (Mobile, 1890), 140; D. Augustus Dickert, *History of Kershaw's Brigade* (Newberry, S.C., 1899), 72, 77. For an example of the high incidence of sickness in the Union army at this time, see G. G. Benedict, *Vermont in the Civil War* (Burlington, 1886), I, 136, 160, 184.

30 Buck, *With the Old Confeds*, 25.

31 *Richmond Daily Dispatch*, Sept. 1 and 7, 1861.

32 Hill to Lucy Hill, Sept. 2, 1861, Hill Papers.

33 L. Franklin Campbell, 13th Va., to "Mary," Sept. 7, 1861, letter in the writer's possession; *Richmond Daily Dispatch*, Sept. 19, 1861; *Winchester Virginian*, Sept. 26, 1861; *Richmond Examiner*, Oct. 24, 1861.

34 Lucy H. Magill to William J. Robertson, undated letter, Hill Papers; *Richmond Daily Dispatch*, Sept. 23, 1861; St. Louis (Mo.) *Republic*, July 12, 1896. The second battle flag is now preserved in the Museum of the Confederacy, Richmond, Va.

35 *Richmond Daily Dispatch*, Sept. 23, 1861; Oliver W. Norton, *Army Letters, 1861–1865* (Chicago, 1903), 26.

36 Macon, *Reminiscences of the Civil War*, 146–47; *Richmond Daily Dispatch*, Nov. 5 and 9, 1861.

37 *Confederate Veteran*, I (1893), 233–34; McKim, *A Soldier's Recollections*, 53.

38 Mugler diary.

39 Goldsborough, *Maryland Line*, 32; Spencer, *Civil War Marriage*, 123.

40 Hill to Dr. ——, Jan. 6, 1862, Monroe F. Cockrell Papers, Duke University.

41 Dickert, *Kershaw's Brigade*, 89; Henry A. Chambers, *Diary of Capt. Henry A. Chambers* (Wendell, N.C., 1983), 9.

42 Hill file, "Compiled Service Records"; *OR*, V, 1058.

43 *SHSP*, XX (1892), 378.

4. WILLIAMSBURG AND A NEW HERO

1 *OR*, LI, Pt. 2, 514–15; William Miller Owen, *In Camp and Battle with the Washington Artillery of New Orleans* (Boston, 1885), 76.

2 *Richmond Daily Dispatch*, Mar. 3, 1862.

3 *Richmond Examiner*, Apr. 21, 1862; Joseph E. Johnston to George B. McClellan, Apr. 29, 1859, McClellan Papers.

4 Charles T. Loehr, *War History of the Old First Virginia Infantry Regiment, Army of Northern Virginia* (Richmond, 1884), 16–17; Susan P. Lee, *Memoirs of*

William Nelson Pendleton, D.D. (Philadelphia, 1893), 176; William W. Bennett, *A Narrative of the Great Revival Which Prevailed in the Southern Armies* (Philadelphia, 1877), 137.

⁵ William Garrett Piston, "Lee's Tarnished Lieutenant: James Longstreet and His Image in American Society" (unpublished dissertation, University of South Carolina, 1982), 147–49; G. Moxley Sorrel, *Recollections of a Confederate Staff Officer* (Jackson, Tenn., 1958), 17.

⁶ *OR*, XI, Pt. 3, 481, 530; LI, Pt. 2, 545.

⁷ William H. Morgan, *Personal Reminiscences of the War of 1861–5* (Lynchburg, Va., 1911), 98–99; Walter Clark, ed., *Histories of the Several Regiments and Battalions from North Carolina in the Great War, 1861–65* (Raleigh, 1901), II, 195–96.

⁸ *Richmond Daily Dispatch*, May 12, 1862; David E. Johnston, *The Story of a Confederate Boy in the Civil War* (Portland, Ore., 1914), 99.

⁹ Morgan, *Personal Reminiscences*, 102.

¹⁰ *Richmond Daily Dispatch*, May 12, 1862; Regis de Trobriand, *Four Years with the Army of the Potomac* (Boston, 1889), 191.

¹¹ Morgan, *Personal Reminiscences*, 102, 105; *OR*, Pt. XI, Pt. 1, 565, 575–76; Loehr, *1st Virginia*, 18.

¹² *OR*, XI, Pt. 1, 564–66, 580, 591; *Richmond Daily Dispatch*, May 12, 1862.

¹³ Morgan, *Personal Reminiscences*, 105.

¹⁴ *OR*, XI, Pt. 1, 576–77; Loehr, *1st Virginia*, 18–21; Morgan, *Personal Reminiscences*, 105–6.

¹⁵ Henry N. Blake, *Three Years in the Army of the Potomac* (Boston, 1865), 74; Johnston, *A Confederate Boy*, 102; *Souvenir: Hill Monument*, 15.

¹⁶ *The Land We Love*, II, (1866–1867), 288; *SHSP*, XVII (1889), 418.

¹⁷ George T. Stevens, *Three Years in the Sixth Corps* (New York, 1870), 57; *OR*, XI, Pt. 1, 567, 577. Thirty years later, when Longstreet wrote his memoirs, after disagreements with Hill later in the war had beclouded his vision, Longstreet did not even mention the presence of Hill's brigade at Williamsburg.

¹⁸ *OR*, XI, Pt. 1, 450, 569, 577–78.

¹⁹ Loehr, *1st Virginia*, 22.

²⁰ Johnston, *A Confederate Boy*, 103.

²¹ *OR*, XI, Pt. 1, 577.

²² Johnston, *A Confederate Boy*, 103; George Wise, *Campaigns and Battles of the Army of Northern Virginia* (New York, 1916), 58, 61.

²³ *Richmond Daily Dispatch*, May 16 and 19, 1862.

²⁴ Hill file, "Compiled Service Records"; *OR*, XI, Pt. 3, 547, 555.

5 · THE LIGHT DIVISION'S FIRST ATTACK

¹ R. J. Wingate to Lawrence O'B. Branch, May 27, 1862, L. O'B. Branch Papers, North Carolina State Archives; *OR*, XI, Pt. 3, 554–55, 589.

² *Richmond Daily Dispatch*, May 24, 1861.

³ [Thomas C. Caffey], *Battle-fields of the South, from Bull Run to Fredericksburg* (New York, 1864), II, 137; Sallie Brock Putnam, *Richmond during the War* (New York, 1867), 199.

⁴ Clark, *N.C. Regiments*, I, 697, 764–65; Walter A. Montgomery, *Life and Character of Major General William Dorsey Pender* (Raleigh, 1894), 5.

⁵ Jennings Cropper Wise, *The Long Arm of Lee; or, The History of the Artillery of the Army of Northern Virginia* (Lynchburg, Va., 1915), I, 113–14; II, 750–54.

6 Joseph H. Crute, Jr., *Confederate Staff Officers, 1861–1865* (Powhatan, Va., 1982), 84–85; *SHSP*, XXVII (1899), 36–37.

7 *Confederate Veteran*, XVIII (1910), 82; *SHSP*, XXVII (1899), 36–37.

8 *OR*, XI, Pt. 1, 681, 685; *Richmond Examiner*, May 29 and 31, 1862; Diary of William James Harriss Bellamy, May 27, 1862, Southern Historical Collection, UNC.

9 Clark, *N.C. Regiments*, II, 654; W. G. Morris to wife, May 30, 1862, William Grove Morris Papers, Southern Historical Collection, UNC.

10 R. J. Wingate to L. O'B. Branch, May 27, 1862; and Hill to Branch, May 28, 1862, Branch Papers, N.C. State Archives; G. W. Smith to W. H. C. Whiting, May 29, 1862, Folder H–483, Museum of the Confederacy.

11 *OR*, XI, Pt. 3, 567.

12 Wayland F. Dunaway, *Reminiscences of a Rebel* (New York, 1866), 210; *Confederate Veteran*, XXIII (1915), 161.

13 J. William Jones, *Stonewall Jackson: A Military Biography* (New York, 1866), 210.

14 John W. Hinsdale diary, June 11, 1862, Hinsdale Family Papers, Duke University. For examples of Hill's inter-division correspondence at this time, see Hill to L. O'B. Branch, June 11, 1862, Branch Papers, N.C. State Archives; *OR*, XI, Pt. 3, 596; Hill to Branch, June 15, 1862, A. P. Hill Papers, North Carolina State Archives.

15 General Order Book, 37th N.C. Troops, 1862–1863, Duke University.

16 Richard C. Morgan to James J. Archer, June 22, 1862, Letterbook of the Light Division, C.S.A., 1862–1863, New York Public Library.

17 *Richmond Daily Dispatch*, July 2, 1862.

18 J. F. J. Caldwell, *The History of a Brigade of South Carolinians Known First as "Gregg's," and Subsequently as "McGowan's Brigade"* (Philadelphia, 1866), 12 [cited hereafter as Caldwell, *S.C. Brigade*]; J. W. Brunson, "Historical Sketch of the Pee Dee Artillery, Army of Northern Virginia," typescript, Pegram-Johnson-McIntosh Papers, Virginia Historical Society, 1; James E. Slaughter, *Settlers, Southerners, Americans: The History of Essex County, Va.* (Salem, W. Va., 1985), 173–74.

19 Armistead L. Long, *Memoirs of Robert E. Lee* (New York, 1866), 167.

20 George B. McClellan, *McClellan's Own Story* (New York, 1887), 167; *OR*, Ser. II, Vol. III, 662–63; McClellan to wife, June 9, 1862, McClellan Papers; Hill to Robert H. Chilton, June 18, 1862, Light Division Letterbook.

21 Mary Newton Stanard, *John Brockenbrough Newton: A Biographical Sketch* (Richmond, 1924), 13.

22 D. H. Hill maintained that Jackson, not he, arrived first at the Dabbs house. Yet evidence is overwhelming that Harvey Hill reached there before the others. Robert U. Johnson and C. C. Buel, eds., *Battles and Leaders of the Civil War* (New York, 1884–1887), II, 347; Douglas S. Freeman, *Lee's Lieutenants: A Study in Command* (New York, 1942–1944), I, 494; Lenoir Chambers, *Stonewall Jackson* (New York, 1959), II, 19.

23 Charles Marshall, *An Aide-de-Camp of Lee* (Boston, 1927), 88–89. The battle plan became General Orders No. 75 (June 24, 1862). A handwritten copy is in the Branch Papers, N.C. State Archives.

24 Lawrence O'Bryan Branch Papers, University of Virginia.

25 *OR*, XI, Pt. 1, 238; William J. Hoke, "Organization and Movements, the Thirty-eighth Regiment, North Carolina Troops," typescript, Southern Historical Collection, UNC, 15; Francis W. Dawson, *Reminiscences of Confederate Service, 1861–1865* (Baton Rouge, 1980), 47.

26 J. R. Sypher, *History of the Pennsylvania Reserve Corps* (Lancaster, Pa., 1865), 205; *Richmond Daily Dispatch*, June 26, 1862.

27 Hoke, "38th North Carolina," 16.

28 *OR*, XI, Pt. 2, 881.

29 *Ibid.*, Pt. 3, 257.

30 Marshall, *Aide-de-Camp of Lee*, 91–92; *OR*, XI, Pt. 2, 835.

31 Judith W. McGuire, *Diary of a Southern Refugee during the War* (New York, 1867), 123.

32 Slaughter, *Essex County*, 176–77; *OR*, XI, Pt. 2, 841.

33 Wise, *Long Arm of Lee*, I, 200–1.

34 Marshall, *Aide-de-Camp of Lee*, 94. Jackson's most famous biographer incorrectly asserted that "a message from Lee, ordering Hill to postpone all further movement, arrived too late." G. F. R. Henderson, *Stonewall Jackson and the American Civil War* (London, 1898), II, 16.

35 *Battles and Leaders*, II, 328. For other firsthand descriptions of the Federal position, see Marshall, *Aide-de-Camp*, 93; John Esten Cooke, *A Life of Gen. Robert E. Lee* (New York, 1871), 79.

36 *Confederate Veteran*, I (1893), 234.

37 Brunson, "Pee Dee Artillery," 2.

38 Sypher, *Pennsylvania Reserve Corps*, 211; *SHSP*, XXIX (1901), 350.

39 Wise, *Long Arm of Lee*, I, 207–8; *OR*, XI, Pt. 2, 835–36.

40 See Freeman, *Lee's Lieutenants*, I, 514–15.

41 Clark, *N.C. Regiments*, II, 680.

42 *OR*, XI, Pt. 2, 507, 899; Edward A. Pollard, *The Lost Cause: A New Southern History of the War of the Confederates* (New York, 1866), 285.

43 Clark, *N.C. Regiments*, I, 756.

44 Robert E. Lee, *The Wartime Papers of R. E. Lee* (Boston, 1961), 213.

45 *OR*, XI, Pt. 2, 836.

46 Hotchkiss, *Confederate Military History—Va.*, 285–86; Joseph P. Cullen, "The Battle of Mechanicsville," *Civil War Times Illustrated*, V (Oct. 1966), 9, 49; *Battles and Leaders*, II, 361; Freeman, *Lee's Lieutenants*, I, 515; Kenneth P. Williams, *Lincoln Finds a General* (New York, 1950–1959), I, 225–26.

47 *OR*, XI, Pt. 2, 882.

48 James Longstreet, *From Manassas to Appomattox* (Philadelphia, 1896), 124; Henry Kyd Douglas, *I Rode with Stonewall* (Chapel Hill, 1940), 100–1; Robert L. Dabney, *Life and Campaigns of Lieut.-Gen. Thomas J. Jackson* (New York, 1866), 441; Sorrel, *Staff Officer*, 81.

49 *Battles and Leaders*, II, 331.

50 *Richmond Examiner*, June 27, 1862.

6. FORGING A REPUTATION ON THE PENINSULA

1 *SHSP*, XXIX (1901), 351.

2 *OR*, XI, Pt. 2, 836.

3 Caldwell, *S.C. Brigade*, 16.

4 *OR*, XI, Pt. 2, 853.

5 Douglas, *I Rode with Stonewall*, 101; *Richmond Daily Dispatch*, Aug. 1, 1862.

6 Anon., "What I Saw of the Battle of the Chickahominy," *Southern Magazine*, X (Jan. 1872), 4; Dabney, *Jackson*, 443.

7 Hotchkiss, *Confederate Military History—Va.*, 288; *OR*, XI, Pt. 2, 836.

8 *Ibid.*

9 Pollard, *The Lost Cause*, 286; Marshall, *Aide-de-Camp of Lee*, 101.

10 *SHSP*, IX (1881), 558.

11 Lee, *Wartime Papers*, 215; *Battles and Leaders*, II, 398. Longstreet later acknowledged that Hill "pressed his battle with great zeal and courage, but he was alone." Longstreet, *From Manassas to Appomattox*, 126.

12 *Battles and Leaders*, II, 337; *OR*, XI, Pt. 2, 837.

13 Walter H. Taylor, *General Lee: His Campaigns in Virginia, 1861–1865, with Personal Reminiscences* (Norfolk, 1906), 67.

14 *OR*, XI, Pt. 2, 855, 864, 873; *SHSP*, XXVIII (1900), 95.

15 La Salle Corbett Pickett, *Pickett and His Men* (Atlanta, 1900), 178; Clark, *N.C. Regiments*, I, 368.

16 *Confederate Veteran*, VIII (1900), 66; John L. Parker, *Henry Wilson's Regiment: History of the Twenty-second Massachusetts Infantry* (Boston, 1887), 119; Brunson, "Pee Dee Artillery," 2.

17 John Esten Cooke, *Hammer and Rapier* (New York, 1870), 78; *OR*, XI, Pt. 2, 837.

18 John S. Robson, *How a One-legged Rebel Lives* (Durham, N.C., 1898), 70.

19 Long, *Memoirs of Robert E. Lee*, 172; Thomas Keith Skinker, *Samuel Skinker and His Descendants* (St. Louis, 1923), 267; *OR*, XI, Pt. 2, 553.

20 Charles Venable, "Personal Reminiscences of the Confederate War," McDowell Family Papers, University of Virginia.

21 *OR*, XI, Pt. 2, 837.

22 Longstreet, *From Manassas to Appomattox*, 129. See also *ibid.*, 657.

23 E. Porter Alexander, *Military Memoirs of a Confederate* (New York, 1912), 131.

24 William G. Morris to wife, June 28, 1862, Morris Papers; Clark, *N.C. Regiments*, IV, 158.

25 *OR*, XI, Pt. 2, 685, 759, 789, 838; *Battles and Leaders*, II, 400.

26 *SHSP*, XIV (1886), 451–52; *Confederate Veteran*, I (1893), 234. Hill officially reported that President Davis "narrowly escaped accident." *OR*, XI, Pt. 2, 838. Longstreet bluntly stated that when shells began exploding in the vicinity of Davis and Lee, "the little opening was speedily cleared of the distinguished group that graced its meagre soil, and it was left to more humble, active combatants." Longstreet, *From Manassas to Appomattox*, 134.

27 *Battles and Leaders*, II, 401; Dickert, *Kershaw's Brigade*, 135.

28 Caffey, *Battle-fields of the South*, II, 177.

29 *OR*, XI, Pt. 2, 901; Sypher, *Pennsylvania Reserves*, 270.

30 *OR*, XI, Pt. 2, 842, 850–51; *Richmond Daily Dispatch*, July 2, 1862.

31 Dunaway, *Reminiscences of a Rebel*, 31–32.

32 Warren H. Cudworth, *History of the First Regiment (Massachusetts Infantry)* (Boston, 1866), 220; Oliver Wendell Holmes, Jr., *Touched with Fire: Civil War Letters and Diary* (Cambridge, Mass., 1947), 59.

33 Pollard, *Lee and His Lieutenants*, 442.

34 *Richmond Times-Dispatch*, Oct. 28, 1934.

35 *OR*, XI, Pt. 2, 838–39.

36 Martin A. Haynes, *A History of the Second Regiment, New Hampshire Volunteer Infantry, in the War of the Rebellion* (Lakeport, N.H., 1896), 113–14; William G. Morris to wife, July 21, 1862, Morris Papers.

37 Lee, *Wartime Papers*, 219; *OR*, XI, Pt. 2, 495.

38 *Battles and Leaders*, II, 388; Bellamy diary, June 30, 1862.

39 Freeman, *Lee's Lieutenants*, I, 587.

40 Caffey, *Battle-fields of the South*, II, 175, 177.

41 *OR*, XI, Pt. 2, 759.

42 *Confederate Veteran*, XXIII (1915), 162.

43 Caldwell, *S.C. Brigade*, 24–25.

44 *OR*, XI, Pt. 2, 492.

45 *Annals of the War, Written by Leading Participants North and South* (Philadelphia, 1879), 698: William P. Snow. *Southern Generals: Who They Are and What They Have Done* (New York, 1865), 378.

46 *OR*, XI, Pt. 2, 839–40.

47 Allen C. Redwood, "With Stonewall Jackson," *Scribner's Monthly*, XVIII (1879), 221.

48 *Richmond Examiner*, June 28 and July 2, 1862.

49 Sorrel, *Staff Officer*, 85–86; Richmond *Whig*, July 11, 1862.

50 William H. Palmer to Murray F. Taylor, Nov. 8, 1902, Petersburg National Battlefield; *OR*, XI, Pt. 3, 939–40.

51 Sorrel, *Staff Officer*, 89; *OR*, LI, Pt. 2, 590.

52 *Richmond Daily Dispatch*, July 25, 1862.

53 *OR*, XI, Pt. 3, 645; LI, Pt. 2, 598; Lee, *Wartime Papers*, 239, 271.

7. HILL'S VICTORY AT CEDAR MOUNTAIN

1 W. Dorsey Pender, *The General to His Lady: The Civil War Letters of William Dorsey Pender to Fanny Pender* (Chapel Hill, 1962), 161, 163.

2 Writing of this period, one of Jackson's favorite aides commented that the general "had a hardness in exacting the performance of military duty which had the flavor of deliberate cruelty." Douglas, *I Rode with Stonewall*, 236.

3 Susan L. Blackford, comp., *Letters from Lee's Army* (New York, 1947), 97; Pender, *Letters*, 164.

4 *OR*, XII, Pt. 2, 222; Blackford, *Letters from Lee's Army*, 99. At that same time, Pender was grumbling that the men in the Light Division "have not the slightest idea what we are to do." Pender, *Letters*, 165.

5 Hoke, "38th North Carolina," 45; *OR*, XII, Pt. 2, 222; Caldwell, *S.C. Brigade*, 26.

6 *OR*, XII, Pt. 2, 215.

7 *Ibid.*, 214; Shelby Foote, *The Civil War, A Narrative* (New York, 1958–1974), I, 599.

8 Freeman, *Lee's Lieutenants*, II, 23.

9 *OR*, XII, Pt. 2, 181, 214–15; Hill to A. D. Pendleton, Mar. 13, 1863, Georgia Callis West Papers, Virginia Historical Society.

10 *SHSP*, XIX (1891), 155; Martin Schenck, *Up Came Hill: The Story of the Light Division and Its Leaders* (Harrisburg, 1958), 142; *OR*, XII, Pt. 2, 181.

11 *Ibid.*, 215.

12 *Ibid.*, 215, 222; *SHSP*, X (1882), 89. For the disappointment of Gregg's men at being left behind, see Caldwell, *S.C. Brigade*, 26.

13 John Berrien Lindsley, ed., *The Military Annals of Tennessee: Confederate* (Nashville, 1886), 234.

14 Dunaway, *Reminiscences of a Rebel*, 35; William J. Pegram to Virginia J. Pegram, Aug. 14, 1862, Pegram-Johnson-McIntosh Papers.

15 Frederic Denison, *Sabres and Spurs: The First Regiment, Rhode Island Cavalry in the Civil War, 1861–1865* (Central Falls, R.I., 1876), 123.

16 John M. Gould, *History of the First-Tenth-Twenty-ninth Maine Regiment* (Portland, 1871), 172; Henderson, *Stonewall Jackson*, II, 94–95.

17 Blackford, *Letters from Lee's Army*, 103, 105.

18 Edwin E. Marvin, *The Fifth Regiment, Connecticut Volunteers: A History*

(Hartford, 1889), 153–54; Jubal A. Early, *Autobiographical Sketch and Narrative of the War between the States* (Philadelphia, 1912), 98–99.

19 William M. Taliaferro manuscript, T. C. Williams Papers, Agecroft Hall, Richmond, Va.

20 Douglas, *I Rode with Stonewall*, 124–25; L. O'B. Branch to wife, Aug. 13, 1862, Branch Papers, University of Virginia. After Branch's men stemmed the Federal onslaught, Jackson rode to their lines and raised his hat in salute. *OR*, XII, Pt. 2, 223. Yet in his official report of the battle, Jackson barely acknowledged Branch's presence on the field.

21 Walter W. Lenoir diary, Jan. 10, 1863, Southern Historical Collection, UNC; *OR*, XII, Pt. 2, 215.

22 *SHSP*, X (1882), 89. During the advance, Hill also stopped to comfort Maj. Snowden Andrews of the artillery, and to ensure that a surgeon and ambulance came to the wounded officer's aid. Tunstall Smith, ed., *Richard Snowden Andrews: A Memoir* (Baltimore, 1910), 65.

23 *OR*, XII, Pt. 2, 137, 215, 218–19; Lindsley, *Annals of Tennessee*, 234.

24 Gould, *1st-10th-27th Maine*, 180–81; W. A. Croffut and John M. Morris, *The Military and Civil History of Connecticut during the War of 1861–1865* (New York, 1868), 218.

25 *SHSP*, XIX (1891), 182.

26 *OR*, XII, Pt. 2, 216.

27 Theodore F. Lang, *Loyal West Virginia from 1861 to 1865* (Baltimore, 1895), 94.

28 *Ibid.*, 184, 216, 232, 239; Early, *Autobiographical Sketch*, 100–1; *Richmond Daily Dispatch*, Aug. 12, 1862.

29 *OR*, XII, Pt. 2, 139, 179–80, 185, 216.

30 Alfred D. Kelly to brother, Aug. 10, 1862, Williamson Kelly Papers, 1852–1882, Duke University; *Richmond Daily Dispatch*, Aug. 13, 1862.

31 Lenoir diary, Jan. 2, 1863.

32 Pender, *Letters*, 167; W. W. Scott, *A History of Orange County, Virginia* (Baltimore, 1974), 155; S. Bassett French, *Centennial Tales: Memoirs of Col. "Chester" S. Bassett French* (New York, 1962), 24. For more on Culpeper's condition at this time, see *Richmond Daily Dispatch*, Aug. 20 and 23, 1862; Alexander D. Betts, *Experience of a Confederate Chaplain, 1861–1864* (n.p., n.d.), 14.

33 *OR*, XII, Pt. 2, 649; Lee, *Wartime Papers*, 260; rough draft of Jackson's charges against Hill, Thomas J. Jackson Manuscripts, Museum of the Confederacy; Jedediah Hotchkiss, *Make Me a Map of the Valley* (Dallas, 1973), 69–70.

34 William J. Pegram to mother, Sept. 4, 1862, Pegram-Johnson-McIntosh Papers.

35 French, *Centennial Tales*, 28; *SHSP*, XIV (1886), 209–10. Two days later, Jackson growled to a Georgia colonel who was not performing to expected standards: "Field officers were intended to be useful as well as ornamental." Hotchkiss, *Make Me a Map*, 71.

36 Blackford, *Letters from Lee's Army*, 125.

37 Douglas, *I Rode with Stonewall*, 130; G. G. Chamberlayne, ed., *Ham Chamberlayne—Virginian: Letters and Papers of an Artillery Officer in the War for Southern Independence, 1861–1865* (Richmond, 1932), 98.

38 *OR*, XII, Pt. 2, 670, 673–74.

39 *Ibid.*, 678; *Battles and Leaders*, II, 532–33.

40 J. William Jones, *Christ in the Camp* (Richmond, 1887), 97.

[41] W. W. Blackford, *War Years with Jeb Stuart* (New York, 1945), 109; *OR*, XII, Pt. 2, 670. For more on the hardships of the march, see Philip F. Brown, *Reminiscences of the War of 1861–1865* (Richmond, 1917), 24–25; Caldwell, *S.C. Brigade*, 30.

[42] *OR*, XII, Pt. 2, 721.

[43] Lindsley, *Annals of Tennessee*, 235.

[44] *OR*, XII, Pt. 2, 260, 401, 643–44.

[45] Robson, *How a One-legged Rebel Lives*, 106.

[46] Caldwell, *S.C. Brigade*, 31.

[47] *OR*, XII, Pt. 2, 670; John Gibbon, *Personal Recollections of the Civil War* (New York, 1928), 58

[48] Stevens, *Sixth Corps*, 230.

[49] Clark, *N.C. Regiments*, IV, 162; *OR*, XII, Pt. 2, 670. Years later, Longstreet incorrectly asserted that Hill marred Jackson's hide-and-seek game by failing "to meet his orders for the afternoon of the 28th." Longstreet, *From Manassas to Appomattox*, 198.

[50] Clark, *N.C. Regiments*, IV, 162.

[51] *OR*, XII, Pt. 2, 670; Goldsborough, *Maryland Line*, 262.

8. FIGHTING POPE—AND JACKSON

[1] Freeman, *Lee's Lieutenants*, II, 321.

[2] *OR*, XII, Pt. 2, 670, 687.

[3] *Ibid.*, 646, 670, 679–80; Caldwell, *S.C. Brigade*, 32.

[4] *OR*, XII, Pt. 2, 311, 676, 693.

[5] Clark, *N.C. Regiments*, II, 656; *OR*, XII, Pt. 2, 670.

[6] Caldwell, *S.C. Brigade*, 36.

[7] *SHSP*, XIII (1885), 30.

[8] *OR*, XII, Pt. 2, 688; Heros von Borcke, *Memoirs of the Confederate War for Independence* (Edinburgh, 1866), I, 147; *Confederate Veteran*, I (1893), 235.

[9] *OR*, XII, Pt. 2, 671; Lee, *Wartime Papers*, 282.

[10] Douglas, *I Rode with Stonewall*, 138.

[11] *SHSP*, XXVIII (1900), 345; *Civil War Times Illustrated*, XVI (Apr. 1977), 14.

[12] W. R. and M. B. Houghton, *Two Boys in the Civil War and After* (Montgomery, Ala., 1912), 25.

[13] *OR*, XII, Pt. 2, 671.

[14] Slaughter, *Essex County*, 179; *SHSP* XIII (1885), 56.

[15] *OR*, XII, Pt. 2, 646, 671, 712.

[16] Douglas, *I Rode with Stonewall*, 138.

[17] Chamberlayne, *Ham Chamberlayne*, 100–1; Early, *Autobiographical Sketch*, 125; *OR*, XII, Pt. 2, 671.

[18] Dunaway, *Reminiscences of a Rebel*, 43–44. Hill put the time of the Federal attack at 2:00 P.M. Lee thought it began at 3:00 P.M.; Jackson asserted that it came an hour later. *OR*, XII, Pt. 2, 557, 647, 671.

[19] *Ibid.*, 671; Hoke, "38th North Carolina," 36.

[20] Pender, *Letters*, 171.

[21] *OR*, XII, Pt. 2, 671.

[22] Francis J. Parker, *The Story of the Thirty-second Regiment, Massachusetts Infantry* (Boston, 1880), 70.

[23] *OR*, XII, Pt. 2, 672, 701.

[24] *Ibid.*, 672, 681; Caldwell, *S.C. Brigade*, 37.

25 *OR*, XII, Pt. 2, 646.

26 *Papers of the Military Historical Society of Massachusetts*, II (1895), 177–78; George Meade, *The Life and Letters of George Gordon Meade* (New York, 1913), I, 322–23.

27 Hassler, *Hill*, 243; *OR*, XII, Pt. 2, 682.

28 William J. Pegram to mother, Sept. 4, 1862, Pegram-Johnson-McIntosh Papers; *OR*, XII, Pt. 2, 672, 714.

29 *OR*, XII, Pt. 2, 698; Schenck, *Up Came Hill*, 184.

30 *SHSP*, XXV (1897), 99. The Federals indeed had trouble with wet gunpowder that afternoon. See *Papers of the Military Society of Massachusetts*, II (1895), 158.

31 *OR*, XII, Pt. 2, 647, 677; William Todd, *The Seventy-ninth Highlanders, New York Volunteers, in the War of the Rebellion, 1861–1865* (Albany, 1886), 216; Rufus R. Dawes, *Service with the Sixth Wisconsin Volunteers* (Madison, 1962), 75.

32 Slaughter, *Essex County*, 179; *Richmond Daily Dispatch*, Sept. 10, 1862; Trobriand, *Army of the Potomac*, 299.

33 Francis A. Walker, *History of the Second Army Corps of the Army of the Potomac* (New York, 1891), 91.

34 *Richmond Examiner*, Sept. 8, 1862; *Battles and Leaders*, II, 638n.

35 *OR*, XII, Pt. 2, 672, 813.

36 Wise, *Campaigns and Battles*, 166; W. W. Lenoir diary, Jan. 2, 1863; Pender, *Letters*, 171.

37 *Confederate Veteran*, XXX (1922), 45.

38 Maury, *Recollections*, 71; William T. Poague, *Gunner with Stonewall* (Jackson, Tenn., 1957), 41, 43; *SHSP*, XXV (1907), 89–90.

39 This account of the Hill-Jackson confrontation is based on the little-known reminiscences of Hill's chief of staff, Col. William H. Palmer, and Jackson's cartographer Jed Hotchkiss, both eyewitnesses to the event. Palmer's account appeared in *Century* magazine, June 14, 1885, that of Hotchkiss in "Lieut. General A. P. Hill," typescript, Jedediah Hotchkiss Papers, Library of Congress. For other versions of the incident, see *SHSP*, XX (1892), 385; Douglas, *I Rode with Stonewall*, 146–47; J. W. Ratchford, *Some Reminiscences of Persons and Incidents of the Civil War* (Richmond, 1909), 54. A fabricated story of the arrest, with Hill referring to Jackson as "that inspired old fool," is in *Confederate Veteran*, VII (1899), 354.

9. ANTIETAM CREEK: "A. P. HILL CAME UP"

1 Clark, *N.C. Regiments*, IV, 165.

2 Douglas, *I Rode with Stonewall*, 148–49; Freeman, *Lee's Lieutenants*, II, 155–56.

3 Clark, *N.C. Regiments*, II, 473; Chamberlayne, *Ham Chamberlayne*, 104; Pender, *Letters*, 173. Various Federal reports had Hill's division fortified at Lovettsville, miles to the west of its actual encampment. *OR*, XIX, Pt. 1, 533, 795; LI, Pt. 2, 794.

4 Caldwell, *S.C. Brigade*, 41.

5 *SHSP*, XIX (1891), 180. Of all the comments written about the Hill arrest, that by historian Kenneth Williams is the most preposterous. He described Hill on the Frederick–Harper's Ferry march by stating: "With nothing to worry about, [Hill] was . . . pondering probably the fortunes of war and the peculiarities of his hard-fighting superior, perhaps thinking as well of the Maryland fried chicken and biscuits which he might have been able to get during his sojourn near Frederick if he had not been in arrest." Williams, *Lincoln Finds a General*, I, 374.

[6] Douglas, *I Rode with Stonewall*, 158; *OR*, XII, Pt. 2, 604. Cf. Hotchkiss, "A. P. Hill," 4. Jackson's rigid demands of discipline, however, did not lessen. On the day after Hill's release, the white-haired and courtly Col. Dixon Barnes of the 12th South Carolina permitted his hungry men to take apples from trees adjacent to the road on which they were marching. Paxton saw this violation of orders and, with Jackson's approval, placed Barnes under arrest. Louise P. Daly, *Alexander Cheves Haskell: The Portrait of a Man* (Norwood, Mass., 1934), 77.

[7] Clark, *N.C. Regiments*, IV, 165.

[8] Raymond L. Ives, National Park Service, to J. Ambler Johnston, July 31, 1970, J. Ambler Johnston Papers, Virginia Polytechnic Institute and State University; Alexander, *Military Memoirs*, 235.

[9] Caldwell, *S.C. Brigade*, 41; *OR*, XIX, Pt. 2, 188, 193, 953, 980.

[10] New York MOLLUS, *Personal Recollections*, IV (1912), 139.

[11] *OR*, XIX, Pt. 1, 953, 980; Caffey, *Battle-fields of the South*, II, 337.

[12] Edith Armstrong Talbot, *Samuel Chapman Armstrong: A Biographical Study* (New York, 1904), 72–73.

[13] *OR*, XIX, Pt. 1, 527, 836, 980.

[14] Daly, *Haskell*, 77–78.

[15] *OR*, XIX, Pt. 1, 987; Edward A. Moore, *The Story of a Cannoneer under Stonewall Jackson* (New York, 1907), 139.

[16] *OR*, XIX, Pt. 1, 980; Mary Anna Jackson, *Memoirs of Stonewall Jackson* (Louisville, 1895), 618.

[17] James H. Clark, *The Iron Hearted Regiment: Being an Account of the Battles, Marches and Gallant Deeds Performed by the 115th Regiment N.Y. Vols.* (Albany, 1865), 19; New York, MOLLUS, *Personal Recollections*, IV (1912), 148.

[18] Hill to Samuel Cooper, July 12, 1864, John Hampden Chamberlayne Papers, Virginia Historical Society; *OR*, XIX, Pt. 1, 980; *SHSP*, XIX (1891), 182; U. R. Brooks, ed., *Stories of the Confederacy* (Columbia, S.C., 1912), 90.

[19] Jones, *Stonewall Jackson*, 325; *OR*, XIX, Pt. 1, 980; *Battles and Leaders*, II, 614.

[20] *OR*, XIX, Pt. 1, 959, 980; Pt. 2, 378, 388, 450. For a Union version of the wagon story, see Benedict, *Vermont in the Civil War*, II, 205–6.

[21] *OR*, XIX, Pt. 1, 951, 955, 960–61, 981; Frederick L. Hitchcock, *War from the Inside* (Philadelphia, 1904), 82. Hill received almost no mention in the stories of the seizure of Harper's Ferry. Richmond's leading newspaper carried two unusually long accounts of the campaign. Hill was cited only as the officer who officially accepted the surrender. *Richmond Daily Dispatch*, Sept. 20 and 23, 1862.

[22] *OR*, XIX, Pt. 1, 951.

[23] Talbot, *Armstrong*, 75.

[24] *Battles and Leaders*, II, 610–11, 655; Clark, *N.C. Regiments*, I, 372.

[25] Caldwell, *S.C. Brigade*, 43; *Richmond Times-Dispatch*, Nov. 11, 1934.

[26] Venable, "Personal Reminiscences of the Confederate War," McDowell Papers.

[27] *SHSP*, XIX (1891), 180.

[28] Lindsley, *Annals of Tennessee*, 237.

[29] Hill's printed official report states that the Light Division began the march at 7:30 A.M. (*OR*, XIX, Pt. 1, 981). Yet the original handwritten draft of that

report asserts that the first elements of the Light Division departed the village at 7:00 A.M. Hill undoubtedly had his troops up and ready before dawn, and it would not have taken more than thirty minutes to begin the march. The original report by Hill is in the Robert Edward Lee Papers, Virginia Historical Society.

30 Caldwell, *S.C. Brigade.* 44; Alexander, *Military Memoirs,* 266; Douglas, *I Rode with Stonewall,* 173.

31 *Confederate Veteran,* XXX (1922), 246.

32 *SHSP,* XIX (1891), 181.

33 Taylor, *General Lee,* 134.

34 Freeman, *Lee's Lieutenants,* II, 222.

35 Freeman, *Lee,* II, 400–1.

36 *Confederate Veteran,* XIX (1911), 429; James Cooper Nisbet, *Four Years on the Firing Line* (Jackson, Tenn., 1963), 108. For a somewhat negative observation of the arrival of Hill's division, see Randolph A. Shotwell, *The Papers of Randolph Abbott Shotwell (Raleigh, 1929–1936),* I, 354–55.

37 *Confederate Veteran,* XX (1912), 204; *OR,* XIX, Pt. 1, 984.

38 Douglas, *I Rode with Stonewall,* 173.

39 *OR,* XIX, Pt. 1, 981.

40 *Ibid.,* 455, 981, 1000–1; *Battles and Leaders,* II, 655; Croffut and Morris, *Connecticut,* 271–72, 276.

41 Caldwell, *S.C. Brigade,* 46; *OR,* XIX, Pt. 1, 992; George H. Allen, *Forty-six Months in the Fourth R.I. Volunteers* (Providence, 1887), 147.

42 Caldwell, *S.C. Brigade,* 46. The next morning, Gregg sat down to eat an ear of corn as his breakfast. When he pulled a handkerchief from his hip pocket to use as a napkin, out fell a bullet, which had been flattened by the impact. Daly, *Haskell,* 82.

43 One of Barnes's compatriots stated that "no officer in the brigade executed so many brilliant and splendid charges as he. . . . No appearances staggered him, no obstacles stayed him." Caldwell, *S.C. Brigade,* 48–49.

44 Clark, *N.C. Regiments,* II, 553–54.

45 Longstreet, *From Manassas to Appomattox,* 261; *OR,* XIX, Pt. 1, 454, 981. There was still animosity between Longstreet and Hill at the time of the battle. Longstreet in his report mentioned only that Hill's attack "was of great value" in maintaining Lee's right. *OR,* XIX, Pt. 1, 841.

46 *Ibid.,* 197, 200, 981, 1001; Alexander, *Memoirs,* 274.

47 Freeman, *Lee,* II, 402; Lee, *Wartime Papers,* 311.

48 *OR,* XIX, Pt. 1, 926.

49 Douglas, *I Rode with Stonewall,* 174; James C. Birdsong, *Brief Sketches of the North Carolina State Troops in the War between the States* (Raleigh, 1894), 54.

50 Robert S. Robertson, *Diary of the War* [Fort Wayne, Ind., 1965], 57; *OR,* XIX, Pt. 1, 981; Greenlee Davidson, *Captain Greenlee Davidson, C.S.A.: Diary and Letters, 1851–1863* (Verona, Va., 1975), 49.

51 *OR,* XIX, Pt. 1, 340, 982. The four Federal regiments that Hill would engage were the 18th and 22nd Massachusetts, 4th Michigan, and 118th Pennsylvania.

52 *SHSP,* XXVII (1899), 215.

53 Edwin C. Bennett, *Musket and Sword; or, The Camp, March and Firing Line in the Army of the Potomac* (Boston, 1900), 96; Varina D. Brown, *A Colonel at Gettysburg and Spotsylvania* (Columbia, S.C., 1931), 43.

54 *OR,* XIX, Pt. 1, 982, 989. Archer likewise termed the Federal bombardment "the heaviest artillery fire I have ever witnessed." *Ibid.,* 1002.

55 *Ibid.*, 986.

56 *Under the Maltese Cross: Campaigns, 155th Pennsylvania Regiment, Narrated by the Rank and File* (Pittsburgh, 1910), 76.

57 Walter H. Taylor, *Four Years with General Lee* (New York, 1878), 74; *OR*, XIX, Pt. 1, 204, 348. See also John L. Smith, *History of the Corn Exchange Regiment, 118th Pennsylvania Volunteers* (Philadelphia, 1888), 56, 62.

58 *OR*, XIX, Pt. 1, 204, 957, 982; John Dooley, *John Dooley, Confederate Soldier: His War Journal* (Washington, 1945), 52.

59 *OR*, XIX, Pt. 1, 982; Chamberlayne, *Ham Chamberlayne*, 116; Hoke, "38th North Carolina," 40.

60 *OR*, LI, Pt. 2, 626.

61 Brunson, "Pee Dee Artillery," 22. Cf. Clark, *N.C. Regiments*, I, 761–62.

62 Pender, *Letters*, 178; *OR*, XIX, Pt. 2, 621.

10. NEAR-DISASTER AT FREDERICKSBURG

1 Hill to R. H. Chilton, Sept. 22, 1862, Light Division Letterbook.

2 Freeman, *Lee's Lieutenants*, II, 243–44.

3 Brown, *Colonel at Gettysburg*, 45; Pender, *Letters*, 179.

4 Freeman, *Lee's Lieutenants*, II, 244.

5 *OR*, XIX, Pt. 2, 729–31. An original copy of Jackson's charges against Hill, with eight supporting witnesses for Hill listed, is in the Henry Brainerd McClellan Papers, Virginia Historical Society.

6 Several sources alleged that Lee ended the rift between Hill and Jackson. Douglas, *I Rode with Stonewall*, 195–96; Maury, *Recollections*, 72; *SHSP*, XX (1892), 385; French, *Centennial Tales*, 24.

7 *OR*, XIX, Pt. 2, 643.

8 *Ibid.*, 683–84, 698–99; XXI, 648; Loehr, *1st Virginia*, 31.

9 Hoke, "38th North Carolina," 38; Caldwell, *S.C. Brigade*, 53.

10 Alfred M. Scales, *The Battle of Fredericksburg: An Address* (Washington, 1884), 5.

11 Caldwell, *S.C. Brigade*, 53; *OR*, XIX, Pt. 1, 660, 674, 981; Wise, *Campaigns and Battles*, 198.

12 *Confederate Veteran*, XXX (1922), 246. The pipe and tobacco pouch are preserved at the Museum of the Confederacy, Richmond, Va.

13 William J. Pegram to Virginia J. Pegram, Oct. 24, 1862, Pegram-Johnson-McIntosh Papers; *Richmond Daily Dispatch*, Oct. 30, 1862; Marietta Minnigerode Andrews, *Scraps of Paper* (New York, 1929), 62–63.

14 C. A. Porter Hopkins, ed., "The James J. Archer Letters," *Maryland Historical Magazine*, LVI (1961), 136; *OR*, XIX, Pt. 1, 982.

15 Samuel H. Walkup to Minnie Walkup, Nov. 10, 1862, Walkup Papers; *Richmond Daily Dispatch*, Nov. 11, 1862.

16 *OR*, XIX, Pt. 1, 707.

17 Hill to J. E. B. Stuart, Nov. 14, 1862, James Ewell Brown Stuart Papers, Virginia Historical Society.

18 Gibbon, *Personal Recollections*, 252.

19 *Richmond Daily Dispatch*, Nov. 17, 1862.

20 Cornelia McDonald, *A Diary with Reminiscences of the War and Refugee Life in the Shenandoah Valley, 1860–1865* (Nashville, 1934), 107.

21 *OR*, XXI, 1025, 1057; Chamberlayne, *Ham Chamberlayne*, 141.

22 *Southern Illustrated News*, Nov. 22, 1862.

23 *OR*, XIX, Pt. 1, 990; John A. Sloan, *Reminiscences of the Guilford Grays,*

Co. B, 27th *N.C. Regiment* (Washington, 1883), 53; Caldwell, *S.C. Brigade,* 55–56; Davidson, *Diary and Letters,* 60. As late as Dec. 9, Federal scouts were still reporting Hill as being in the Snicker's Gap area. *OR,* XIX, Pt. 2, 568.

24 Pender, *Letters,* 191; Davidson, *Diary and Letters,* 61.

25 Ellsworth Eliot, *West Point in the Confederacy* (New York, 1945), 245.

26 Richard C. Morgan to mother, Dec. 15, 1862, and Jan. 27, 1863, Morgan Papers, Morgan–Hunt House, Lexington, Ky.

27 Davidson, *Diary and Letters,* 62; *OR,* XXI, 645.

28 Dabney, *Jackson,* 610.

29 *Ibid.,* 636–37, 653–54, 676; Von Borcke, *Memoirs of the Confederate War,* II, 105–6.

30 Von Borcke, *Memoirs of the Confederate War,* II, 113–14; John H. Worsham, *One of Jackson's Foot Cavalry* (Jackson, Tenn., 1964), 93.

31 Trobriand, *Army of the Potomac,* 364; *OR, XXI,* 645; *Battles and Leaders,* III, 139.

32 Charles S. Wainwright, *A Diary of Battle* (New York, 1962), 142.

33 *OR,* XXI, 646.

34 *Ibid.,* 655; William G. Morris to wife, Dec. 18, 1862, Morris Papers.

35 Early, *Autobiographical Sketch,* 172; *OR,* XXI, 646, 656–57, 659; *Battles and Leaders,* III, 140.

36 St. Clair A. Mulholland, *The Story of the 116th Regiment, Pennsylvania Infantry* (Philadelphia, 1899), 59; Caldwell, *S.C. Brigade,* 59.

37 *OR,* XXI, 646, 651–52.

38 *Ibid.,* 487; Clark, *N.C. Regiments,* I, 665.

39 *OR,* XXI, 647, 653; Scales, *Battle of Fredericksburg,* 14.

40 Trobriand, *Army of the Potomac,* 369; Abner R. Small, *The Road to Richmond* (Berkeley, Cal., 1939), 67.

41 Caldwell, *S.C. Brigade,* 61; *SHSP,* XL (1915), 218; *OR,* XXI, 634, 647.

42 *OR,* XXI, 139–40, 481, 635, 648.

43 *Confederate Veteran,* I (1893), 235; *OR,* XXI, 646. Gregg's remains received a hero's welcome in Richmond. See *Richmond Daily Dispatch,* Dec. 17, 1862. One of his officers eulogized: "Although not so rigid and minute in his discipline and management as many others, he excelled most officers of equal rank in efficiency. He was an excellent drillmaster, a constant maintainer of good order and regularity, and . . . always succeeded in inspiring confidence in himself and in imparting to others the magnetism of his own enthusiasm."

44 Edward K. Gould, *Major-General Hiram G. Berry* (Rockland, Me., 1899), 220–21; Donald L. Smith, *The Twenty-fourth Michigan of the Iron Brigade* (Harrisburg, Pa., 1962), 66.

45 *OR,* XXI, 632, 646; Hopkins, "Archer Letters," 139.

46 McDonald, *Diary,* 115.

11. "THIS SLUMBERING VOLCANO"

1 Clark, *N.C. Regiments,* IV, 175–76; James W. Milgram, "John Woodzell Writes Home," Society of Philatelic Americans *Journal,* XLII (1979–1980), 170.

2 Oliver C. Bosbyshell, *The 48th in the War, Being a Narrative of the Campaigns of the 48th Regiment, Pennsylvania Veteran Volunteers, during the War of the Rebellion* (Philadelpia, 1895), 101.

3 Pender, *Letters,* 195; Chamberlayne, *Ham Chamberlayne,* 151, 154; *SHSP,* XLIII (1920), 37.

4 William G. Morris to wife, Dec. 28, 1862, Morris Papers.

5 *Richmond Daily Dispatch*, Jan. 26, 1863; U.S. National Archives, comp., "Compiled Service Records of Confederate Soldiers Who Served in Organizations from the State of Virginia" (Washington, 1961), Microfilm Roll No. 358; Hill to Osmun Latrobe, undated letter, Lee Papers.

6 *OR*, XXV, Pt. 2, 602; Skinker, *Skinker Descendants*, 257–68; Hotchkiss, *Make Me a Map*, 107.

7 R. C. Morgan to mother, Jan. 27, 1863, Morgan Papers.

8 *OR*, XXIX, Pt. 2, 731–32.

9 Henderson, *Stonewall Jackson*, II, 641.

10 Hill to Robert E. Lee, Jan. 29, 1863, Light Division Letterbook.

11 Douglas, *I Rode with Stonewall*, 215; Hill to A. S. Pendleton, Mar. 13, 1863, West Papers.

12 Hotchkiss, "A. P. Hill," 6; Hill to Robert E. Lee, Mar. 11, 1863, Light Division Letterbook.

13 *OR*, XXV, Pt. 2, 786–87.

14 Douglas, *I Rode with Stonewall*, 215; Hill to A. S. Pendleton, Apr. 23, 1863, Light Division Letterbook; Hill to Robert E. Lee, Apr. 23, 1863, *ibid.*

15 Hill to A. S. Pendleton, Nov. 13, 1862, West Papers.

16 Colonel Palmer declared that in late April Lee tried in vain to end the dispute. Freeman, *Lee's Lieutenants*, II, 512–14; Eliot, *West Point in the Confederacy*, 245.

17 Joseph H. Saunders to cousin, Jan. 26, 1863, Joseph H. Saunders Papers, Southern Historical Collection, UNC; *Richmond Daily Dispatch*, Jan. 2, 1863.

18 *Richmond Enquirer*, Jan. 27, 1863.

19 *Ibid.*, Feb. 11, Mar. 20, and Mar. 25, 1863; Francis Kennedy diary, Southern Historical Collection, UNC, entry of Mar. 22, 1863.

20 Susan W. Benson, ed., *Berry Benson's Civil War Book* (Athens, 1962), 34–35; Calier G. Hamilton to father, Mar. 15, 1863, Hamilton Letters, Southern Historical Collection, UNC; William H. Stewart, *A Pair of Blankets* (New York, 1911), 78.

21 Caldwell, *S.C. Brigade*, 71; *Richmond Dispatch*, Apr. 15, 1863; *OR*, XXV, Pt. 2, 696.

22 Skinker, *Skinker Descendants*, 276; Pender, *Letters*, 221; Lenoir (N.C.) *News-Topic*, Oct. 5, 1923, in Samuel Finlay Harper Letters, N.C. State Archives.

23 Hotchkiss, *Make Me a Map*, 109; *Richmond Daily Dispatch*, Feb. 17, 1863.

24 Percy G. Hamlin, ed., *The Making of a Soldier: Letters of General R. S. Ewell* (Richmond, 1935), 119; Hill to Lucy Hill, Feb. 14, 1863, Hill Papers.

25 Pender, *Letters*, 213; Hill to C.S. War Dept., Apr. 6, 1863, Light Division Letterbook.

26 *OR*, XXV, Pt. 1, 654.

27 Heth, *Memoirs*, ix, lviii.

28 Pender, *Letters*, 226, 229.

29 Caldwell, *S.C. Brigade*, 73; Chamberlayne, *Ham Chamberlayne*, 171; *OR*, XXV, Pt. 1, 138; Pt. 2, 253, 316; Calier G. Hamilton to father, May 17, 1863, Hamilton Letters.

12. CROSSROADS AT CHANCELLORSVILLE

1 H. P. Griffith, *Variosa: A Collection of Sketches, Essays and Verses* (Gaffney, S.C., 1911), 50.

2 *Confederate Veteran*, XII (1904), 492; *OR*, XXV, Pt. 1, 890.

3 Griffith, *Variosa*, 58–59.

4 *Battles and Leaders*, III, 204.

5 David Gregg McIntosh, *The Campaign of Chancellorsville* (Richmond, 1915), 30; *SHSP*, VI (1878), 230; XX (1892), 187.

6 Robert Stiles, *Four Years under Marse Robert* (New York, 1903), 168.

7 Caldwell, *S.C. Brigade*, 76; Stiles, *Marse Robert*, 169; Calier G. Hamilton to father, May 17, 1863, Hamilton Letters.

8 *OR*, XXV, Pt. 1, 941; McIntosh, *Chancellorsville*, 35–36; *SHSP*, VI (1878), 231.

9 John R. Boyle, *Soldiers True: The Story of the One Hundred and Eleventh Regiment, Pennsylvania Veteran Volunteers* (New York, 1903), 93–94.

10 *OR*, XXV, Pt. 1, 798, 941.

11 Thomas C. Parramore *et al.*, eds., *Before the Rebel Flag Fell* (Mufreesboro, N.C., 1968), 55.

12 Captain R. E. Wilbourn of Jackson's staff, in Early, *Autobiographical Sketch*, 213; *Confederate Veteran*, XXVIII (1920), 96.

13 *OR*, XXV, Pt. 1, 916; McClellan, *Stuart*, 241–42.

14 Calier G. Hamilton to father, May 19, 1863, Hamilton Letters; *The Land We Love*, I (1866), 181; *SHSP*, VIII (1880), 494.

15 *Confederate Veteran*, XII (1905), 232; Murray Forbes Taylor typescript reminiscences, Hill Papers, 5–6; *SHSP*, XXIX (1901), 333. According to one of Jackson's bodyguards, the general's climactic directive to Hill was: "Order the whole line to advance, General Hill, but slowly, with great caution, and without noise." *Ibid.*, 332.

16 John Esten Cooke, *Stonewall Jackson: A Military Biography* (New York, 1866), 419–20.

17 *SHSP*, VI (1878), 279; Clark, *N.C. Regiments*, V, 99; *The Land We Love*, I (1866), 181.

18 Taylor reminiscences, 14; *Confederate Veteran*, XII (1904), 493; XVIII (1910), 82.

19 This account of Hill's ministrations to Jackson is a composite of testimonies by several eyewitnesses. See Hotchkiss, *Make Me a Map*, 138; *SHSP*, VI (1878), 232–33, 269, 279; XXIX (1901), 335; XLIII (1920), 52; *Confederate Veteran*, IV (1896), 308.

20 Luther W. Hopkins, *From Bull Run to Appomattox* (Baltimore, 1908), 80; VI (1878), 270.

21 *OR*, XXV, Pt. 1, 799, 890; *Confederate Veteran*, XIII (1905), 233. For varying references to Hill's wounding, see *Richmond Daily Dispatch*, May 7, 1863; Clark, *N.C. Regiments*, II, 38. The Union fire came from Capt. Justin E. Dimick's battery. The following day, Dimick was mortally wounded. Abner Doubleday, *Chancellorsville and Gettysburg* (New York, 1882), 40.

22 "Record of William H. Palmer," Charles T. Palmer Papers, Museum of the Confederacy.

23 Taylor reminiscences, 9; *Confederate Veteran*, XXVI (1918), 23.

24 *OR*, XXV, Pt. 1, 803, 887; *SHSP*, VII (1879), 575.

25 *OR*, XXV, Pt. 1, 886, 889, 891–92, 935; *Richmond Enquirer*, May 15, 1863.

26 Caldwell, *S.C. Brigade*, 83–84.

27 *Confederate Veteran*, XII (1904), 494; *Richmond Enquirer*, May 15, 1863.

28 *OR*, XXV, Pt. 2, 782; Hotchkiss, *Make Me a Map*, 142; Caldwell, *S.C. Brigade*, 88.

29 Samuel W. Fiske, *Mr. Dunn Browne's Experiences in the Army* (Boston, 1866), 151.

[30] *OR*, XXV, Pt. 1, 192, 807; Poague, *Gunner with Stonewall*, 66; Slaughter, *Essex County*, 186.

[31] *OR*, XXV, Pt. 1, 885.

[32] Hunter McGuire and George L. Christian, *The Confederate Cause and Conduct in the War between the States* (Richmond, 1907), 228–29.

[33] William J. Pegram to Mary E. Pegram, May 11, 1863, Pegram-Johnson-McIntosh Papers.

[34] Hotchkiss, "A. P. Hill," 9; Douglas, *I Rode with Stonewall*, 196; Hotchkiss, *Make Me a Map*, xxv; Pender, *Letters*, 237.

[35] *OR*, XXV, Pt. 2, 810; Lee, *William Nelson Pendleton*, 272.

[36] *Richmond Examiner*, May 28, 1863.

[37] *Battles and Leaders*, III, 245, 355; Alexander, *Military Memoirs*, 367.

[38] *Confederate Veteran*, I (1893), 235.

[39] *OR*, XXV, Pt. 1, 1003.

13. GETTYSBURG: THE FIRST DAY

[1] *OR*, XXIV, Pt. 3, 355; Francis Vinton Greene, *The Mississippi* (New York, 1881), 187.

[2] Sorrel, *Recollections*, 136.

[3] Hassler, *Hill*, 143; Freeman, *Lee's Lieutenants*, II, 698–99.

[4] Wise, *Long Arm of Lee*, II, 566, 569, 571–72, 736; Poague, *Gunner*, 63.

[5] *Souvenir, Hill Monument Unveiling*, 19.

[6] Pender, *Letters*, 244–45.

[7] Betsy and John D. P. Fuller, eds., *Green Mount, A Virginia Plantation Family during the Civil War* (Lexington, Ky., 1962), 233; Moore, *Story of a Cannoneer*, 177–78.

[8] Norton, *Army Letters*, 156.

[9] Caldwell, *S.C. Brigade*, 95; Spencer G. Welch, *A Confederate Surgeon's Letters to His Wife* (New York, 1911), 55.

[10] Lee, *Wartime Papers*, 501–2.

[11] Pender, *Letters*, 242.

[12] Chamberlaine, *Memoirs*, 62; *OR*, XXVII, Pt. 2, 294; Pickett, *Pickett and His Men*, 257; Caldwell, *S.C. Brigade*, 91.

[13] *OR*, LI, Pt. 2, 723; Clark, *N.C. Regiments*, II, 341.

[14] *Richmond Enquirer*, June 23, 1863; Westwood A. Todd, "Reminiscences of the War between the States," typescript, Southern Historical Collection, UNC.

[15] Lucy R. Buck, *Sad Earth, Sweet Heaven: The Diary of Lucy Rebecca Buck* (Birmingham, Ala., 1973), 202; Thomas A. Ashby, *The Valley Campaigns* (New York, 1914), 241–42.

[16] W. A. Alexander diary, Southern Historical Collection, UNC, June 17–25, 1863; Abner Perrin, "A Little More Light on Gettysburg," *Mississippi Valley Historical Review*, XXIV (1938), 521.

[17] Arthur J. L. Fremantle, *Three Months in the Southern States* (London, 1863), 229–30.

[18] *OR*, XXVII, Pt. 3, 909; Hoke, "38th North Carolina," 67.

[19] Freeman, *Lee*, III, 53–54.

[20] Edmund D. Patterson, *Yankee Rebel: The Civil War Journal of Edmund DeWitt Patterson* (Chapel Hill, 1966), 110; *SHSP*, XIV (1886), 15–16.

[21] Freeman, *Lee*, III, 54–55; Carnot Posey to wife, June 27, 1863, Mississippi Room Papers, Museum of the Confederacy.

[22] Pender, *Letters*, 253; *SHSP*, XXVI (1898), 120.

[23] Freeman, *Lee*, III, 59–60; *SHSP*, XXIII (1895), 226–27; Marshall, *Aide-de-Camp*, 225.

[24] Pender, *Letters*, 254–55.

[25] *OR*, XXVII, Pt. 2, 317, 607, 637; Heth, *Memoirs*, 174.

[26] John B. Hood, *Advance and Retreat: Personal Experiences in the United States and Confederate States Armies* (New Orleans, 1880), 55. For a scathing indictment of Stuart by Lee's chief of staff, see Taylor, *Four Years*, 93.

[27] *SHSP*, IV (1877), 157; Clark, *N.C. Regiments*, V, 116–17. Cf. Heth, *Memoirs*, 173.

[28] *OR*, XXVII, Pt. 2, 607.

[29] Pickett, *Pickett and His Men*, 272–73; Fremantle, *Southern States*, 260.

[30] *SHSP*, VI (1878), 122; Ken Bandy and Florence Freeland, comps., *The Gettysburg Papers* (Dayton, O., 1978), I, 432; Taylor, *Four Years*, 93.

[31] *The Land We Love*, II (1866–1867), 42.

[32] *OR*, XXVII, Pt. 2, 637.

[33] Thomas M. Aldrich, *The History of Battery A, First Regiment, Rhode Island Light Artillery, in the War to Preserve the Union, 1861–1865* (Providence, 1904), 193; *Confederate Veteran*, XIV (1906), 308; XVIII (1910), 460.

[34] Military Order of the Loyal Legion: Minnesota Commandery, *Glimpses of the Nation's History*, IV (1898), 340–41.

[35] Dawes, *6th Wisconsin*, 173; Minnesota MOLLUS, *Glimpses of the Nation's History*, IV (1898), 343.

[36] *OR*, XXVII, Pt. 2, 638; *Richmond Enquirer*, July 21, 1863.

[37] *SHSP*, III (1877), 126; Cooke, *Lee*, 301–2; Taylor, *General Lee*, 187.

[38] Clark, *N.C. Regiments*, IV, 178.

[39] *SHSP*, IV (1877), 158.

[40] *OR*, XXVII, Pt. 2, 317. The combined divisions of Heth and Pender numbered about 16,000 men. Add to that another 16,000 troops, whom Ewell was rushing down from the north, plus a total of 25 batteries of artillery between the two corps, and it was a formidable force indeed. Opposed to them were elements of the I and XI Corps, about 15,000 men and 7 batteries. *Ibid.*, Pt. 1, 151; Pt. 2, 287–90.

[41] Clark, *N.C. Regiments*, II, 351–52.

[42] William W. Strong, *History of the 121st Regiment, Pennsylvania Volunteers* (Philadelphia, 1893), 45–46; *OR*, XXVII, Pt. 2, 643.

[43] Heth, *Memoirs*, 175–76.

[44] *OR*, XXVII, Pt. 2, 656–57; Perrin, "Gettysburg," 522. Perrin exaggerated slightly. It is only a mile from Herr Ridge to Seminary Ridge.

[45] Wainwright, *Diary of Battle*, 235–36.

[46] *OR*, XXVII, Pt. 2, 669–70; Gordon, *Reminiscences*, 114; Perrin, "Gettysburg," 522; Walker, *Second Army Corps*, 266–67.

[47] *OR*, XXVII, Pt. 2, 607.

[48] Long, *Memoirs*, 277.

[49] John S. Mosby, *Stuart's Cavalry in the Gettysburg Campaign* (New York, 1908); 135–69; *SHSP*, IV (1877), 155.

[50] Hotchkiss, *Confederate Military History—Va.*, 403; Alexander, *Military Memoirs*, 381; Robert M. Stribling, *Gettysburg Campaign and Campaigns of 1864 and 1865 in Virginia* (Petersburg, 1905), 45.

[51] *OR*, XXVII, Pt. 2, 308.

[52] *Ibid.*, 607; LI, Pt. 2, 811; Benjamin F. Cook, *History of the Twelfth Massachusetts Volunteers* (Boston, 1882), 101.

[53] David G. McIntosh, *Review of the Gettysburg Campaign* (n.p., 1909), 48–49.

14. BYSTANDER TO DEFEAT

[1] John L. Black, ed., *Crumbling Defenses; or, Memoirs and Reminiscences of John Logan Black, Colonel, C.S.A.* (Macon, Ga., 1960), 37; Fremantle, *Southern States*, 263.

[2] *OR*, XXVII, Pt. 2, 607–8.

[3] *Ibid.*, 608.

[4] Poague, *Gunner with Stonewall*, 71.

[5] Fitzgerald Ross, *Cities and Camps of the Confederate States* (Urbana, Ill., 1958), 50.

[6] Marginal note by Col. Thomas T. Munford in the Museum of the Confederacy's copy of McIntosh, *Gettysburg Campaign*, 27.

[7] Chamberlain, *Memoirs*, 70; Pickett, *Pickett and His Men*, 290; Owen, *Washington Artillery*, 246.

[8] For the discrepancies in orders relative to Hill's use of Anderson in this battle, see *OR*, XXVII, Pt. 2, 308, 318–19, 608.

[9] *Ibid.*, 608, 624.

[10] *Ibid.*, 333, 619; *SHSP*, IV (1877), 116; Hassler, *Hill*, 161.

[11] John S. Lewis to mother, July 21, 1863, Harry Lewis Papers, Southern Historical Collection, UNC.

[12] Jacob Hoke, *The Great Invasion of 1863* (Dayton, O., 1887), 355.

[13] *SHSP*, VII (1879), 92; XL (1916), 40.

[14] Clark, *N.C. Regiments*, I, 543; *SHSP*, IV (1877), 103; VII (1879), 92.

[15] Wainwright, *Diary of Battle*, 249; *Richmond Enquirer*, July 24, 1863.

[16] *SHSP*, V (1877), 44.

[17] Thomas W. Hyde, *Following the Greek Cross; or, Memoirs of the Sixth Army Corps* (Boston, 1894), 155–56.

[18] T. J. Canton to John R. Lane, June 22, 1890, John Randolph Lane Papers, Southern Historical Collection, UNC.

[19] Walker, *Second Army Corps*, 297–98; Ross, *Cities and Camps*, 58; *OR*, XXVII, Pt. 2, 608.

[20] Clark, *N.C. Regiments*, I, 590; *Confederate Veteran*, XVII (1909), 110; Lane address, Lane Papers; Alfred M. Scales to wife, Aug. 10, 1863, Alfred M. Scales Papers, N.C. State Archives; W. H. Blount to "Miss Bettie," July 3, 1863, Steed and Phipps Family Papers, Southern Historical Collection, UNC.

[21] Robert K. Krick, comp., *The Gettysburg Death Roster* (Dayton, O., 1981), 13–16.

[22] *Battles and Leaders*, III, 420; Freeman, *Lee*, III, 133.

15. EBB TIDE AT BRISTOE STATION

[1] Caldwell, *S.C. Brigade*, 104–5; Todd, "Reminiscences," 135; *Scribner's Monthly*, XXII (1881), 648.

[2] George Lewis, *The History of Battery E, First Regiment, Rhode Island Light Artillery* (Providence, 1892), 221; Clark, *N.C. Regiments*, II, 661–62.

[3] James B. Sheeran, *Confederate Chaplain: A War Journal* (Milwaukee, 1960), 49–50.

[4] *OR*, XXVII, Pt. 2, 640, 667.

[5] Heth, *Memoirs*, 178; Val C. Giles, *Rags and Hope: The Recollections of Val C. Giles* (New York, 1961), 189.

[6] *OR*, XXVII, Pt. 2, 323, 640.

7 James M. Simpson to wife, July 16, 1863, Allen and Simpson Family Papers, Southern Historical Collection, UNC; Caldwell, *S.C. Brigade*, 107.

8 Edmund W. Jones to father, July 17, 1863, Edmund Walter Jones Papers, Southern Historical Collection, UNC; W. R. Bond, *Pickett or Pettigrew? An Historical Essay* (Weldon, N.C., 1888), 23; Clark, *N.C. Regiments*, II, 376.

9 W. H. Blount to "Miss Bettie," Aug. 2, 1863, Steed and Phipps Family Papers; Worsham, *Jackson's Foot Cavalry*, 109; L. Minor Blackford, *Mine Eyes Have Seen the Glory* (Cambridge, Mass., 1954), 220.

10 *The Land We Love*, III (1867), 255–56.

11 Samuel Harper, 22nd N.C., in Lenoir (N.C.) *News-Topic*, Oct. 5, 1923; *OR*, XXVII, Pt. 2, 609; Scales, *Battle of Fredericksburg*, 16.

12 *OR*, XXVII, Pt. 2, 609; *Richmond Daily Dispatch*, Aug. 1, 1863.

13 *OR*, XXVII, Pt. 2, 609; W. H. MacNamara, *The Irish Ninth in Bivouac and Battle* (Boston, 1867), 215.

14 Archibald T. Robertson, *Life and Letters of John A. Broadus* (Philadelphia, 1901), 203.

15 *OR*, XXVII, Pt. 2, 653; Wise, *Long Arm of Lee*, II, 693, 709.

16 *Richmond Enquirer*, Aug. 15 and 21, 1863.

17 Alfred M. Scales to wife, Aug. 10, 1863, Scales Papers; Caldwell, *S.C. Brigade*, 111–12.

18 *Richmond Daily Dispatch*, Aug. 31, 1863; Todd, "Reminiscences," 140.

19 *Richmond Enquirer*, Aug. 18, 1863; Caldwell, *S.C. Brigade*, 112–13; Elias Davis to Georgia Davis, Sept. 8, 1863, Elias Davis Papers, Southern Historical Collection, UNC.

20 *Richmond Times-Dispatch*, June 11, 1905; Robertson, *Broadus*, 207.

21 A tenth soldier in Lane's brigade was executed on Nov. 4. Kennedy diary, Sept. 12, Sept. 28, Nov. 4, 1863; Alfred M. Scales to wife, Oct. 1, 1863, Scales Papers.

22 Leonidas L. Polk to wife, Sept. 23, 1863, Leonidas L. Polk Letters, Southern Historical Collection, UNC; *OR*, XXIX, Pt. 2, 201–2. See also Elias Davis to Georgia Davis, Sept. 11, 1863, Davis Papers.

23 *OR*, XXX, Pt. 3, 872, 874.

24 Katherine Morgan Hill to Cornelis Wise Moore [Oct. 1863], Wise Moore Papers, Jones Memorial Library, Lynchburg, Va.

25 *OR*, XXIX, Pt. 1, 405–6; Pt. 2, 781; *Richmond Enquirer*, Oct. 16, 1863.

26 Marsena R. Patrick, *Inside Lincoln's Army* (New York, 1964), 296.

27 James A. Graham, *The James A. Graham Papers, 1861–1884* (Chapel Hill, 1928), 160.

28 Caldwell, *S.C. Brigade*, 115.

29 *OR*, XI, Pt. 2, 842; Clark, *N.C. Regiments*, III, 69; IV, 45, 536; *Richmond Enquirer*, Oct. 24, 1863.

30 Clark, *N.C. Regiments*, I, 545.

31 *OR*, XXIX, Pt. 1, 426; Poague, *Gunner*, 79.

32 Alfred D. Kelly to brother, Oct. 24, 1863, Kelly Papers; Clark, *N.C. Regiments*, II, 444; *OR*, XXIX, Pt. 1, 426, 430; Chamberlaine, *Memoirs*, 82.

33 *OR*, XXIX, Pt. 1, 426, 438; Clark, *N.C. Regiments*, II, 441.

34 Sloan, *Guilford Grays*, 69.

35 *Ibid.*, 69, 71; *OR*, XXIX, Pt. 1, 427; Clark, *N.C. Regiments*, I, 743.

36 Graham, *Papers*, 157; *Richmond Enquirer*, Oct. 20, 1863; Patrick, *Inside Lincoln's Army*, 299.

37 *OR*, XXIX, Pt. 1, 427, 431; Sloan, *Guilford Grays*, 70; Mugler diary.

38 *OR*, XXIX, Pt. 1, 426, 431, 437.

[39] *Ibid.*, 428; Clark, *N.C. Regiments*, II, 443; IV, 505.

[40] W. G. Bean, *Stonewall's Man: Sandie Pendleton* (Chapel Hill, 1959), 150; Taylor, *Four Years*, 116; Clark, *N.C. Regiments*, II, 45, 773; III, 92; *Richmond Enquirer*, Oct. 20, 1863.

[41] *OR*, XXIX, Pt. 1, 427–28.

[42] Thomas L. Livermore, *Days and Events, 1860–1866* (Boston, 1920), 295; Chamberlaine, *Memoirs*, 83; Cooke, *Lee*, 355. For differing versions of Lee's statement to Hill, see Heth, *Memoirs*, 180; Moore, *Cannoneer*, 205; Sloan, *Guilford Grays*, 74.

[43] *OR*, XXIX, Pt. 1, 226.

[44] *Confederate Veteran*, XXX (1922), 246.

16. PLEASANT FAMILY DIVERSIONS

[1] Lee, *Wartime Papers*, 611; Ada Bruce Desper Bradshaw, ed., "Civil War Diary of Charles William McVicar" (typescript, privately printed, 1977), 31.

[2] Hassler, *Hill*, 181.

[3] *OR*, XXIX, Pt. 2, 371; Adam S. Bright, *"Respects to All": Letters of Two Pennsylvania Boys in the War of the Rebellion* (Pittsburgh, 1962), 49; William Clark Corson, *My Dear Jennie* (Richmond, 1982), 113; Leonidas L. Polk to wife, Oct. 28, 1863, Polk Letters; *Richmond Times-Dispatch*, Oct. 28, 1934.

[4] The cradle is preserved at the Museum of the Confederacy, Richmond.

[5] *OR*, XXIX, Pt. 1, 823, 830; Poague, *Gunner with Stonewall*, 81.

[6] Patrick, *Inside Lincoln's Army*, 313; *Richmond Daily Dispatch*, Nov. 27, 1863.

[7] *OR*, XXIX, Pt. 1, 895–96; LI, Pt. 2, 788; Small, *Road to Richmond*, 117–18.

[8] Cooke, *Lee*, 368; *OR*, XXIX, Pt. 1, 896.

[9] Taylor, *General Lee*, 226–27; *Richmond Times-Dispatch*, Nov. 4, 1934.

[10] Caldwell, *S.C. Brigade*, 119; Alfred S. Roe, *The Thirty-ninth Regiment, Massachusetts Volunteers, 1862–1865* (Worcester, 1914), 126; *Richmond Daily Dispatch*, Dec. 8, 1863.

[11] *OR*, XXIX, Pt. 1, 896.

[12] Vivian Minor Fleming, *Campaigns of the Army of Northern Virginia* (Richmond, 1928), 111; *Richmond Daily Dispatch*, Dec. 8 and 11, 1863.

[13] *Ibid.*, Feb. 12, 1864. The spurs are part of the Hill memorabilia at the Museum of the Confederacy.

[14] Hill to Lucy Hill, Dec. 14, 1863, Hill Papers.

[15] *Richmond Daily Dispatch*, Dec. 19, 1863; Clark, *N.C. Regiments*, I, 673. The Alabama brigade of the Third Corps went on a similar Christmas spree. Elias Davis to Georgia Davis, Jan. 1, 1864, Davis Letters.

[16] *Richmond Enquirer*, Jan. 8, 1864; *Richmond Daily Dispatch*, Jan. 9, 1864; Mary B. Chesnut, *Mary Chesnut's Civil War Diary* (New Haven, 1981), 534.

[17] *Richmond Daily Dispatch*, Jan. 11, 1864; Roger Tusken, "In the Bastille of the Rebels," *Journal of the Illinois State Historical Society*, LVI (1963), 329–30.

[18] *Richmond Daily Dispatch*, Jan. 11–14, 1864.

[19] Scott, *Orange County*, 207; Eva Browning to W. J. Robertson, Oct. 30, 1931, Hill Papers; *OR*, XXXII, Pt. 2, 149, 151; XXXIII, 1075, 1124.

[20] Hill to Henry Heth, Jan. 13, 1864, Henry Heth Papers, Museum of the Confederacy.

[21] Hill to "My Dear Georgia," Mar. 19, 1864, Robert Martin Hughes Papers, College of William and Mary.

[22] Hill to George S. Palmer, Mar. 30, 1864, George S. Palmer Papers, Museum of the Confederacy.

23 Hill to Richard C. Morgan, Apr. 26, 1864, Morgan Family Papers.

24 *Annals of the War*, 486.

25 *Richmond Daily Dispatch*, Jan. 29, 1864; W. H. Blount to "Miss Bettie," Feb. 1, 1864, Steed and Phipps Family Papers.

26 Theophilus Frank to wife, Mar. 24, 1864, Frank Family Letters, 1863–1865, Southern Historical Collection, UNC. See also W. H. Blount to "Miss Bettie," Mar. 24, 1864, Steed and Phipps Family Papers.

27 *Richmond Daily Dispatch*, Mar. 28, 1864; Samuel H. Walkup diary, Mar. 28, 1864, Samuel Hooey Walkup Papers, Southern Historical Collection, UNC; Kennedy diary, Apr. 1, 1864.

28 Alfred M. Scales to wife, Apr. 24, 1864, Scales Papers.

29 Eva B. Browning to W. J. Robertson, Mar. 14, 1931, and Lucy H. Magill to W. J. Robertson, Oct. 5, 1931, Hill Papers; *Richmond Times-Dispatch*, Nov. 4, 1934.

30 *Richmond Daily Dispatch*, Mar. 9, 1864; Joseph C. Robert, ed., "A Ring Tournament in 1864: A Letter from a Mississippian in the Army at Northern Virginia," *Journal of Mississippi History*, III (1941), 294.

31 *Annals of the War*, 487; Caldwell, *S.C. Brigade*, 126.

32 *OR*, XXXVI, Pt. 1, 1070.

33 William L. Royall, *Some Reminiscences* (New York, 1909), 28; William Meade Dame, *From the Rapidan to Richmond* (Baltimore, 1920), 71–72.

17. WILDERNESS AND SICKNESS

1 Louis N. Beaudrye, *Historic Records of the Fifth New York Cavalry* (Albany, 1863), 122–23; *Annals of the War*, 489; Clark, *N.C. Regiments*, II, 446.

2 *Annals of the War*, 492; J. William Jones, *Army of Northern Virginia Memorial Volume* (Richmond, 1880), 219–20.

3 Royall, *Some Reminiscences*, 29.

4 Thomas Chamberlin, *History of the One Hundred and Fiftieth Regiment, Pennsylvania Volunteers* (Philadelphia, 1895), 190.

5 Benedict, *Vermont in the Civil War*, I, 424.

6 Caldwell, *S.C. Brigade*, 127–28.

7 Clark, *N.C. Regiments*, II, 665; W. S. Dunlop, *Lee's Sharpshooters: Or, the Forefront of Battle* (Little Rock, 1899), 31; *OR*, XXXVI, Pt. 1, 615.

8 Military Historical Society of Massachusetts, comp., *The Wilderness Campaign: May–June, 1864* (Boston, 1905), 144.

9 Charles A. Humphreys, *Field, Camp, Hospital and Prison in the Civil War, 1863–1865* (Boston, 1918), 42; Charles A. Page, *Letters of a War Correspondent* (Boston, 1899), 50.

10 Morris Schaff, *The Battle of the Wilderness* (Boston, 1910), 196; Royall, *Some Reminiscences*, 29.

11 *Annals of the War*, 272.

12 Lenoir (N.C.) *News-Topic*, Oct. 5, 1923; Royall, *Some Reminiscences*, 29; Heth, *Memoirs*, 183.

13 Royall, *Some Reminiscences*, 30; Jones, *Army of Northern Virginia*, 220.

14 Stribling, *Gettysburg Campaign*, 93–94.

15 Clark, *N.C. Regiments*, III, 75, 305.

16 *OR*, XXVI, Pt. 1, 420; Carlton McCarthy, *Detailed Minutiae of Soldier Life in the Army of Northern Virginia, 1861–1865* (Richmond, 1882), 104.

17 Dunlop, *Lee's Sharpshooters*, 32.

18 *Battles and Leaders*, IV, 123; Clark, *N.C. Regiments*, II, 173; Heth, *Memoirs*, 183–84; Jones, *Army of Northern Virginia*, 221, 228.

19 Royall, *Some Reminiscences*, 30; *Annals of the War*, 495.

20 Royall, *Some Reminiscences*, 30–31.

21 Quoted in Dunlop, *Lee's Sharpshooters*, 443.

22 *Battles and Leaders*, IV, 123; Royall, *Some Reminiscences*, 31.

23 *Ibid.*; R. E. Lee to C.S. War Dept., May 7, 1864, Robert Edward Lee: Official Telegrams, 1862–1865, Duke University; Caldwell, *S.C. Brigade*, 134.

24 *Ibid.*, 133; *SHSP*, VIII (1880), 108; XIV (1886), 525; Alexander, *Military Memoirs*, 503; Freeman, *Lee*, III, 286.

25 Gibbon, *Personal Recollections*, 215.

26 Royall, *Some Reminiscences*, 31–32.

27 Cf. Jones, *Army of Northern Virginia*, 229; Clark, *N.C. Regiments*, I, 547–48.

28 Dame, *Rapidan to Richmond*, 85.

29 Jones, *Army of Northern Virginia*, 233; *SHSP*, XIV (1886), 525; Benedict, *Vermont in the Civil War*, I, 429; Trobriand, *Army of the Potomac*, 572.

30 Royall, *Some Reminiscences*, 33–34.

31 Freeman, *Lee*, III, 289.

32 Sorrel, *Staff Officer*, 237.

33 Joseph P. Cullen, *Where a Hundred Thousand Fell* (Washington, 1966), 45; Benedict, *Vermont in the Civil War*, I, 434; Caldwell, *S.C. Brigade*, 136.

34 For accusations that Hill was solely to blame for the chaos of May 6, see *SHSP*, XIV (1886), 525; Longstreet, *Manassas to Appomattox*, 560. Among the strong critics of Longstreet's actions that day are Long, *Memoirs of Robert E. Lee*, 329; Poague, *Gunner with Stonewall*, 91.

35 Royall, *Some Reminiscences*, 35; *OR*, XXXVI, Pt. 1, 1041, 1071.

36 Dame, *Rapidan to Richmond*, 148; *Contributions to a History of the Richmond Howitzer Battalion* (Richmond, 1883–1886), II, 242; *Richmond Enquirer*, May 17, 1864, *The Land We Love*, II (1866–1867), 288; Lee, *Wartime Papers*, 725; *OR*, XXXVI, Pt. 2, 974.

37 Jones, *Army of Northern Virginia*, 59.

38 *Richmond Daily Dispatch*, May 17, 1864; Walker, *Second Army Corps*, 451.

39 Jubal A. Early, *A Memoir of the Last Year of the War for Independence* (Lynchburg, Va., 1867), 22–24; *Richmond Enquirer*, May 14, 1864; *OR*, XXXVI, Pt. 1, 332.

40 *Richmond Daily Dispatch*, May 17 and 20, 1864.

41 Heth, *Memoirs*, 186–87.

42 "Palmer Record," C. T. Palmer Papers; *Richmond Enquirer*, May 20, 1864.

43 Clark, *N.C. Regiments*, II, 571; *SHSP*, IX (1881), 146; *Richmond Daily Dispatch*, May 16, 1864.

44 Dunlop, *Lee's Sharpshooters*, 70.

45 Freeman, *Lee*, III, 331.

46 *Richmond Enquirer*, May 23, 1864; *The Land We Love*, II (1866–1867), 288–89; *Confederate Veteran*, I (1893), 235.

18. NORTH ANNA TO PETERSBURG

1 *OR*, XXXVI, Pt. 3, 814–15; Taylor, *Four Years*, 134.

2 Milgram, "John Woodzell," 367; *Richmond Daily Dispatch*, May 24, 1864.

3 George M. Neese, *Three Years in the Confederate Horse Artillery* (New York, 1911), 274–75.

4 Chamberlin, *150th Pennsylvania*, 202.

⁵ *SHSP*, IX (1881), 241–43; Clark, *N.C. Regiments*, II, 55; IV, 196; *Richmond Daily Dispatch*, May 27, 1864.

⁶ Freeman, *Lee*, III, 355.

⁷ Taylor, *General Lee*, 249; Hotchkiss, *Confederate Military History—Va.*, 460.

⁸ Jones, *Army of Northern Virginia*, 61.

⁹ Walkup diary, May 29, 1864.

¹⁰ *OR*, XXXVI, Pt. 1, 1031–32; LI, Pt. 2, 969.

¹¹ *Richmond Howitzer Battalion*, II (1883), 261; Clark, *N.C. Regiments*, III, 95; *Richmond Enquirer*, June 7, 1864.

¹² *OR*, LI, Pt. 2, 983.

¹³ Quoted in Joseph P. Cullen, *Richmond National Battlefield Park, Virginia* (Washington, 1961), 33.

¹⁴ Edward O. Lord, *History of the Ninth Regiment, New Hampshire Volunteers, in the War of the Rebellion* (Concord, 1895), 426–27; Chamberlayne, *Ham Chamberlayne*, 226–27.

¹⁵ Dame, *Rapidan to Richmond*, 203; Walker, *Second Army Corps*, 510–11.

¹⁶ Cooke, *Lee*, 406.

¹⁷ Clark, *N.C. Regiments*, III, 120.

¹⁸ Trobriand, *Army of the Potomac*, 585; Alexander, *Military Memoirs*, 542.

¹⁹ Theophilus Frank to wife, June 11, 1864, Frank Letters.

²⁰ Lee, *Wartime Papers*, 759–60.

²¹ *Richmond Daily Dispatch*, June 15, 1864; Alexander diary, June 13–14, 1864.

²² Hoke, "38th North Carolina," 76; Alfred M. Scales to wife, June 14, 1864, Scales Papers; *Richmond Enquirer*, June 17, 1864.

²³ Caldwell, *S.C. Brigade*, 161; *OR*, XXXVI, Pt. 1, 1035; LI, Pt. 2, 1017.

²⁴ Asheville (N.C.) *Gazette-News*, Aug. 29, 1908; *OR*, XL, Pt. 2, 663; *SHSP*, XX (1892), 202.

²⁵ Caldwell, *S.C. Brigade*, 162.

²⁶ James G. Scott and Edward A. Wyatt IV, *Petersburg's Story: A History* (Petersburg, 1960), 186.

²⁷ *SHSP*, XX (1892), 202.

19. THE BESIEGED STRIKE BACK

¹ Taylor, *General Lee*, 274.

² David MacRae, *The Americans at Home* (New York, 1952), 162; Johnson Hagood, *Memoirs of the War of Secession* (Columbia, S.C., 1910), 288–89.

³ *SHSP*, II (1876), 273–74; Mulholland, *116th Pennsylvania*, 244.

⁴ Horace H. Shaw, *The First Maine Heavy Artillery, 1862–1865* (Portland, 1903), 131.

⁵ Thomas D. Marbaker, *History of the Eleventh New Jersey Volunteers* (Trenton, 1898), 200; George A. Bruce, *The Twentieth Regiment of Massachusetts Volunteer Infantry, 1861–1865* (Boston, 1906), 409; Gibbon, *Personal Recollections*, 246.

⁶ A postwar account by Mahone, in John D. Smith, *The History of the Nineteenth Regiment of Maine Volunteer Infantry, 1862–1865* (Minneapolis, 1909), 211. In his official report of the battle, Mahone wrote only that "General Wilcox is now behind me, but it is too late to push farther." *OR*, LI, Pt. 2, 1026.

⁷ *Ibid.*, XL, Pt. 1, 14; Walker, *Second Army Corps*, 544; Petersburg paper quoted in *Richmond Daily Dispatch*, June 24, 1864.

⁸ *OR*, LI, Pt. 2, 1027–28.

⁹ *Ibid.*, XL, Pt. 3, 762; Caldwell, *S.C. Brigade*, 166; John H. Rhodes, *The History of Battery B, First Regiment, Rhode Island Light Artillery, in the War to Preserve the Union, 1861–1865* (Providence, 1894), 305.

¹⁰ For example, see *OR*, XXXVII, Pt. 2, 185, 257, 401; XL, Pt. 3, 147, 159, 165, 177, 196.

¹¹ William J. Pegram to Virginia J. Pegram, July 14, 1864, Pegram-Johnson-McIntosh Papers.

¹² Lord, *9th New Hampshire*, 462.

¹³ *Richmond Daily Dispatch*, July 25, 1864.

¹⁴ Henry Pleasants, Jr., *The Tragedy of the Crater* (Boston, 1938), 32.

¹⁵ *SHSP*, XVIII (1890), 4.

¹⁶ Hyland C. Kirk, *Heavy Guns and Light: A History of the 4th New York Heavy Artillery* (New York, 1890), 299.

¹⁷ Michael Hanifen, *History of Battery B, First New Jersey Artillery* (Ottawa, Ill., 1905), 119.

¹⁸ *SHSP*, XX (1892), 203.

¹⁹ Taylor, *General Lee*, 257; Stewart, *A Pair of Blankets*, 154; W. Gordon McCabe, in Jones, *Army of Northern Virginia*, 158–59.

²⁰ John S. Wise, *The End of an Era* (Boston, 1901), 361.

²¹ *SHSP*, II (1876), 291–92; XXVIII (1900), 205–6; Todd, "Reminiscences," 236.

²² *SHSP*, XXXIII (1905), 362.

²³ William J. Pegram to Virginia J. Pegram, Aug. 7, 1864, Pegram-Johnson-McIntosh Papers; Stewart, *A Pair of Blankets*, 155.

²⁴ Todd, "Reminiscences," 236.

²⁵ Elias Davis to Georgia Davis, Aug. 3, 1864, Davis Papers.

²⁶ Lee, *Wartime Papers*, 828; *OR*, XL, Pt. 1, 752, 788; Alexander, *Military Memoirs*, 572.

²⁷ *Richmond Daily Dispatch*, Aug. 16, 1864.

²⁸ Sidney Lanier, *Sidney Lanier: Letters, 1857–1868* (Baltimore, 1945), VII, 164.

²⁹ Lord, *9th New Hampshire*, 514; R. E. Lee to C.S. Sec. of War, Aug. 1, 1864, Lee Telegrams; *Richmond Daily Dispatch*, Aug. 3, 1864.

³⁰ Marbaker, *11th New Jersey*, 200.

³¹ Caldwell, *S.C. Brigade*, 168; C.S. War Dept.: Subsistence Dept. Papers, Virginia Historical Society.

³² *OR*, XLII, Pt. 2, 1175, 1273–75.

³³ *SHSP*, XX (1892), 203.

³⁴ Goldsborough, *Maryland Line*, 135.

³⁵ Heth, *Memoirs*, 190–91.

³⁶ *Under the Maltese Cross*, 315; Petersburg paper quoted in *Richmond Daily Dispatch*, Aug. 22, 1864.

³⁷ *OR*, XLII, Pt. 1, 940.

³⁸ *Ibid.*, 858, 936; Smith, *Corn Exchange Regiment*, 502.

³⁹ *OR*, XLII, Pt. 2, 421.

⁴⁰ E. B. Long, *The Civil War Day by Day: An Almanac, 1861–1865* (Garden City, N.Y., 1971), 558.

⁴¹ Lee, *Wartime Papers*, 845.

⁴² *Papers of the Military Historical Society of Massachusetts*, IV (1905), 467. For good descriptions of the Union lines at Reams's Station, see Walker, *Second Army Corps*, 582–83; Mulholland, *116th Pennsylvania*, 258.

⁴³ Walker, *Second Army Corps*, 588. Other accounts of Hill as being in, or not in, the battle are in *OR*, XLII, Pt. 1, 224; Pt. 2, 484; *SHSP*, II (1876), 297n.; Bruce, *20th Massachusetts*, 420.

[44] Walker, *Second Army Corps*, 590; Todd, "Reminiscences," 255; Kirk, *Heavy Guns and Light*, 339.

[45] Rhodes, *Battery B*, 328.

[46] Clark, *N.C. Regiments*, II, 447–48; III, 97; Walker, *Second Army Corps*, 594.

[47] Gibbon, *Personal Recollections*, 257; Bruce, *20th Massachusetts*, 422.

[48] Aldrich, *Battery A*, 379.

[49] Todd, "Reminiscences," 255; *OR*, XLII, Pt. 1, 131.

[50] *Richmond Daily Dispatch*, Aug. 30, 1864; U. R. Brooks, *Butler and His Cavalry in the War of Secession, 1861–1865* (Columbia, S.C., 1909), 306.

[51] George Baylor, *Bull Run to Bull Run; or, Four Years in the Army of Northern Virginia* (Richmond, 1900), 236; Finley Harper to sister, Aug. 26, 1864, Harper Letters.

20. "HE IS NOW AT REST"

[1] *Richmond Daily Dispatch*, Sept. 1, 1864; *OR*, XLII, Pt. 2, 1030, 1214. "The Army of Northern Virginia needs reinforcement to its fighting *materiel*," the *Richmond Daily Dispatch* editorialized on Sept. 12. 1864. "This reinforcement must come at once! . . . Let not our authorities and our newspaper press lay the flattering unction to their hearts that victories can be achieved without men."

[2] Richard J. Sommers, *Richmond Redeemed: The Siege at Petersburg* (Garden City, N.Y., 1981), 214.

[3] William J. Pegram to Mary Pegram, Sept. 24, 1864, Pegram-Johnson-McIntosh Papers; *Richmond Times-Dispatch*, Nov. 4, 1934.

[4] Hagood, *Memoirs*, 303–4.

[5] Dunlop, *Lee's Sharpshooters*, 212.

[6] *History of the Thirty-fifth Regiment, Massachusetts Volunteers, 1862–1865* (Boston, 1884), 298; Lord, *9th New Hampshire*, 525; *Richmond Daily Dispatch*, Oct. 3, 1864.

[7] William J. Pegram to Mary Pegram, Oct. 5, 1864, Pegram-Johnson-McIntosh Papers.

[8] *OR*, XLII, Pt. 3, 1134.

[9] William J. Pegram to Mary Pegram, Oct. 5, 1864, Pegram-Johnson-McIntosh Papers; *OR*, XLII, Pt. 3, 1140.

[10] Lee, *Wartime Papers*, 863.

[11] James I. Robertson and Richard M. McMurry, eds., *Rank and File: Civil War Essays in Honor of Bell Irvin Wiley* (San Rafael, Cal., 1976), 129.

[12] Chamberlaine, *Memoirs*, 109.

[13] Sorrel, *Staff Officer*, 89, 276.

[14] William J. Pegram to mother, Oct. 28, 1864, Pegram-Johnson-McIntosh Papers.

[15] Jefferson Davis, *Jefferson Davis, Constitutionalist: His Letters, Papers and Speeches* (Jackson, Miss., 1923), VI, 430.

[16] William J. Pegram to mother, Oct. 28, 1864, Pegram-Johnson-McIntosh Papers.

[17] Wainwright, *A Diary of Battle*, 477.

[18] *OR*, XLII, Pt. 1, 854; *Richmond Daily Dispatch*, Oct. 29 and Nov. 1, 1864; Hassler, *Hill*, 233.

[19] Hill to Wade Hampton, Oct. 28, 1864, Wade Hampton Papers, Virginia State Library.

[20] *OR*, XLII, Pt. 1, 854; *Richmond Daily Dispatch*, Nov. 9 and 22, 1864; Alfred M. Scales to wife, Nov. 12, 1864, Scales Papers.

21 Todd, "Reminiscences," 261.

22 Mrs. Roger A. Pryor, *Reminiscences of Peace and War* (New York, 1904), 191, 320, 326; Chamberlayne, *Ham Chamberlayne*, 299; Freeman, *Lee*, III, 527.

23 Todd, "Reminiscences," 265; Dunlop, *Lee's Sharpshooters*, 222.

24 For example, see Pendleton, *Memoirs*, 379.

25 Hill to Lucy Hill, Dec. 17, 1864, Hill Papers.

26 *Annals of the War*, 703.

27 George W. Tucker typescript reminiscences, Petersburg National Battlefield; Wise, *End of an Era*, 331; Gordon, *Reminiscences*, 379.

28 Clark, *N.C. Regiments*, III, 154.

29 Lee, *Wartime Papers*, 886; *OR*, XLVI, Pt. 2, 387, 1145.

30 Walkup diary, Feb. 21 and Mar. 27, 1865.

31 Robert E. Lee to John C. Breckinridge, Feb. 28 and Mar. 8, 1865, Lee Papers; *OR*, XLVI, Pt. 2, 1254.

32 *SHSP*, II (1876), 302; Murray Forbes Taylor to mother, Mar. 3, 1865, Murray Forbes Taylor Papers, Virginia Historical Society.

33 *SHSP*, XI (1883), 565; *The Land We Love*, II (1866–1867), 289; *Confederate Veteran*, I (1893), 236.

34 *SHSP*, XIX (1891), 185.

35 Freeman, *Lee*, IV, 37; Foote, *The Civil War*, III, 875.

36 Samuel H. Walkup to Minnie Walkup, Mar. 30, 1865, Walkup Papers.

37 Louis H. Manarin and Weymouth T. Jordan, comps., *North Carolina Troops, 1861–1865: A Roster* (Raleigh, 1966–   ), X, 7.

38 Finley Harper to father, Mar. 31, 1865, Harper Letters.

39 Tucker reminiscences.

40 Caldwell, *S.C. Brigade*, 217.

41 Susan B. Harrison to William J. Robertson, Nov. 2, 1931, Hill Papers.

42 Undated newspaper clipping from the Philadelphia *Weekly Times*, Millns Collection; William H. Palmer to Murray Forbes Taylor, Nov. 8, 1902, Petersburg National Battlefield.

43 *SHSP*, XII (1884), 186; XXVII (1899), 29; *OR*, XLVI, Pt. 1, 902; Taylor, *Four Years*, 149.

44 Unless otherwise cited, the details and quotations relative to Hill's activities and death on Apr. 2 are taken from accounts by Tucker and Venable in *SHSP*, XI (1883), 564–69, and XII (1884), 181–87, respectively.

45 *OR*, XLVI, Pt. 1, 903–4.

46 *SHSP*, XX (1892), 349–51; XXVII (1899), 35–38.

47 *Ibid.*, XIX (1891), 184–85; XXVII (1899), 32; *OR*, XLVI, Pt. 1, 993, 1007–8. More erroneous statements exist about Hill's death than about the end of any other Confederate figure. As examples, see Clark, *N.C. Regiments*, II, 61; Catherine A. D. Edmonston, *"Journal of a Secesh Lady": The Diary of Catherine Ann Devereux Edmonston, 1860–1865* (Raleigh, 1979), 694; Frederick C. Floyd, *History of the Fortieth (Mozart) Regiment, New York Volunteers* (Boston, 1909), 247; Longstreet, *Manassas to Appomattox*, 605; *SHSP*, XX (1892), 383.

48 *SHSP*, XII (1884), 184; *Confederate Veteran*, XXVII (1919), 342.

21. EPILOGUE

1 "Report of the Committee Appointed by A. P. Hill Camp, Sons of Confederate Veterans, To Locate the Place of the Death of Gen. A. P. Hill," typescript, Petersburg National Battlefield, 13–14; *SHSP*, XII (1884), 187; XXVII (1899), 32.

2 William H. Palmer to Murray Forbes Taylor, Nov. 8, 1902, Petersburg National Battlefield; postwar interview with Dolly Hill in St. Louis (Mo.) *Republic*, July 12, 1896.

3 Unidentified newspaper clipping, Petersburg National Battlefield; Eva Browning to William J. Robertson, Nov. 2 and 12, 1931, Hill Papers. An overabundance of myths ultimately arose over the disposition of Hill's body during the April 2–4 period. Typical misrepresentations are in Adam Badeau, *Military History of Ulysses S. Grant* (New York, 1885), III, 532; Pollard, *Lee and His Generals*, 446; Page, *Letters*, 324; *Papers of the Military Historical Society of Massachusetts*, XIV (1918), 140.

4 Eva B. Browning to William J. Robertson, Oct. 2, 1931, Hill Papers; *SHSP*, XIX (1891), 183–85. The cemetery is on the outskirts of modern-day Bon Air.

5 Eva B. Browning to William J. Robertson, Nov. 2, 1920, and Lucy H. McGill to William J. Robertson, Oct. 5, 1931, Hill Papers; Catherine Thom Bartlett, comp., *"My Dear Brother": A Confederate Chronicle* (Richmond, 1952), 186, Dolly Hill's pardon is preserved at the Museum of the Confederacy.

6 Richmond *Dispatch*, Feb. 16, 20 and 27, 1867; July 2, 1891; Daniel Grimsley typescript reminiscences, Hill Papers; Mary H. Mitchell, *Hollywood Cemetery: The History of a Southern Shrine* (Richmond, 1985), 114. Cf. *SHSP*, XVII (1889), 418.

7 James D. Birchfield, University of Kentucky Libraries, to writer, Nov. 26, 1984; E. Baptist Hill to Robert E. Lee, Apr. 30, 1868, Lee Papers.

8 Lucy H. McGill to William J. Robertson, undated letter, Hill Papers; Lexington *Daily Press*, Sept. 9, 1875; *Kentucky Gazette*, Sept. 11, 1875. A factually garbled account of Mrs. Hill's third marriage is in Eva B. Browning to William J. Robertson, Nov. 20, 1920, Hill Papers.

9 Freeman, *Lee*, IV, 492; *SHSP*, XX (1892), 385–86.

10 *Annals of the War*, 704.

11 Roland Galvin to writer, Mar. 28, 1984.

12 Richmond *Times*, June 25, and July 2, 1891; *Richmond Dispatch*, July 2, 1891.

13 *SHSP*, XIX (1891), 267–68; Burton Milward to writer, Dec. 10, 1984.

14 *SHSP*, XX (1892), 353, 367–68, 376.

15 See Mrs. B. A. C. Emerson, *Historic Southern Monuments* (New York, 1911).

16 Miscellaneous papers, Petersburg National Battlefield.

17 Eva B. Browning to William J. Robertson, Oct. 2 and Nov. 2, 1931, Hill Papers; undated newspaper clipping, Millns collection.

18 *Lexington Leader*, Mar. 23, 1920; *Lexington Herald*, Mar. 26, 1920; James D. Birchfield to writer, Nov. 26, 1984.

19 St. Louis *Republic*, July 12, 1896; Winchester (Va.) *Evening Star*, Nov. 17, 1904; undated newspaper clipping, Millns collection.

20 Lucy H. McGill to William J. Robertson, undated letter, Hill Papers.

21 *SHSP*, XX (1892), 386.

22 *The Land We Love*, II (1866–1867), 289.

23 *SHSP*, XII (1884), 187.

Works Cited

MANUSCRIPTS

Alexander, W. A. Diary. Southern Historical Collection, University of North Carolina.

Allen and Simpson Family Papers. Southern Historical Collection, University of North Carolina.

Bellamy, William James Harriss. Diary. Southern Historical Collection, University of North Carolina.

Branch, Lawrence O'Bryan. Papers. North Carolina State Archives.

———. Papers. University of Virginia.

Brunson, Joseph W. "Historical Sketch of the Pee Dee Artillery, Army of Northern Virginia." Pegram-Johnson-McIntosh Papers. Virginia Historical Society.

Campbell, L. Franklin. Letter to "Mary," Sept. 7, 1861. In possession of James I. Robertson, Jr.

Campbell Papers. College of William and Mary.

Chamberlayne, John Hampden. Papers. Virginia Historical Society.

Cockrell, Monroe F. Papers. Duke University.

C.S. War Department: Subsistence Papers. Virginia Historical Society.

Cullum, George Washington. File Letters. U.S. Military Academy.

Davis, Elias. Papers. Southern Historical Collection. University of North Carolina.

Frank Family Letters, 1863–1865. Southern Historical Collection, University of North Carolina.

General Order Book, 37th N.C. Troops, 1862–1863. Duke University.

Hamilton, Calier G. Letters. Southern Historical Collection, University of North Carolina.

Harper, Samuel Finlay. Letters. North Carolina State Archives.

Heth, Henry. Papers. Museum of the Confederacy.

Hill, Ambrose Powell. Letter to "Miss Carrie," Apr. 30, 1856. Duke University.

———. Papers. North Carolina State Archives.

———. Papers. Virginia Historical Society.

Hinsdale, John W. Diary. Hinsdale Family Papers. Duke University.

Hoke, William James. "Organization and Movements, the Thirty-eighth Regiment, North Carolina Troops." Southern Historical Collection, University of North Carolina.

Hotchkiss, Jedediah. "Lieut. General A. P. Hill." Jedediah Hotchkiss Papers. Library of Congress.

Hughes, Robert Martin. Papers. College of William and Mary.

Jackson, Thomas Jonathan. Manuscripts. Museum of the Confederacy.

Johnston, James Ambler. Papers. Virginia Polytechnic Institute and State University.

Jones, Edmund Walter. Papers. Southern Historical Collection, University of North Carolina.

Kelly, Alfred D. Letters. Williamson Kelly Papers, 1852–1882. Duke University.

Kennedy, Francis. Diary. Southern Historical Collection, University of North Carolina.

Lane, John Randolph. Papers. Southern Historical Collection, University of North Carolina.

Lee, Robert Edward. Official Telegrams, 1862–1865. Duke University.

———. Papers. Virginia Historical Society.

Lenoir, Walter W. Diary. Southern Historical Collection, University of North Carolina.

Letterbook of the Light Division, C.S.A., 1862–1863. New York Public Library.

Lewis, Harry. Papers. Southern Historical Collection, University of North Carolina.

McClellan, George Brinton. Papers. Library of Congress.

McClellan, Henry Brainerd. Papers. Virginia Historical Society.

McDowell Family Papers. University of Virginia.

Millns, Henrietta. Collection of Hill Papers. Raleigh, N.C.

Morgan Family Papers. Morgan-Hunt House, Lexington, Ky.

Morris, William Grove. Papers. Southern Historical Collection, University of North Carolina.

Mugler, Henry J. Diary. West Virginia University.

Munford, Beverly Bland. Papers. Virginia Historical Society.

Palmer, Charles Turner. Papers. Museum of the Confederacy.

Palmer, George S. Papers. Museum of the Confederacy.

Palmer, William Henry. Letter to Murray F. Taylor, Nov. 8, 1902. Petersburg National Battlefield.

Pegram-Johnson-McIntosh Papers. Virginia Historical Society.

Petersburg National Battlefield. Miscellaneous Papers.

Piston, William Garrett. "Lee's Tarnished Lieutenant: James Longstreet and His Image in American Society." Doctoral dissertation, University of South Carolina, 1982.

Polk, Leonidas L. Letters. Southern Historical Collection, University of North Carolina.

Posey, Carnot. Letter to wife, June 27, 1863. Museum of the Confederacy.

"Report of the Committee Appointed by A. P. Hill Camp, Sons of Confederate Veterans, To Locate the Place of the Death of Gen. A. P. Hill." Typescript, Petersburg National Battlefield.

Saunders, Joseph H. Papers. Southern Historical Collection, University of North Carolina.

Scales, Alfred Moore. Papers. North Carolina State Archives.

Smith, Gustavus Woodson. Letter to W. H. C. Whiting, May 29, 1862. Museum of the Confederacy.

Steed and Phipps Family Papers. Southern Historical Collection, University of North Carolina.

Stuart, James Ewell Brown. Papers. Virginia Historical Society.

Taylor, Murray Forbes. Papers. Virginia Historical Society.

———. Typescript reminiscences. Ambrose Powell Hill Papers, Virginia Historical Society.

Todd, Westwood A. "Reminiscences of the War between the States." Southern Historical Collection, University of North Carolina.

Tucker, George W. Typescript reminiscences. Petersburg National Battlefield.

U.S. Adjutant General's Office. Endorsements, 1851–1870. U.S. National Archives.

———. Letters Sent Relating to Nominations in the Army, 1837–1876. U.S. National Archives.

U.S. Military Academy. Adjutant's Letters Received (Unregistered, 1845–1852) —Cadet Letters. U.S. Military Academy.

———. Cadet Application Papers, 1805–1866. U.S. National Archives.

———. Monthly Class Reports and Conduct Rolls, 1831–1866. U.S. National Archives.

———. Staff Records, IV (1845–1850). U.S. Military Academy.

U.S. National Archives, comp. "Compiled Service Records of Confederate Soldiers Who Served in Organizations from the State of Virginia."

———. "Compiled Service Records of General and Staff Officers, Corps, Division and Brigade Staffs, Non-Com. Staffs and Bands."

U.S. Quartermaster Consolidated Correspondence File. U.S. National Archives.

Venable, Charles Scott. Papers. University of Virginia.

Walkup, Samuel Hooey. Papers. Southern Historical Collection, University of North Carolina.

West, Georgia Callis. Papers. Virginia Historical Society.

Williams, T. C. Papers. Agecroft Hall, Richmond, Va.

Wise Moore Papers. Jones Memorial Library, Lynchburg, Va.

PERIODICALS

Asheville (N.C.) *Gazette-News,* 1908
Century Magazine, 1885
Confederate Veteran, 1892–1932
Kentucky Gazette, 1875
Land We Love, The, 1866–1869
Lenoir (N.C.) *News-Topic,* 1923
Lexington (Ky.) *Daily Press,* 1875
Lexington (Ky.) *Herald,* 1920
Lexington *Kentucky Statesman,* 1859
Lexington (Ky.) *Leader,* 1920
Richmond Daily Dispatch, 1860–1864

Richmond *Dispatch*, 1867, 1891
Richmond *Enquirer*, 1863–1864
Richmond *Examiner*, 1861–1863
Richmond *Times*, 1891
Richmond *Times-Dispatch*, 1905, 1934
Richmond *Whig*, 1861–1862
St. Louis (Mo.) *Republic*, 1896
Southern Historical Society Papers, 1876–1952
Southern Illustrated News, 1862
Winchester (Va.) *Evening Star*, 1904
Winchester Virginian, 1861

PRIMARY PRINTED SOURCES

Aldrich, Thomas M. *The History of Battery A, First Regiment, Rhode Island Light Artillery, in the War to Preserve the Union, 1861–1865*. Providence: Snow & Farnham, 1904.

Alexander, E. Porter. *Military Memoirs of a Confederate*. New York: Charles Scribner's Sons, 1912.

Allen, George H. *Forty-six Months in the Fourth R.I. Volunteers*. Providence: J. A. & R. A. Reid, 1887.

Andrews, Marietta Minnigerode. *Scraps of Paper*. New York: E. P. Dutton & Co., 1929.

Annals of the War, Written by Leading Participants North and South. Philadelphia: The Times Publishing Co., 1879.

Bartlett, Catherine Thom, comp. *"My Dear Brother": A Confederate Chronicle*. Richmond: The Dietz Press, 1952.

Baylor, George. *Bull Run to Bull Run: Four Years in the Army of Northern Virginia*. Richmond: B. F. Johnson Publishing Co., 1900.

Beaudrye, Louis N. *Historic Records of the Fifth New York Cavalry*. Albany: J. Munsell, 1863.

Benedict, G. G. *Vermont in the Civil War*. 2 vols. Burlington: Free Press Assn., 1886.

Bennett, Edwin C. *Musket and Sword: or, The Camp, March, and Firing Line in the Army of the Potomac*. Boston: Coburn Publishing Co., 1900.

Bennett, William W. *A Narrative of the Great Revival Which Prevailed in the Southern Armies*. Philadelphia: Claxton, Remsen & Haffelfinger, 1877.

Benson, Susan W., comp. *Berry Benson's Civil War Book*. Athens: University of Georgia Press, 1962.

Betts, Alexander D. *Experience of a Confederate Chaplain, 1861–1864*. N.p., n.d.

Birdsong, James C. *Brief Sketches of the North Carolina State Troops in the War between the States*. Raleigh: Josephus Daniel, 1894.

Black, John L. *Crumbling Defenses; or, Memoirs and Reminiscences of John Logan Black, Colonel, C.S.A.* Macon, Ga.: J. W. Burke Co., 1960.

Blackford, L. Minor. *Mine Eyes Have Seen the Glory*. Cambridge: Harvard University Press, 1954.

Blackford, Susan L., comp. *Letters from Lee's Army*. New York: Charles Scribner's Sons, 1947.

Blackford, W. W. *War Years with Jeb Stuart*. New York: Charles Scribner's Sons, 1945.

Blake, Henry N. *Three Years in the Army of the Potomac.* Boston: Lee and Shepard, 1865.

Borcke, Heros von. *Memoirs of the Confederate War for Independence.* 2 vols. Edinburgh, Scot.: W. Blackwood and Sons, 1866.

Bosbyshell, Oliver C. *The 48th in the War, Being a Narrative of the Campaigns of the 48th Regiment, Pennsylvania Veteran Volunteers, during the War of the Rebellion.* Philadelphia: Avil Printing Co., 1895.

Boyle, John R. *Soldiers True: The Story of the One Hundred and Eleventh Regiment, Pennsylvania Veteran Volunteers.* New York: Eaton & Mains, 1903.

Bradshaw, Ada Bruce Desper, ed. "Civil War Diary of Charles William McVicar." Typescript privately printed, 1977.

Bright, Adam S. *"Respects to All": Letters of Two Pennsylvania Boys in the War of the Rebellion.* Pittsburgh: University of Pittsburgh Press, 1962.

Brooks, U. R. *Butler and His Cavalry in the War of Secession, 1861–1865.* Columbia, S.C.: The State Co., 1909.

——, ed. *Stories of the Confederacy.* Columbia, S.C.: The State Co., 1912.

Brown, Philip F. *Reminiscences of the War of 1861–1865.* Richmond: Whittet & Shepperson, 1917.

Bruce, George A. *The Twentieth Regiment of Massachusetts Volunteer Infantry, 1861–1865.* Boston: Houghton, Mifflin Co., 1906.

Buck, Lucy R. *Sad Earth, Sweet Heaven: The Diary of Lucy Rebecca Buck.* Birmingham, Ala.: The Cornerstone, 1973.

Buck, Samuel D. *With the Old Confeds: Actual Experiences of a Captain in the Line.* Baltimore: H. E. Houck & Co., 1925.

[Caffey, Thomas C.]. *Battle-fields of the South, from Bull Run to Fredericksburg.* 2 vols. New York: J. Bradburn, 1864.

Caldwell, J. F. J. *The History of a Brigade of South Carolinians Known First as "Gregg's," and Subsequently as "McGowan's Brigade."* Philadelphia: King & Baird, 1866.

Chamberlaine, W. W. *Memoirs of the Civil War.* Washington: Byron S. Adams, 1912.

Chamberlayne, G. G., ed. *Ham Chamerlayne—Virginian: Letters and Papers of an Artillery Officer in the War for Southern Independence, 1861–1865.* Richmond: Dietz Printing Co., 1932.

Chamberlin, Thomas. *History of the One Hundred and Fiftieth Regiment, Pennsylvania Volunteers.* Philadelphia: J. B. Lippincott Co., 1895.

Chambers, Henry A. *Diary of Capt. Henry A. Chambers.* Wendell, N.C.: Broadfoot's Bookmark, 1983.

Chesnut, Mary B. *Mary B. Chesnut's Civil War Diary.* New Haven: Yale University Press, 1981.

Clark, James H. *The Iron Hearted Regiment: Being an Account of the Battles, Marches and Gallant Deeds Performed by the 115th N.Y. Vols.* Albany: J. Munsell, 1865.

Clark, Walter, ed. *Histories of the Several Regiments and Battalions from North Carolina in the Great War, 1861–'65.* 5 vols. Raleigh: E. M. Uzzell, 1901.

Contributions to a History of the Richmond Howitzer Battalion. 4 vols. Richmond: C. McCarthy, 1883–1886.

Cook, Benjamin F. *History of the Twelfth Massachusetts Volunteers.* Boston: Twelfth (Webster) Regiment Assn., 1882.

Cooke, John Esten. *Hammer and Rapier.* New York: Carleton, Publisher, 1870.

Corson, William Clark. *My Dear Jennie.* Richmond: The Dietz Press, 1982.

Croffut, W. A., and Morris, John M. *The Military and Civil History of Connecticut during the War of 1861–1865.* New York: Ledyward Bill, 1868.

Cudworth, Warren H. *History of the First Regiment (Massachusetts Infantry).* Boston: Walker, Fuller and Co., 1866.

Dame, William Meade. *From the Rapidan to Richmond.* Baltimore: Green-Lucas Co., 1920.

Davidson, Greenlee. *Captain Greenlee Davidson, C.S.A.: Diary and Letters, 1851–1863.* Verona, Va.: McClure Press, 1975.

Davis, Jefferson. *Jefferson Davis, Constitutionalist: His Letters, Papers and Speeches.* 10 vols. Jackson: Mississippi Department of Archives and History, 1923.

Dawes, Rufus R. *Service with the Sixth Wisconsin Volunteers.* Madison: State Historical Society of Wisconsin, 1962.

Dawson, Francis W. *Reminiscences of Confederate Service, 1861–1865.* Baton Rouge: Louisiana State University Press, 1980.

Denison, Frederic. *Sabres and Spurs: The First Regiment, Rhode Island Cavalry, in the Civil War, 1861–1865.* Central Falls, R.I.: E. L. Freeman Co., 1876.

Dickert, D. Augustus. *History of Kershaw's Brigade.* Newberry, S.C.: E. H. Aull Co., 1899.

Dooley, John. *John Dooley, Confederate Soldier: His War Journal.* Washington: Georgetown University Press, 1945.

Doubleday, Abner. *Chancellorsville and Gettysburg.* New York: Charles Scribner's Sons, 1882.

Douglas, Henry Kyd. *I Rode with Stonewall.* Chapel Hill: University of North Carolina Press, 1940.

Dunaway, Wayland F. *Reminiscences of a Rebel.* New York: The Neale Publishing Co., 1913.

Dunlop, W. S. *Lee's Sharpshooters: or, the Forefront of Battle.* Little Rock: Tunnah & Pittard, 1899.

Early, Jubal A. *Autobiographical Sketch and Narrative of the War between the States.* Philadelphia: J. B. Lippincott Co., 1912.

———. *A Memoir of the Last Year of the War for Independence.* Lynchburg, Va.: Charles W. Button, 1867.

Edmonston, Catherine A. D. *"Journal of a Secesh Lady": The Diary of Catherine Ann Devereux Edmonston, 1860–1866.* Raleigh: Division of Archives and History, 1979.

Eggleston, George Cary. *A Rebel's Recollections.* New York: Hurd and Houghton, 1875.

Fiske, Samuel W. *Mr. Dunn Browne's Experiences in the Army.* Boston: Nichols and Noye, 1866.

Floyd, Frederick C. *History of the Fortieth (Mozart) Regiment, New York Volunteers.* Boston: F. H. Gilson Co., 1909.

Fremantle, Arthur J. L. *Three Months in the Southern States.* London: William Blackwood and Sons, 1863.

French, S. Bassett. *Centennial Tales: Memoirs of Col. "Chester" S. Bassett French.* New York: Carlton Books, 1962.

Fuller, Betsy and John D., eds. *Green Mount: A Virginia Plantation Family during the Civil War.* Lexington: University Press of Kentucky, 1962.

Gibbon, John. *Personal Recollections of the Civil War.* New York: G. P. Putnam's Sons, 1928.

Giles, Val C. *Rags and Hope: The Recollections of Val C. Giles.* New York: Coward-McCann, 1961.

Goldsborough, W. W. *The Maryland Line in the Confederate Army, 1861–1865*. Baltimore: Press of Guggenheimer, Weil & Co., 1900.

Gordon, John B. *Reminiscences of the Civil War*. New York: Charles Scribner's Sons, 1904.

Gould, Edward K. *Major-General Hiram G. Berry*. Rockland, Me.: Press of the Courier-Gazette, 1899.

Gould, John M. *History of the First-Tenth-Twenty-ninth Maine Regiment*. Portland: Stephen Berry, 1871.

Graham, James A. *The James A. Graham Papers, 1861–1884*. Chapel Hill: University of North Carolina Press, 1928.

Grant, Ulysses S. *The Papers of Ulysses S. Grant*. Vol. I. Carbondale: Southern Illinois University Press, 1967.

Griffith, H. P. *Variosa: A Collection of Sketches, Essays and Verses*. Gaffney, S.C.: H. P. Griffith, 1911.

Hackley, Woodford B. *The Little Fork Rangers: A Sketch of Company "D," Fourth Virginia Cavalry*. Richmond: The Dietz Printing Co., 1927.

Hagood, Johnson. *Memoirs of the War of Secession*. Columbia, S.C.: The State Co., 1910.

Hamlin, Percy G., ed. *The Making of a Soldier: Letters of General R. S. Ewell*. Richmond: Whittet & Shepperson, 1935.

Hanifen, Michael. *History of Battery B, First New Jersey Artillery*. Ottawa, Ill.: Republican-Times, 1905.

Haynes, Martin A. *A History of the Second Regiment, New Hampshire Volunteer Infantry, in the War of the Rebellion*. Lakeport, N.H.: Martin A. Haynes, 1896.

Heth, Henry. *The Memoirs of Henry Heth*. Westport, Conn.: Greenwood Press, 1974.

History of the Thirty-fifth Regiment, Massachusetts Volunteers, 1862–1865. Boston: Mills, Knight & Co., 1884.

Hitchcock, Frederick L. *War from the Inside*. Philadelphia: J. B. Lippincott Co., 1904.

Hoke, Jacob. *The Great Invasion of 1863*. Dayton, O.: W. J. Shuey, 1887.

Holmes, Oliver Wendell, Jr. *Touched with Fire: Civil War Letters and Diary*. Cambridge: Harvard University Press, 1947.

Hood, John B. *Advance and Retreat: Personal Experiences in the United States and Confederate States Armies*. New Orleans: Hood Orphan Memorial Fund, 1880.

Hopkins, C. A. Porter, ed. "The James J. Archer Letters." *Maryland Historical Magazine*, LVI (1961).

Hopkins, Luther W. *From Bull Run to Appomattox*. Baltimore: Fleet-McGinley Co., 1908.

Hotchkiss, Jedediah. *Confederate Military History: Virginia*. Atlanta: Confederate Publishing Co., 1899.

———. *Make Me a Map of the Valley*. Dallas: Southern Methodist University Press, 1973.

Houghton, W. R. and M. B. *Two Boys in the Civil War and After*. Montgomery, Ala.: The Paragone Press, 1912.

Humphreys, Charles A. *Field, Camp, Hospital and Prison in the Civil War, 1863–1865*. Boston: George H. Ellis Co., 1918.

Hyde, Thomas W. *Following the Greek Cross; or, Memories of the Sixth Corps*. Boston: Houghton Mifflin Co., 1894.

Jackson, Mary Anna. *Memoirs of Stonewall Jackson*. Louisville: Courier-Journal Job Printing Co., 1895.

Johnston, David E. *The Story of a Confederate Boy in the Civil War*. Portland, Oreg.: Glass D. Prudhomme, 1914.

Johnston, Joseph E. *Narrative of Military Operations Directed during the Late War between the States*. New York: D. Appleton and Co., 1874.

Kirk, Hyland C. *Heavy Guns and Light: A History of the 4th New York Heavy Artillery*. New York: C. T. Dillingham, 1890.

Lanier, Sidney. *Sidney Lanier: Letters, 1857–1868*. Baltimore: The Johns Hopkins Press, 1945.

Lee, Robert E. *The Wartime Papers of R. E. Lee*. Boston: Little Brown, 1961.

Lee, Susan P. *Memoirs of William Nelson Pendleton, D.D.* Philadelphia: J. B. Lippincott, 1893.

Lewis, George. *The History of Battery E, First Regiment, Rhode Island Light Artillery*. Providence: Snow & Farnham, 1892.

Lindsley, John Berrien, ed. *The Military Annals of Tennessee: Confederate*. Nashville: J. M. Lindsley & Co., 1886.

Livermore, Thomas L. *Days and Events, 1860–1866*. Boston: Houghton Mifflin Co., 1920.

Loehr, Charles T. *War History of the Old First Virginia Infantry Regiment, Army of Northern Virginia*. Richmond: William Ellis Jones, 1884.

Long, Armistead L. *Memoirs of Robert E. Lee*. New York: J. M. Stoddart & Co., 1886.

Longstreet, James. *From Manassas to Appomattox*. Philadelphia: J. P. Lippincott Co., 1896.

Lord, Edward O. *History of the Ninth Regiment, New Hampshire Volunteers, in the War of the Rebellion*. Concord: Republican Press Assn., 1895.

McCarthy, Carlton. *Detailed Minutiae of Soldier Life in the Army of Northern Virginia*. Richmond: C. McCarthy and Co., 1882.

McClellan, George B. *McClellan's Own Story*. New York: Charles L. Webster & Co., 1887.

McDonald, Cornelia. *A Diary with Reminiscences of the War and Refugee Life in the Shenandoah Valley, 1860–1865*. Nashville: Cullom & Gherter, 1934.

McGuire, Hunter and Christian, George L. *The Confederate Cause and Conduct in the War between the States*. Richmond: L. H. Jenkins, 1907.

McGuire, Judith W. *Diary of a Southern Refugee during the War*. New York: E. J. Hale & Son, 1867.

McIntosh, David Gregg. *The Campaign of Chancellorsville*. Richmond: William Ellis Jones' Sons, 1915.

———. *Review of the Gettysburg Campaign*. N.p., 1909.

McKim, Randolph H. *A Soldier's Recollections*. New York: Longmans, Green, and Co., 1910.

MacNamara, W. H. *The Irish Ninth in Bivouac and Battle*. Boston: Lee and Shepard, 1867.

Macon, Emma C. R. and Reuben C. *Reminiscences of the Civil War*. N.p.: privately printed, 1911.

Manarin, Louis H., and Jordan, Weymouth T., comps. *North Carolina Troops, 1861–1865: A Roster*. Raleigh: Division of Archives and History, 1966–

Marbaker, Thomas D. *History of the Eleventh New Jersey Volunteers*. Trenton: MacCrellish & Quigley, 1898.

Marshall, Charles. *An Aide-de-Camp of Lee*. Boston: Little, Brown, 1927.

Marvin, Edwin E. *The Fifth Regiment, Connecticut Volunteers: A History.* Hartford: Wiley, Waterman & Eaton, 1889.

Maury, Dabney H. *Recollections of a Virginian in the Mexican, Indian and Civil Wars.* New York: Charles Scribner's Sons, 1894.

Meade, George G. *The Life and Letters of George Gordon Meade.* 2 vols. New York: Charles Scribner's Sons, 1913.

Milgram, James W. "John Woodzell Writes Home." Society of Philatelic Americans *Journal*, XLII (1979–1980).

Military Historical Society of Massachusetts. *Papers.* 14 vols. Boston: Houghton Mifflin Co., 1895–1918.

Military Order of the Loyal Legion: Minnesota Commandery. *Glimpses of the Nation's History.* 6 vols. St. Paul: St. Paul Book and Stationery Co., 1887–1909.

————: New York Commandery. *Personal Recollections of the War of the Rebellion.* 4 vols. New York: New York Commandery, 1891–1912.

Moore, Edward A. *The Story of a Cannoneer under Stonewall Jackson.* New York: The Neale Publishing Co., 1907.

Morgan, William H. *Personal Reminiscences of the War of 1861–5.* Lynchburg, Va.: J. P. Bell Co., 1911.

Mulholland, St. Clair A. *The Story of the 116th Regiment, Pennsylvania Infantry.* Philadelphia: F. McManus, Jr. & Co., 1899.

Neese, George M. *Three Years in the Confederate Horse Artillery.* New York: The Neale Publishing Co., 1911.

Nisbet, James Cooper. *Four Years on the Firing Line.* Jackson, Tenn.: McCowat-Mercer Press, 1963.

Norton, Oliver W. *Army Letters: 1861–1865.* Chicago: O. L. Deming, 1903.

Owen, William Miller. *In Camp and Battle with the Washington Artillery of New Orleans.* Boston: Ticknor and Co., 1885.

Page, Charles A. *Letters of a War Correspondent.* Boston: L. C. Page and Co., 1899.

Parker, Francis J. *The Story of the Thirty-second Regiment, Massachusetts Infantry.* Boston: C. W. Calkins & Co., 1880.

Parker, John L. *Henry Wilson's Regiment: History of the Twenty-second Massachusetts Infantry.* Boston: Rand Avery Co., 1887.

Parramore, Thomas C., *et al.*, eds. *Before the Rebel Flag Fell.* Murfreesboro, N.C.: Johnson Publishing Co., 1968.

Patrick, Marsena R. *Inside Lincoln's Army.* New York: Thomas Yoseloff, 1964.

Patterson, Edmund D. *Yankee Rebel: The Civil War Journal of Edmund DeWitt Patterson.* Chapel Hill: University of North Carolina Press, 1966.

Pender, William Dorsey. *The General to His Lady: The Civil War Letters of William Dorsey Pender to Fanny Pender.* Chapel Hill: University of North Carolina Press, 1962.

Perrin, Abner. "A Little More Light on Gettysburg." *Mississippi Valley Historical Review*, XXIV (1938).

Pickett, LaSalle Corbett. *Pickett and His Men.* Atlanta: The Foot & Davies Co., 1900.

Poague, William T. *Gunner with Stonewall.* Jackson, Tenn.: McCowat-Mercer Press, 1957.

Pryor, Mrs. Roger A. *Reminiscences of Peace and War.* New York: The Macmillan Co., 1904.

Putnam, Sallie Brock. *Richmond during the War.* New York: G. W. Carleton & Co., 1867.

Ratchford, James Wylie. *Some Reminiscences of Persons and Incidents of the Civil War*. Richmond: Whittet & Shepperson, 1909.

Redwood, Allen C. "With Stonewall Jackson." *Scribner's Monthly*, XVIII (1879).

Rhodes, John H. *The History of Battery B, First Regiment, Rhode Island Light Artillery, in the War to Preserve the Union, 1861–1865*. Providence: Snow & Farnham, 1894.

Robert, Joseph C., ed. "A Ring Tournament in 1864: A Letter from a Mississippian in the Army of Northern Virginia." *Journal of Mississippi History*, III (1941).

Robertson, James I., ed. *Proceedings of the Advisory Council of the State of Virginia, April 21–June 19, 1861*. Richmond: Virginia State Library, 1977.

Robertson, Robert S. *Diary of the War*. [Fort Wayne, Ind.: Charles Walker, 1965].

Robson, John S. *How a One-legged Rebel Lives*. Durham, N.C.: Educator Co., 1898.

Ross, Fitzgerald. *Cities and Camps of the Confederate States*. Urbana: University of Illinois Press, 1958.

Royall, William L. *Some Reminiscences*. New York: The Neale Publishing Co., 1909.

Scales, Alfred M. *The Battle of Fredericksburg: An Address*. Washington: R. O. Polkinhorn & Son, 1894.

Schaff, Morris. *The Battle of the Wilderness*. Boston: Houghton Mifflin Co., 1910.

Schofield, John M. *Forty-six Years in the Army*. New York: The Century Co., 1897.

Shaw, Horace H. *The First Maine Heavy Artillery, 1862–1865*. Portland, Me., 1903.

Sheeran, James B. *Confederate Chaplain: A War Journal*. Milwaukee: The Bruce Publishing Co., 1960.

Shotwell, Randolph A. *The Papers of Randolph Abbott Shotwell*. 2 vols. Raleigh: N.C. Historical Commission, 1929–1936.

Sloan, John A. *Reminiscences of the Guilford Grays, Co. B, 27th N.C. Regiment*. Washington: R. O. Polkinhorn, 1883.

Smith, John D. *The History of the Nineteenth Regiment of Maine Volunteer Infantry, 1862–1865*. Minneapolis: Great Western Printing Co., 1909.

Smith, John L. *History of the Corn Exchange Regiment, 118th Pennsylvania Volunteers*. Philadelphia: J. L. Smith, 1888.

Smith, Tunstall, ed. *Richard Snowden Andrews: A Memoir*. Baltimore: Sun Job Printing Office, 1910.

Sorrel, G. Moxley. *Recollections of a Confederate Staff Officer*. Jackson, Tenn.: McCowat-Mercer Press, 1958.

Spencer, Carrie E. *et al.*, comps. *A Civil War Marriage in Virginia: Reminiscences and Letters*. Boyce, Va.: Carr Publishing Co., 1956.

Stevens, Charles A. *Berdan's United States Sharpshooters in the Army of the Potomac, 1861–1865*. St. Paul, Minn.: Price-McGill Co., 1892.

Stevens, George T. *Three Years in the Sixth Corps*. New York: Van Nostrand, 1870.

Stewart, William H. *A Pair of Blankets*. New York: Broadway Publishing Co., 1911.

Stiles, Robert. *Four Years under Marse Robert*. New York: The Neale Publishing Co., 1903.

Stribling, Robert M. *Gettysburg Campaign and Campaigns of 1864 and 1865 in Virginia.* Petersburg: The Franklin Press Co., 1905.

Strong, William W. *History of the 121st Regiment, Pennsylvania Volunteers.* Philadelphia: Press of Burk & McFetridge Co., 1893.

Sypher, Josiah R. *History of the Pennsylvania Reserve Corps.* Lancaster, Pa.: Elias Barr & Co., 1865.

Taylor, Walter H. *Four Years with General Lee.* New York: Appleton and Co., 1878.

———. *General Lee: His Campaigns in Virginia, 1861–1865, with Personal Reminiscences.* Norfolk: Nusbaum Book and Art Co., 1906.

Todd, William. *The Seventy-ninth Highlanders, New York Volunteers, in the War of the Rebellion, 1861–1865.* Albany: Brandow, Barton & Co., 1886.

Trobriand, Regis de. *Four Years with the Army of the Potomac.* Boston: Ticknor and Co., 1889.

Tusken, Roger. "In the Bastille of the Rebels." *Journal of the Illinois State Historical Society,* LVI (1963).

Under the Maltese Cross: Campaigns, 155th Pennsylvania Regiment, Narrated by the Rank and File. Pittsburgh: 155th Regimental Assn., 1910.

U.S. War Dept., comp. *War of the Rebellion: A Compilation of the Official Records of the Union and Confederate Armies.* 128 vols. Washington: Government Printing Office, 1880–1901.

Wainwright, Charles S. *A Diary of Battle.* New York: Harcourt, Brace & World, 1962.

Walker, Francis A. *History of the Second Army Corps of the Army of the Potomac.* New York: Charles Scribner's Sons, 1891.

Welch, Spencer G. *A Confederate Surgeon's Letters to His Wife.* New York: The Neale Publishing Co., 1911.

"What I Saw of the Battle of the Chickahominy." *Southern Magazine,* X (Jan. 1972).

Wise, George. *Campaigns and Battles of the Army of Northern Virginia.* New York: The Neale Publishing Co., 1916.

Wise, John S. *The End of an Era.* Boston: Houghton, Mifflin Co., 1901.

Worsham, John H. *One of Jackson's Foot Cavalry.* Jackson, Tenn.: McCowat-Mercer Press, 1964.

OTHER SOURCES

Ashburn, Percy M. *A History of the Medical Department of the United States Army.* Boston: Houghton Mifflin Co., 1929.

Ashby, Thomas A. *The Valley Campaigns.* New York: The Neale Publishing Co., 1914.

Badeau, Adam. *Military History of Ulysses S. Grant.* 3 vols. New York: D. Appleton and Co., 1885.

Bandy, Ken, and Freeland, Florence, comps. *The Gettysburg Papers.* 2 vols. Dayton, O.: Press of Morningside Bookshop, 1978.

Barker-Benfield, G. J. *The Horrors of the Half-known Life.* New York: Harper & Row, 1976.

Bean, W. G. *Stonewall's Man: Sandie Pendleton.* Chapel Hill: University of North Carolina Press, 1959.

Bond, W. R. *Pickett or Pettigrew? An Historical Essay.* Weldon, N.C.: Hall & Sledge, 1888.

Brooks, Stewart. *Civil War Medicine.* Springfield, Ill.: Charles C. Thomas, 1966.

Brown, Varina D. *A Colonel at Gettysburg and Spotsylvania.* Columbia, S.C.: The State Co., 1931.

Brown, William J., et al. *Syphilis and Other Venereal Diseases.* Cambridge: Harvard University Press, 1970.

Chambers, Lenoir. *Stonewall Jackson.* 2 vols. New York: William Morrow & Co., 1959.

Cooke, John Esten. *A Life of Gen. Robert E. Lee.* New York: D. Appleton and Co., 1871.

———. *Stonewall Jackson: A Military Biography.* New York: D. Appleton and Co., 1866.

Crute, Joseph H., Jr. *Confederate Staff Officers, 1861–1865.* Powhatan, Va.: Derwent Books, 1982.

Cullen, Joseph P. "The Battle of Mechanicsville." *Civil War Times Illustrated,* V (Oct. 1966).

———. *Richmond National Battlefield Park, Virginia.* Washington: National Park Service, 1961.

———. *Where a Hundred Thousand Fell.* Washington: National Park Service, 1966.

Dabney, Robert L. *Life and Campaigns of Lieut.-Gen. Thomas J. Jackson.* New York: Blelock & Co., 1866.

Daly, Louise P. *Alexander Cheves Haskell: The Portrait of a Man.* Norwood, Mass.: Plimpton Press, 1934.

Davis, William C. *Battle at Bull Run.* Baton Rouge: Louisiana State University Press, 1977.

DeLeon, Thomas C. *Belles, Beaux and Brains of the 60's.* New York: G. W. Dillingham Co., 1907.

———. *Four Years in Rebel Capitals.* Mobile: Gospel Printing Co., 1890.

Dowdey, Clifford. *Lee's Last Campaign.* Boston: Little, Brown and Co., 1960.

Eliot, Ellsworth. *West Point in the Confederacy.* New York: G. A. Baker & Co., 1945.

Emerson, Mrs. B. A. C. *Historic Southern Monuments.* New York: The Neale Publishing Co., 1911.

Fleming, George T. *Life and Letters of Alexander Hays.* Pittsburgh: Gilbert Adams Hays, 1919.

Fleming, Vivian Minor. *Campaigns of the Army of Northern Virginia.* Richmond: William Byrd Press, 1928.

Foote, Shelby. *The Civil War, A Narrative.* 3 vols. New York: Random House, 1958–1974.

Freeman, Douglas S. *Lee's Lieutenants: A Study in Command.* 3 vols. New York: Charles Scribner's Sons, 1943–1944.

———. *R. E. Lee: A Biography.* 4 vols. New York: Charles Scribner's Sons, 1934–1935.

Green, Russell P. "A. P. Hill's Manic Depression." *Virginia Country,* VIII (Mar./Apr. 1985).

Greene, Francis Vinton. *The Mississippi.* New York: Charles Scribner's Sons, 1881.

Haller, John S., Jr. and Robin M. *The Physician and Sexuality in Victorian America.* Urbana: University of Illinois Press, 1974.

Hanson, Joseph Mills. *Bull Run Remembers . . . The History, Traditions and Landmarks of the Manassas (Bull Run) Campaigns before Washington, 1861-1862.* Manassas, Va.: National Capitol Publishers, 1953.

Hassler, William W. *A. P. Hill: Lee's Forgotten General.* Richmond: Garrett & Massie, 1957.

————. "A. P. Hill: Mystery Man of the Confederacy." *Civil War Times Illustrated,* XVI (Oct. 1977).

Henderson, George F. R. *Stonewall Jackson and the American Civil War.* 2 vols. London: Longmans, Green and Co., 1898.

Holland, Cecil Fletcher. *Morgan and His Raiders.* New York: The Macmillan Co., 1942.

Iobst, Richard W. *The Bloody Sixth.* Raleigh: Confederate Centennial Cmmn., 1965.

Jones, J. William. *Army of Northern Virginia Memorial Volume.* Richmond: J. W. Randolph & English, 1880.

————. *Christ in the Camp.* Richmond: B. F. Johnson & Co., 1887.

————. *Life and Letters of Robert Edward Lee.* New York: The Neale Publishing Co., 1906.

————. *Stonewall Jackson: A Military Biography.* New York: D. Appleton and Co., 1866.

Krick, Robert K., comp. *The Gettysburg Death Roster.* Dayton, O.: Morningside Bookshop, 1981.

Lang, Theodore F. *Loyal West Virginia from 1861 to 1865.* Baltimore: The Deutsch Publishing Co., 1895.

Long, E. B. *The Civil War Day by Day: An Almanac, 1861-1865.* Garden City, N.Y.: Doubleday & Co., 1971.

MacRae, David. *The Americans at Home.* New York: E. P. Dutton, 1952.

Mitchell, Mary H. *Hollywood Cemetery: The Story of a Southern Shrine.* Richmond: Virginia State Library, 1985.

Montgomery, Walter A. *Life and Character of Major General William Dorsey Pender.* Raleigh: Edwards & Broughton, 1894.

Mosby, John S. *Stuart's Cavalry in the Gettysburg Campaign.* New York: Moffat, Yard & Co., 1908.

Myers, William Starr. *General George Brinton McClellan.* New York: D. Appleton-Century Co., 1934.

Paludan, Philip Shaw. *Victims: A True Story of the Civil War.* Knoxville: University of Tennessee Press, 1981.

Pleasants, Henry J. *The Tragedy of the Crater.* Boston: Christopher Publishing House, 1938.

Pollard, Edward A. *Lee and His Lieutenants.* New York: E. B. Trent & Co., 1867.

————. *The Lost Cause: A New Southern History of the War of the Confederates.* New York: E. B. Trent & Co., 1866.

Robertson, Archibald T. *Life and Letters of John A. Broadus.* Philadelphia: American Baptist Publication Society, 1901.

Robertson, James I., and McMurry, Richard M., eds. *Rank and File: Civil War Essays in Honor of Bell Irvin Wiley.* San Rafael, Cal.: Presidio Press, 1976.

Roe, Alfred S. *The Thirty-ninth Regiment, Massachusetts Volunteers, 1862-1865.* Worcester: The Commonwealth Press, 1914.

Rosebury, Theodor. *Microbes and Morals: The Strange Story of Venereal Disease.* New York: The Viking Press, 1971.

Schenck, Martin. *Up Came Hill: The Story of the Light Division and Its Leaders.* Harrisburg: The Stackpole Co., 1958.

Scott, James G., and Wyatt, Edward A., IV. *Petersburg's Story: A History.* Petersburg: Titmus Optical Co., 1960.

Scott, W. W. *A History of Orange County, Virginia.* Baltimore: Regional Publishing Co., 1974.

Skinker, Thomas Keith. *Samuel Skinker and His Descendants.* St. Louis: Thomas Keith Skinker, 1923.

Slaughter, James E. *Settlers, Southerners, Americans: The History of Essex County, Va.* Salem, West Va.: Don Mills, Inc., 1985.

Smith, Donald L. *The Twenty-fourth Michigan of the Iron Brigade.* Harrisburg: The Stackpole Co., 1962.

Snow, William P. *Southern Generals: Who They Are and What They Have Done.* New York: C. B. Richardson, 1865.

Sommers, Richard J. *Richmond Redeemed: The Siege at Petersburg.* Garden City, N.Y.: Doubleday & Co., 1981.

Souvenir: Hill Monument Unveiling, May 30th 1892. [Richmond: 1892].

Squires, W. H. T. *The Land of Decision.* Portsmouth, Va.: Printcraft Press, 1931.

Stanard, Mary Newton. *John Brockenbrough Newton: A Biographical Sketch.* Richmond: privately printed, 1924.

Swiggett, Howard. *The Rebel Raider.* Indianapolis: The Bobbs-Merrill Co., 1934.

Talbot, Edith Armstrong. *Samuel Chapman Armstrong.* New York: Doubleday, Page & Co., 1904.

Tucker, Glenn. *High Tide at Gettysburg.* Indianapolis: Bobbs-Merrill, 1958.

Walker, Francis A. *General Hancock.* New York: D. Appleton and Co., 1894.

Warner, Ezra J. *Generals in Gray.* Baton Rouge: Louisiana State University Press, 1959.

Williams, Kenneth P. *Lincoln Finds a General.* 5 vols. New York: The Macmillan Co., 1950–1959.

Wise, Jennings Cropper. *The Long Arm of Lee: or, The History of the Artillery of the Army of Northern Virginia.* 2 vols. Lynchburg, Va.: J. B. Bell Co., 1915.

Index

Note: Place names are listed as they were at the time of the Civil War.

ALL FOR THE UNION:
The Civil War Diary and Letters of Elisha Hunt Rhodes,
edited by Robert Hunt Rhodes, foreword by Geoffrey C. Ward

"One of the best first-hand accounts...of campaigning and combat in the Civil War" (James M. McPherson).

"One of the most remarkable diaries I have ever read.... [Rhodes's] diary represent[s]...the spirit of the Union soldier."
—Ken Burns, writer and director of *The Civil War*

Civil War History/0-679-73828-2/$11.00

BOLD DRAGOON:
The Life of J. E. B. Stuart
by Emory M. Thomas

The leader of the cavalry of the Army of Northern Virginia until his death in 1864 is brought to life through Emory M. Thomas's use of letters, newspaper stories, war dispatches, and diaries.

"Jeb Stuart has been the subject of several biographies over the past century, but this is the first one based on exhaustive research and the extensive use of primary sources.... *Bold Dragoon* is now the basic reference for the Confederacy's most famous cavalry chief."
—James J. Robertson,
C.P. Miles Professor of History,
Virginia Polytechnic Institute and State University

Civil War History/0-394-75775-0/$10.95

THE BROTHERS' WAR:
Civil War Letters to Their Loved
Ones from the Blue and Gray,
edited by Annette Tapert

Ninety letters, chronologically arranged from the onset of hostilities in 1861 to the assassination of Lincoln in 1865—startling, often moving documents of the Civil War, written on its battlefields, by combatants from both sides.

Civil War History/0-679-72211-4/$10.00

THE CIVIL WAR: A NARRATIVE
Volume I: Fort Sumter to Perryville
Volume II: Fredericksburg to Meridian
Volume III: Red River to Appomattox
by Shelby Foote

"Here, for certainty, is one of the great historical narratives of our century, a unique and brilliant achievement, one that must be firmly placed in the ranks of the masters...a stirring and stupendous synthesis of history."

—*Chicago Daily News*

"This, then, is narrative history—a kind of history that goes back to an older literary tradition...[It is] one of the historical and literary achievements of our time."

—*Washington Post Book World*

Civil War History/Volume I: 0-394-74623-6/$24.00; Volume II: 0-394-74621-X/$24.00; Volume III: 0-394-74622-8/$24.00; 3-volume boxed set: 0-394-74913-8/$72.00

THE CIVIL WAR DICTIONARY
by Mark M. Boatner III

The definitive reference book on the war between the states has more than 4,000 entries, all alphabetically arranged and precisely cross-indexed.

"This remarkable book constitutes an encyclopedia of the Civil War."

—*The New York Times*

American History/Reference/0-679-73392-2/$18.00

THE GENERALS:
Ulysses S. Grant and Robert E. Lee
by Nancy Scott Anderson and Dwight Anderson

An engrossing dual biography—based on eyewitness accounts, diaries, and memoirs—that follows both Lee and Grant from their childhoods, through West Point, into their individual careers in and out of the Army, and, finally, to their confrontation in the Civil War.

"Lively biography...rich and satisfying."

—*Chicago Tribune*

"A well-crafted and extremely readable dual biography."

—*Washington Post Book World*

Civil War History/0-394-75985-0/$15.00

LINCOLN AND HIS GENERALS
by T. Harry Williams

The story of Lincoln's search for a winning general, and of his own emergence as a master strategist and great commander-in-chief.

"The author's conclusions about Lincoln's war strategy are sometimes controversial, but his presentation is convincing. As a scholar Mr. Williams has drawn his facts from fundamental sources, and as a story-teller he displays a craftsmanship that holds the reader in suspense even when he knows exactly how the incident ends."
—*The New York Times*

Civil War History/0-394-70362-6/$9.00

LINCOLN RECONSIDERED
by David Donald

A brilliant reinterpretation of Civil War issues and personalities, *Lincoln Reconsidered* is "a gentle assessment, a common sense, witty, and erudite analysis of certain unrealities which have grown to be accepted as Gospel truths in the average American's thinking about Lincoln and the Civil War. It is a book which had to be written, and it could not have been written with more wisdom, better documentation or more charm" (*The Atlantic*).

Civil War History/0-679-72310-2/$9.95

THE LONG SURRENDER
by Burke Davis

The last days of the Confederacy, retold with the immediacy of an eyewitness account—one that includes the dramatic capture of Jefferson Davis and his family and Davis's ignominious treatment by his captors.

"Burke Davis tells the story of a little-known aspect of the Civil War and handles it with an eye for narrative detail that turns history into storytelling."
—*The New York Times Book Review*

Civil War History/0-679-72409-5/$9.95

SHERMAN'S MARCH
by Burke Davis

The vivid narrative of General William T. Sherman's devastating sweep through Georgia and the Carolinas in the closing days of the Civil War.

"What gives this narrative its unusual richness is the author's collation of hundreds of eyewitness accounts."

—*New Yorker*

Civil War History/0-394-75763-7/$11.00

VINTAGE ✸ BOOKS